AMERICAN BEAUTY

AMERICAN
BEAUTY

Lois W. Banner

THE UNIVERSITY OF CHICAGO PRESS
CHICAGO AND LONDON

The University of Chicago Press, Chicago 60637
The University of Chicago Press, Ltd., London

© 1983 by Lois W. Banner
All rights reserved. Published 1983
University of Chicago Press edition 1984
Printed in the United States of America

93 92 91 90 89 88 87   2 3 4 5

Published by arrangement with Alfred A. Knopf, Inc.

Library of Congress Cataloging in Publication Data

Banner, Lois W.
    American beauty.

    Bibliography: p.
    Includes index.
    1. Women—United States—History.   2. Beauty,
Personal—History.   I. Title.
[HQ1410.B36   1984]   305.4′2′0973   84-2562
ISBN 0-226-03700-2 (pbk.)

*To all my sisters,
especially to
Lila*

Contents

Illustrations follow page 180.

Acknowledgments

A number of institutions and individuals have aided in the writing of this book. For their generous and insightful criticism I want to thank Ann Douglass, Kirk Jeffrey, David Grimsted, Lewis Erenberg, Linda Kerber, Elizabeth McLachlan, and especially James McLachlan and James M. Banner, Jr. Frances Chen of the Princeton University Library was indefatigable in the search for materials through interlibrary loan. Helen Wright of Princeton University cheerfully and with great skill typed the manuscript for me, as she has for all my books. Yvonne Steiner taught me how to find illustrations. Doreen Bolger Burke of the Metropolitan Museum of Art tracked down several elusive portraits, and the staffs of the Atlanta, Chicago, St. Louis, and Oregon historical societies were helpful in finding material on beauty contests for me. My thanks also for the assistance of the staffs of the Harvard Theatre Collection, the New York Public Library Theatre Collection, the New-York Historical Society, and the Library of Congress. In the final stages of the work, Susan Erb was an indispensable research assistant. Finally, the Bunting Institute of Radcliffe College and the Humanities Division of the Rockefeller Foundation provided generous fellowship support.

AMERICAN BEAUTY

Introduction

The pursuit of personal beauty has always been a central concern of American women. Even in Puritan Massachusetts, where sumptuary laws prohibited excessive adornment, fashionable women appeared in makeup, dyed hair, and elegant attire. In the nineteenth century, feminist Elizabeth Cady Stanton, despite her radical rhetoric and advocacy of dress reform, loved fine dress and was vain about her appearance, particularly her thick, curly hair. Twentieth-century reformer Jane Addams was considerably embarrassed when, upon arriving in Russia to meet Leo Tolstoy, a symbol of the natural life to her generation, his first remark to her was to express amazement at the size of her fashionable sleeves. Dancer Isadora Duncan, who usually wore simple white tunics modelled after classical attire, fell prey to what she called the "fatal lure" of beautiful gowns when a lover took her to the Parisian salon of renowned designer Paul Poiret.[1]

The pursuit of beauty and of its attendant features, fashion and dress, has more than any other factor bound together women of different classes, regions, and ethnic groups and constituted a key element in women's separate experience of life. Conversely, varying standards of beauty have been important factors in the differentiation of classes and groups. One thinks of the Quakers, with their plain, subdued attire, and of the women at the Transcendentalists' Brook Farm or at John Humphrey Noyes's Oneida community, who wore short hair, shifts, and trousers in a variation on what was later known as bloomer dress. For both men and women appearance is a primary mark of identification, a signal of what they consider themselves to be.

Yet the literature of American history includes no scholarly investigation of the subject and only modest explorations into the history of fashion. English and Continental historians, dealing with smaller territories and more rigid class structures in which differences in dress and deportment have been more readily apparent, have more often explored the relationship of fashion and culture, and analysts like James Laver and Cecil Willett Cunnington have devoted much of their careers to the subject of fashions in dress.

Characteristically they have paid little attention to the United States, implicitly assuming that the new nation, in fashion as in other areas of art and culture, was naturally a follower rather than a leader, an imitator rather than an originator. And to some degree their assumption is correct. Decades after American writers and artists had declared their independence and—with talents like James Fenimore Cooper and Thomas Cole—established indigenous American styles, American fashions in face, figure, and dress followed European modes. Not until 1890 did the Gibson girl of Charles Dana Gibson successfully challenge European hegemony over popular standards of beauty and create a new international type. Not until the 1920s and the triumph of the movies did the United States gain domination over international beauty ideals. Yet even in the decades when the United States copied trends set in Europe, modifications in styles and manners reverberated back to their source—hence the significant and underestimated American role in certain fashion revolutions, notably in the genesis of simplified working women's garb in the late nineteenth century.

But this book is about beauty, not about dress alone; and before the more comprehensive category even European historians have hesitated. Thus I have had to formulate categories and draw conclusions primarily from contemporary diaries, autobiographies, novels, fashion magazines, beauty and etiquette manuals, foreign travellers' accounts of their own society and that of the United States, and general periodical literature. The search for evidence has not been easy. Standards of personal beauty fall into the realm of cultural conventions that are so pervasive and are taken so completely for granted that commentators assume widespread familiarity with them. At the same time, to determine why particular features of face or body—like upturned noses or large breasts—came into fashion requires such distance from one's own culture-bound perceptions that contemporaries generally deal glancingly with the whole issue.

In addition, although a dominant standard of beauty existed in every age, alternative models in a minority position always vied for precedence. Sometimes they gained sufficient authority that women attempting to be beautiful might adopt two or three styles at once and thus further complicate the problem of analysis. In the 1850s, for instance, the dominance of the frail, thin, and pale model of beauty prompted fashionable women to cultivate the palest possible complexions and sometimes to go so far as to paint their faces white. Yet at the same time voluptuousness was coming to be considered beautiful, and so fashionable women padded their bosoms.

Finally, some circles were beginning to regard an aspect of independence and even athleticism as attractive. Therefore white-faced women with padded bosoms were likely to stride the streets in a manner that combined femininity with sensuality and yet contained more than a hint of assertiveness.

The study of the history of beauty is made additionally difficult by the fact that it is transnational and that it intersects with many other segments of culture and society, including art, medicine, the theater, business, advertising, and the professions. Nevertheless, despite the difficulties in analysis, general patterns in the history of beauty can be discerned. Between 1800 and 1921, American fashions of face and figure can be divided into four periods. In the antebellum years, the frail, pale, willowy woman enshrined in the lithographs of fashion magazines predominated. I have chosen to call this model of beauty the "steel-engraving lady." In the decades after the Civil War she was challenged by a buxom, hearty, and heavy model of beauty who made her first major appearance on the British music hall stage and then, brought to the United States by a burlesque troupe known as the British Blondes, gained the height of popularity in this country in the person of Lillian Russell, the greatest star of the popular musical stage in the late nineteenth century. I call this model of beauty the "voluptuous woman." In turn, she was challenged by the tall, athletic, patrician Gibson girl of the 1890s, whose vogue was superseded in the 1910s by a small, boyish model of beauty exemplified by Mary Pickford and Clara Bow.

This "flapper" model of beauty was predominant throughout the 1920s. By 1930 a new, less youthful and frivolous beauty ideal came into being and remained popular through the 1950s, culminating in a renewed vogue of voluptuousness that bore resemblance to nineteenth-century types. That same decade, however, a youthful, adolescent model reappeared and continued in popularity through the 1960s, a decade that witnessed a significant rebellion, not only against the commercial culture of beauty and fashion, but also against the whole notion of a single or standard ideal of beauty based on Western European types. Black women began to be portrayed as beauties within the white community; women of distinctive characteristics, such as Barbra Streisand with her Mediterranean looks, created new manners of appearance.

Why such changes in the standards of beauty occurred is a complex issue in the interaction of class, women's changing expectations, social modernization, medical points of view, and other factors. As sociologists of fashion have pointed out, since the appearance of changeable fashions in dress in the Middle Ages, European cultures have demonstrated an inclination toward variations in styles of behavior and personal appearance not characteristic of non-European cultures. Yet aside from this broad principle of variation, what constitutes and influences fashion is the particular constellation of forces—social, medical, artistic—that happen to be predominant in a given period.[2]

Moreover, as a force, fashion is apparent in a wide variety of human endeavors, not just dress. And changes in styles of dress do not necessarily correlate with fashion changes in other areas. Fashions in physical appearance, for example, sometimes exhibit an independence from fashions in dress, seemingly their obvious accompaniment. The voluptuous style of physical appearance emerged in the 1860s just about the time that styles in dress underwent a major transformation from bell-shaped skirts, fashionable since the 1820s, to closely shaped, clinging skirts that culminated in a hump at the rear known as a bustle. Yet such correlations between changes in dress and those in physical appearance do not always occur. Small mouths, for example, remained the fashion throughout the period from 1800 to 1921; there was no change in the 1860s.

Indeed, standards of beauty have generally remained in vogue longer than fashions in dress. This phenomenon is partly the result of the relatively late commercialization of the cosmetic industry, which did not reach major dimensions until the late nineteenth century. In contrast, dressmakers and, later, couturiers wielded considerable power over the determination of fashions in dress throughout the nineteenth century. In addition, the existence of variant models of beauty reduced the pressures for change in the ruling look of the times. During the dominance of the steel-engraving lady, for instance, one can find models that resembled each of the three types of beauty that succeeded her.

Yet this study is historical, not sociological. One of its implied purposes is to evaluate the studies of fashion in which limited evidence is brought to bear to substantiate wide-ranging conclusions. These have been written primarily by social scientists—among them Thorstein Veblen, whose *Theory of the Leisure Class* launched the twentieth-century study of the meaning of fashion and whose theories still dominate the field. Veblen located the source of fashion change among the elites, arguing that fashion percolated downward through the class structure—a position that recent sociologists have modified by including the middle class as a fashion innovator. At first glance, Veblen's theories ring true, particularly for the nineteenth-century world that was the focus of his analysis. The steel-engraving lady, the model of beauty who dominated the age, was a symbol of gentility and elite status, as Veblen saw her. But later models of beauty were related to groups outside the elites and even the middle class.[3]

The interaction of classes out of which fashion was often forged since at least 1800 included the workers as well as the wealthy, the lower classes as well as the middle and upper classes. This point is graphically apparent in the matter of language. Slang almost always emerges from among the lower or outsider groups or, more precisely, from among those sectors of the population whose behavior is more unfettered than the rest: the sporting set, the theatrical world, and those who frequent saloons and gaming parlors. In this book this group is denominated a "subculture of sensuality" because of its more liberated moral codes and erotic styles of dress and behavior. The voluptuous model of beauty of the mid-nineteenth century arose from this milieu, which also formed the source of a sensual rebellion that began in the 1890s and reached its peak in the 1920s.

Moreover, any analysis of social classes must take account of the fact that classes themselves divide into special interests when it comes to fashion change. Veblen himself recognized—albeit vaguely—that certain sectors of the upper classes often renounce fashion competition and take up simple modes of dress and behavior. Old wealth, it is said, has the security to abjure engaging in the kind of conspicuous consumption that characterizes the nouveau riche. But sectors of the elites can just as easily become fashion innovators in areas other than those involving material display. Thus a group of young New York aristocrats rebelled against the restrictive rules of their elders to take up sports in the 1890s and a new sensual style in the 1900s. Portions of the middle classes diligently copied French fashions, while other sectors adopted reform dress, worn by almost all women as standard street costume. Still other sectors were innovators in the area of sports, apparent on college campuses before elite women took it up. Here, indeed, the class model breaks down: the introduction of sports on college campuses was related not to class, but to the sense of innovative mission of these institutions and to medical attacks on the health of the women attending them.

Broad principles of human psychology and social behavior may lie behind society's standards of physical appearance and fashionable attire, but for too long the emphasis has been on using the evidence of fashion to substantiate theories rather than to write history. Even so basic a source as the fashion magazines has never been thoroughly examined. Nor have fashion analysts systematically attempted to evaluate the comments of contemporaries about fashion and its meaning in their societies. Indeed, recent interpretations of past styles often differ from contemporary analyses. In the case of drawings and photographs, for example, nineteenth-century observers did not necessarily see what twentieth-century commentators see. Women whom they considered beautiful we would find plain; nuances in the representations of both the steel-engraving lady and the Gibson girl apparent to contemporaries easily escape us.[4]

What concerns me most about fashion and physical appearance is how they interact with other social and cultural events and institutions and particularly what they tell us about changing behavior over time. One of the weaknesses in recent writing on the history of women in the nineteenth century has been to regard the century as a seamless whole, failing to discern any significant changes once the basic industrialization of the early century occurred and the "Victorian synthesis," with its doctrine of domesticity for women, came into being. My own study indicates that Victorianism was in the process of being undermined almost as soon as it appeared; that a new kind of "liberated" woman appeared in the 1850s; and that the post–Civil War era witnessed a wave of sensuality that heralded a new freedom of sorts for women. In turn, this new sensuality stimulated a new repressiveness, which was symbolized by Anthony Comstock and which represented the "real" bedrock Victorianism of the age. By the 1890s, it, too, was in retreat, and the rise of the "new woman" represented the triumph of the new, modern age.

Each of these main episodes in the history of women corresponds to a significant change in the styles of beauty. The frail, suppressed Victorian model gave way to the voluptuous woman of the 1860s, who was in turn superseded in the 1890s by the Gibson girl, a major exemplar of the new woman. Behind these style changes lay a conflict between feminism and fashion, a central motif of the age made even more complex by its relationships to new expressions of sensuality. Most writings on feminism's opposition to fashion focus on the unsuccessful bloomer movement and fail to realize the important effect of the feminist critique throughout the century. By the time of the Civil War, working women were wearing suits modelled after male attire; and by the 1890s the garb of the Gibson girl mirrored that of the new woman: blouses and skirts for sports, suits for street wear. Nourished by a popular health movement and a new athleticism, feminist ideals of free garb and of standards of beauty based on healthy bodies and useful lives provided powerful competition to commercial standards peddled by the growing commercial beauty culture. The reform impulse of the Progressive era, which coincided with a resurgent feminism, spilled over into a wide number of areas not usually associated with those years. Two of these subsidiary reforms were the muckraking crusade against the commercial beauty culture and the feminist attempt to provide a new, liberated model of beauty for women. Here, as elsewhere, popular and high culture intersected in a powerful manner generally overlooked by historians.

II

Since the early nineteenth century, beauty has been seen as a special category of women's experience. In keeping with the bifurcation of men's and women's spheres of behavior, nineteenth-century Americans viewed the preservation and inculcation of beauty, in addition to religion and spiritual values in general, as women's special concern. It is a woman's duty, wrote the author of a popular beauty manual in 1890, to beautify the earth and to counteract "any sordid or unlovely interests that are ever struggling for mastery." Within the home she was to create a pleasing environment, in keeping with her presumed superiority in interior decoration, "in the arrangement of a house, and in the introduction of ornamental furniture and articles of bijouterie." An appreciation of music and painting and the arts in general, devoted to the pursuit of ideal beauty, was also viewed as woman's special province outside the home. "In a country where men are incessantly occupied at their business or profession," wrote English visitor James Bryce in 1893, "the function of keeping up the level of culture devolves upon women." Orchestra conductor Walter Damrosch wrote that "there has never been a country whose musical development has been fostered so exclusively by women." In the United States, wrote Anna Rogers in 1907, "the whole higher culture is feminized." According to Rogers, the vast majority of book readers as well as art gallery and theater patrons were women.[5]

Although most major nineteenth-century writers and composers were men, the most acclaimed stage performers, dancers, and singers were women. The nineteenth-century ballet was dominated by the ballerina, whose male partner became the *porteur,* the carrier who facilitated the ballerina's display of grace and beauty. The great opera singers were "prima donnas," but no such title developed for their male counterparts. In the acting profession, too, women were more renowned and earned higher salaries than men. Few male performers could boast the accolades given to actresses Charlotte Cushman, Ellen Terry, or Sarah Bernhardt. Only women, it was believed, were capable of the high emotionalism that fine acting required. Elizabeth Linn Linton, a British essayist widely read in the United States, asserted in 1868 that women had conquered art: "Nature educates her into a being of her own, sensitive above all to the beauty of thought and color."[6]

Similarly, personal beauty was defined as an attribute that only a woman could possess. "Beauty is particularly a female perfection." "Woman embodies the ideal of beauty." "Woman is the beauty principle." "Beauty, unquestionably, is the master-charm of that sex." Such aphorisms echoed from the pulpit, the press, and the pens of poets and philosophers and were repeated in hundreds of beauty manuals and advice books for women written over the course of the century. "It is a woman's *business* to be beautiful," *Godey's Lady's Book* declared categorically in 1852. "Beauty of some kind is so much the attribute of the sex, that a woman can hardly be said to feel herself a woman who has not, at one time of her life, at all events, felt herself to be fair."[7]

The identification of women with beauty has a lengthy tradition in Western culture. The word "beauty" itself derives from the Latin *bellus,* a diminutive of *bonus,* meaning good. It was first applied only to women and children; later it was used ironically to describe men. Before the Romans, the Greeks assumed that men and women possessed different virtues, with ambition, for example, being distinctly a male virtue and beauty being a female virtue, a particular indication of good character. The late medieval cult of chivalry, which arose in opposition to the brutal warfare of the early Middle Ages, revolved around the adoration of women and their beauty as the symbol of the pacific virtues of love, truth, and charity. Neo-Platonic Renaissance artists and poets carried the notion of women's moral superiority even further and saw women as a link to the divine: Dante worshipped Laura from afar and made Beatrice his guide to union with the Godhead.[8]

Beginning with the Renaissance, artistic depictions of the naked human form most often were of women. By the nineteenth century the convention became even stronger: to speak of a "nude" meant to refer primarily to a woman. Indeed, by the nineteenth century, the prevailing artistic esthetic came to locate the highest beauty in the human form and to define women as by nature more beautiful than men. The link between beauty and the human body resulted from the classical revival of the late eighteenth century, particularly from the writings of archeologist Johann Winckelmann, who publicized throughout Europe the discoveries at Pompeii and identified the figures of Greek and Roman art as pure beauty personified. The notion that women were by nature more beautiful than men originated with eighteenth-century painter William Hogarth, who argued that a curved line was naturally more beautiful than a straight one.[9]

Hogarth's "line of beauty" was in fact a complex metaphor encompassing his preference for variety over sameness and the unusual over the usual. But a half century later his notion was being used to support the simple argument that the female body, provided naturally with more curves than the male's, was more beautiful. Thus philosopher Edmund Burke in his influential *Philosophical Inquiry Into the Origin of Our Ideas of the Sublime and the Beautiful* noted his agreement with the "very ingenuous Mr. Hogarth"

about the line of beauty and added to it the notion that smallness, smooth-
ness, and delicacy were also indices of beauty, qualities that he found greatest "in the female sex." In addition to philosophers like Burke, fashion designers and self-styled experts on physical beauty regularly referred to
Hogarth's line of beauty. "Ancient and modern authors agree," wrote one
beauty specialist, "that the outlines of the perfect female form constitute the
highest type of beauty to be found anywhere in nature," for "the curved line
is the line of beauty." Ralph Waldo Emerson claimed that "beauty reaches
its perfection in the human form" and "its height in women."[10]

The nineteenth-century fixation with beautiful women reverberated
among Romantic poets and philosophers, who saw beauty as their central
quest. Novelists often characterized women as closer to nature because of
their recurring physiological cycles and their presumed intuitive powers and
made them the center of their analyses of emotion and personality. Hawthorne's Zenobia and Hester Prynne were paralleled by Poe's Ulalume and
Ligeia. Sir Walter Scott, along with Byron the favorite European author of postrevolutionary Americans, coined the word "glamorous," which
would haunt the beauty culture of the modern age and established the convention of splitting the female personality into two characters: Rebecca and
Rowena, one dark and sensuous, the other blonde and virtuous.[11]

To male authors woman was perplexing. Her sexuality made her a suspect seductress; her position as virgin and mother gave her a special spirituality. Since Plato, the love of beauty had been seen as the source of human
creativity, "provoking and furthering our social and sympathetic feelings,
quickening a pulsation of balanced, harmonious feeling," in the words of
the earl of Shaftesbury, the eighteenth-century esthetic theorist. By the nineteenth century the beauty that presumably inspired such sensitivities was
identified with women. All authors of the period, even when their work
centered on male characters, chose to represent their muse, or the creative
power on which they relied, as female. In 1832 Goethe wrote the memorable lines that ended his epic *Faust:* "The eternal female leads us on."

The Romantic fascination with the medieval age often focused on the
cult of chivalry, which revolved around women and their beauty as a moral
symbol. Such ideas became preeminent among midcentury pre-Raphaelite
painters—radicals rebelling against industrialism, materialism, and the pace
of the modern world created by men. The pre-Raphaelites located their ideal
age in medieval times and often painted women as a symbol of their rebellion. They greatly influenced Charles Du Maurier and through him Charles
Dana Gibson, America's foremost lithographer of beautiful women at the
turn of the twentieth century and the creator of a dominant ideal of physical appearance for women in that period.

In his widely read essay "Of Queen's Gardens," John Ruskin provided
the classic analysis of woman as chivalric object. Men, he argued, were to
protect and advance the interests of home and state; women, to cherish and
adorn both spheres: "What the woman is to be within her gates, as the
centre of order, the balm of distress, and the mirror of beauty; that she is
also to be without her gates, where order is more difficult, distress more im-
minent, loveliness more rare." The conservative Ruskin was not alone in
such ideas. Feminists also regarded beauty as a special goal of women. "It is
indeed our duty to be as beautiful as we can," wrote dress reformer Frances
Russell in 1892. Such attitudes should not seem surprising, since both conservatives and feminists believed in women's moral superiority, although
they differed in their recommendations on its social application. Conservatives wanted women to inculcate traditional morality within the home; feminists wanted them to promote freedom and social responsibility in the
world outside.[12]

Yet their prescriptions for the attainment of beauty often were similar.
Both groups characteristically described beauty in spiritual rather than physical terms. "Straight is the line of duty/Curved is the line of beauty," wrote
Russell, echoing Hogarth and a century of writers on beauty. But Russell's
beauty esthetic drew on Puritan rather than sensual values. "Follow the first
[duty] and thou shalt see/The second [beauty] ever following thee." Ruskin, despite his belief in women's mental inferiority, also advocated such behavior. "The perfect loveliness of a woman's countenance," he contended,
"can only consist in that majestic peace, which is founded in the memory of
happy and useful years." Like many during his age, Ruskin believed that
physical beauty in a woman reflected moral sensitivity.

That moral goodness was a special attribute of women had been a sta-
ple of Western thought since Plato, and the dislocations of the French Revolution and the advent of industrialism made the idea even more powerful
in the nineteenth century. But there was an obverse side to the traditional
view of woman as redeemer—as the Virgin Mary—and that was woman as
enchantress, Circe, the daughter of Eve come to tempt men. Keats's muse
may have been female, but so were his wicked seductresses. Hawthorne's
Zenobia lost her beloved to the frail Priscilla and killed herself at the end of
The Blithedale Romance, but her authority, when she was alive, was real and
compelling. By the late nineteenth century woman as seductress had become a powerful figure in Western art, apparent in the figure of Salome, the
personification of destructive female desires, and, according to some commentators, in the writhing, distorted women of art nouveau. Whether a reaction to emerging feminism or a reflection of the late-century decline of
Victorian prudery, such personifications of woman stood in opposition to
the idea that she was innately good; and they paved the way for another

definition of beauty, one more concerned with sensuality and with surface features of face and body as a way of attracting men.[13]

In fact, throughout the beauty literature of the nineteenth century lay another central theme: that beauty for women represented not morality, but power. "From the memorable day when the queen of Sheba made a formal call on the lamented King Solomon, the power of beauty has controlled the fate of dynasties and the lives of men," wrote etiquette authority John Wesley Hanson, Jr. Such arguments represented more than a consolation accorded to women by conservatives who realized that men held the world's real power. Like Hanson, most writers who used the power argument expressed it in extravagant terms. Female beauty, noted the *Denver Post* in 1900, represents a "power more absolute and more intoxicating than any other earthly despotism." Because of the power of women's beauty, claimed a face cream advertisement in the 1901 *Chicago Tribune,* "kings have been dethroned and dynasties perished." Writers combed the historical record for beautiful women whose physical appearance had given them power over important men: Delilah, Cleopatra, the queen of Sheba, Madame Pompadour, the Empress Josephine.[14]

What is important about the claim for women's superior power (which feminists did not employ) was that power was viewed not as a way of advancing humanitarian ends, but rather as a narcissistic device; women should use their beauty to advance their own interests, it was argued. And they should do so in the context of relationships with men. Beauty represented neither morality nor goodness, but rather a means of self-aggrandizement through "admiration, homage," and, ultimately, association with a powerful man. Woman was not only an Eve figure, but also an individual obsessed with self, with physical relationships with men, and with the eternal pursuit of beauty through whatever means.

III

To feminists and moral reformers beauty lay in the possession of spiritual qualities like honesty and devotion. To commercial fashion leaders, what mattered was dress, hair style, and physical conformity to the prevailing fashionable model of beauty. Throughout the nineteenth century the two groups were in opposition: feminism opposed fashion, and as cultural archetypes, the "fashionable woman" opposed the "natural woman."

Still, behind their conflict lay the reality that personal beauty, however defined, remained a central feature of women's separate culture. It was women who curled their hair and dyed it, who painted their faces and fingernails, who tightlaced their corsets and wore tiny shoes that pinched their toes, who tried in a variety of ways to be beautiful. In doing so, they participated in rituals as central to women's separate experience of life as childbirth or the domestic chores on which historians have usually focused. And of all the elements that have defined women's separate culture, the pursuit of beauty, then as now, transcended class and racial barriers. Until recently, minorities followed the dominant model, based on white European types. In this regard, it is revealing that the first black millionaire in the United States was a woman, Madame C. J. Walker, who discovered a way of straightening hair and established a string of beauty salons to market her invention. Indeed, to develop a fashionable physical appearance has been an important part of the process of modernity for women, of that transition from traditional to modern values that many historians believe to be the central event in the histories of nations and their populations.[15]

As presented in the idealistic vision of feminists in the Progressive era, beauty was a liberating force for women. Nor can one deny the role in women's lives of the fantasy of being beautiful in soothing personal discontents and providing strength. Yet of all the elements of women's separate culture, the pursuit of beauty has been the most divisive and, ultimately, the most oppressive. In trying to be beautiful, women have been prey to unattractive qualities of narcissism and consumerism. Beauty has also been a powerful force in dampening social discontent. Early in the nineteenth century, a Cinderella mythology became for women the counterpart of the self-made-man mythology for men. Just as it was commonly believed that for men hard work and perseverance would bring success, beauty was supposed to attract wealthy and powerful men into marriage. Young men in business dreamed of rising to the top through entrepreneurial skill. Young working women dreamed of marrying the boss's son.

By the late nineteenth century an elaborate system of symbols, rules, and rewards had arisen to reinforce the Cinderella mythology. Popular working-class novels focused on marriages between working women and wealthy men. Newspapers and magazines featured the lives of actresses—increasingly powerful style setters—who had often risen to prominence from humble backgrounds. By 1900 the chorus girl had become a major exemplar of beauty's success, for she was generally of working-class background and, after her day of glamour, usually married a millionaire, according to popular belief. At the same time, the commercial beauty culture provided increasingly complex makeup, coiffures, and clothes by means of which the ordinary woman could copy the heroine of the hour. Finally, in the early nineteenth century the category of "beauty" or "belle" developed among both working and wealthy women to denominate style setters in the area of physical appearance. In the wake of this development, hundreds of beauty contests occurred to ritualize beauty competition among women.

The writing of this book has taken a long and circuitous path, and not the least of my wanderings involved time spent in writing a biography of Elizabeth Cady Stanton, the nineteenth-century feminist leader. Yet what I thought would be a digression turned out to be central to the present work. In many ways the effort to understand Cady Stanton provided me with the tools of analysis to understand fashion in the nineteenth century as well as its interaction with feminism. As a cultural commentator, Cady Stanton had few superiors; as an analyst of fashion, she had few peers. Thus her name and her ideas figure prominently in the present work.

Other clarifications are necessary. I have, for example, used the term "Victorian" to refer to that cultural construct of prudery and propriety that existed during the nineteenth century and influenced the behavior of many sectors of the American population. As I have previously implied, however, I am not certain that the dominant morality of the age was Victorian in content. In fact, insofar as I can determine, nineteenth-century commentators on the prudish point of view did not use the term "Victorian." Rather, they called moral repression "Puritan" and generally considered it a holdover from earlier ages of Puritan domination, an atavism that waxed and waned throughout the century. Their point of view conflicts with more recent interpretations of colonial Puritanism as liberal in the area of sexuality and underscores the point that Victorian codes of behavior may have represented a minority, not a majority, point of view.[16]

Moreover, I should also make clear that I am not concerned in this work with the subject of private sexuality and the concomitant issues of birth control and fertility, which have recently been of substantial interest to historians. Rather, my focus is on what I call "sensuality," or the public expression of sexuality through behavior that could be termed erotic. Sensual behavior bears an obvious relationship to private sexuality, but its strong expression does not necessarily indicate a change in private sexuality.

In addition, much of my analysis of fashion and cultural behavior focuses on New York City. The immensity of my unexplored subject made such geographic narrowing necessary. Moreover, New York was the fashion center of the nation and, as such, its influence over the ways in which women throughout the nation viewed themselves and others was of signal importance. And, although much of this work focuses on women, I have written a chapter on men's looks, both as an initial exploration into the subject and as a way of offering a comparative perspective on women and beauty. I have also included an analysis of women and old age, concentrating on the late nineteenth and early twentieth centuries, when the growth of an emphasis on youth as the model of beauty created both new opportunities and a new oppression for older women.

The bulk of this work is concerned with the nineteenth and early twentieth centuries. It was during these years that the major institutions of the American beauty culture were established. The decades from the 1920s to the 1980s involved the further development of trends and institutions already established before World War I. Of all the years of this century, 1921 was a pivotal date in the history of women's looks. Not only did a major shift in beauty standards occur about that time, but that year also marked the start of Atlantic City's Miss America pageant, the most famous and longest-running of all American beauty contests. The event made a national ritual of the by then powerful notion that the pursuit of beauty ought to be a woman's primary goal. It also marked a substantial triumph of the fashion culture over feminism. Feminists' sense of unlimited possibility in freeing women from cultural constraints had led them to argue that every woman could be beautiful; the fashion culture turned the argument on its head by contending that beauty was available to all who used the right cosmetic or wore the right hair style. The 1920s witnessed a significant rebellion against restrictive Victorian dress, but it was also the decade in which the hairdressing and cosmetic industries fully came into their own. Increased liberation had occurred, but only at the cost of the further commercialization of beauty. This dynamic marked the history of the American beauty culture from the 1920s until the 1960s, when feminism and reform again issued a challenge to the dominance of fashion.

1

The Fashionables

During the summer of 1835, twelve-year-old Marian Gouverneur, the
daughter of wealthy New Yorkers, vacationed with her family in
Newport, Rhode Island, already a favorite seaside resort of the New
York elite. Her most vivid memory of the summer's stay was neither the
scenery, the sun, nor the recreation. What impressed her most was the dress
and demeanor of Mrs. James L. Petigru of South Carolina, a fellow guest at
the boarding house where she stayed. In contrast to the women in her previous experience, Gouverneur recalled, Mrs. Petigru wore the latest fashions,
rouged her cheeks, carried herself in a suggestive manner, stayed up late to
dance, and slept late in the mornings. Fascinated, Gouverneur watched the
first "lady of fashion" she had ever seen. She had encountered the type in
novels, particularly those of Maria Edgeworth, but never before had she
come into contact with a woman whose life seemed devoted to the pursuit
of fashion.[1]

The young girl's reaction to Mrs. Petigru is revealing of varying
American attitudes toward fashion during the nation's early years. That the
daughter of a wealthy New Yorker could remain sheltered from knowledge
of fashionable styles and modes of behavior as late as 1835 was not inconceivable. Puritan asceticism and revolutionary and republican idealism had
made national virtues of simplicity of style and demeanor in the postrevolutionary period. American periodicals in the 1790s were filled with attacks on
fashion, and prominent public leaders often wore homespun on ceremonial
occasions to reinforce their commitment to republican ideals. Dolly Madison was renowned during her husband's presidency for her fashionable attire. But after 1800, in keeping with republican simplicity, many leaders of
Washington society scorned fashionable dress. In 1818, radical Frances
Wright was pleased to see that New York women wore modest dresses and

had unaffected manners. In her opinion the dress and behavior she saw were proof of the success of republicanism in the new nation.[2]

Yet Mrs. James Petigru—not Marian Gouverneur—and Dolly Madison—not Frances Wright's republicans—were harbingers of the dominant style of American women in dress and demeanor by 1840. Simplicity in dress seemed a style of the past, and fashionable display had triumphed over republican frugality. By the late 1830s social commentators, native and foreign, stressed the American woman's striking attention to fashion. Novelist Maria McIntosh noted that while foreigners praised the political institutions of the United States, they found appalling the ostentatious displays of finery everywhere apparent. "I do not think I ever saw so large a proportion of highly dressed women," remarked English writer John Robert Godley. "How the ladies dress," wrote Charles Dickens. "What rainbow silks and satins! What fluttering of ribbons and silk tassels, and displays of cloaks with gaudy hoods and linings!" "They never walk on the streets but in the most showy and extreme toilet," noted eminent actress Frances Kemble.[3]

Even rural, working-class, frontier, and immigrant women attempted to follow the mode. In 1854 the nation's preeminent woman's rights journal, the *Lily,* reported with concern that women of all classes and in all areas—West as well as East—wore fashionable "furbelows and flounces." German émigré Francis Lieber was amazed to find women fashionably dressed in Buffalo and Cincinnati. Frenchman Michel Chevalier found the "fashionables" even in Missouri villages, and Francis and Theresa Pulsky met them in the log cabins of back-country Pennsylvania. In West Virginia in 1826 traveller Anne Royall found that farmers still made homespun, but then took it to the local stores and traded it for fashionable attire. Or, upon occasion, they delivered produce to the spas and springs where the well-to-do vacationed and, when back home, reproduced as best they could in their own clothes the fashions they saw. Women on the Western frontier adopted bloomers and male attire during the difficult months of the overland trail and early settlement. But as soon as possible, they subscribed to fashion magazines, established social circles and discussed fashion, and tried to dress in the latest styles.[4]

"The City lady," wrote one foreign resident of New York City in 1842, "is distinguished [from countrywomen] by close adherence to Parisian fashions." Author Caroline Gilman made the contrast between the urban fashionable woman and the unaffected country girl one of the main themes of her *Recollections of a New England Bride and of a Southern Matron.* Yet the contrast was easily overdrawn. As early as 1832, Reverend Adoniram Judson, the nation's first foreign missionary, expressed dismay at the fine clothing of women from the farms and small towns of New England who were coming to his Burma station as the wives of missionaries. He called for the formation of "Plain Dress Societies" to end what he called the "Idiocy" of fashion.[5]

By many accounts, fashionable dress had a particular relationship to religion. Both in city and country, fashion information was transmitted particularly at church services. Most women wore their fanciest dresses to church; "Sunday best" was an old term indicating women's desire to display their finery on important occasions. "In our town," wrote the chronicler of a childhood in rural Connecticut, "you never dressed up much to make calls; parties were few and small. . . . In church everyone saw your clothes, that was where you wore your best." And even though piety decreed that no one at church should pay attention to dress, "we could sing out of hymnbooks looking right at the notes and tell whose ruffle was cut in the new way and how Abby Norton's sleeve was set." Furthermore, by midcentury the practice of wearing a new dress on Easter was widespread. And in New York City there were unofficial parades of finery down Fifth Avenue on Sundays and on Easter.[6]

A regular stop on the itinerary of foreign travellers to the United States was the city of Lowell, Massachusetts, where cotton mill owners had essayed a famous experiment in hiring young women in their mills. Accounts of Lowell indicate that fashion among the workers was a powerful force. For work in the mills the young women wore simple black dresses with coarse aprons. But they donned finery outside. In 1844 one young woman who came from a Vermont farm to work in the mills was astonished by the fashionable dress of women on Lowell streets. Spanish traveller Domingo Sarmiento found a similar situation in 1847, although Frederika Bremer thought that some of the Lowell girls were "not well clad; others too fine." Michel Chevalier was struck by the surprising number of dressmakers in Lowell. And Lucy Larcom, at one time a mill worker, remembered that the mill girls all subscribed to *Godey's Lady's Book,* the day's most important fashion magazine.[7]

Immigrant women, too, were not immune to the attraction of fashion. They often wore their best clothing when arriving in the new land. Returning by ferry from breakfast at a Staten Island café, English visitor Francis Grund passed a packet ship with travellers from Europe and noted that the steerage passengers were all dressed in their "Sunday best." Newly arrived families might be encountered wandering up Broadway in traditional costume after landing at Castle Garden at the foot of the street; but as speedily as possible, many immigrant women acquired some fashionable clothing. Observers noted the absence in the United States of the national and class dress characteristic of European societies: the drive to be fashionable permeated the social order. Edward Abdy, an Englishman living in New York in 1833, wrote that he knew of families who were living in garrets and borrowing money for the necessities of life while their daughters were "vying on Broadway with the wives of wealthy merchants." Servants copied the clothing their employers wore; when walking in the streets, according to one commentator, they were "scarcely to be distinguished from their employers."[8]

Working women scrimped on food and lodging to have money for clothes. At the office of a Washington newspaper, Francis Grund was surprised to find women setting type and operating the presses. He was even more surprised to find that they were dressed in the height of fashion. Observers noted that schoolteachers also wore fashionable dress. Even Susan B. Anthony could not resist wearing modish attire when, as a young woman, she first started teaching school. Even the woman "whose monthly wages scarcely suffice to keep her comfortably clad in the coarsest and cheapest materials" managed to afford finery. Among those better off, many spent two or three months' wages on a fine bonnet or a silk dress. "I have known young ladies supporting themselves," wrote Anne Royall, "sit up til 12 o'clock at night, to complete a suit of clothes, the proceeds of which was to purchase a fine cap, or a plume of feathers, to deck herself for church. Hundreds of those females thus maintain themselves in a style of splendor; no ladies in the city dress finer. A ten dollar hat, a thirty dollar shawl, with silk and lace, is common amongst the poorer class of females." When hoop skirts were in fashion, many factory women in New York City wore them to work, despite the difficulties involved and the pleas of some employers that, for efficiency and comfort, they wear bloomer dress. One manufacturer of painted window shades was compelled to fire his women employees and hire men because the women's voluminous skirts brushed against the wet shades. Even black servants on New York streets, wrote Francis Lieber, were well dressed in heavy silks, fashionable hats, fine gloves, worked stockings, elegant parasols, and lace veils. Some of them, according to Lieber, looked like caricatures of their employers, but the clothes of many were indistinguishable from those of their masters. Lieber traced their expensive attire to their excellent wages.[9]

Yet the wages of most working women in American cities were extremely low. Seamstresses made 25¢ to 30¢ a day, or $1.25 to $1.50 a week. Male laborers made $1.25 a day, or $5.25 a week. An 1833 Philadelphia survey of women's work concluded that three-quarters of the city's women workers earned less for seventy-eight hours of work a week than journeymen received for one ten-hour day. In her 1863 study of working women in New York City, Virginia Penny wrote of the flattened chests, pale faces, and scanty wardrobes of the many unemployed or seasonally employed women, the victims of a labor market with a surplus of young women seeking work.[10]

Nevertheless there existed an aristocracy of working women who were paid sufficient wages to support a taste for fancy clothes. Women who worked in hoop skirt factories, for example, were paid $4 to $5 a week, according to Penny, and they spent so much money on clothing that their employers considered starting a savings bank for them. Women typesetters earned as much as $8 a week; forewomen in ladies' underwear factories earned $6 to $12 a week. At fashionable millinery and dress shops, women employees earned from $3 a week for beginners to $12 a week for forewomen. Yet there were both danger and opportunity in working at such occupations. Women employed in the making and selling of clothing, according to Penny, often developed a personal interest in dressing fashionably. At the same time they developed expertise in making their own clothing and gained contacts in the fashion world that enabled them to save money on materials.[11]

So great was the passion for dress in the United States that most observers, native as well as foreign, concluded that American women followed the mode more carefully than the women of any other nation. Secretary of State William Marcy in 1853 decreed that members of the diplomatic corps had to wear plain attire, in keeping with the American democratic creed. But no such directive governed their wives' dress. They continued to clothe themselves, whether at home or abroad, in fashionable attire, inappropriately looking like "duchesses" and "queens," according to one observer. Others called the American woman's fascination with dress a "mania" and an "obsession." Fashion was universally called a "tyrant" or, because of its constant changes, a "fickle goddess." Its followers were often called "slaves."[12]

Surveying the century, one 1880 writer on etiquette observed that all writers on behavior invariably singled out the United States as the country in which "excessive dress" was so ubiquitous that it was a "reproach." Florence Howe Hall, daughter of feminist Julia Ward Howe and an authority on etiquette in the first decades of the twentieth century, remembered a "certain spring season" in her childhood in the 1850s "when every woman between 12 and 50 wore a yellow straw bonnet trimmed with green ribbon on the outside and pink ribbon on the inside." In 1849 English traveller Emmeline Stuart-Wortley, famed for her Near Eastern travels, noted that in New York City the women were all wearing large white shawls, a fashion she found very unattractive because they reminded her of tablecloths, ghosts, and Arabs in burnooses. She consoled herself with the thought that white shawls, following the inevitable swing of fashion, would probably disappear by the time she returned.[13]

Elizabeth Cady Stanton, the century's preeminent American feminist, judged the woman of fashion to be a major enemy of woman's rights. Her diatribes against wealthy women who lived for fashion and display off the labors of hard-working husbands equalled her most vituperative outbursts against the tyranny of men. These women, in her view, constituted an "aristocracy of women" as destructive to the development of women as any elite based on class or on male superiority. Fashionable women, she noted, objected to the woman's rights movement because they deemed it immodest to speak from a platform or to have their names printed in the newspapers. Yet in the Newport, Rhode Island, hotel lobby where the woman's rights forces held their 1868 convention, she watched them reading in the morning newspapers, "with evident satisfaction, the personal compliments and full descriptions" of their dresses at the last ball. "I presume that any one of you," she later said to some who approached her, "would have felt slighted if your name had not been mentioned in the general description."[14]

In 1857 Barbara Bodichen, an English woman's rights pioneer, found the situation appalling. Throughout the nation the women she met regarded her simple wool and linen dresses as so outmoded in contrast to the elaborate silk creations they were wearing that they hesitated to be seen with her. Even reformers, charged Sarah Grimké, were not immune to the prevailing passion for dress. Many of them were not exceeded "by the butterflies of the ballroom in their love of curls, artificial flowers, embroidery, and gay apparel." "The feminine mind is occupied by clothes—and nothing but," wrote dress reformer Abba Woolson in 1873. According to Woolson, most women, following fashion's dictates, redid their wardrobes four times a year. Since each change required about three months of work, many women were left with little time for anything else. Even the sewing machine was no help, according to Woolson and many others, for its advent had simply resulted in a vast expansion of the amount of trimming and decoration on fashionable clothes. "Dress has become primary, woman secondary," wrote reformer Celia Burleigh. "You ask a friend to describe the entertainment he went to last night and he will tell you what the men said and did and what the women wore."[15]

Ministers and reformers, fashion editors and etiquette writers, conservatives and liberals—all railed at the American woman's fixation with dress. Yet nothing, it seemed, could be done. As late as 1901 the authoritative *Ladies' Home Journal* expressed a common sentiment: "We are all hypnotized by some evil magician whose spell we cannot break."[16]

II

The vogues of fashion flew in the face of republicanism, but the growth of fashion consciousness was in keeping with the rampant individualism, materialism, and search for status and success that were as much a part of basic American values as the egalitarianism traditionally associated with the rise of nineteenth-century democracy. Ironically, the unsurpassed American commitment to getting ahead helps explain the commitment to fashion on the part of American women that foreign travellers found so inappropriate in the world's preeminent republic.

In the young nation, men flooded the professions, embarked on new commercial ventures, and vied for the riches of an expanding economy. They sought new opportunities in the city and on the frontier. In the process of forming a nation "whose population is the most active and industrious in the world," they abandoned the traditional values of a rural, deferential culture to take on the attributes of self-control, enterprise, and self-interest that characterize men in modern societies. The Jacksonian era witnessed the birth of the United States as a modern nation; the Jacksonian men became modern men.[17]

Yet women, confined to housewifery by convention and admitted to the work force in low-level occupations, were denied access to power and success through male-dominated enterprise. Many retreated to the culture of women, which the nineteenth-century bifurcation of sex roles solidified. They found the significance of their lives in women's traditional role as homemaker and mother. So completely did these women conform to the ideal of domesticity that foreign travellers marvelled at the identification of American married women with their homes. They provided to others a comforting reassertion of traditional values in the midst of rapid change, while their diligence in pursuing their role was a female dimension of the contemporary male pattern of industrious application to the challenge at hand.

Many women, living with husbands, fathers, and brothers infused with the work ethic, could not avoid the attraction of the capitalist creed. "Go-aheadism," wrote one commentator, "is as common among women as men." Ambitious women sought ways to carve out roles that would fulfill their own strivings and yet not violate cultural conventions about women's role. In their quest they expanded domesticity and childrearing into elaborate occupations; they took up volunteer work; they made the pursuit of fashion into a career. According to Harriet Beecher Stowe, to be a "belle" was nothing other than a "profession."[18]

Among the possible options for distinction and advancement for women, fashion had a powerful appeal. It provided intricate paths to influence and achievement; its complexities equalled those of masculine businesses and professions. Competition was its hallmark, as women vied for preeminence over their peers. "Among rival candidates for fashionable fame," asserted a contemporary observer, there are "heart-burnings and competitions." Indeed, fashion competition could be as cutthroat as any in the business world. Writers on fashion often puzzled over whether women dressed to attract men or to display their superiority over other women, and they often concluded that the latter was the case. Only the most extreme devotees of fashion thought the excessive hoop skirts of the mid-1860s were attractive, for they were so large that women could hardly enter through regular doors or sit down on regular chairs. Satirized in the newspapers and regularly denounced by male commentators as ugly, hoop skirts grew to such impractical size, in the eyes of many analysts, because of fashionable women's desires to outdo their rivals in the world of style.[19]

Yet the pursuit of fashion could also be fulfilling. By its very nature it presumed leisure—the demonstration of which was a major responsibility of wives of successful men. By definition, a woman of fashion did not work. And fashion implied pleasure and self-indulgence. It was an outgrowth of the cosmopolitan milieu of cities, particularly of Paris, already a transatlantic symbol of fascinating sophistication and vice. It was emblematic of the way elite life was supposed to be: "a dainty, bonbon, spun-sugar world," a setting of "endless carnival," where dress was a "round of disguises." "The glitter of fashion," according to Maria Cummins in *The Lamplighter,* a bestselling novel of the 1860s, had a "dazzling, blinding effect." Its hallmark was glamour—a word grounded in the ancient Scottish culture of magic, witches, and spells and transmogrified into the modern meaning of elusive, sophisticated attraction.[20]

The fashionable woman's career promised challenge as well as pleasure. "Women of fashion," noted William Dean Howells, an important commentator on social behavior, worked and sacrificed for their ideal. "Their resolution, their suffering for their ideal, . . . their energy in dressing and adorning themselves, the pains they were at to achieve the trivialities they passed their lives in" testified to their dedication. Yet frustration always threatened. Charles Worth, the century's preeminent dress designer, told an interviewer from the *Ladies' Home Journal* in 1894 that only the woman of impeccable social position and reputation for elegance could achieve the ultimate goal of fashionable people: the introduction of a new fashion. Worth's statement was not entirely accurate, yet it underscored the ultimate problem that the pursuit of fashion posed. The challenge was not only to reach an "impeccable social position and reputation for elegance," but also to know when one had attained it.[21]

Men like John Jacob Astor and Cornelius Vanderbilt developed a national economy and built powerful financial empires. In no less astute and aggressive ways, their wives and daughters constructed an intricate elite society, built around elaborate dinners and balls, mansions and carriages; around the proper schools and dancing masters for children; and, for themselves, around fashionable clothes, the principal indicator of status at places away from home. Through fashion, even women of moderate means signalled their participation in American prosperity and fulfilled the fantasy of being wealthy.

Like elite women, working-class, immigrant, and rural women also followed fashion because of the sophistication and modernity it implied. Growing up in rural Maine in the 1860s, Kate Douglas Wiggin, author of the classic Rebecca stories of the early twentieth century, never forgot the visit one afternoon of Martha Ripley, a friend of her mother's who had travelled extensively and had translated several works from French into English. More than anything else, Wiggin remembered the fashionable blue belt that Ripley wore. To the small-town girl, it symbolized the world of adventure and success that the visitor inhabited. Within a week nearly every woman in the village had copied it. "O! that intoxicating belt!" wrote Wiggin. "It spelled Parisian fashion and *Godey's Lady's Book*."[22]

Immigrants brought traditional values from the Old World and resisted assimilation to the homogenizing culture of the New. Yet many of them, also influenced by the mythology of social mobility, expected a better life. Such expectations were especially characteristic of young Irish women, many of whom emigrated singly or with friends and so, in contrast to immigrant women of other nationalities coming with families, were not subject to family discipline as daughters, nor committed to domesticity as wives and mothers. With bodies not yet made shapeless by poor diet, heavy work in the fields, and frequent maternity, they could signal their independence and their hope for a better life by the dress they wore. "The same aristocratic feeling which pervades our fashionable women operates on girls in lower walks of life," wrote Francis Grund, "only there it is called independence." Young Irish women, according to a number of observers, seemed to be dressed in fashionable clothes as soon as they stepped off the boats at Castle Garden.[23]

Even more for young women working in shops and factories, dress was a primary means of status distinction. "Girls in shops and factories," wrote English resident James Burn, "turn up their genteel noses at those among them whose dress does not come up to standard." In addition, stylish dress might attract an upward-striving husband—the ultimate goal of most working women. For these reasons, both schoolteachers and typesetters dressed fashionably. Schoolteachers in particular had to cope with the insecurity common to pioneers in any profession. Although they were better educated than most individuals in the communities that employed them, they nonetheless occupied an uncertain station as suspect women outside the domestic circle in which proper women belonged. Fashionable dress was a way of displaying their literacy, of laying claim to social respect, and of signalling their adherence to the new order of things.[24]

Historians trace the advent of modernization in the United States to the burgeoning urbanization and industrialization in the 1820s and 1830s. Modern traits were no less evident, if not so dominant, among women than among men, and they were particularly evident among women in their growing attention to fashion. Students of colonial dress point out that men and women clothed themselves according to their social station and occupation, wearing traditional attire rather than creating new modes in the New World. By the 1820s and 1830s, the pull of custom had greatly weakened, and women had abandoned traditional dress to wear what was fashionable, what was new.[25]

The self-reliant heroines of the popular women's novels of the antebellum years, with their simple dresses made of muslin—an inexpensive fabric widely used by all classes—were depicted by their creators as upholders of traditional values. It was the women of fashion in these novels who represented the new and alarming trend of self-indulgence in an increasingly secular, consumer-oriented society. Women writers of the antebellum years often called their belles and their women of fashion "modern" women. For like the hard-driving businessmen and professionals with whom they were often linked, the fashionables represented to them the growing force of secular, capitalist values. Elizabeth Linn Linton was not sympathetic to the woman of fashion, but she recognized the type as a symbol of modernity: "It is the vague restlessness, the fierce extravagance, the neglect of home, the indolent fine-ladyism, the passionate love of pleasure which characterizes the modern woman."[26]

These traits were the result of a fundamental change in American values and self-definition evident in many areas of social attitudes and behavior. And like changes in politics, ideology, and the economy, a change in women's views of themselves and in their aspirations seems to have taken place in the 1820s and 1830s. In an insightful memoir of her grandmother's life in North Stonefield, Connecticut, Bertha Damon traced the change partly to advancing technology and new mass-produced goods. New magazines printed recipes for fancy dishes. Furniture and cloth made in manufactory situations were readily available. No longer did women have to weave their own cloth or their husbands have to make the family furniture. It was increasingly easy to follow the fashions.[27]

But there was more to the new mode of behavior than a change in production from home to workshop. A change in women's attitudes about themselves and others was also involved. No longer were women satisfied to follow their mothers' roles. No longer were they content to be only housewives with their lives encompassed within a large kitchen that served as dining room, living room, nursery, and library. By the 1830s North Stonefield women wanted to be "ladies." They wanted to be fashionably dressed, to have the latest furniture, to cook the latest recipes, to show off by having many separate rooms in their houses filled with furniture and knickknacks. In community after community the effort to follow fashion and become ladies became compelling. With its triumph, one important aspect of the modern age for women had arrived.

2

Beauty as Business
The Early Development of the
Commercial Beauty Culture

To translate the dictates of French fashion into American terms, entrepreneurs of fashion appeared in the United States early in the nineteenth century. They included dressmakers, department store owners, hairdressers, and cosmeticians, and they were linked together most strongly by the commercial values to which they all subscribed. Despite protestations that their goal was to enhance women's self-esteem, they were intent on selling products for which the demand was largely artificial. The enterprising, they knew, could reap substantial rewards. Asked one commentator, "Who makes fortunes faster among the working classes than those who minister to the desire for beauty?"[1]

In the early part of the century, dressmakers in particular played a key role in deciding how women would look. By 1835 ready-made clothing for men was an important industry in Philadelphia, Boston, and New York, and artisans' shops produced such women's items as gloves and corsets in volume. When it came to dresses and hats, however, women either made their own or went to dressmakers or milliners.[2] Self-styled experts on dress, these individuals took care to subscribe to French fashion magazines or to arrange for correspondents in Paris to dress dolls in the latest styles and send them across the Atlantic. "There are few even third or fourth rate mantua makers, in any of the larger places, who have not their *Petite Courrier des dames de Paris*," wrote Francis Lieber. Even before the appearance in the 1850s of Charles Worth, generally credited as the creator of the modern French couture, the names of French designers were known in the United

States, and their fame lent authority to the imitative creations of American dressmakers. In 1833 English traveller Thomas Hamilton wrote that the fame of Parisian modiste Madame Maradan "is diffused over the New [World]." In 1853 New York society journalist Nathaniel Parker Willis contended that American women regarded "the productions of Herbault, Boivin, and Manieri, as translations of the Talmud on the inspired text."[3]

Because American dressmakers were neither educated nor especially self-reflective, their world view has by and large been lost to the historical record. Yet from passing commentary in beauty manuals and magazines and from the memoirs of their clients, the dimensions of their role can be reconstructed. And all evidence points in the same direction: just as they were often tyrannical to the young women they employed as seamstresses, the most successful had also mastered the relationship between salesperson and client and were effectively able to manipulate their patrons by a subtle mixture of flattery and imperiousness—a combination still characteristic of successful fashion and beauty salespeople. "The dictation of the milliner," wrote one commentator, "can impose anything." By dint of dressmaker persuasiveness and the American woman's craze for fashion, dressmakers had become "a power in the land."[4]

To secure their position, dressmakers affected French names and manners, even though most of them, according to one analyst, were Irish and came from working-class backgrounds. All the fashionable dressmakers in the United States, noted English resident James Bell, seemed to be French. Their shops were called "Magasins de Nouveautés"; their goods were "distinguées, recherchés, nouveaus." No dressmaker was considered "orthodox" if she did not have "a prefix of Madame" or call herself a "modiste." Ellen Demorest of small-town Schuylerville, New York, was inspired to be a designer by a childhood spent near the fashionable spa of Saratoga. When she established herself in New York City she became Madame Demorest, and the distribution agencies she established for her products were called "Magasins de Modes." Olive Logan's fictionalized elite dressmaker in Long Branch, New Jersey, a popular summer resort, naturally had a French name. Madame Penelon's establishment occupied a large and luxurious house, "over whose broad portal the magic word *Penelon* was inscribed in gilt. Her charges were ruinous, yet her clientele was enormous and always increasing."[5]

Not only fashionable dressmakers, but also those of lesser status found ways to exert control over clients. Anna Cora Mowatt's popular play *Fashion,* which satirized the attempts of nouveau riche New Yorkers to be modish, indicated the ways in which clever maids could control aspiring mistresses, particularly if the maids were shrewd Frenchwomen. "I teach

Madame les modes de Paris, and Madame set de fashion for all of New York," gloated Mademoiselle Seraphina. "You see ... dat it is me, moi-même, dat do lead de fashion for all de American beau monde." Even in the Colorado mining country, one town's dressmaker talked freely of Paris fashion and of "balls" she had attended to clients who had never been to Paris and who were familiar only with "dances."[6]

Elizabeth Cady Stanton's *Revolution* in 1871 told the story of Mary, a thrifty housewife, who employed "Miss Midge" to make her dresses in her home "in an old-fashioned style" rather than going to the expensive Madame Perrine, as did her more extravagant neighbors. Yet in her way Miss Midge was as powerful as Madame Perrine. Even though she was poorly paid and had no life of her own, travelling from house to house as a boarder while she sewed clothes, the very privations of her existence hardened her determination to have her way. "For her hungry nature" she had "just one outlet: the furbelowing of dresses." Few were the customers who could resist "passively giving themselves into Miss Midge's hands to be moulded, brought up, or squeezed down into the right shape." Miss Midge even used French phrases from time to time.[7]

In addition to Parisian names and a manipulative personal style, dressmakers also used advertising and other sales techniques to advance their products. Occasionally they advertised in newspapers; more often they distributed printed cards that detailed their services. By the 1850s some displayed mannequins in their windows, and some even employed live women who slowly revolved to display their creations to potential customers. Long before Worth is said to have begun the practice of using models to show his clothes to customers, astute New York dressmakers employed young assistants for the purpose. By 1869 New York City dressmakers held regular fall and spring "opening days" to publicize their latest designs for each season. They issued invitations to these shows and served refreshments. The most fashionable modistes were located on Broadway; among them a Mrs. Duel cleverly arranged for a popular sewing guide to recommend a visit to her Broadway shop for knowledge of the latest fashions. When Adah Isaacs Menken in the late 1850s emerged as a star of the New York stage, several prominent dressmakers offered her a new wardrobe if they could advertise her as a patron. Menken finally came to terms with a Madame Marguerite. From then on Madame Marguerite's cards bore the legend "dressmaker to Miss Adah Isaacs Menken."[8]

Yet despite their acumen as advertisers and analysts of human character, dressmakers were not really astute businesswomen. They did not, for example, move into the potentially lucrative field of women's ready-to-wear clothing, despite the increasing numbers of women entering the work force throughout the nineteenth century. Part of their hesitation may have stemmed from their identification with French designers, whose products were based on painstaking hand sewing closely overseen by the designer and who themselves were not venturesome in business marketing. Despite the large market for French designs in the United States, for example, there was only one business representative from a major French design house in New York City in 1857. But there was much more to dressmakers' hesitation than any vision of themselves as French modistes. A sex-role division had long characterized the production of outer clothing. Male tailors made men's suits and shirts, and female dressmakers made women's dresses. By the 1830s the entrepreneurial spirit inspired the former to move into large-scale artisanal production, while the latter, bound by convention, remained locked into traditional business practices.[9]

It is true that the complex construction of fashionable dresses made volume production difficult, even after the development of the sewing machine in 1846 had vastly stimulated the men's ready-to-wear industry. Yet it is telling that it was male tailors and not female dressmakers who in the years before the Civil War set up the first large-scale arrangements for making cloaks, the first item of women's outer clothing to be produced on a volume basis. Indeed, according to the standard history of the clothing industry in New York, employees in both the factory and the home workshop situations that characterized the New York ready-to-wear production were women, cheap laborers who replaced the expensive, trained journeymen who had preceded them as workers in the tailoring trade. More than this, when male tailors set up cloakmaking workshops, they hired women as foremen, in deference to the clothesmaking tradition that women should make women's clothing. Furthermore, in keeping with the belief that the best dressmakers were French, they advertised specifically for Frenchwomen for these positions. But the dressmaker-forewomen did not set up their own workshops.[10]

As the century progressed, such trends in women's ready-to-wear continued. As skirts and suits were added to the ready-to-wear repertoire by the 1870s, again it was male tailors who set up factory and home workshop units. Bound by convention, women dressmakers displayed a limited entrepreneurial sense characteristic of women in this period who, if forced into earning a living by widowhood or spinsterdom, usually thought of earning a competence rather than of making a fortune.

Yet this point cannot be carried too far. In the field of cosmetics, women like Harriet Hubbard Ayer became major entrepreneurs, and Madame Demorest showed a singular business skill in the mass marketing of paper patterns. For a full understanding of the issue, both the nature of the clothes industry and the cultural attitude toward the dress as an item of clothing must be explored. It is crucial to realize that most women's ready-to-wear apparel in the nineteenth century—cloaks, suits, shirtwaists—was based on male attire. Thus tailors who had long made women's mannish riding habits, for example, legitimately moved into these areas of production, particularly since it was commonly believed (as it is today) that male tailors were superior to women dressmakers in achieving the close fit that jackets and suits require.

Moreover, women's ready-to-wear clothing was especially designed for working women, who did not have the time to sew their own clothes or to undergo dressmaker fittings. Their very existence, in addition to the kinds of clothing they wore, threatened the traditional craft of dressmaking, geared toward the dress as its primary product and toward women with leisure time for shopping and styling. At some point in the mid-nineteenth century, types of women's clothing took on symbolic meanings for Americans. The dress was feminine: it meant either domesticity or frivolity. Work was a masculine sphere, and for justification in entering it, women borrowed masculine attire. The simple dress, which might logically have become work attire for women, never became such except in limited situations—for example, among Lowell mill workers. And, ironically, although dressmakers were pioneers among women workers and potentially important models of independent behavior for women, they remained votaries of fashion who often assumed false identities (such as French names and backgrounds) to indoctrinate American women into an overweening concern with physical appearance and dress.

II

No less than dressmakers, department store proprietors played a major role in furthering the culture of beauty in the nineteenth century. As early as 1829, in the rapidly growing frontier city of Cincinnati, Frances Trollope had built a large commercial emporium where a variety of items were sold in separate booths. The rapid failure of her "bazaar," however, had probably impeded the development of the department store idea among American retailers, although the fanciful Moorish structure she built influenced later department store architecture. Alexander Turney Stewart of New York City is generally acknowledged to have been the first successful entrepreneur in the field, and his direct inspiration came from Continental precedents. His store, known as Stewart's, was completed in 1846.[11]

Before Stewart's was built, most urban retail stores, including the previous ones Stewart himself had owned, had been small and specialized. Reflecting the limited vision of retailers, their status was depreciated: the commercial world called them "mongers," in contrast to ship owners and importers, who were known as "merchants." But the spaciousness of Stewart's 1846 store, the amount and variety of his stock, and the innovations in organization necessary to bring formerly specialized goods into one merchandising operation and to establish a buying network in Europe indicated an entrepreneurial shrewdness equal to that of the New York shippers and importers who had established Manhattan's commercial preeminence and diminished old social designations. Although Stewart's rough-hewn manner did not endear him to the old Knickerbocker aristocracy, the mansion that he built at Thirty-fourth Street and Fifth Avenue in 1867 was for its day the largest dwelling in New York City, and it was the predecessor of the private palaces along Fifth Avenue that the New York wealthy built in later decades.

Stewart's merchandising techniques were a boon to women consumers. He reversed the prevailing trend toward specialty shops—a trend that, according to New Yorker Natalie Dana, had reached such annoying extremes that one merchant on Chatham Street sold nothing but combs. Whereas previously a woman might have had to search in numerous stores for material, buttons, lace, and trimmings (if her dressmaker did not have them), now these items were available in a wide variety in a single place. Moreover, Stewart's catered to women. There was, for example, no barrel of whiskey for men—a feature that was characteristic of many retail shops and had developed from stores established by early shipping entrepreneurs who had sold rum (designated "wet goods") on one side of their enterprise and fabric and other dry goods on the other. Instead Stewart kept his women customers "in a perpetual tizzy, with imports of new laces and fabrics from Europe, fashion exhibitions, and special sales." And he chose his salesmen for their "gentlemanly" manners and pleasing appearance and expected them to remain apprised of the latest fashions. Catering to women customers even further, the general manager greeted each entrant at the door and assigned her, if she desired, a special salesman who escorted her through the store. As much as possible, Stewart made visiting his store a pleasant, protected experience.[12]

At the same time the experience was intended to be exciting. By establishing fixed prices for his merchandise, Stewart eliminated the bartering over price that was common in stores of the period and may have been increasingly offensive to genteel women. But he retained the excitement of trying to secure bargains by introducing regular sales on his merchandise. On one occasion he went so far as to rent Niblo's Garden, a popular New York theater, for a sale of shawls. He extended credit to his customers and held fashion exhibitions. To display the cloaks and jackets that he began to sell in the 1850s, he hired women as models for the customers.[13]

The architecture and interior design of Stewart's were meant to dazzle the customers and even to uplift them. Stewart's was the first commercial building in New York City to have a marble exterior as well as plate glass windows with displays of goods behind them. Its four stories made it the largest retail store in New York City. Mirroring the rise of a mercantile aristocracy rejecting republican austerity and desirous of the trappings of royalty, its Italian palazzo architectural style was in sharp contrast to the previously dominant Greek revival style. It was popularly called the "Marble Palace." The interior featured a columned portico leading to a four-storied, domed rotunda. Each floor extended out from the rotunda, which formed a large hollow in the center. There were circular staircases, walls lined with mirrors and frescoes, large chandeliers, mahogany showcases and counters, and a special promenade gallery. On the second floor was a "Ladies' Parlor," where women could view themselves in new merchandise in front of full-length mirrors. Like others, Emmeline Stuart-Wortley thought that Stewart's was one of the finest buildings she had ever seen.[14]

In 1862 Stewart completed a new building of steel and stone—a precursor of the later iron skyscraper construction. The new Stewart's was eight stories high and covered an entire Broadway block. Employing two thousand individuals, it was the largest retail store in the world. Henry James described the edifice as "vast, marmoreal, plate-glassy."[15]

By midcentury Stewart's came to be part of the mythology of New York City. A subject of song and story, like Delmonico's restaurant or Niblo's Garden, it became a regular tourist stop. More than anything else, however, Stewart's success was apparent in the numbers of storekeepers who, like Samuel Lord, George Taylor, and Arnold Constable, speedily copied his architectural and merchandising innovations—as did Potter Palmer in Chicago and John Wanamaker in Philadelphia. Even in outlying areas, storekeepers were influenced by the urban entrepreneurs. Aspiring Pittsburgh entrepreneur Isaac Roberts advertised the dry goods and dresses that he sold as "in the latest fashion" and averred that he had "opened a correspondence with one of the best taylors in Philadelphia, whom he can depend on for the fashions being regularly sent to him." In Reading Town, Pennsylvania, the proprietor of the local store, O'Brien's, also kept up with the latest French fashions and ordered fashionable materials for his demanding patrons from Philadelphia. And as towns developed into cities, department stores were not far behind.[16]

As for New York City, in 1854 George William Curtis thought that "Broadway was fast becoming a street of palaces." Curtis's use of the term "palace" was important, for it indicated the role that department stores were assuming in the lives of American women. Shopping had always been a favorite avocation of fashionable women. The new department stores—safe, exciting, and uplifting environments—legitimized and extended that pursuit. In the eighteenth century, churches and government buildings had dominated urban landscapes; by the mid-nineteenth century, banks and department stores challenged them. The latter structures signified the increasing commercial dominance of American life and indicated the roles that men and women were expected to play in that civilization. Banks were male preserves at the heart of mercantile expansion, while department stores were women's places devoted to consumption. In New York City for many years department stores were located along Broadway, accessible by horse-drawn trolleys from residential areas, close enough to river docks for easy transport for foreign goods, but clustered together, away from the business district, constituting a separate space where women could congregate. Department stores were palaces bringing an upper-class style to the people; they were also shrines commemorating women's shopping ritual.[17]

As further indication of their function within women's separate culture, Stewart's and the other early department stores carried only dry goods and clothing accessories. It was not until the 1870s that Rowland H. Macy pioneered in adding furniture, crockery, and the diverse lines of goods characteristic of modern department stores. In addition, in the area of direct advertising, Stewart was also not especially innovative, perhaps because of the discreet, upper-class tone of his enterprise. Startling, eye-catching advertising was utilized by less well known entrepreneurs, who also contributed to the development of consumerism as women's special concern. Contemporaries were fascinated, for example, by the exploits of Monsieur Genin, initially a lowly dealer in inexpensive men's hats who decided to become a fashionable milliner. The brother-in-law of Phineas T. Barnum and the proprietor of a shop located next to Barnum's museum, Genin utilized Barnum-style tactics to secure his ends. He became famous overnight when in 1850 he paid $225 for the first seat at Jenny Lind's epic Castle Garden concert, thereby outbidding millionaire John Jacob Astor. During the summers he sent dozens of boys throughout the city to distribute free Chinese fans bearing directions to his shop. In 1860 visitor Lillian Foster remembered that his establishment rivalled Stewart's in the magnificence of his merchandise. Foster called him the "Napoleon of costumers."[18]

In addition to Genin, there was also the otherwise unexceptional dry goods firm of Bogert and Mecamly, which, as early as 1839, persuaded Julia Gardiner, a "reigning belle" of New York society, to allow her picture to appear in an advertising flyer with a caption asserting that she shopped at Bogert and Mecamly. New York high society was scandalized; and although Gardiner went on to marry widowed President John Tyler, no other nineteenth-century woman of wealth was willing to replicate Gardiner's open association with trade and the sale of goods.[19]

In novel advertising as well as other merchandising innovations, by midcentury R. H. Macy was outdistancing his competitors. His sales were more frequent; his bargains were better than those of his competitors. His newspaper advertising managed to be fresh and compelling. As women's ready-to-wear apparel became popular, he introduced it into his store and as early as 1860 was marketing it under his own label. If the less well-to-do had any hesitancy about frequenting the new department stores, Macy clearly welcomed them. And Macy, in contrast to his competitors, employed a woman as second in command. She was Margaret Getchell, and she had a reputation in the trade for energy and daring. But Getchell never set up her own store or took over Macy's; the example of Frances Trollope apparently did not influence her. Another area of women's activity in the world of fashion was controlled and directed by men.

III

As disseminators of commercial values in the field of fashion, dress designers and department store entrepreneurs were joined in the antebellum era by hairdressers and cosmeticians—all members of the growing population of urban shopkeepers and small business people. By the late nineteenth century the latter two groups would prove to be especially innovative in the business of beauty. The beauty parlor in particular would be their creation. In the antebellum era, however, Victorian decorum and the prevailing styles of simplicity in hair arrangement and innocence in facial features hampered the growth of professionals devoted to hair and face.

In the eighteenth century, hairdressers had been indispensable to styling the fashionable, elaborate hair arrangements and wigs that included false hair, pads, and feathers in their construction. But from 1800 to the 1870s, hair styles close to the head were in vogue, and hairdressers were not needed to style them. In the early part of this period the hair was parted in the middle and drawn into a cluster of curls over each ear. Later, a bun at the nape of the neck (the so-called chignon) replaced the curls. Moreover, in contrast to European hairdressers, American stylists never had a guild organization to sustain them in times of hardship. They functioned independently and thus were prey to market forces: in this case the lessened demand for their services. Furthermore, as early as 1810, many American barbers adopted the practice of calling themselves hairdressers, in imitation of the eighteenth-century male women's hairdressers. This new title reflected in part the propensity of postrevolutionary American workers to improve their status by adopting inflated titles. But it also indicated that male hairdressers who had catered to women and were now out of work because of the new hair styles invaded the barbering trade and brought their titles with them. In retaliation to this threat to their own status, the few remaining male women's hairdressers began to call themselves "artistes in hair."[20]

Yet, for certain purposes and occasions, women still resorted to hairdressers. Even though prevailing styles dictated a hairdo close to the head, the hair itself was supposed to appear wavy. Thus most nineteenth-century women curled their hair, either by putting it up overnight in pins or rags and sleeping on it or by crimping it with heated curling irons. In country districts another, more primitive method was used: women braided their hair in and out of a loop of thick cord, then put their heads down on a table and pressed their hair with a clothes iron. And in order to attain just the right sort of curls or chignon, some women resorted to using false hair. Hairdressers were skilled in the techniques of curling hair with heated irons without burning the hair or scalp. It was they who made and sold false hair and were expert at the task of intermixing it with regular hair so that it did not show. Moreover, for evening entertainments and other special occasions, upswept hairdos ornamented by flowers and feathers remained in vogue, and their arrangement remained another source of employment for women's hairdressers. And, although the French Revolution had disrupted the hairdressing business in France, renowned Parisian hairdressers were again ascendant by the 1820s and 1830s. By the 1840s *Godey's* was reporting on them to its American readers, thus reinforcing the notion of hairdresser expertise.[21]

According to Virginia Penny, in her detailed 1863 study of women's employment in New York City, both men and women were involved in the business of dressing women's hair, although the most respected hairdressers were men. By the 1850s Monsieur Martelle was New York's most fashionable coiffeur. He was "a dainty half Spanish or French octoroon, endowed with exquisite taste, a ready wit, and a saucy tongue," wrote Julia Ward Howe, then growing up among the New York elite. "He was the Figaro of the time, and his droll sayings were often quoted among his lady customers." "What girl dares wear curls when Martelle prescribes puffs or bandeaux?" asked George William Curtis.[22]

William Dibbee ran a close second to Martelle. His renown stemmed from his having styled Jenny Lind's hair during her triumphant 1850 tour of the United States. So popular was he that on at least one occasion he went to Washington, D.C., to dress the hair of Jessie Benton Frémont, wife of the military hero and presidential aspirant and a social figure in the nation's capital in her own right. Frémont probably summoned Dibbee because the principal fashionable hairdresser in Washington, François, was unavailable. Employed by a Madame DeLarue, the proprietor of a hat and glove shop, François was popular among Washington women because he discussed in detail the intimate lives of European royalty whose hair he had presumably coiffed.[23]

Even in New York City, most hairdressers did not own their own shops. To build up a steady clientele was not easy, according to Virginia Penny, and the accouterments of the trade called for considerable capital. Moreover, although learning simple ways of dressing hair required only two or three lessons, a full knowledge of the trade could take as long as two years. Apprentices to established hairdressers were not well paid, and most, according to Penny, became discouraged and quit before they finished their training. Penny also noted that many hairdressers were attached to hotels and served out-of-town visitors. But she cited only one example of such a coiffeur—at the Fifth Avenue Hotel—who had an actual salon which women patronized. *Godey's Lady's Book* in the 1850s noted the existence of hairdressing establishments for women in New York City. Consistent with Penny's information, the salons that *Godey's* mentioned were owned by men who employed women assistants. During their unoccupied hours, these women made false hairpieces which the hairdressers then attempted to sell to their clients.[24]

Most women used hairdressers only on special occasions: on their confirmation or wedding days, for example. And, for the most part, hairdressers went to patrons' homes. Even William Dibbee, despite his popularity, made his way from house to house the night before a ball or other such occasion, putting up his patron's hair in curlers or pins. The next morning he returned, combed out each customer's hair, and arranged the finished hair style. Some wealthy women employed a hairdresser full-time; most expected that their personal maids would know how to arrange hair. Chambermaids in hotels often took lessons in hairdressing so that they might perform such a service for hotel guests.[25]

The capricious nature of the hairdressing business was particularly apparent in the crush whenever a major event occurred, for then the supply of hairdressers, normally greater than the demand for their services, became woefully inadequate. Such was the case on New Year's Day in New York City, when, following an old Dutch custom, well-to-do men visited in turn their women acquaintances, who provided drinks and elaborate buffets. For the New Year's Day celebration, the hairdressers began their rounds on New Year's Eve and worked straight through until noon the next day, when the visiting began. To save time, they often crimped their customer's hair with heating irons rather than curling it, and customers who were coiffed at the beginning of their rounds had to sit up all night to make certain that they did not spoil their hairdos.[26]

More than anything else, Victorian rectitude made the male hairdresser's shop suspect. The public association of men and women in physical contact was in this case too obvious to seem respectable. Moreover, by the early nineteenth century, in New York and elsewhere, barbershops for men had become increasingly elaborate both in decor and in service, encouraging a male sybaritism that the culture normally associated with women of questionable reputation. Foreign travellers in the 1830s and 1840s were consistently astonished by the size and sumptuousness of barbershops, but they made no reference to similar establishments for women. In keeping with the proud title of "hairdresser" that former barbers assumed, barbershops were mirrored and gilded. They were perhaps the first example of the ornamental decor that would later become characteristic of department stores, hotels, theaters, beauty parlors, and other commercial institutions of mass culture that catered to the aristocratic fantasies of the upwardly mobile who could afford their services. In addition, never far distant from the barbershops was the aura of aggressive male sexuality that Victorians condemned. Just as they went to saloons, men went to barbershops to exchange gossip, tell risqué stories, and, in the later years of the century, read the semipornographic *Police Gazette*. The nature of male barbershops made suspect similar establishments for women.[27]

Some well-established hairdressing firms and other new and innovative ones did try to attract a clientele of women. From 1831 on, C. Fouladous of Philadelphia advertised himself as the "Ladies' Fashionable Hairdresser from Paris," "with a Ladies' Private Dressing Room and a Gentlemen's Hair-Cutting Room." Lemuel Burr of Boston in 1846 began to circulate flyers announcing that his artistes would cut both men's and women's hair and curl women's hair. When Elizabeth Cady Stanton donned the bloomer dress in 1851, she had James, the town barber in Seneca Falls, cut her hair short. After a dozen women followed her example, James fitted out a special room for women and advertised his availability to cut and shampoo their hair. Yet in every instance in which male hairdressers tried to attract women customers, they paid obeisance to Victorian convention by making clear that they would attend to female customers in a different room from that used for male customers. Moreover, hairdresser advertising directed toward women always stressed that the stylists were also available to cut children's hair.[28]

Even hairdressers who styled hair in their clients' own homes were subject to suspicion. Cady Stanton contended that all men who entered occupations catering to women inevitably lowered their status; "man-milliner," she said, was a term of opprobrium. Discussing his work in 1817, one New York hairdresser cautioned his colleagues to be circumspect. "He who lives in the boudoir," wrote Monsieur Lafoy, "whose 'flying fingers' are incessantly revolving around charms the most delicate and bewitching," must pay attention to "the most minute essential of propriety. Obliged to con-

demn to long and tedious inaction the animated form which he embel-
lishes, has he not need on his part of a wit, at once prompt, chastened, and
eloquent, and of a language at once pure and refined?" Lafoy counselled the
hairdresser to cultivate a special bearing, both reserved and confiding, obse-
quious and controlling. It was a potent prescription for the personality that
dressmakers assumed to manipulate their patrons and the beginning of the
intimate relationship between hairdresser and client that would intensify in
our own age.[29]

IV

The sexual divisions of labor in the culture of beauty varied among its fields
of entrepreneurship. The elite dressmakers had long been women; not until
1850 did Charles Worth enter the field in France, come to dominate it, and
establish the presumed superiority of the male couturier. The profession of
hairdressing had first emerged in the seventeenth century as a subsidiary occupation of the male wigmakers who made and groomed the elaborate wigs
that both men and women wore. At elite levels, hairdressing has remained a
male occupation until the present day. Such was not true, however, of the
manufacturers and retailers of cosmetics, some of whom were women
throughout the history of the industry.[30]

Despite the widespread use of cosmetics by fashionable women from
the sixteenth century on, a special profession devoted to their expert application did not arise, in contrast to hairdressing. On the contrary, the manufacture of cosmetics was casual and haphazard. In the early nineteenth century its development was hindered by the republican identification of
powder and paint with aristocracy, the increasing Victorian identification of
these products with prostitution, and the growing knowledge that many
skin whiteners and rouges contained poisonous lead and arsenic.

The extent to which women used cosmetics in the early nineteenth
century is difficult to determine. Even contemporaries could not always tell
whether or not women were using them. Mrs. William Seaton, of Washington, D.C., wife of the editor of the *National Intelligencer,* wrote to a friend in
1816 that the "belles of Washington spoke of using rouge and pearl powder" with great familiarity. Yet although Dolly Madison was supposed to
use rouge, Mrs. Seaton did not believe the rumors, "as I am well assured I
saw her color come and go at the naval ball." For centuries a smooth, fair
complexion had been fashionable, in part because the high incidence of
smallpox, the epidemic disease that scarred the skin, had made an unblem-
ished face a rarity. To attain such a look, fashionable women since the Eliza-

bethan age had painted their faces white, using enamels made from egg whites or a combination of lead and vinegar, called ceruse. The ideal woman of the antebellum era, however, was not supposed to look artificial. Her white skin was supposed to have a natural delicacy. Thus women wore hats and bonnets to shield their faces from the darkening rays of the sun; they carried parasols; they kept curtains pulled and avoided the out-of-doors. "The tenderness and whiteness . . . of the celery are produced by carefully excluding the plant while growing from the rays of light," noted *Harper's* sarcastically. "Women make themselves white and tender by a similar process."[31]

Such practices indicate women's reluctance to use the cosmetics that would have produced a similar, although less natural, effect. The avoidance of paint was also evidenced by the practices of eating vinegar, chalk, or even arsenic to obtain a delicate complexion. Had cosmetics been in vogue, there would have been no need to take such substances internally. Arsenic eating, the most bizarre of these practices, resulted from garbled reports of the discoveries of an eminent Austrian biologist, Johann Frederick Blumenbach, who by 1795 had collected a famous assortment of skulls and skeletal remains of various racial types according to which he constructed a widely accepted racial classification. In his classification the European stock was the original racial type from which all other races had degenerated. Since Blumenbach's earliest skulls came from the Caucasus, he devised the term "Caucasian" to denote his preeminent racial type.

Blumenbach's work seemed to give scientific support to the long-standing popular belief that among the world's women, the Circassians, who dwelt in the Caucasus, were particularly beautiful. The Circassians refused to intermarry with any of the other Balkan tribes and thus maintained their ethnic purity; for centuries their women had been noted for beauty and had been much in demand for harems. In the 1830s, reports circulated that the Circassian women were eating arsenic to preserve their vaunted complexions, and, according to fashion magazines, at least some fashionable women took up the potentially deadly practice.[32]

The preference for natural skin rather than painted faces was partly the luxury of a culture that no longer suffered from smallpox, particularly once the successful inoculations of the Napoleonic armies had conclusively proved the efficacy of vaccination. Yet facial blemishes must have been common in a society whose diet depended heavily on fatty meats and potatoes fried in grease. Robert Tomes, editor of *Harper's Bazar* at midcentury, wrote of the acne common to young people at the time of puberty. For such conditions, physicians often prescribed Fowler's Solution, an arsenic-based medication that, applied externally, gave such a translucent tone to the skin that some women used it as a face cream. Until the twentieth century no

legislation restricted the sale of such poisonous compounds, and antebellum
doctors were so poorly trained that many did not know the dangers of using
them. Beauty manuals of midcentury warned that lead and mercury were
used in commercial skin creams; but it was easy to discount these publications, since many were written to spread the reputations of their authors
and to promote sales of their own products.[33]

In 1835 Frances Trollope contended that American women "powdered
themselves immoderately with pulverized starch," but she noticed no rouge.
Cosmetics were still associated with the *ancien régime* or with prostitutes,
who used them to attract customers. "When a woman rouges," wrote one
observer, "it is considered in this country *prima facie* evidence that her character is frail." In 1859 etiquette authority Eliza Leslie counselled women
when travelling to avoid saying anything to women "in showy attire, with
painted faces." Yet by the late 1850s, at least in the cities, such attitudes
about cosmetics were largely reversed. The change was the result of new
Parisian styles, which included heavy cosmetics, and of the appearance of a
bolder generation of American women. Later in the century attitudes about
cosmetics would shift once again in a negative direction, but for the several
decades surrounding the Civil War, even respectable women painted their
faces.[34]

Whatever prohibitions existed against cosmetics in the early part of the
century did not extend to creams and lotions that softened the skin and left
no apparent residue. Sunburned skin, freckles, and facial hair, for example,
were regarded as problems that women had the right to eradicate. The
household recipe books that women passed down from generation to generation and that contained treasured remedies for a variety of household
problems also contained recipes for lotions to keep skin soft. Similarly, the
many nineteenth-century beauty manuals, which, like etiquette books,
flooded the market from the 1830s on, universally condemned the use of
commercial cosmetics as dangerous and expensive while providing a variety
of recipes for homemade creams and powders designed to provide a soft,
white skin.[35]

Moreover, even in the postrevolutionary years enterprising Americans
exploited the potential market for commercial cosmetics. In particular, peddlers brewed and sold soaps and lotions in imitation of aggressive patent-
medicine vendors and in response to the growing importance of cleanliness
as a cultural virtue. Many of the early cosmetic firms developed from commercial soap companies. Colgate, Palmolive, Peet was a late-century merger
of local firms initially established by peddlers, one of whom, William Colgate, had pioneered in the field as early as 1806. By 1830 B. T. Babbitt began
to sell cakes of soap with his name on the wrapper, the first entrepreneur to

establish such a trademark in the cosmetic line. In 1846 peddler Theron Pond developed and started to sell his Pond's Extract.

By the mid-1840s these early cosmetic entrepreneurs began to enlarge the scope of their ventures. In 1847 itinerant Solon Palmer left New Hampshire and moved to Cincinnati, where he developed a line of cosmetics that included cologne, perfume, hair oil, and powder. Several decades before Ellen Demorest and E. L. Butterick essayed a new marketing venture by distributing paper dress patterns through their own sales forces, Palmer hired agents nationwide to sell his products, and riders of the newly organized Pony Express even carried his products to California. But men were not solely responsible for the development of commercial cosmetics. Some women dressmakers in New York City manufactured creams and lotions for their customers. Ellen Demorest's ventures in the 1860s included a line of cosmetics that she marketed through her nationwide distribution agencies. Among her products, invented by chemists whom she employed, were hair curling lotions, perfumes, and a skin cream called Madame Demorest's Roseate Bloom for the Complexion.

From the earliest years, manufacturers of commercial cosmetics regularly employed advertising to sell their products. Among these early advertisers, perfume makers were perhaps the most aggressive. By the 1840s a number of Frenchmen had come to the United States specifically to manufacture perfumes, and they vied actively with native American producers. By 1858 there were no less than six perfume manufactories in New York City. To advertise their products, perfume manufacturers distributed advertising cards soaked in scent. In the cards that still exist the scent has disappeared, but the names of the products and the drawings on the cards reveal much about the industry. By the mid-nineteenth century, perfumers had developed advanced production techniques and were importing exotic materials like ambergris to achieve subtle scents that women could not attain on their own. But perfume, like rouge or mascara, was easily associated with prostitution. Thus perfumers concentrated on sweet scents like lilac and violet, called their products Cream of Lily and Violet Blossoms, and typically used pictures of blonde, angelic-looking children on their advertising cards.[36]

Because early nineteenth-century newspapers and magazines did not carry full-page, colored advertising spreads, we must not assume that advertising was not an important part of marketing. To further knowledge of their products, businessmen used cards, posters, banners, placards, and display wagons. Writing about New York City in 1844, Lydia Maria Child asserted that advertising permeated the life of the city. Not only were signs and advertising wagons everywhere, but newspapers carried all sorts of advertising and specialists had come into being to write sales copy. Underscor-

ing the importance of cosmeticians as early advertisers, Child cited the case
of the advertisements of a Dr. Gouraud, the maker of a depilatory powder.
Like later purveyors of cosmetics, Gouraud promoted his product by linking it to a legendary beauty, in this case the queen of Sheba. But Gouraud
also involved Solomon, her famed paramour. "Solomon, it is well-known,
was celebrated for his wisdom" went a typical Gouraud advertisement. "But
it is not so generally known that he invented a powder, highly beautifying,
for the Queen of Sheba. Such, however, is the fact, according to Mahome-
tan commentaries. With Solomon the secret of the preparation died; but
now, singular as it may appear, after the lapse of many centuries, it has been
discovered by Dr. Gouraud, whose Poudre Subtile will effectually remove
every appearance of beard from the lips." Gouraud was also a pioneer in the
use of celebrity endorsement. An 1868 sheet advertising his Oriental Cream,
or Magical Beautifier, includes testimonials from "the eminent tragedienne
Mrs. D. P. Bowers," and from "Fannie Stockton, Prima Donna of the
Opera House."[37]

By the 1860s the old prohibitions against the use of cosmetics would
end. By that decade fashionable women not only creamed and powdered
their faces, but they also used rouge, lipstick, and mascara. Professionals in
the application of cosmetics, known as enamellers, began to appear. Increasingly elaborate hairdos and peroxided blonde hair became the vogue, and
the use of false hair spread widely. Wealthy women began to patronize
Turkish baths. Although the health reform movement was partly responsible for their appearance, in the hands of commercial entrepreneurs such
baths became places of luxurious pleasure where women not only steamed
their bodies, but also had their hair shampooed and curled in a foretaste of
the later beauty parlor.[38]

By the last decades of the nineteenth century the catalogue of A. Simonson, importer and dealer in false hair and cosmetics, could marvel that
"there was a time when the wearing of a hair switch was regarded as sinful;
cosmetics with horror." But the fascination of fashion, the force of modernity, and the power of the emerging beauty industry had seriously undermined, if they had not ended, such attitudes. So powerful was the world of
fashion by midcentury that new, complimentary words were coined to describe both its products and the appearance of its devotees, and the words
became part of the language. "Elegant" dated from 1845; "stunning" from
1849; "chic" from 1856. Each word ratified the authority and assured the
future of fashion in the lives of American women.[39]

3

The Ideal Woman
The Steel-Engraving Lady

F ashion in physical appearance took a number of forms in the nine-teenth century. Predominant among these was the fragile and sub-missive maiden of the Victorian stereotype. Nathaniel Hawthorne gave her epic representation in the dovelike Hilda of *The Marble Faun* and the manipulated Priscilla of *The Blithedale Romance*. Poems and stories hymned her praises, and she was the central character in the lyrics of the parlor songs that constituted the major popular music of the day. Above all, her dimensions were personified in the drawings of ethereal maidens that appeared in the illustrations of fashion magazines like *Godey's Lady's Book* and in the mass-produced lithographs marketed by firms like Currier and Ives. One late-century analyst aptly called her the "steel-engraving lady," re-ferring both to the lithographic process by which she was created and to the element of moral rectitude in her character.[1]

"When I speak of her as a beauty," wrote Charles Astor Bristed, grand-son of John Jacob Astor and an important observer of New York society, "you must dismiss all ideas of voluptuousness, commanding figure, June mien and the like, and summon up such associations as you have been ac-customed to connect with the words sylph and fairy." To observers, Ameri-can women appeared "sylphlike," "ultra-attenuated," "etherealized," "frag-ile," "frail," and "slight." They had a "wax-doll prettiness"; groups of them resembled butterflies. Frances Kemble thought they looked as though "a puff of wind would break them in half or a drop of water soak them through." James Fenimore Cooper expressed astonishment at the extent to which this model of beauty had permeated the class structure. Attending the 1822 New York City Castle Garden ball in honor of the marquis de Lafayette during the French veteran's triumphal tour of the United States, Cooper noted that of some three thousand women present, "not a sixth of the whole number belonged to those classes that, in Europe, are supposed to compose society's elite." "Again and again I asked myself the question," wrote Cooper, "could those fair, graceful creatures be the daughters and wives of the mechanics and tradesmen of a provincial town in North America?" He concluded: "There is something in the bloom, delicacy, and innocence of one of these young things, that reminds you of the conceptions which poets and painters have taken of the angels."[2]

Such descriptions reflect the physical features of the steel-engraving lady of the fashion magazines and the popular lithographs. Her face is oval or heart-shaped. Her eyes gaze into the distance or are downcast. Her chin is soft and retreating. Her mouth is tiny, resembling a "beestung cupid bow" or a "rosebud," as contemporaries described it. Her body is short and slight, rounded and curved. Her shoulders slope; her arms are rounded; a small waist lies between a rounded bosom and a bell-shaped lower torso, covered by voluminous clothing. Her hands are small, her fingers tapering. Her feet, when they protrude, are tiny and delicate. When her pictorial representation is colored, her complexion is white, with a blush of pink in her cheeks.

The etherealized woman personified by the steel-engraving lady was not a new ideal of beauty. She had first emerged in the late Middle Ages, a product of Eastern influences brought home to Europe by the crusaders and of the veneration of women that was central to the cult of chivalry. Renaissance artists enshrined for their own age the spiritualized, chivalric version of femininity. The lean body of Botticelli's *Birth of Venus* exemplified the dominant female image of the mannerist school of those years. In succeeding eras, however, the earthy, voluptuous type of female beauty made its appearance, especially during the ages of expansion, conquest, and the rise of nation states in the sixteenth and seventeenth centuries. In the art of these centuries "size, weight, dynamic movement, were what mattered," and artists like Rembrandt and Rubens painted "full, weighty, solid beings."[3]

Yet by the eighteenth century the ideal of feminine frailty was once again dominant. Women in the rococo paintings of Watteau and Fragonard, for example, were buxom, yet small and delicate, their sensuality coy and indirect. They personified in the pictorial sphere part of the attributes of the new, feminine, domestic woman of eighteenth-century fiction—a woman exemplified particularly in the heroine of Samuel Richardson's *Pamela,* who had, in Richardson's description, "more beauty, generosity, and prudence than any aristocrat." She was the one angel "come down for this thousand years." Numerous historians have argued that the Victorian lady had her beginnings in this eighteenth-century type, represented in *Pamela* as an impoverished young woman of genteel background, in contrast to the novel's sensual, rakish aristocrats. Mary Wollstonecraft wrote her epochal *Vindication of the Rights of Woman* to refute the many contemporary writers who, she argued, had contributed "to make women mere artificial, weak characters," who were "gentle and docile" and who exhibited a "spaniel-like affection" and feigned "a sickly delicacy."[4]

Height and weight as defining features of beauty in women returned to predominance during the French Revolution and the era of Napoleon. Josephine de Beauharnais, though slender, was tall; and Mademoiselle George, the greatest star of the French stage during the early decades of the century and a significant model of beauty, was tall but, unlike Josephine, sturdy and buxom. To a certain extent, Britons in particular never abandoned these standards, even during the period of the steel-engraving lady's dominance. In his widely used etymology of the English language, first published in the opening decade of the nineteenth century and still in print in the 1900s, George Crabb drew careful distinctions between types of beauty in women. Although Crabb himself thought that "pretty" women possessed the greatest beauty because of their delicacy, still "beautiful," "fine," and "handsome" women existed, and these categories of physical appearance implied height, health, and solidity.[5]

By the 1830s Crabb's "pretty-woman" model was solidly in place, and nowhere was she more evident than in the United States. "We in America," wrote Harriet Beecher Stowe, "have got so far out of the way of a womanhood that has any vigor of outline or opulence of physical proportions, that, when we see a woman made as a woman ought to be, she strikes us as a monster. Our willowy girls are afraid of nothing so much as growing stout; and if a young lady begins to round into proportions like the women in Titian's or Gorgione's picture . . . she is distressed above measure, and begins to make secret enquiries into reducing diet, and to cling desperately to the strongest corset."[6]

"Genteel women never seem to be hungry," noted one observer. Some commentators, marvelling at how young women never seemed to eat meals, suspected that they snacked in secret. Whatever women's private behavior, important public censors enforced abstinence. Travelling in the South, Frederick Law Olmsted noted that neither young white mistresses nor their black slaves ate much in public because "it ain't stylish for young courting gals to let on like they have any appetite." Feminist Abba Gould Woolson noted that older girls enforced dieting on their younger sisters. Once young women had donned long dresses and declared their maturity, "to eat as much at the tea-table as hunger craves would subject them to a sarcastic lecture from their older sisters."[7]

In addition to dieting, as Harriet Beecher Stowe suggested, women also corseted themselves to appear thin. Since early times, corsets had been a standard item of fashionable women's attire. Even when the French Revolution brought loose, flowing styles, many women buttressed their dresses with stays that dug into their waist and hips. Proper Victorians believed that a woman's frail body required the support of a corset. Even Elizabeth Cady Stanton's *Revolution* recommended wearing a light corset as support for a woman's muscular structure.[8]

Yet fashion decreed much more than simply wearing a corset. The imperative to thinness included exact dimensions and, like so much else in the competitive culture of fashion, the prescribed dimensions were difficult to attain. Throughout most of the century, from the 1820s on, the stylish circumference was eighteen inches, a waist measurement so out of line with normal body dimensions that most women could achieve it only by tightlacing their corsets, a practice that caused headaches and fainting spells and may have been a primary cause of the uterine and spinal disorders widespread among nineteenth-century women, as many contemporary doctors and reformers contended.

Tightlacing was difficult to accomplish. Throughout the century women's corsets, like their dresses, fastened in the back. Well-to-do women had their servants cinch them in—a practice immortalized in Margaret Mitchell's *Gone With the Wind*. But without a servant, to tie the laces that held the corsets together by oneself was difficult enough, but to exert sufficient pressure to achieve a circumference of eighteen inches was nearly impossible. The *Revolution*'s Miss Midge recommended using the bedpost for leverage, a practice substantiated in contemporary autobiographies. Marion Harland remembered that the procedure took at least a half hour and was very difficult to complete successfully.[9]

Yet time, comfort, and even health did not seem to matter to nineteenth-century fashionables so long as they resembled the ideal of beauty. To attain a milk-white skin, they used creams and powders and stayed out of the sun. To underscore their presumed delicacy, they wore light dresses and short sleeves with only a shawl as covering, even in inclement weather. As late as the 1860s fashionable women scorned rubber boots and waterproof cloaks, which had been introduced in the 1830s, for thin silk and kid slippers, even in cold northern winters. "Thirty or forty years ago," wrote fashion editor Jane Cunningham Croly in 1887, "daughters of the well-to-do froze in insufficient clothing because it wasn't ladylike to wear flannels or woolens."[10]

To appear beautiful, women paid careful attention to body movements and facial expression as well as to physical appearance and attire. Conforming to prevailing esthetic theory and reproducing Hogarth's curve of beauty, the steel-engraving lady was usually posed in magazine illustrations with her head to one side and her arms and body slightly bent so that the line of her figure was curved. *Harper's Bazar* declared that there was no better measure of female beauty than Hogarth's curve and advised careful attention to making all gestures and movements round. "The graceful woman never crosses the room in an unbroken straight line," counselled the magazine. Rather, "she curves. She does not thrust a letter nor a cup of tea." She should move slowly, gracefully bend her arm when lifting the tea kettle, and, when pouring the tea, carefully crook her little finger in imitation of the line of the tea spout.[11]

Moreover, women went to elaborate lengths to attain the small "bee-stung" mouth often described as the most important feature of the beautiful face. The common practice was to repeat in sequence a series of words beginning with *p;* this would have the effect of rounding and puckering the mouth. "Peas, prunes, and prisms" were the most popular words in the sequence, although "potatoes" and "papa" were sometimes added. It was common for a "belle of bygone days," according to a 1913 etiquette manual, to come into a room with the word "prisms" just fading on her lips. Elizabeth Cady Stanton commented that she did not bother to give feminist literature to any woman who had the "prunes and prisms" expression on her face. In posing their subjects, nineteenth-century photographers did not ask them to smile or say "cheese," but rather to repeat the *p* words.[12]

Concern about physical appearance is a constant in women's lives. As Erving Goffman has argued, modern women display their gender in a variety of subtle ways, expressing their femininity, often unconsciously, through the way they move and show their bodies. In the nineteenth century such gender indication was equally complex. Encased in voluminous clothing, held rigid by tight corsets, women were also encircled by a set of requirements governing their physical movements and their personal behavior. Victorianism as a social code was based on a separation between masculine and feminine spheres of life; and one of its main underpinnings was fashion's code about what women were to wear and how they were to move. Yet the ambiguities in this code and the extent to which women rebelled against it from its introduction indicate the shaky foundations on which Victorianism was constructed.[13]

II

On all sides, medical and scientific theories lent legitimacy to the steel-engraving model of beauty for women. By the 1830s, medical advice books, like etiquette and beauty manuals, flooded from the presses in this age of increased literacy, advanced technology, and an expanding publishing industry. Most of these works viewed women as destined by nature to passivity and dependence. Many viewed the physiological processes involved in their life cycles—puberty, menstruation, childbirth, and menopause—as difficult and draining experiences, when women must rest and shepherd the limited energies of their delicate bodies. Many doctors endorsed the popular notion that a woman's digestive system was so delicate that she could not eat heavy meats and potatoes, but must subsist on small amounts of light nourishment: toast, tea, a bit of chicken or bouillon.[14]

The scientific community lent its weight to these medical theories. Anatomists and physiologists concurred, on the basis of height, weight, and cranial measurements, that woman was the weaker sex. To explain the ubiquity of the steel-engraving type of beauty among American women, popular theories originating with Montesquieu and claiming that climate had a particular influence on appearance and behavior were invoked. According to these theories, the severe climate in the United States foreordained that American women would be physically frail and psychologically delicate. Even so sensitive an observer as Elizabeth Cady Stanton subscribed to these ideas on occasion. "Owing to the general difference in climate [between England and the United States]," she wrote, "our women are nervously more highly wrought, physically more delicate and slender, their voice pitched in a higher key."[15]

Other scientific theories of the day upheld the idea of women's greater spirituality rather than her innate weakness, but they nonetheless reinforced the steel-engraving lady look. Drawing on Blumenbach's racial categories, popular geographies of the period displayed the face of a beautiful white woman with delicate features to represent the Caucasian stock and surrounded her by swarthy individuals meant to exemplify the other races. Among popular scientific theorists of the period, phrenologists, who studied the shape and configurations of the human skull (the so-called bumps of the head), drew no particular distinction between male and female. But physiognomists, who argued that character could be determined through the size, shape, and configuration of facial features, displayed a notable bias in favor of the steel-engraving type of beauty as the indication of womanly perfection. Originating with the Swiss Johann Lavater, the "science" of physiognomy played an important role in shaping people's attitudes toward physical appearance. Contemporary beauty manuals referred to Lavater's theories; references in autobiographies and other writings indicate a general cultural awareness of his ideas, which foreshadowed the twentieth-century theories of Cesare Lombroso and others about facial indications of criminal types of people. With regard to women, physiognomists argued that small features indicated virtue and "great delicacy of sentiment"; large features indicated sensuality and slothfulness.[16]

Novelists and poets were also influential in the creation and dissemination of the steel-engraving ideal of beauty in women. The model woman of Samuel Richardson, apparent also in the writings of Goethe and Rousseau, reappeared in Romantic and Victorian authors. "She was a vision of delight" to Wordsworth, a "milk white lamb that bleats for man's protection" to Keats. "Longfellow, Tennyson, and the whole tuneful throng," wrote Abba Woolson, "immortalize the maidens of their verses as slender and wandlike." Sensual, passionate women—like Zenobia of *The Blithedale Romance* or Hester Prynne of *The Scarlet Letter*—were not excluded from their portrayals, but it was the delicate, spiritual woman who was held up as the ideal. Writing in 1915, Amy Reed called the cult of the delicate woman of physical frailty but superior morality "the finer-clay theory." This view "was well established at the end of the eighteenth century," noted Reed, "and was given fresh emphasis in Wordsworth, Keats, and Shelley."[17]

What was true of high fiction was also characteristic of popular literature. In the many romances she read as a young woman, remembered Lucy Larcom, the heroines always had "high white foreheads" and "cheeks of a perfect oval" and were pale and pensive-looking. According to their most recent analyst, the stories in *Godey's Lady's Book* were written in line with a "tremulous" formula whereby women under pursuit by evil men or faced with a desperate fate sickened and died or, alternatively, overcame difficult situations through their superior spirituality. Both the heroines who died and the ones who triumphed had delicate "flowerlike" natures. In the *Revolution,* Helen Ekin Starrett claimed that the steel-engraving lady look was popular precisely because young women wanted to resemble the ethereal heroines of the novels and stories they constantly read.[18]

So powerful was the desire for delicacy that it became fashionable to appear ill, according to contemporary observers. Abba Gould Woolson contended that "the ill are studiously copied as models of female attractiveness." Mirroring contemporary attitudes, Hawthorne's Priscilla in *The Blithedale Romance* had "an impalpable grace [that] lay so singularly between disease and beauty." Behind this vogue of illness as fashion lay the reality of seemingly alarming rates of illness among American women. In the early 1850s Catharine Beecher conducted a rudimentary survey among the hundreds of women she met in her nationwide travels in order to support her observation that middle-class women were always ill—an observation validated by recent historians. American women were prey to gynecological ailments that doctors could not treat, to emotional disorders that were brought on by boring, powerless lives, to illnesses accentuated by a lack of exercise and physically damaging dress.[19]

Moreover, consumption, the epidemic disease of the nineteenth century that the medicine of the day could neither prevent nor cure, was both age- and sex-linked. It affected the young, and particularly young women, in rates disproportionate to their ratio within the population. Consumption was a frightening ailment. Unlike other epidemic diseases it occurred constantly and not at intermittent times: one could not flee from it by temporarily moving away from its locale. Everyone had a relative or a friend who suffered from consumption. In contrast to cholera and the other epidemic ailments of the age, consumption was lingering. One could suffer from it for months or even years without dying, experiencing a combination of agony and euphoria that were the disease's primary symptoms. In Christian terms, tuberculosis seemed to result in a special, Christlike suffering. Again in contrast to cholera or smallpox, whose victims were rendered ugly, those who suffered from tuberculosis seemed to become more beautiful. Their frailty and translucent skin suggested a special spirituality.[20]

It might be argued that society coped with the disease's threat by investing its victims with a special grace, by seeing in them the ultimate expression of the sacrificial spirituality expected of all women. The consumptives who appear throughout the pages of nineteenth-century literature—Little Eva in *Uncle Tom's Cabin,* Beth in *Little Women,* even the courtesan Camille in Alexandre Dumas's *La Dame aux camélias* and Mimi in Puccini's *La Bohème*—are heroic figures whose self-sacrificing lives culminate in death. Indeed, perhaps the attempt to cope with the threat of consumption went even further than glorifying its victims: women may have triumphed over the fear of infection by affecting its symptoms and, by thus unconsciously expressing solidarity with all female sufferers, may have anesthetized its dread impact.

Yet the steel-engraving lady as the dominant model of beauty would have come into being even if consumption had not existed. What is curious about contemporary writings on the ethereal woman of the Victorian ideal is how rarely pulmonary disease is mentioned as an essential element in the creation of her characteristics. By and large, most analysts charged that women themselves were responsible for their illnesses. Women chose to tightlace, to avoid exercise, to eat and dress improperly. If consumption was mentioned, it was seen most often as the result of improper care of the body and not as a force over which women had no control. Some writers borrowed from the argument that climate was responsible for the appearance of American women and placed the blame for women's invalidism on it. But few writers dwelt on this idea. Writing in the *Revolution,* Helen Ekin Starrett went so far as to charge that women "feigned" exhaustion and delicacy: "That fatigue of which she complains, and which causes her to recline so gracefully upon the sofa may either be constitutional laziness, or it may be a feminine stratagem for securing an expression of sympathy from some person of the other sex."[21]

Behind the medical, scientific, and literary ideas about women's ideal appearance lay the fact that the steel-engraving model of beauty was an embodiment of the restrictive, middle-class Victorian view of woman's role. In a turbulent, rapidly industrializing society, where the pursuit of the main chance monopolized men's attention, and in a period of conservatism, which the entire Western world had entered following the upheavals of the French Revolution, women were designated the representatives of order, morality, and repose. They were to display in face and attire as well as attitude their adherence to the qualities of purity, piety, domesticity, and submission that formed the core of the nineteenth-century "cult of true womanhood," the analogue of the "feminine mystique" of modern times.[22]

But the steel-engraving lady represented not only the middle-class mode. All dominant models of physical appearance encompass in their features a wide variety of cultural meanings: it is this inclusive character which guarantees them hegemony. Thus a central characteristic of the steel-engraving lady—and one that contrasted with previous beauty models—was that she was young. Her youth underscored her purity and reflected both the nineteenth-century romanticization of childhood and its tendency to infantilize women, to view them as creatures of childlike disposition. But her youth was also related to the revolutionary and romantic rebellion against the Old Regime, in which both men and women, identifying with age, had worn white wigs. Thus in this guise the steel-engraving lady became a symbol for the rejuvenation of the nineteenth-century natural order, for the optimism implicit in romantic revolutionism, and for the often youthful quality of its proponents, not unrelated to the emergence of adolescence as a distinct stage of life.

There is even more to the meaning of the steel-engraving lady. As much as she personified the Victorian need for stability and security and the romantic quest for change, she embodied even more the common American drive for high status. The features of the steel-engraving lady were in line with what the culture viewed as aristocratic. Small hands and feet had long been considered a mark of nobility. Slim waists were the luxury of a social class that did not have to live on a heavy starch diet. Small noses and mouths, too, were seen as signs of superior gentility, as was a pale complexion. And the latter, like all the features of the steel-engraving lady, was easily carried to extremes. Forced to prepare dinner because her cook had suddenly left, one New England woman was deeply embarrassed that "the kitchen fire had deepened my complexion beyond the delicacy of beauty."[23]

The fragility of the steel-engraving lady and the languor that surrounded her were also perceived as indications of aristocratic refinement. In early capitalist cultures, where men were absorbed by the marketplace, family wealth and status were displayed by the sumptuous dress of wives and daughters, by their physical approximation to an upper-class ideal, and by the leisure of their lives. "Nothing would prove so fatal to a lady's reputation for gentility," reported one observer, "as the character of a working woman." Even tasks associated with housewifery and childrearing were viewed as vulgar by the fashionables. "It is not genteel for mothers to wash and dress their own children, or make their clothing, or teach them, or romp with them in the open air," wrote Lydia Maria Child. "To be a good housewife, is degrading in the extreme." This prohibition went so far that all exercise, aside from dancing, was interdicted to fashionable women. In country as well as city, observed English visitor William Baxter in 1855, they sat all day in rocking chairs—an American invention he thought characteristic of the American avoidance of exercise. The only physical activities he saw women participating in were bowling and driving trotting horses. "They would regard anyone who proposed vigorous physical exercise as a madman." Even at seaside resorts, American women seemed "victimized by inertia."[24]

"The more opulent would appear to consider walking to be suited only to such females as are compelled by necessity to labor for their bodily sustenance," wrote one commentator. Women's skirts trailed on the ground, according to Harriet Beecher Stowe and others, so that the well-to-do could demonstrate by their clean hems that they used carriages. Yet the distinctions could be intricate. In New York City women walked on Broadway because they could not adequately display their clothing if they rode in carriages. But they never carried the goods they bought home with them because they might too closely resemble milliners' assistants delivering parcels. To carry a music roll, however, was "perfectly genteel," for it signified that the individual not only could play an instrument—then considered a refined accomplishment—but also could afford to buy the latest music.[25]

To nineteenth-century Americans, gentility was the measure of proper behavior and "genteel" the word that arbiters of etiquette commonly used. It was an old word, long associated with the characteristics of persons of high class and with what was perceived as refinement and elegance. But by the late eighteenth century the emerging middle classes had appropriated the genteel norm as their own and had added their own brand of high moral tone—of decorum and respectability—to its meaning, further confusing old, ambiguous definitions of what made ordinary people gentlefolk. In England a rigid class structure provided at least some fixed standards, but the fluidity of American society, the universal striving after success, the lack of a titled aristocracy, and the modest past of most Americans created a situation of vast confusion. Mrs. Basil Hall was astounded in 1827 by the extent to which the cult of gentility had permeated American life. Never before, in

England or on the Continent, had she observed such adherence to a standard that she herself found absurd. Americans' favorite descriptive phrase, she wrote, was "very ungenteel"; in the new land everything was "genteel" or "ungenteel."[26]

Foreign observers of genteel manners in the United States were astounded at the extent to which the bowdlerization of the language in the New World had proceeded to include circumlocutions for words that the English would never dream of considering prurient. Such prudery in language was the primary evidence of Victorian repressiveness in the United States, according to many foreign observers. In 1877 *Harper's Bazar* traced the prudery to American social mobility, to the fact that "our American progenitors . . . like all half cultivated but aspiring people, who are only too conscious of vulgarisms from their lowly associations, made overstrained efforts to avoid them." By the mid-nineteenth century in England the word "genteel" had acquired a sarcastic connotation implying that those who aspired to its nomenclature attached exaggerated importance to spurious indications of social superiority or demonstrated a ridiculous fear of being considered lower-class. But in the United States, where few were free from such status competition, it retained its power. Ultimately it became associated with the post–Civil War publishers, writers, and editors who controlled American letters and tried to enforce a proper moral code. The "genteel" writers, they are called.[27]

It is a truism of fashion history that any prevalent style normally develops into an extreme expression of its form before another style replaces it. Thus the leg-of-mutton sleeves of the 1830s became so large that women had to enter rooms sideways because they could not fit through regular doors frontward, and the hoop skirts of the 1850s evolved into a similar stage of ridiculousness. Such a perspective in particular sheds light on the antebellum phenomenon of invalidism as the epitome of fashion. Sensitivity and delicacy had long been regarded as particular marks of gentility. In classic European folk mythology the princess proved her identity not only by the smallness of her foot (like Cinderella), but also by her sensitivity to discomfort, like the princess who was unable to sleep because there was a pea under the pile of mattresses on which she was lying.

By the nineteenth century, frailty had expanded to permeate all areas of physical life and to become identified with sensitivity. In Maria Cummins's *Haunted Hearts,* a romance set during the Revolution, the beautiful farm girl, Angevine Cousin, learns from an elegant British officer at a country dance that a genteel woman is so sensitive that she cannot endure a chilly room. "These farmers and milkmaids may be able to endure it, but you are more delicately constituted." She listened, amazed. "It had never occurred to her before that a frail constitution was a mark of refinement." By the

nineteenth century, however, such beliefs were widespread, communicated
by novelists, by information in fashion magazines, and even by tales in
school textbooks. In a typical textbook story, the aunt of fictional Ruth
Penway complains to her niece's teacher that the young girl is becoming
"vulgarly robust" because of the physical activities encouraged by the
school. "Who wishes to see such a rude state of health as hers? It may do for
a washerwoman, but not for Ruth Penway."[28]

Among the fashionables, invalidism became another competitive cir-
cumstance with even higher stakes than the competition over dress, physical
appearance, or splendid possessions, for here one's life might ultimately be
on the line. "Our fine ladies," wrote Abba Gould Woolson, "aspire to be
called *invalides*; and the long French accent with which they roll off this
word seems to give it special charm. If you happen on a group of them
conversing on a bright summer afternoon, you will be sure to find them en-
deavoring to outshine one another in the recital of past illnesses." Sara J.
Lippincott, a popular essayist who wrote under the pseudonym Grace
Greenwood, remembered how in her Rochester, New York, school days she
had become the envy of her classmates after she donned a corset and
achieved an extremely small waist. Even though she developed fainting
spells and a cough, the discomfort was worth the admiration. She was in-
comparably pale and willowy, in contrast to the "chunky," corsetless girls at
the school.[29]

Josephine DeMott, a bareback rider and star of the circus who in the
1870s married wealthy Cincinnatian John Robinson, provides another example. DeMott quickly adapted to the role of lady that her new position
demanded. She learned to walk slowly and to sit and fold her hands elegantly. She laced her corsets to eighteen inches and then carefully became ill
all the time, as were most of the women in her new circle. She bought herself an expensive cut-glass smelling salts bottle topped by a diamond that
she carried to revive her after fainting attacks. She visited doctors and discussed her medical problems with all her friends. "It was a thrilling game,"
she remembered, "and in order to compete with any ability, you had to be
ready with illnesses—the worse they were, the more operations you had to
your name, the higher you ranked."[30]

Behind the pale face and the slim form of the steel-engraving lady lay a
generalized hypochondria. Spirituality as style had gotten out of hand, and
illness as an expression of the mode represented competition in fashion carried to absurdity and the cult of gentility grown to its outermost limits.
Moreover, as Grace Greenwood and Josephine DeMott indicated, illness
was a role, not necessarily a fixed condition. One could move in and out of
it or, alternatively, adopt some of its features and not others. Thus a white
complexion and a delicate frame did not necessarily mean a listless personal-

ity or an abdication of energy in other areas of life. The Victorian woman might assiduously diet and avoid the sun, but duty and prudery did not necessarily govern other areas of her dress and behavior.

III

Despite the dominance of the steel-engraving lady, other models of beauty emerged in the antebellum era to challenge her hegemony. Primary among these were a plump and sturdy type depicted in lithographs in the popular British humor magazine *Punch* by John Leech, the predecessor of George Du Maurier. Leech's drawings reflected a physical type common in England, whose women did not follow French fashions as closely as American women and among whom the squirearchy tradition of physical exercise was still strong. Many commentators remarked on the striking contrast between the physiques of American and English women. "Travellers have remarked over and over again," noted the *Revolution* in 1870, "the fragile contrast which the American woman presents to the well-developed and healthy women of England and Europe." The faces of English women, wrote Francis Lieber, were immediately discernible in the United States because of their florid color. Englishman George Towle found the physiques of English women "round" in comparison to American women and their general appearance "ruddy."[31]

Many foreign travellers extolled the frail beauty of American women, but some were critical of it. Echoing George Crabb's definitions of beauty, James Buckingham contended that there were more "pretty" women in the United States than in England but few "fine" women with tall, full, and commanding figures—a beauty model that Buckingham preferred. Moreover, noted Buckingham and many European visitors, the frailty of American women produced an unfortunate physical characteristic as common among American women by their early thirties as their beauty in their teens. "Premature physical decay," some European observers called the phenomenon. It seemed to involve a loss of skin tone, sagging muscles, and a body deterioration that not even tightlacing could conceal. Isabella Bird observed that the "sylphlike" and "elegant" figures of young American women became "unpleasantly angular" by the time they were thirty. Other commentators described them as "gaunt" and "sallow and scrawny."[32]

Sensitive to criticism, Americans bridled at assertions that American women quickly lost their beauty. Nathaniel Hawthorne, long resident in England, in retaliation called British women "beefy," and, to his embarrassment, the description stuck throughout the century. The adjective was especially utilized in the 1860s when troupes of British music hall stars—all of considerable girth—invaded the American popular stage, and press reports initially described them as beefy.[33]

British visitors to the United States were often plump and healthy; so, too, were German women immigrants to the New World. Among antebellum immigrants, the Germans must be differentiated from the Irish. Not only was there a language barrier for the Germans but also they migrated in family units and thus did not include large numbers of single men and women outside the government of the family and more exposed to the influence of American culture. Young unmarried German women who worked did so alongside fathers and mothers, particularly in tailoring workshops, which had already taken on a tenement-centered character among the Germans who dominated them.[34]

German women did not adopt fashionable modes of dress or physical appearance. Among many peasant cultures where starvation was an ever-present possibility, a full frame was an indication of prosperity. Commenting on the physical appearance of the peasant women of Germany, English traveller William Howitt noted that the young women were built "broad and strong" and that "in spite of modern notions" they had a "wholesome, heartsome, agreeable, and good-natured look" with bodies "which seemed ready to burst with plumpness." The old women, however, differed strikingly in appearance. In contrast to English women, Howitt noted, the peasant women of Germany worked in the fields, and this activity affected their bodies. Long years out of doors, he wrote, made them "wrinkled, lean, gray, and stooping." They looked, in his estimation, like "all our personal ideas of witches." No wonder that, with a diet based on beer and potatoes, Germans found plumpness a sign of prosperity.[35]

In contrast to the Irish, viewed as unkempt and "wild," the Germans generated a positive image. Most of them, with financial resources, employment skills, or individual initiative, rose quickly within the occupational hierarchy. Their rates of crime and admissions to public hospitals were low, and the cleanliness of their housekeeping appealed to middle-class Americans drawn to such standards. Ultimately, the German influence on American mores would be substantial, particularly through their pleasure ethic, *Gemütlichkeit,* "the joy of living," apparent in their beer gardens, their music societies (which in many cities introduced public choruses and instrumental performances), and their *Turnvereine,* or patriotic gymnastic clubs for physical improvement, founded to reinvigorate Germans after the Napoleonic conquest. Later in the century neurologist George Beard wrote approvingly of the "Germanicization" of the United States—a development that he saw encouraging outdoor exercise and providing a healthy example of calmness to nervous, overachieving Americans. Others wrote of the German influence in softening Puritan asceticism and providing a rationale for carnivals and other public entertainments. Their styles of physical appearance, too, did not go unnoticed.[36]

The Germans were not the only group to find plumpness in women attractive. Lecturing in the United States in the late 1850s, Lola Montez, the famed dancer and adventuress whose conquests included kings, pointed out that only Western Europeans held the model of a "Lilliputian dame" as their ideal of beauty in women. According to Montez, the Dutch, Spanish, Greeks, and other Mediterranean peoples held that "corpulency is the most perfect beauty." For her part, Montez thought that the women of the English aristocracy were the age's preeminent beauties. They were "large and magnificent" and "very voluptuous."[37]

As a word, "voluptuous" was of old origin. Originally it meant sensual and luxurious and was applied to a style of life or behavior. By the 1830s it took on a new, more modern meaning as an adjective referring to the shape of a woman's body. Voluptuous now meant fleshy, with full hips and bosoms shaped and displayed to arouse. The appearance of the word indicated the emergence of another standard of beauty.[38]

That is to say, as the power of the steel-engraving lady moved across two continents, some groups paid little heed to its imperatives. Many artists, for example, abandoned the coyness of Fragonard and Watteau to paint and sculpt large and fleshy nudes. Ingres, a leading painter of the period, turned for inspiration to the corpulent nudes of Titian and Raphael. Following the Romantic vogue of orientalism, French painters, like French writers, were inspired by Eastern modes, which prized fleshiness in women. The nudes of Gustave Courbet, the influential French realist painter of midcentury, had large buttocks and breasts, and such models of appearance, although not featured in works by native American artists, were present in paintings that Americans viewed—even in this early period. In 1830 two Biblical canvases, *The Temptation* and *The Expulsion* by Claude Marie Dubufe, with large, fleshy figures, travelled throughout the United States, drawing large crowds. During the social dislocations following the German revolutions of 1848, a large collection of paintings by prominent Düsseldorf artists was brought to the United States and exhibited at a gallery on Broadway for at least a decade. The female figures of the acclaimed Düsseldorf school were large and fleshy; contemporary art critic Edward Strahan contended that they "formed the aesthetic fashion of the epoch."[39]

Perhaps the most important artistic representation of size and natural contour as an ideal of appearance for women, however, was Hiram Powers's sculpture, The Greek Slave, which toured the country in 1847, drawing enormous crowds of men and women wherever it was displayed. It became a national icon, repeatedly mentioned throughout the century in novels,

plays, and memoirs. The figure's association with the popular Greek rebellion against Turkish tyranny as well as its classical style legitimized its nudity and allowed prudish Victorians to violate their principles in viewing
the statue. The figure had the sturdy breasts and hips characteristic of classical female statuary, modified somewhat to accord with the smaller bulk of
the steel-engraving lady. Popular writer Ned Buntline described the heroine
of his *G'Hals of New York* as having a form "chastely beautiful and match-
less as Powers' Greek Slave," thereby indicating the figure's transitional position between voluptuousness and "chaste" fragility. George Ellington asserted that the figure of the Greek Slave became the century's model of
beauty for women.[40]

Painterly standards of voluptuous beauty in women were also followed
by actresses and prostitutes, women whose roots lay in the working-class
culture from which artists often drew their models. For example, waitresses
at the concert saloons of New York City, who functioned as prostitutes on
the side, according to journalists who observed them, had well-defined busts
and carmine red lips. Ned Buntline's *G'Hals of New York* featured two
thriving prostitutes. One was a "tall, dashing, magnificent creature, with
well-defined features, cheeks glowing with health and passion's fever; a bold
voluptuous bust." The other was "a bewitching little blonde, petite in figure, but full and plump as a partridge."[41]

Actresses also used their bodies to attract audiences, and a voluptuous
appearance, then as now, could be a significant factor in male attendance.
Hiram Fuller, a journalist who wrote popular travel books under the pseudonym Belle Brittain, described an actress he thought particularly beautiful.
She had "a remarkably sculpturesque bust; beautifully rounded arms, with
dimples at the elbows" and "cherry-ripe and sensuous lips." Writing in
1868, George Ellington recorded a conversation with the principal dancer of
a popular ballet company on the subject of women's bodies and their attractiveness to men. She pointed out to him that the years of rigorous physical
training required to become a first-rank ballerina changed a woman's
body; it became thin, taut, and muscular. For this reason, men often preferred the minor dancers in the company, who still possessed the soft
curves and voluptuous appearance that she thought men preferred in
women.[42]

Central to such an appearance were large hips and breasts. Whether
American women knew it or not, tightlacing was designed to increase the
size of the bosom and hips by reducing the size of the waist and pushing
excess flesh upward and downward. By the 1830s, padding was also used to
attain the proper form. Actresses and prostitutes, generally in advance of the
mode when it came to erotic effects, were already padding not only their
bosoms and hips, but even their arms and thighs to be certain they were

properly rounded. It is difficult to determine exactly when American women began to use padding. Foreign travellers in the 1830s and 1840s commonly remarked on the "flatness" of American women. Jane Cunningham Croly, a sensitive observer of such matters, dated the widespread use of padding to the late 1860s, although Thomas Grattan indicated that urban women were using padding by the late 1850s. In later decades Henry Collins Brown remembered how women wore a "gay deceiver," a rubber device inflated with air which occasionally popped at parties, creating merriment among the partygoers and mortification for the wearer.[43]

As much as women attempted to appear frail and delicate in the antebellum years, fashionable styles of dress often betrayed them. In the late 1820s and early 1830s, skirts hung to the ankles and feet clearly showed, while the flamboyant hats and full sleeves of that period gave women a defiant, even aggressive look. The sloping sleeves, bonnets, and crinolined skirts of the 1840s lent an appearance of frailty and dependence, but the hoop skirt, invented in 1856, introduced a new element. Held out by its lightweight frame, skirts swung to and fro, responding to their wearer's every movement and providing regular glimpses of feet and legs. This erotic feature, coupled with padded breasts, was considerably at variance with the presumed delicate look of the steel-engraving lady.

By the 1850s, feminist critics of nineteenth-century fashion excoriated the eroticism of women's dress. "Man's passions are unduly stimulated all the time by a woman's attire," wrote Elizabeth Cady Stanton. By the 1870s, with the disappearance of the bell shape in favor of tight-fitting dresses highlighted by a bustle in the back, the situation, in the eyes of feminists, was even worse. "We have long been accustomed to think of the dress of woman as unhealthful, inconvenient, absurdly complicated, extravagant," wrote dress reformer Celia Burleigh, "but we have not thought of it as immodest." Although "the imprisoned skirts proclaim helplessness," continued Burleigh, they also suggested mystery, and when these were lifted in crossing a street or getting into a carriage, "underclothing catches the eye and fires the imagination." One observer noted that the very fact that current fashion "emphasizes the distinct features of the feminine organization, that it is full of sensuous suggestions, points directly to its lack of modesty."[44]

Yet implicit in the image of the steel-engraving lady herself had always been a hint of "sensuous suggestions." One of the major curiosities of contemporary analyses of the derivation of the steel-engraving lady is the extent to which they traced this fragile model of beauty to Byron. Over and over, writers on fashion and beauty held Byron responsible for the pale cheeks and the wan form of the steel-engraving lady. Such judgments were not without authority. According to Byron scholars, the vogue for the English poet was even greater in the United States than in England, and he remained popular in the young nation long after Keats and Shelley had usurped his place in England. A self-conscious rebel, in flight from the conventions of his age, he seemed to personify some secret craving in the heart of otherwise respectable Victorians for adventure and passion. In the United States, as in England, the details of his personal life were as popular as his poetry, and young people in particular copied his dress and behavior. What is more, if we can believe the fashion magazines, young women copied Byron as much as did young men. Because a story circulated that Byron washed his hair in cold water every morning and allowed it to dry in short curls, women all over the United States followed his example. Fashion commentators in the latter part of the century traced the then current interest in manicuring to the fact that Byron had beautiful hands and nails and took special care of them. Above all, Byron himself had a natural tendency toward gaining weight and, to counter this, he constantly dieted. The popularity of drinking vinegar to lose weight can be traced directly to Byron, whose most popular regimen, according to some accounts, was to subsist for some days on vinegar and water.[45]

Yet according to most nineteenth-century fashion commentators, Byron's central influence was spread through his statement that he found disgusting the sight of a woman eating. Because of this remark, women in Europe and the United States took up systematic fasting. That Byron made such a remark is without doubt: his troubled relations with women, which ruined his reputation and drove him, a pariah, from England, led him to make venomous remarks about the female sex. That such misogyny dominated his attitude toward women and was his chief legacy to the women of his age is, however, questionable. The women in Byron's poems are voluptuous and sensual, fiery yet tender, the full partners in the flesh of his wandering, tempestuous men. Leila and Zuleika were his ideal; his criterion of beauty was derived from Spain and the Near East, to which his wanderings early took him, and the supple, sensuous odalisque was his ideal. In *Childe Harold* Byron wrote sarcastically of the pale women of the North: "How poor their forms appear! How languid, wan, and weak." To a friend he wrote that he detested thin women and that he liked "rounded forms."[46]

American women, avid readers of fiction, knew Byron's works. They were as familiar with his voluptuous females as they were with the details of his personal life, with his dieting, and with whatever misogynous remarks he made. That contemporary fashion analysts placed so much emphasis on a statement motivated by personal irritation reflected more than anything else their own prudery and their desire to downplay the sensuality that was Byron's real message.

But they could never entirely do so. One of the striking features of the

Victorian model of beauty, despite her delicacy, was her dark hair. In all the fashion plates of the period the women have dark, not blonde, hair, a clear indication to nineteenth-century culture of an underlying sensuality and possibly the greatest influence that Byron had on the model of the steel-engraving lady. For centuries European culture had identified dark hair with passion, blonde hair with purity. In 1878 *Harper's Bazar* noted that the heroines of sentimental romantics like Tennyson and Browning were blonde, but the women that Scott and Byron preferred had dark hair. The steel-engraving lady was demure in face and figure, but her hair indicated a different attribute. "Jeannie with the Light Brown Hair," as Stephen Foster described it, was the preferred hair color of the day; even Lavater thought that blonde women were insipid.[47]

An incipient sensuality permeated the ideal beauty of the Victorian period on a number of levels. The existence of such a quality, as well as its complex relationship to the dominant attribute of purity, is strikingly revealed in the image of the ballerina. More than any other figure, she was the direct model of beauty for the steel-engraving lady. Her popularity, like that of Byron, reached the dimensions of a craze in the 1830s not only in France and England, but also in the United States.

For some time male dancers who excelled in vigorous, athletic movements had dominated ballet. In the 1820s and 1830s, however, a number of gifted ballerinas, aided by choreographers intent on change, had revolutionized the art. Utilizing the discovery of dancing *en pointe,* or on toe, which was introduced in the 1820s, they had developed a new kind of dancing based on deliberate and graceful movements, geared to what the culture viewed as women's naturally superior bodily grace and beauty. They "have discovered that the line of beauty in dancing is like that of Hogarth in painting," wrote a contemporary. Among the great Romantic ballerinas, Maria Taglioni was lionized throughout the Western world, and Fanny Elssler, the major one to visit the United States, received an extraordinary reception in 1840, surpassed only by that of singer Jenny Lind in 1850.[48]

The great ballerinas of the Romantic ballet varied in body type, but contemporaries often described them as slender and elegant, and that is the way they appeared in their widely distributed lithographic representations. The American dancer who discussed the matter of body type with George Ellington contended that her company's minor dancers were voluptuous in appearance but that the years of training first-rank ballerinas underwent produced thin, muscular frames. Hiram Fuller wrote that the dancers in the Ronzoni Ballet company, which toured the United States in the 1850s, were so thin that they looked like "open umbrellas with two pink handles." Thinness was part of the ethereal image the Romantic ballerinas wanted to portray: they were birds in flight, angels come to earth. Dressed in white, hair sleekly drawn to the backs of their heads, they were the personification of innocent spirituality characteristic of the ideal Romantic woman. Ethereal in white tulle, they defied gravity by dancing birdlike on their toes. In the ballets in which they performed, they were often spirits or fairies—unattainable beings with whom mortal men, replicating the Romantic quest for the ideal, fell in love. Or, in a variation of the Cinderella mythology with its satisfying denial of class divisions and its reinforcement of the power of men over women, they were ordinary women partnered with princes.[49]

Yet as with the Romantic women, whose image they played an important role in creating and disseminating, sensuality was not absent from their milieu. The typical Romantic ballet was set in a mysterious landscape peopled with exotic, magical creatures, among whom were evil fairies and witches. Too, many of these ballerinas, despite their lithographs, were in actuality heavy and curvaceous in body type, foreshadowing the kind of physical appearance that Lydia Thompson would later popularize in the United States. Maria Taglioni, for example, was known for having introduced a new modesty as well as grace in her dancing, but according to Nathaniel Parker Willis, her figure was "rounded to the very last degree of perfection." And her great rival, Fanny Elssler, was a different sort of performer. Influenced by traditional Spanish folk dances, she developed a staccato style that contemporaries experienced as seductive and sensuous.[50]

It was Elssler, known for her fiery dancing, and not Taglioni, the exemplar of the etherealized ballerina, who toured the United States to a thunderous welcome. Crowds thronged Elssler's passage through the streets of the major cities in which she played; her performances were mobbed; lithographs of her quickly sold out; and everything from confections to articles of clothing was named after her. The Senate and House of Representatives cancelled sessions so that their members could attend performances. Despite her checkered past, she was welcomed by New York society. According to theatrical producer Frederick Wemyss, the enthusiasm for Elssler and her dancing was a "mania."

Like Jenny Lind ten years later, Elssler had an agent, Chevalier Wikoff, who used every possible advertising technique to enhance her popularity. And, according to some analysts, she lengthened her dresses and toned down her dances so as not to offend the conventional sensibilities of American audiences. Still, her welcome reflected the curiosity of Americans who wanted to see this exemplar of Victorian womanhood and fashion style setter in the flesh. And the sensual display of her European performances was not absent from her American dances. The manager of the New Orleans theater in which she performed called her movements "ethereal" and her form "classic." Famed American voluptuary Sam Ward, however, found her dancing "sensual, her ensemble the incarnation of seductive attractiveness."[51]

If one views the steel-engraving lady from the perspective of Byron and the ballerina, the underlying sensuality of her face and form becomes clearer. Her dark hair is no accident; nor is the roundness of her figure simply an expression of girlish innocence. Finally, her very innocence itself can be viewed as erotic. In his treatise on beauty, Alexander Walker wrote that the nineteenth-century art of flirting "adopts a general concealment which it well knows can alone give a sensual and seductive power to momentary exposure." As feminists realized, the long skirts and covered arms of Victorian fashion were seductive precisely because they were constructed in such a way that a momentary glimpse of ankle or wrist might show through. Producers and directors of musical comedy in the late nineteenth century realized this principle of human nature when they abandoned the risqué, abbreviated costumes of the variety entertainers and clothed their principal singers and dancers in long, full skirts that could easily be lifted or kicked aside to offer an occasional, brief display of ankle or leg.[52]

In his pioneering *Psychology of Sex,* written in Victorianism's waning years, Havelock Ellis provided not the universal definition of female sexual attractiveness that he thought he had discovered, but rather a statement of characteristics that nineteenth-century men found attractive in women. According to Ellis, those qualities were modesty and innocence. Modesty, he argued, "is the chief secondary [sexual] characteristic of women. Even in abnormal, as well as normal erotic passion, the desire is for innocence." Yet for many men, voluptuousness in women was singularly appealing. Nineteenth-century writers noted how married men liked to boast that they could encircle their wives' waists with the fingers of their hands held together. Such a boast not only indicated male domination, but also was a scarcely concealed declaration of erotic intent, since tiny waists were increasingly combined with large bosoms and hips. Innocence and modesty may have remained predominant in the antebellum years, but the arrival of the British Blondes, with their voluptuous bodies and their assertive ways, indicated the emergence of a powerful, competing model of sexuality and of beauty in women.[53]

4

The Underside of Fashion

W hen contemporaries analyzed the forces behind fashion's domination, they often stressed the drive on the part of individuals of all social classes to emulate the wealthy. "The wife of the bank clerk, or of the young business man just making a start in life aims at dressing as stylishly as does the wealthiest among her acquaintances," wrote one observer. "The sewing girl and the shopgirl, nay even the chambermaid and the cook, must in turn have flounced silk dresses and velvet cloaks for Sunday use." Long before Thorstein Veblen published his classic analysis of fashion in *The Theory of the Leisure Class* in 1899, nineteenth-century predecessors realized the intense desire among many people to identify with the upper classes and their patterns of leisure, fashion, and consumption.

The drive for upper-class status was an important motivation behind fashionable behavior as well as a determinant of the characteristics of the steel-engraving lady. Yet it was difficult then—as it is for historians now—to determine who constituted the upper classes in the mobile society of the United States. Moreover, the initial source of American fashions lay across an ocean. Exactly who held the mandate to translate Parisian fashions into American terms was not always clear. Even dressmakers, often upwardly mobile with insecure status, had to be sensitive to social trends.[1]

Observers of American social behavior left a wealth of descriptions of the dress and behavior of women on New York City streets. From their observations a panorama of the behavior of real women in actual life situations can be reconstructed. And it is clear from their accounts that, by the 1850s, the stereotype of the modest Victorian maiden did not always apply, that women did not always follow Parisian fashion, and that the upper classes, at least in the United States, did not always set the prevailing style.

Since the time of Louis XIV, Paris had been the fashion center of the Western world. The participation of French aristocrats like the marquis de

Lafayette in the American Revolution had stimulated a taste for French products, and many Americans identified France in the 1790s as a comrade in revolution and a leader of worldwide republicanism. The French revolutionary experience had produced a simplified style in dress based on classical models—the so-called Empire style, as it came to be known in the Napoleonic era. This style appealed to Americans, who were steeped in the classics and who identified their republic with the republics of the classical world. But French influence over American fashion persisted long after republicanism in dress had ended.

French fashions were transmitted to the United States in a variety of ways. Before the advent of regular fashion magazines, like *Godey's Lady's Book,* European dressmakers and other correspondents dressed dolls in the latest fashions and sent them to American women and their dressmakers to indicate the current Continental mode. Sometimes they sent drawings and descriptions and occasionally gowns themselves, although this more expensive method was risky before the advent of standardized body measurements for clothing in the post–Civil War period. Men and women not directly connected with the fashion industry were also responsible for the transmission of fashion to the United States. For instance, American women who visited Europe brought back the latest styles. Louisa Jay, wife of jurist and statesman John Jay, introduced Parisian fashions to New York society in 1789 on her return from accompanying her husband to Paris, where he had helped negotiate the peace treaty that ended the revolutionary war. In 1836 an unnamed "Virginia lady" just back from Paris wore the first fashionable tight sleeves in the United States after the seven-year reign of the enormous leg-of-mutton variety. She first displayed the style at Carusi's, the fashionable dancing master's quarters in Washington, D.C., where elite society held its balls. William Thomson, the American consul at Southampton, England, developed a remarkable sense for female fashions and sent the first striped petticoats, which became fashionable in 1858, to friends in Washington.[2]

Fashionable women introduced stylistic innovations in dress at dinner parties, at balls, and in church. Moreover, every city had its fashionable street, like New York's Broadway, where elite shops and dressmakers were located and where women promenaded in the afternoons, providing a daily fashion panorama. Theaters, too, by the 1850s were becoming places of fashion dissemination, as their managers began to follow innovations in interior design first introduced in opera houses. They eliminated the third tier of seats traditionally reserved for prostitutes and replaced the cheap seats at orchestra level with more expensive ones, thereby eliminating the "pit," formerly a center of rowdy behavior that dominated theaters. Slowly but surely theater going became popular among the well-to-do, and theater managers did all they could to enhance the possibilities for the display of dress—an activity appealing to women patrons. They built special lobbies where women could promenade between the acts, and they kept the lights half on during performances so that people in the audience could observe one another. The manager of the Bowery Theatre went so far as to paint the backs of the boxes light pink so that women's dresses would be set off to best advantage.[3]

Hotels were also beginning to be places where women displayed modish dress. In the early decades of the nineteenth century, women usually dined and entertained at home. But for women travelling with husbands, as well as for those women who had taken up permanent residence in hotels with their families, the public rooms of hotels became stages for fashionable display. Long before George Boldt, manager of the Waldorf-Astoria, in 1897 constructed in his hotel the long hall that was known as Peacock Alley, which became famous as a place for fashionable display, some women were using the dining rooms, corridors, and ladies' parlors of hotels for this purpose. "At dinner takes place the grand daylight display," wrote one observer of hotel behavior. "Here it is that the ambition, the ostentation, the panting struggle for superiority in mere external appearance, which is the essence of the life of the fashionable woman, is displayed." After dinner, according to French traveller Oscar Comettant, hotel parlors were filled with elegant women, reading, playing the piano, flirting, with no concern that strangers could see and hear them.[4]

In addition to hotels and theaters, summer resorts had by the 1840s become important places where styles were developed and disseminated. Saratoga and Newport were especially popular among the wealthy; but the well-to-do of Boston frequented the nearby seacoast of Nahant during the summer months; New Jerseyans and New Yorkers went to Long Branch and Long Island; and White Sulphur Springs and other southern mineral spas were popular among wealthy southern urbanites and plantation owners.

Removed from regular social circles, the spas offered women freedom to experiment with new styles of dress and behavior. It was not unique, for example, that New York debutante Celia Wall in 1867 chose Saratoga as the place to introduce the so-called Grecian bend, which was then newly in vogue in Paris and which involved an extreme S-shaped silhouette, with bulging hips and buttocks and a tightly bound waist. At the spas, vacationers stayed not in private residences, but rather in public boarding houses and hotels, where domestic duties were at a minimum. Bringing people together from a variety of areas, conceived as places of pleasure where conventional restraints were relaxed, the spas were regarded as arenas of romance conducive to courtship, as husband-hunting grounds where it was important that a young woman look her best to find a husband—or a bored matron to find a lover.[5]

Even before the Civil War, when only the elites could afford the spas, women predominated there. Husbands joined their families on weekends. At the spas, noted Lillian Foster, "the entire government is in the hands of women." Boredom and numerical dominance created among the women a competitive situation that centered around dress. At Saratoga's many hotels, fashion competition was so intense on the nights when balls were held that a steady stream of women and their escorts walking or riding in carriages passed from one hotel to another to see what other women at the resort were wearing. "Nothing can exceed the display of restless ostentation observable at the watering places," wrote Harriet Martineau.[6]

Moreover, the frequent appearance of southerners at northern spas intensified the competition by adding a sectional dimension. Although many historians note that women on plantations, involved with day-to-day management of huge estates, did not have time to keep up with the latest fashions, personal pride and sectional jealousy prompted attention to style when they left the South. And wealthy southern women from sophisticated cities like Charleston and New Orleans had long been renowned for their knowledge of fashion. Mrs. James L. Petigru, who fascinated Marian Gouverneur at Newport, represented the dominant type of southern woman at northern spas; she was determined to make a stir and establish southern leadership in another area concerned with the aristocratic world that southerners claimed they represented.

Yet there were other sources for the transmission of fashion, and these were not connected with the elites. Actresses and other stage performers often introduced fashions. Ballerinas were important models for the steel-engraving type of beauty. Actresses found that their appeal was enhanced, and more women came to see them, if they dressed in the latest styles. Josephine Shaw, a member of Lester Wallack's respected New York repertory company, is usually credited with having begun the practice of stylish dress in the 1850s after she married John Hooey, one of New York City's wealthiest merchants, and thereby gained social standing and more money for clothing, although Philadelphia producer Frederick Wemyss noted that several successful actresses who played at his theater wore the latest modes before Shaw did so. Nineteenth-century actresses were responsible for providing their own costumes—a requirement that could entail considerable expense, but also encouraged responsiveness to audience demand in the area of dress. When the eminent French tragedienne Rachel came to tour the United States in 1855, her costumes had been well publicized in advance, and she brought forty-two trunks of clothing with her. By the end of the century, so close was the association of actresses and fashion that the heroines even of historical dramas were costumed in modern style, and audience expectation of seeing lavish, fashionable dress on stage was an element behind the vogue for period plays in the late nineteenth and early twentieth centuries.[7]

The point is that actresses as well as society women set the fashion, and actresses were not usually of the elites. Fashionable women set the fashions, but exactly who the fashionable women were at any given time is not so easy to determine as suggested by beauty writers in the early nineteenth century or by Thorstein Veblen toward its close.

II

Victorian prudery and the widespread pursuit of fashion both appeared in a time of rapid economic, urban, and industrial growth—a period from 1830 to 1860 that encompassed the most rapid urbanization in the nation's history. In New York City, the nation's fashion center, the influx of population plus economic growth and change produced a chaotic social situation.

As nineteenth-century analysts realized, the fluid class structure of American society made aspiration universal and, at the same time, the drawing of social distinctions difficult. "There are no distinctive classes, as in aristocratic lands," wrote Catharine Beecher. "Thus, the person of humble means is brought into contact with those of vast wealth while all gradations between are placed side by side. Thus, too, there is a constant comparison among equals, and a constant temptation presented to imitate the customs, and to strive for the enjoyments of those who possess larger means." The common mythology had it that there were no class divisions in the United States. "There being no positive acknowledged degrees of rank among them," noted English observer James Bell, "all the world wish to hide their humble stations as much as possible by imposing externals."[8]

Recent research on the Jacksonian period indicates, however, that during the 1830s and 1840s, despite much evidence of social flux, a redistribution of wealth did not occur. Several of the wealthiest men in New York City, including fur trader and real estate entrepreneur John Jacob Astor and commercial magnate Alexander Turney Stewart, came from humble backgrounds. But in general the old elites maintained their position and wealthy new entrepreneurs came mainly from the well-to-do. Nevertheless, as the closest scholar of Jacksonian mobility has found, 10 percent of New York's financial elite rose from poverty to riches. Their number partly explains why so many contemporary observers thought that most wealthy Americans were nouveau riche.[9]

The economic expansion of the antebellum years also gave rise to a new group of upwardly striving, middle-level entrepreneurs in business and the professions who saw elite status as their right and who lived beyond their means. "No sooner do they find that their husbands or fathers have laid up a couple of thousand dollars in the bank," wrote Francis Grund, "than they set up for ladies of the *ton*." Social critics like Charles Astor Bristed, Nathaniel Parker Willis, and Anna Cora Mowatt unmercifully satirized New York's nouveau riche. They found the plebeian pasts of these people still apparent in their "coarse faces, loud voices, bad English, and vulgar manners." According to George Foster, "For the most part our parvenue aristocracy, who live in magnificent houses and whose families ride in beautiful carriages . . . are of the lowest grade of vulgarity." Francis Grund charged that "they ride in their own carriages; live in expensive houses, give parties to which they invite people whom they have never met before; rake up a relationship with some colonel in the revolutionary army, or some noble family in Europe; hang up the portraits of their ancestors in the parlors; make the tours of the springs in the summer. . . ." For their benefit appeared the scores of etiquette books that flooded the market, guides useful in a society where, as Eliza Farrar put it, "talents and education carry people into the most refined circles, without any previous training in manners."[10]

In 1854 Anna Cora Mowatt graphically repeated these charges in her popular and still performed play *Fashion*. The central character, Mrs. Tiffany, made hats in a millinery shop when she first met Mr. Tiffany, a peddler who sold silks and ribbons and initially carried his wares "in a pack on his own shoulders." By shrewd dealings Tiffany has made a fortune in the dry goods business. During the action of the play, business preoccupies him, while his wife attempts to become a woman of fashion. Yet because of her humble beginnings she constantly violates correct etiquette. Eventually her brother, a virtuous, rural Yankee of the heroic type often introduced into plays of the period, shows her the error of her ways, but not before Mowatt has demonstrated the foolishness of Mrs. Tiffany's fixation with dress, consumption, and social climbing.[11]

As new groups sought advancement, new social barriers appeared. In Boston and New York invitational balls organized by a small group of self-constituted families defined the highest social circle; in Philadelphia residence in the right section of the city became especially important. But such attempts at exclusion in no way lessened the drive of those rejected to penetrate the barriers and to create circles of their own. In Philadelphia, for example, Andrew Bell claimed in 1838 that there were "nine or ten distinct ranks, beginning at the lower class of traders and ending in the dozen or so who keep . . . a large establishment; each of these circles, repelling and repelled, carefully keeps itself apart, and draws a line that no one of doubtful status may pass." In Boston, as Francis Grund described it, "if you belong to the first society you must not by any chance accept an invitation to the second. . . . If you belong to the second, if you are seen with the third, you are done with the second, and so on." Even to contemporaries the basis of social distinctions seemed frivolous. According to one analyst, wholesale merchants and importers thought themselves superior to retail merchants, while downtown retailers disdained their uptown competitors. "How edifying to see the auctioneer asserting his superior gentility to the grocer," commented the *New York Review* in 1838, "and the wife and daughters of the man who sells by the bale in Pearl Street refusing to associate with the wife and daughters of the man who sells by the yard on Broadway." In New York City, Nathaniel Parker Willis was completely confused as to who constituted elite society: "The uncertainty as to who the fashionables are is sometimes increased, too, by their great number, as no recognized circle ever comes twice together, and no twenty fashionables would agree as to the fashionableness of twenty more."[12]

Even if they were unable to afford the necessary appointments of wealth like carriages, servants and stylish homes, particularly with the severe housing shortages in burgeoning cities, aspirants to the world of fashion found other ways to assert their claims. Many families took lodging in the boarding houses that were a distinct feature of urban life before the late-century appearance of apartment buildings. Boarding houses constituted the main form of urban housing in antebellum America; even large, prestigious hotels offered boarding arrangements. "I have lived in American hotels where three or four hundred people sat down to dinner of whom not one hundred were travellers," wrote one observer. Both George Ellington and David Mitchell estimated that 75 percent of the population of New York City lived in boarding houses. The American people were, according to Walt Whitman, a "boarding people."[13]

Emancipated from housekeeping, ignored by husbands involved in work, boarding house women often made fashion the center of their lives. A new type of woman had come into existence in America's cities, wrote one commentator. By and large she came from the nouveau riche and lived in hotels and boarding houses, places of "aimless idleness." She travelled, she haunted the fashionable spas, she was prominent at the opera and at public balls—"wherever she can show herself and her clothes." English feminist Barbara Bodichen wrote that women in boarding houses reminded her "of certain women I have seen in seraglios, whose whole time was taken up with dressing and painting faces."[14]

Women who lived in boarding houses, often frustrated in their drive for social advancement by the nature of their living arrangements, were particularly intent on asserting their identity. Moreover, New York's economic growth in this period was partly based on the expansion of the dry goods and clothing industries. Many of the newly wealthy—like Mrs. Tiffany in *Fashion*—had a special connection with the fabric and dress business that gave them a temerity they might otherwise have lacked. Their challenge to elite control of the mode is particularly apparent in the innumerable descriptions of women on New York City streets as looking "gaudy," as dressed in bright colors and flashy trimmings. From 1830 to 1850 the Parisian mode called for soft, subdued colors, and the cult of gentility required that women muffle themselves in shawls and bonnets when on the streets. In the 1830s and 1840s the observations of many social commentators indicated that women were following these dictates. Abram Dayton remembered "the delicate mantling of the cheek, the half-closed eyelid, the slightly stooped position, the noiseless, sliding step, the subdued tone." George Foster described the typical women riders on New York City omnibuses: "With fluttering morning robes and thick green veils," they were "muffled inscrutably from sight, and as careful of being seen as the inmates of the harem."[15]

By the 1850s, however, the appearance and behavior of women on New York City streets had changed. "The wives and daughters of free-born Americans seem to think they have a right to sport their silks and satins at what hour of the day they please, whether in the boudoir, public sitting-room, or on Broadway," wrote one observer. "They look like tinselled butterflies born for show. If anyone needs their services, it is P. T. Barnum." In 1852 Frances Kemble noted that women on New York City streets walked with a kind of shuffle that was in vogue in France and was, in her opinion, partly the result of wearing shoes that were too tight. *Harper's Magazine* described the walk as "mincing." But by 1859 the walk of New York women had changed. Thomas Grattan, long-term British consul in Boston, wrote that "the flaunting airs of the ladies, their streaming feathers and flowers, silks and satins of all colors, and a rapid, dashing step as they walk along, give foreigners a wildly mistaken idea of them." Grattan thought they resembled no other group of European women as much as prostitutes. Anthony Trollope had a similar opinion in 1865. He found American women wiggling their hips in imitation of "a peculiar step often seen on the French boulevards."[16]

The newly well-to-do, neophytes in the world of fashion, came from modest backgrounds in which clothing was made of dark fabrics that did not show dirt or of cheap fabrics that quickly lost their color. Bright colors and gaudy display offered a strong fashion statement that seemed to attract them. Some commentators claimed that clever American cloth merchants imported the leftover, brightly colored fabrics that Parisian women wore only in ball gowns and successfully sold them to unknowing Americans as suitable for everyday wear. Others thought that Parisian modistes foisted their most extravagant fashions, which they had difficulty selling in Paris, on an unsophisticated American clientele. Whatever the truth, middle-class women on some level knew exactly what they were doing when they wore "gaudy" clothes. Their costumes were a statement of rebellion against the elites, an attempt to preempt the latter's position by assuming fashion leadership. Journalist George Foster observed in 1850 how differently dressed were women of elite and middle-class station. Although some might think the shawls and dresses of the middle-class women "a little too exuberant," Foster found their dress more attractive than that of wealthier women.[17]

Some groups of working-class women also challenged elite control of fashion. They could do so because, except for years like 1836 when skintight sleeves suddenly replaced balloon sleeves, and 1867 when the S-line replaced the bell-shaped curve, fashions changed gradually from year to year, and a clever seamstress could replace ruffles with bows and flounces with ribbons or readjust waistline gathers for fuller or tighter skirts. By the 1850s, *Godey's* employed a regular correspondent in Paris to gain the newest fashion information, which, issued monthly in its pages, was as fresh as that which dressmakers received. Styles in accessories set by actresses were often produced in large quantities as a means of publicity, and they were available to the public immediately after a successful debut. Thus working women also could appear quickly on New York streets in their own variations of the current mode.

The most determined group of working-class women to challenge elite control of fashion were the "Bowery G'Hirls," female counterparts of the "Bowery B'Hoys." By the 1850s the tough and aggressive Bowery B'Hoys, generally members of the volunteer fire companies that alternately protected and terrorized New Yorkers, had become well-known symbols of urban masculinity. In those years, according to Charles Haswell, New York was sufficiently small that types like the Bowery B'Hoy and G'Hirl gained speedy recognition. Their fame was spread nationally by a series of plays featuring them as main characters. The first of these plays, Frank Chanfrau's *Glance at New York,* was produced in 1848.[18]

Like the Bowery B'Hoy, the Bowery G'Hirl was independent and self-reliant. Often she was a dressmaker's assistant, and her elevated position within the hierarchy of working women in the fashion world gave her special access to fashion information and training in the skills of style. Like the Bowery B'Hoy, she expressed her rebellious nature in her behavior and dress. Her walk was mischievous and defiant. Her voice was loud and hearty. Her dress copied, while parodying, prevailing styles. Like the newly rich on Broadway and the Bowery, she wore bright colors and gaudy decoration, but her decorations were even more elaborate and her colors brighter than those of wealthier women. She defied "all laws of harmony and taste." Drawing on fashions that had been popular in the 1820s, she typically wore a bright yellow shawl, red dress, and a bonnet trimmed with flowers and feathers, gigantic bows, and long streamers of tricolored ribbons resting on the back of her head so that her face clearly showed. She paid little attention to current conventions that fashionable women ought to be thin and pale-faced. "It may be true," wrote George Foster, "that these plump and hearty divinities betray some little bizarrie in the selection of colors and the cut of their dresses . . . [but] whenever they take the trouble to think of the poor, pale-faced creatures of Broadway, they actually and heartily pity them."[19]

What is more, in a statement of insurgency, Bowery G'Hirls wore their skirts at ankle length, then considered shockingly short. Young girls commonly wore skirts at this length, as did ballerinas and, by the 1850s, women on ice skates. Shortened skirts were part of certain national costumes, particularly German ones. But since the late 1830s, only prostitutes had bared their ankles for street wear. The skirts of genteel women swept the streets. In New York City short skirts had become identified with the waitresses at the "concert saloons" on Broadway and the Bowery, who practiced prostitution on the side. Yet many working-class women paid no heed to such views. Among them, public dances were a main form of entertainment and here, in particular, they wore whatever they pleased: "no sleeves; balloons; sacks; the long dress, the short dress, the high and the low."[20]

Along with the wealthy, prostitutes also promenaded Broadway, frequenting shops and openly soliciting customers, even during the day. George Foster reported the convention that the sunny side of the street was theirs: before Alexander Stewart daringly built his emporium on Broadway's suspect side, a woman could lose her reputation if she appeared on the wrong sidewalk. By 1848, in his massive report on prostitution in New York City, William Sanger found high-class prostitutes walking along even the fashionable side of Broadway. Five Points, the city's most notorious pre–Civil War slum and the center of lower-class prostitution, and the area of Thomas, Duane, and Church streets, where New York City's elegant bordellos were centered, were only a few blocks from the fashionable Broadway shopping center; both were visible from the corner in front of Barnum's Broadway museum. For half a century, according to Matthew Hale Smith, the streets parallel to Broadway on either side, from Canal to Bleecker, were the abode of streetwalkers.[21]

Prostitutes from the lower and middle ranks often wore gaudy colors or heavy cosmetics or dressed in some fashion to make their purpose clear to potential customers. Yet the costumes of the new wealthy and the Bowery

G'Hirl must have made the prostitutes' displays less easily discernible. Many concert hall waitresses wore red boots with their short skirts, but so did waitresses in the German beer halls on the Bowery, places of respectable family entertainment, and these women were not prostitutes. By the mid-1850s fashionable women themselves were wearing makeup as well as gaudy attire. One observer of women on New York City streets wrote that "there was a time when a mode of dressing to display every personal charm was peculiar to an unfortunate class of beings, regarded as lost to all the modesty and dignity of the sex; but it is a melancholy truth, that this distinction between the lost and the reputable no longer exists in our great cities, where leaders of fashion . . . are most remarkable for the solicitude with which they prepare their lovely persons to be gazed at and admired, in all their proportions. . . ." Ultimately the streetwalkers took to smoking cigarettes as a way of indicating their occupation. And upper-class prostitutes, who did not ply their trade on the streets, did not separate themselves from the women on Broadway and other streets. Possessing financial reserves, they could afford the costly fashions. To the Broadway panorama, they added another element of extravagant display.[22]

Housing patterns in large, growing cities, in which upper- and middle-class residential districts had not yet been sorted out, contributed to fashion's perplexing message. Middle-class boarding houses and working-class tenements were situated side by side with the mansions of the wealthy; and here the class challenge to high fashion was visible and direct. Even Broadway presented problems in class and fashion interaction. Nathaniel Parker Willis, whose office was located on Broadway across from Barnum's museum, thought his office window was an excellent place from which to observe "street habits." Writing in 1848, he was particularly interested in the women who promenaded the avenue after five o'clock. "The crowd is unlike the morning crowd," he wrote. "There is as much or more beauty, but the fashionable ladies are not out. You would be puzzled to discover who these lovely women are. Their toilets are unexceptional, their style is a *very* near approach to *comme il faut.*" Willis indicated they were not prostitutes; in all probability they were working women able to display themselves only after they had finished work. Characterized by behavior that would become common among all Broadway promenaders by the 1850s, they were bold and provocative. "They look perfectly satisfied with themselves, and they do (what fashionable ladies do *not*) meet the eye of a promenader with a coquettish confidence he will misinterpret if he be green or a puppy."[23]

To achieve clarity in class definition, the wealthy sometimes introduced fashions that even the middle classes could not afford. Cashmere shawls, woven by hand from the rare fleece of Kashmir goats and originally brought to Europe during the Napoleonic wars, were very expensive. Wealthy women also purchased handkerchiefs either so finely woven that the fabric was scarcely visible or fringed with rows of the most expensive lace, which they ostentatiously held in the tips of their fingers as they promenaded the fashionable streets and shopped in the fashionable stores. One observer during the crinoline craze of the 1860s—as skirts grew wider and the expense of making them greater—speculated that the only way working-class women could possibly afford what they were wearing was by engaging in part-time prostitution. Yet increasingly, for example, fine machine-made lace was produced, and reputable imitations of the cashmere shawl were developed, at first in Paisley, England. Ultimately, certain sectors of the upper classes dropped completely out of the competition, made simplicity their hallmark, left fashion competition to others, and added another confusing element to the fashion scene. "The better sort of ladies," wrote Anne Royall, "are easy in manners, plain in equipage and dress, and seldom seen on the streets." The women who promenaded daily on Broadway were not of the upper classes, she contended. That Marian Gouverneur, daughter of elite New Yorkers, could live in New York City without encountering a woman of fashion until she went to Newport in the 1830s was probably because she came from this group of the secluded wealthy.[24]

Etiquette arbiter Mary E. Sherwood, of old New York lineage, graphically depicted the confrontation between old and new wealth in the arena of fashion in her novel, *A Transplanted Rose*. The book's heroine, Rose, a country heiress, comes to live with her aristocratic aunt in New York City. Naturally intelligent and beautiful, Rose nevertheless possesses neither sophistication nor genteel manners. Above all, her taste in dress, by Sherwood's standard, is nouveau riche. Preparing for her first society ball, she hires an "enameller" to rouge and powder her face; to the ball she wears an elaborate brocade dress. She is, of course, a failure. Scorned and teased at the ball, to which all the other young women wear diaphanous white, she can explain to her aunt only that she thought all the well-to-do women in New York used cosmetics and wore showy dress. Such was the popular impression.[25]

At the height of the crinoline craze, reporter Hiram Fuller noted that the broadest skirts emerged from "equivocal localities." In 1850 Parisians began to wear long-sleeved, tailored, tight-fitting jackets over their full-skirted dresses. The jackets were called "polka" jackets, in honor of the new popular dance, or "monkey" jackets, because they resembled the jackets worn by monkeys accompanying the ubiquitous organ grinders in Paris and New York. Yet upper-class New York City women refused to wear this new costume commonly sported by the middle classes. They cited the "immorality" of a woman wearing male attire and the "dangers of overstepping the barrier which separates persons of 'position in society' from the more common vulgar herd."[26]

Determined like many of their husbands to achieve success, middle-class women were more "modern" in the world of fashion than their upper-class counterparts. Indeed, the evidence of their dress and street behavior indicates that the cult of gentility among them was a complex phenomenon that may not have extended beyond the area of language and certain conventions in male-female interaction. The gaudy women on New York streets simply do not fit the common Victorian stereotype of constraint. Surveying the urban scene in 1868, George Ellington could write only with wonder at the way the middle class was supposed to be—a pattern of behavior much at variance with what he observed.

> The middle classes are supposed to be the moral classes. All the virtues are centered in them, or, if not centered in them, they are commonly supposed to be more virtuous and moral than either the higher or the lower classes. The wicked fashionable and the wicked poor sin always, but the middle classes keep a medium in morality and goodness as they do in wealth, and, if guilty at all, are only guilty of occasional transgressions of the moral code. They are supposed to have the best sense in everything, to avoid all extremes in everything.

Yet uplifting, moral behavior did not always characterize the middle class Ellington observed in New York City.[27]

By the 1850s, many contemporaries were noting the appearance of a new kind of American woman. Not only did she wear gaudy clothes and appear aggressive, but her entire behavior was characterized by a new freedom. The new ideal came partly from Paris, where the delicate woman of the 1830s as the model of beauty was challenged in the 1840s by the "lionne"—the woman patterned after the heroines of George Sand, who "could ride like an arab ... fence, shoot with pistols, smoke a cigar...." But the roots of the new woman of the 1850s were also American, and they proceeded from the successful attempts of working- and middle-class women to gain some control over setting fashionable styles.[28]

III

Even at the height of the popularity of the steel-engraving lady, a new kind of American woman was emerging to challenge her hegemony. Her outlines were apparent in the regular complaints of foreign travellers and native observers that American women were not polite in public places. Critics especially noted that women expected men to give up their seats in public conveyances and to allow them to enter buildings first without evincing a hint of thanks. Foreign travellers marvelled at the deference American men paid to women; Nathaniel Parker Willis asserted that it was popularly called the "American Homage to Women." Most analysts traced the origins of American chivalry to the colonial period and saw it as a result of women's participation in the work of colonization and of their numerical minority within the colonial population. By the mid-nineteenth century, however, many analysts thought that women were abusing their privileges, that rudeness, not respect, was coming to characterize women's public behavior.[29]

In 1857, *Harper's Magazine* expressed the common concern: "Where does woman have, in any other nation, a bolder air in public than with us? Where does she flaunt her charms so freely? Where does her eye look with a steadier gaze on man? Where does her voice sound louder, and her laugh ring more sonorously? There is an eye bearing steadily the gaze of man, and having a conscious look of experience that by right belongs only to the wife, but which by some means or other has got into the heads of our most useful vestals." In 1879 Henry James in *Daisy Miller* sketched a classic portrait of the independent, self-willed young American woman. Because the work seemed to capture the concerns of Americans about the behavior of their daughters, it became an overwhelming success, invariably noted by later analysts of adolescent women. Yet long before James's work was published, contemporary commentators noted the appearance of the "fast young woman," of " 'hoydenish,' laughing, giggling, romping, flirting behavior among young American women." In Boston, Philadelphia, New York, and Baltimore, Oscar Comettant saw women behaving exactly like the "lionnes" of Paris. In the 1860s this new style of woman became known as the "girl of the period," an appellation popularized by English social critic Elizabeth Linn Linton.[30]

Many American women in the 1850s and 1860s were bold and provocative in public. Contrary to common impression, external controls on their conduct were limited. Chaperonage and other formalized attempts to monitor the behavior of young men and women in the courting years were not enforced with any degree of success until well after the Civil War. During these earlier years a young woman could walk throughout much of New York unescorted. Frances Kemble observed the "hoydenish" young women in New York City streets, between the ages of ten and eighteen, "screaming at the top of their lungs, running in and out of shops, spending lots of time lounging about in the streets," apparently with no adult attempting to restrain their behavior.[31]

Relations between young men and women were similarly free. Women could accompany male friends alone to ice cream parlors, balls, or the theater. They could go driving with men and meet them for walks. "The youthful Jones," according to one commentator, "who may have polked a night with the youthful Araminta Brown or been introduced in the street by the youthful Annabella Smith," would be welcomed into the homes of his new female friends. Nor would parents oversee their conversation. According to feminist Abba Woolson, "European society considers our girls little short of Amazons. They walk home from parties with gentlemen escorts; they go about by day in the streets unattended." Spaniard Domingo Sarmiento was astonished by what he found as early as 1847. The Americans, he wrote, "have developed customs which have no parallel and which are unprecedented on this earth. The unmarried woman, or 'man of the feminine sex,' is as free as a butterfly until marriage. She travels alone, wanders about the streets of the city, carries on several chaste and public love affairs under the indifferent eyes of her parents, receives visits from persons who have not been presented to her family, and returns home from a dance at two o'clock in the morning accompanied by the young man with whom she has waltzed or polkaed exclusively all night."[32]

Aboard the Staten Island ferry en route to breakfast at a café on the island, Francis Grund noted not only steerage passengers in their Sunday best, but also young women passengers with male escorts. According to Grund, they were escaping the heat of the city before returning to promenade on Broadway during the fashionable afternoon hours. Girls at boarding school, according to another commentator, were allowed to come and go at will and to make friends indiscriminately. Prince Napoleon was particularly shocked by the daytime dress of young American women who bared their necks and shoulders, a décolletage that in France would not be permitted until evening.[33]

English travellers, accustomed to the English practices of separate swimming areas at beaches and of bathing machines for women, were astonished at the freedom of behavior at American beaches. At Cape May and Long Branch, popular middle-class resorts on the Jersey shore, women displayed no temerity in bathing with men, "making regular engagements, as for a dance, to meet them on the beach or among the breakers." Even at Newport, which some sources cite for decorum, an astonished Baron Rothschild saw unmarried men and women returning unchaperoned at ten in the evening from walking, driving, or horseback riding, and he observed men and women making engagements to swim together.[34]

The freedom of young American women in the antebellum years was particularly apparent in their public flirtations, which shocked foreign visitors from the 1850s on. The word "flirt" is of old derivation, dating from the sophisticated sexual encounters that characterized court circles in England during the seventeenth-century Restoration. Yet it had particular relevance for the nineteenth century. In an age that presumably circumscribed sexuality, the ways in which individuals circumvented the prohibitions on sensuality without incurring censure is important in evaluating the actual functioning of those codes.

"It would be almost impossible to exaggerate," wrote Thomas Grattan, "in describing this rage for flirtation which prevails among American females." Domingo Sarmiento wrote that "women of all social stations loiter around the streets and byways flirting." Elizabeth Cady Stanton's *Revolution* corroborated his judgment: "The flirting which is carried on between strangers in omnibuses, horse cars, and on ferry boats . . . is open and patent." "Everywhere in public establishments, in buses, steamboats, railroads," wrote Oscar Comettant, flirtatious conversations, often initiated by women, could be observed. In some public places, Comettant asserted, physical intimacy was common. Young men could be seen with arms around their sweethearts' waists; at Barnum's museum couples strolled around the galleries with arms intertwined; and in the small, dark museum theater they could be observed embracing.[35]

Many commentators on women's behavior thought flirting an innocent activity. Marion Harland wrote that the well-bred girl of the 1850s "might enjoy life with abandon" and gain a reputation for being "dashing," but she was never "fast." By 1870 *Godey's Lady's Book* even argued that flirting was beneficial. The flirt, according to *Godey's,* was always the person who thought up interesting amusements at boring parties; her personality was open, undisguised, and affable; her romances enhanced her ability to contract a successful marriage. In reflecting on her Victorian upbringing, Caresse Crosby, a leader of the 1920s American colony in Paris, called flirtation the "minuet of love." It took "grace and precision and a time of ease." Behind it lay sentimentality and stealth. "It was words written on a cotillion card, a sleigh ride to Fraunces Tavern, a handkerchief cherished, flowers pressed, a kiss at the foot of the staircase." It involved innocent promiscuity: "One could flirt with a dozen admirers at once." Its delights, in contrast with the pairings that Crosby thought characterized the 1920s youth, were nonthreatening and "frivolous."[36]

Most foreign and native analysts of flirting behavior, however, regarded it as sophisticated and serious. Thomas Grattan drew a distinction between flirting, which he regarded as innocent, and coquetry, which by his description was self-conscious and manipulative and characterized the behavior of most young American women. The flirt set out to interest men indirectly; the coquette was openly bent on conquest and had no temerity in initiating encounters. The "business" of a young American woman's life, according to Grattan, was to secure a young man "as a partner for the balls, or an escort to the lectures of the season, or a companion for walking around the streets." Moreover, "to reckon the number of her 'beaux' is her pride; to cast them off, her pastime." "Girls here lead a very free life," wrote Henryk Sienkiewicz, "and there are few whose past does not contain an episode resulting from too much 'flirtation.' "[37]

The adolescent Julia Newberry, forced by illness to take on the role of a spectator at social events, in her diary noted the incidence of flirting among the young American women she encountered in 1870 in Chicago, New York, and abroad. Personally conservative, Newberry found the "style in which girls try to captivate young men nowadays peculiar." For rather than waiting for the appearance of swains, her friends actively sought them. "They seem to think they must make opportunities," and they even indulged in what Newberry called "violent" flirtations. *Harper's Bazar* again and again criticized the "want of respectful reserve among young people of both sexes, their interchange of slang phrases, their audacious and dangerous flirtations." A central feature of the character of the belle in antebellum women's novels was her flirtatious ways; the widespread criticisms of the flirt in the publications of the day indicated her popularity. "Did you ever hear of a nice girl that was not [a flirt]?" retorted the fictional Daisy Miller to criticisms of her character.[38]

Such behavior was not universally sanctioned. Internalized standards and the force of community sentiment limited, without stopping, its practice. In the early twentieth century, the *Ladies' Home Journal* published a number of autobiographical accounts of restrictive nineteenth-century childhoods, with the implication that the experiences recounted were typical of their time. Raised in a small New England town, one woman remembered how she always walked through the center of the town with downcast eyes because she was not supposed to look into the barbershop or the hotel. Nonetheless, she was severely criticized for going riding alone with a man. Scores of etiquette books interdicted sensuous behavior, cautioning women that they must never be alone with a man before marriage nor allow any liberties in their associations with them. In *Little Women,* Louisa May Alcott provided a major example of the subtle ways in which restrictive pressures were brought to bear on young American women.[39]

Breaches in the application of this moral code, however, were not uncommon. In the early nineteenth century kissing games were a common activity at young people's parties, especially in New England. Englishman George Towle traced the practice to old peasant customs and thought that the rural folk he observed were freer in their behavior than city people, that they threw themselves with abandon into their dances and "indulged in frank lovemaking." Even in areas where prudery governed behavior, there were families and groups with freer behavior codes. In *Little Women* the March sisters are taught rigid behavior standards. Yet, they are nonetheless attracted to the Moffat family, with their interest in fashion, their loud assertive manner, and their lack of prohibitions. Spending a weekend at the Moffat house, Meg is almost corrupted into accepting their ways. Subsequently, Marmie will not allow her daughters to have anything to do with Ned Moffat, the vibrant son who might threaten their innocence. Only long acquaintance, his generosity, and his evident self-control make Laurie by contrast acceptable, for Alcott hints that as a young man he, too, has not kept entirely away from drinking and gambling.[40]

Moreover, the strictures of etiquette books should be seen as a reaction to such freer behavior, not as a description of the way in which people actually behaved. They were prescriptive attempts to persuade people to adopt restrictive behavior, and careful reading of them often reveals descriptions of the behavior they wanted to eliminate. Eliza Farrar's long list of recommended cautions to young women included refusing to "join us in any rude plays, that will subject you to being kissed or handled in any way." "Do not suffer your hand to be held or squeezed." "Accept no unnecessary assistance in putting on cloaks, shawls, over-shoes." Eliza Leslie admitted that young men and women were "generally incautious."[41]

Antebellum American society not only accorded young women considerable freedom, but also gave them social power. All commentators, in fact, agreed that social sets in many cities revolved around young women, who made the decisions about balls, parties, and other events. "Our girls," wrote Francis Grund, "who have nothing to do but to walk Broadway in the forenoon and to go to a party in the evening, 'govern society.'" Marianne Finch, who observed the same phenomenon in Boston, noted that the domination of young women there accounted for the fact that balls, where young women could indulge their love of dancing, were the main social entertainments. During the Civil War, New York reformers asked society matron Maria Daly to try to persuade wealthy New York women to discontinue entertaining for the duration of the war. She replied that she doubted she could have any influence, for young women were the real arbiters of New York elite society, and she was certain they would not listen to her. "However they may differ in other particulars, European travellers have expressed themselves with wonderful unanimity on this subject," wrote William Baxter. "Young ladies who, in all other civilized countries would be regarded as mere boarding-school misses, in whom modesty is regarded as the most essential requirement, in the United States, casting off all restraint, not only act an independent part and display an ease of manner savouring painfully of pertness and pretension ... but actually assume the lead in society to the neglect of married women."[42]

If such comments were not so universal, they would seem questionable in a society that moulded its young women for marriage and presumably held up innocence as the model of beauty. But Daisy Miller was "an inscrutable combination of audacity and innocence," and so were her forerunners earlier in the nineteenth century. Alexis de Tocqueville asserted that "nowhere [as in the United States] are young women surrendered so early or so completely to their own guidance. The great sense of the world is constantly open to her view; far from seeking concealment, it is everyday disclosed to her more completely, and she is taught to survey it with a firm and calm gaze." "I have been frequently surprised," continued Tocqueville, "at the singular address and happy boldness with which young American women contrive to manage their thoughts and their language amidst all the difficulties of stimulating conversation."[43]

Some analysts traced the freedom of young American women to their mothers' heavy domestic responsibilities, which impeded oversight of adolescent daughters. Others attributed it to the general veneration afforded American women whereby there was little danger for women in public places. Still others thought the phenomenon was restricted primarily to daughters of families that lived in boarding houses, where discipline easily broke down. Some commentators argued that the more rigorous education young women were receiving in the new postrevolutionary academies had somehow emboldened them. Alexis de Tocqueville held democracy accountable, with its disordered society in which parents decided that rather than "hiding the corruptions of the world from her, they prefer she should see them at once and train herself to shun them."[44]

The appearance of the girl of the period marked a new development in the history of American women. In one of the time's most perceptive travel accounts, Frederick Oldmixon contended that the 1850s witnessed a rebellion of American youth, a rebellion particularly directed against Puritan prohibitions. In politics the nationalist movement known as "young America" appeared. Attracted by urban economic possibilities, young men and women flooded into the cities, dominating society. Even in old-style Boston, wrote Oldmixon, "the youth nightly, en masse, fill the theatres, concert-rooms, and auction marts to overflowing. The softer sex try to make a compromise; and if they dance and sing and run about all week they are careful in church attendance." Ultimately, according to Oldmixon, the liberalism of the new generation would triumph over the Victorianism of the old. "All these small states and towns of New England are the strongholds of fanaticism and teetotalism, but it is, as in Boston, forced to give way before the rising generation which . . . is extremely fast and noisy."[45]

Generational conflict is a constant in human experience, and this generation of the 1850s would, in several decades, evidence no less conservatism than that of its parents. Yet, taken on its own terms, a new assertiveness was an important characteristic of the generation of young women in the 1850s and 1860s. Like Frederick Oldmixon, Elizabeth Cady Stanton also thought that a "revolution" of young women was occurring, although she was uncertain about what direction the rebelliousness would take. In her case, however, she hoped to lead it toward the ends of feminism, not of fashion.[46]

5

The Feminist Challenge and Fashion's Response

I n Seneca Falls, New York, in the spring of 1851, feminists Elizabeth
Cady Stanton and Amelia Bloomer launched a crusade against fashionable dress by donning costumes consisting of dresses shortened to midcalf and worn over baggy trousers. Bloomer described their decision to wear
reform dress as an "accident" triggered by a series of unforeseen events, the
first of which was a local newspaper's satirical article on women's dress that
had jokingly suggested that women should wear short skirts and Turkish
pantaloons. Incensed, Bloomer had written a rebuttal to the publication's
antifeminist stance in the *Lily,* the temperance journal she edited. Coincidentally, Elizabeth Smith Miller, Cady Stanton's second cousin and close
friend, had paid a visit dressed in a costume resembling the one the newspapers had described. Miller had designed her reform attire out of distaste for
gardening, doing housework, and walking along dusty streets in long, confining fashionable dress. Inspired by Miller's attire, Cady Stanton made a
copy for herself and persuaded Bloomer to do likewise. Within a few
months, most feminists were wearing the reform attire.[1]

The dress itself was labelled "bloomer" by journalists who identified it
with Bloomer's newspaper, and the appellation stuck, despite feminists' efforts to substitute a more dignified name. Yet Cady Stanton was the guid-
ing force behind the adoption of the costume. She often acted on impulse
(as she had in introducing the resolution for woman's suffrage before the
resistant 1848 Seneca Falls Convention), but calculation usually lay behind
her seemingly impulsive actions. In the case of the bloomer costume, Cady
Stanton's intention probably involved a desire to cement her relationship

with Amelia Bloomer, a conservative on woman's rights whom she had been trying to liberalize for some time.

Cady Stanton was already known for her role in the Seneca Falls Convention, which had received national publicity. It was not surprising, then, that newspapers throughout the states publicized the new bloomer dress, particularly after stories about it appeared in Bloomer's *Lily* and in the influential *New York Tribune,* edited by Horace Greeley, the two feminists' friend and reform associate. Yet what began as favorable publicity quickly became irksome notoriety as vicious caricatures of a dress that journalists found neither attractive nor seemly appeared and as stories circulated about how men jeered and young boys threw stones at those who wore it. Cady Stanton's sister wept at the reaction, her father requested that she not visit him, and her sons at boarding school were distressed. Henry Stanton, her husband, initially favored the reform, quipping that the men he knew secretly approved it because they could find out whether their women friends had fat or thin legs. Eventually he opposed it, perhaps believing that his 1851 defeat in a race for the New York State Senate had been due to his wife's bold break with fashion.[2]

Despite attacks upon her initiative, Elizabeth Cady Stanton remained committed to the reform for several years, writing in 1853 to her faltering friend Elizabeth Smith Miller that she should "stand firm a little longer." By the end of that year, however, Cady Stanton herself gave up the costume, probably influenced by her June 1853 defeat as president of the New York State Woman's Temperance Society, a position from which she had tried to bring temperance women into the woman's rights fold. Although protesting, Susan Anthony went back to regular dress. Elizabeth Smith Miller, once the waverer, wore the bloomer costume for nine more years. She was supported by both her husband and her father, reformer Gerrit Smith, who maintained stoutly that women could never be fully emancipated until they no longer displayed their oppression in the clothes they wore.[3]

The fame of the brief bloomer campaign has fostered the impression that the Seneca Falls feminists speedily devised and quickly abandoned the new costume and that the episode represented all there was of antebellum dress reform agitation. The truth is that a widespread consensus on the need to modify fashionable dress styles existed among doctors, educators, women novelists, editors of women's magazines, writers of advice literature, and feminists and reformers. According to Cady Stanton, even journalists who deprecated the bloomer were in favor of some sort of dress reform; they simply did not like the costume the Seneca Falls feminists devised. In 1851 Cady Stanton thought that simplified dress was not a radical enthusiasm, but rather a reform whose time had come. There existed among the general public, she believed, "a serious demand for some decided steps, in the direction of a rational costume for women." Her comment was a not unrealistic appraisal of the situation. Yet because the ideologies and approaches of those who supported dress reform varied considerably and because these groups never achieved unity of action, their common interest has by and large been lost to the historical record.[4]

Many feminists had long contemplated dress reform. Cady Stanton for years had discussed the difficulties of fashion with Elizabeth Smith Miller and had designed a loose-fitting costume when on a Scottish hiking vacation with her husband in 1840. Sarah Grimké included dress reform in her pathbreaking *Letters on the Equality of the Sexes* in 1838, and the masculine garb worn by popular actress Frances Kemble received wide publicity. From their own experience, feminists had to be aware that women at the beach and on skates wore shortened dresses and that Near Eastern women wore trousered costumes. The Greek revolution and other Near Eastern agitations had produced stories and pictures of Mediterranean women in pantaloons, and American sailors in the Mediterranean had brought back native dresses that their wives and daughters wore to costume balls.[5]

An interest in dress reform pervaded the reform community of the period and constituted another matrix out of which Cady Stanton's commitment grew. Lucretia Mott and Sarah and Angelina Grimké regularly wore the simple, dark dresses with white collars and cuffs that were the insignia of Quaker commitment to reform. "Lucretia Mott," wrote a Quaker descendant, "would cease to be the treasured picture we carry in our memory, were she divested of her simple, unchanging, Quaker garb." A sizable community of Hicksite, or reform, Quakers lived near Seneca Falls. Among them were Jane Hunt and Mary Ann McClintock, who were closely associated with Cady Stanton and Mott in planning the Seneca Falls meeting. No record exists of what women at the 1848 convention wore, but one assumes that its large proportion of Quakers in simple dress must have impressed others present. In 1851 Quaker Amelia Willard became Cady Stanton's beloved housekeeper, and that same year, at the Second National Woman's Rights Convention in Worcester, Massachusetts, Susan Anthony led a successful protest against the election of novelist Elizabeth Oakes Smith to the presidency because she was wearing fashionable dress. Instead, Lucretia Mott, the symbol of simplicity, was elected to the post.[6]

It was perhaps natural that reformers in this age of evangelical and millennial enthusiasm would take up dress reform, both as an outgrowth of their all-encompassing reformism and because simplified dress symbolized allegiance to the reform cause. Health reformer Mary Gove Nichols contended that many radicals and reformers wore simplified dress of their own design. Elizabeth Cady Stanton wrote about the individualistic, even outlandish, attire of many radical abolitionists. At communitarian settlements like Brook Farm, Oneida, and New Harmony, women gave up corsets, shortened their skirts, and added long pantaloons to cover their legs. In the early 1840s Cady Stanton visited Brook Farm; she must have seen the reform dress of its women inhabitants.[7]

Health reformers also advocated simplified dress, adding the persuasive authority of physiological science to the dress reform argument. Whether homeopaths, Thompsonians, Grahamites, or hydropaths, the irregular medical sects' modifications of standard medical practices and their closer relationship to folk techniques led them to emphasize the prevention of illness as well as its treatment and to pay attention to exercise, diet, and proper dress.

In the 1830s, Sylvester Graham's popular lectures on physiology inspired the formation of ladies' physiological societies, devoted to ending prevailing prudery about the body and to eliminating unhealthy dress. His emphasis was continued by the hydropaths, or water-cure advocates, who devised a system of medical treatment based on the extensive use of water (taken internally and applied in the form of baths and cold compresses) and who absorbed the failing Grahamite movement in the 1840s after Graham's death. At the sanitariums that the hydropaths established and that were popular among women reformers, women wore loose dresses and pantaloons. According to a late-century writer in *Godey's* who was searching for the origins of bloomer dress, a Mrs. William L. Chaplin had first designed it as a water-cure costume and had introduced it at her sanitarium well before the Seneca Falls initiative.[8]

Many early woman's rights leaders came to feminism by way of the popular health movement. Mary Gove Nichols, a disciple of Sylvester Graham who became a water-cure leader, wrote stories for *Godey's Lady's Book* and lectured on physiology throughout the nation in the 1840s as did Paulina Wright Davis, who edited the *Una,* an important antebellum woman's rights journal. Cady Stanton knew both; they probably stayed with her when in the Seneca Falls area. Reform doctor Harriot Hunt asserted that Cady Stanton agreed with her that health reform was the basic feminist reform; in taking up bloomer dress, Cady Stanton perhaps signalled partial adherence to this point of view.[9]

Dress reform was also a part of the physical exercise movement, which allied itself to the popular health reform while remaining distinct from it. Phrenologists believed that health required a sound body as well as mind and thus provided a major rationale for physical exercise as well as simplified dress. George Combe, the acclaimed Scottish philosopher of the movement, and his brother Andrew, a physician who wrote popular medical guides, also spread the exercise message. Scores of editions of their works appeared; reformist beauty and advice writers regularly quoted from them.

When touring the United States in 1838, George Combe asserted that physiological knowledge about dress, diet, and exercise was readily available and was taught in all women's seminaries. His implication was that American women chose ill health in defiance of contrary medical advice.[10]

In addition, influenced by the arguments of European émigrés familiar with European state-supported systems of physical instruction, some colleges and women's seminaries began to add physical exercise to their curricula by the 1820s. In keeping with the prevailing belief in women's weaker physique, however, the seminaries designed special moderate systems of exercise for women, called "calisthenics," to distinguish them from male gymnastics, which involved vigorous exercise using heavy apparatus. Calisthenics called for lighter exercise and equipment like wands and dumbbells. Catharine Beecher introduced calisthenics into her Hartford Female Seminary in 1823, and Emma Willard did the same at her Troy Female Seminary in 1831—at a time when Elizabeth Cady Stanton was attending the school. By that year, according to acting principal Almira Phelps, such exercise instruction was becoming "a regular branch of women's education." Catharine Beecher's *Physiology and Calisthenics,* published in 1856, became the standard textbook for women's physical education courses.[11]

In addition to Catharine Beecher, the most important leader of the women's exercise movement of this period was Dio Lewis, a homeopathic physician who took up exercise as his major interest after his wife recovered from both consumption and spinal curvature seemingly through following an exercise regimen he devised. His exercises drew upon those devised by Catharine Beecher, but were more rigorous and for this reason drew Beecher's criticism as too "vigorous" and "ungraceful" for young ladies. In 1861 Lewis established the Boston Normal Institute for Physical Education, which trained teachers in the new discipline. At the same time, he founded a women's seminary at Lexington, Massachusetts, which admitted only young women in poor health and specialized in body development as well as academic work. Catharine Beecher, Theodore Weld, and Angelina Grimké taught there for a time. Lewis's students wore short, loose dresses of his own design; they attended calisthenic classes every day, square-danced at night, and took weekly five- to ten-mile walks. Lewis believed that the improvement in his students' health by the time of their graduation was "magical." Teachers trained by Lewis took physical education positions and established similar schools elsewhere.[12]

Even *Godey's Lady's Book* was an advocate of moderate exercise for women, "however unfashionable the sentiment will appear to some of our more than usually romantic and fastidious readers." *Godey's* rated housework as the best exercise for women, but the magazine from time to time featured exercise alternatives, including calisthenic systems. In 1849, *Godey's* averred that in its view the end of calisthenics was "to counteract nervousness and invalidism, not to make athletes." Yet the women pictured exercising with wands in this same article were wearing simple, loose dresses that, in spite of the prudery the magazine elsewhere displayed, rose above the ankle.[13]

A number of popular cultural institutions also disseminated the message of the benefits of exercise. Chief among these was the circus, one of whose central entertainments was the gymnastic feats of acrobats and bareback riders. In addition, acrobats and gymnasts also performed on the stage, where an evening of legitimate theater was usually interspersed with variety acts. The Ravel family, a troupe that combined acrobatics with pantomime and dance, was probably the most popular single attraction of the antebellum stage. Circus bareback rider Josephine DeMott avowed that among circus performers good health was a "religion," and Dio Lewis was strongly influenced by circus and stage acrobats in designing his system of exercise. Even in rural New England in the mid-1830s, Harriet Martineau noted the fame of a Stockbridge, Massachusetts, acrobatic troupe of "rosy, graceful girls, and active women."[14]

In addition to circus and stage acrobats, the German *Turnvereine* advertised the benefits of exercise—and indirectly of simplified dress. The *Turnvereine* had appeared in the wake of the Napoleonic conquest of Germany; they were gymnastic societies that advocated national rejuvenation through physical fitness. Established in the United States by German immigrants in the 1840s, the *Turnvereine* numbered over 150 in American cities by the time of the Civil War. In San Francisco beer gardens, where the *Turnvereine* met, rooms with gymnastic equipment were made available to patrons. Yearly parades and athletic demonstrations in every city brought the *Turnvereine* public attention.[15]

The dress reform movement included not only feminists and health and exercise reformers, but also other, more conservative individuals and groups. Moral reform societies, whose members concentrated on the elimination of prostitution and the improvement of general moral standards, castigated fashionable dress in their reports and contended that women's love of finery was a major motivation for prostitution. Many regular doctors also assailed women's attire and counselled exercise for their patients. Even the editors of the major fashion magazines of the day—Sarah Josepha Hale of *Godey's,* Jane Cunningham Croly of *Demorest's Weekly,* and Mary L. Booth of *Harper's Bazar*—were all critical of restrictive women's fashions.[16]

The majority of writers of nineteenth-century advice literature also scorned the woman of fashion and called for simple modes of dress and behavior. Imbued with the republican ideology strong in the postrevolutionary years, writers like Eliza Farrar saw motherhood as woman's primary goal and did not favor radical dress reform or vigorous physical exercise. But they added a voice to the consensus that found fashion detrimental to women and the nation, and they proposed alternatives to the steel-engraving lady as models of beauty. Primary among these was Martha Washington, who in their characterizations made no attempt to follow fashion, whose entertainments were simple, and who was "eminently domestic." Queen Victoria was also a favored figure, particularly after marriage and motherhood ended her love of fashionable dress and entertainment and made her a model of domesticity and wifely decorum.[17]

Perhaps the most important critics of nineteenth-century dress and fashionable behavior were the popular women novelists of the period, Hawthorne's "damned scribbling women" who pre-empted the market Hawthorne thought should have been his. From Susanna Rowson and the novel of seduction to Louisa May Alcott and the novel of adolescent exploration, a central theme of the works of these women is the danger and lure of fashion, which in their presentations threatens to undermine family cohesion, democratic procedures, and the simple virtues of regularity, trust, and modesty that defined national greatness. On the road to self-reliance and republican marriage that the heroines of these novels typically follow, it is fashion above all that threatens their successful quest and is thus the potential despoiler, not only of their own innocence, but of the innocence of the social order that they represent.[18]

The plot of these novels occasionally involves a heroine who has already been corrupted by the world of fashion before the story begins and who finds her way back to a simple, virtuous life during the course of the narrative. Most often, however, a virtuous, uncorrupted heroine is counterposed against a young, fashionable woman—sometimes designated a coquette and sometimes a belle—whose beauty is greater than that of the heroine and whose sensual dress and behavior initially make her more attractive to the men of the story. The belle represents the world of fashion, initially vivacious and comely, but artificial and conniving behind her beautiful façade. The belle is interested only in having pleasure, displaying clothes, marrying well, and, above all, luring men into infatuation. "A perpetual child," "a spoiled baby," she is pleasant only when attention is lavished on her, incapable of being a good wife once she finally marries. Ada Montrose, the belle of Mary Jane Holmes's *Meadowbrook,* reacts to her new husband's professional difficulties by taking to her bed and becoming a chronic invalid. Lillie Ellis of Harriet Beecher Stowe's *Pink and White Tyranny* follows the same path. Neither woman can handle difficulty; both expect to lead luxurious, pampered lives.[19]

In general, the belles are considerably older than the heroines. Usually they lie about their ages—prevarications that underscore the falsity of their characters. Sometimes, however, their age has made them wise and thus even more deadly because experienced in the ways of the world. In Catharine Sedgwick's *Clarence,* Grace Layton, "a belle of forty," may look like "a Parisian artificial flower," but she speaks of society "like bubbles catching the sun's rays." She makes the heroine, Gertrude Clarence, feel that the latter's simple life is a "paralyzed, barren existence," and Grace comes close to attracting the young hero of the story into marriage. Only Gertrude Clarence's natural virtue, her "practical, rational, dutiful, efficient, direct, and decided" character (with "only a touch of the romantic in it"), makes her realize the falseness of Layton's standards and ultimately persuades the hero to choose her. The point about her superiority is made precise by the hero's musings—after he has decided in her favor—that she is really not beautiful. "When I first knew her, I did not think her handsome, and now I do not think she is beautiful; but the thoughts that beam from her eyes, and the kind words that drop from her lips, the true jewels of the fairy tale, infuse into her face the very essence of beauty." Character, not exterior appearance, is what counts.[20]

In all these antebellum novels, the heroines are so noble that they often fail to realize the danger posed by the belles, who lie and cheat to gain their ends. The belles read Byron and are genteel. The heroines like Scott for his defiant peasant women, like Meg Merrilies, or they read Maria Edgeworth because of her criticism of the world of fashion. The heroines are independent and healthy, and they exercise. They often work as teachers, dressmakers, or governesses before they marry. The belles are indolent and dependent on money earned by others. The heroines wear white muslin; the belles dress in the height of fashionable display. The belles are usually blonde, and the heroines have dark hair. Harriet Beecher Stowe describes her heroines as having features classical in type, to underscore both their independence and their simple tastes. On the other hand, the ideal women in the works of Catharine Sedgwick and Augusta Stephens have small features in keeping with their eventual domestic role; it is the women of fashion who are "heathen" and "Junoesque" in appearance. But whether genteel or classical in looks, as Catharine Sedgwick declares in *Clarence,* the belles are personifications of the "artificial construction of society" with its "perpetual discussions of relative gentility," "its secret envy and manifest contempt"—all of which is "mortifying" in republican America. Still, most authors call the belles "modern" women; the heroines uphold traditional values.[21]

Despite the widespread criticism of fashion in novels, advice books, and writings on physiology and health, by the 1850s women's fashionable dress had become particularly unreasonable. Skirts were so long that they dragged in the mud. Corsets were so tightly laced that breathing was constricted. The stiff wool and horsehair petticoat, or crinoline, which had been introduced in 1842 to reduce the number of petticoats women wore, had simply been added to the rest, producing a mass of heavy undergarments, a "sea" of petticoats, as one contemporary described it. The situation was impossible. By 1851 there seemed to be, as Elizabeth Cady Stanton wrote, "a serious demand for some decided steps, in the direction of a rational costume for women."[22]

II

If a widespread consensus in favor of dress reform existed in antebellum America, why was the bloomer dress a failure? Initially, in the first months after its introduction, it seems to have achieved considerable success. Amelia Bloomer remembered that she and Cady Stanton received hundreds of letters inquiring about the dress and that subscriptions to the *Lily* substantially increased. Frederick Oldmixon saw many young women wearing bloomers in Philadelphia, despite the jeering crowds surrounding them. In Washington, D.C., Varina Clay wrote that "Bloomers are 'most as plenty as blackberries.'" Women in the Lowell mills wore bloomers for a time, and in his survey of antebellum American life Thomas Low Nichols contended that "thousands" of women nationwide had worn them.[23]

Negative reactions, however, quickly set in. The late-century *Encyclopedia of Social Reform* argued that bloomers had in fact been quite popular when first introduced, but when the press revealed that its designers had no connection with Paris and were in fact "strongminded" (a term of opprobrium in antebellum America), women speedily abandoned it. Some moderates argued that the bloomer dress might have succeeded had a society leader or an actress introduced it or had it been designated for a particular use during the day, such as for exercising or doing housework, rather than as general attire for all occasions. Some reformers charged that dressmakers and dry goods merchants, fearing a drop in their sales, had hired prostitutes to wear outrageous versions of the costume and vagrants to taunt women wearing the reform dress.[24]

Moreover, although a general consensus existed on the need to modify fashionable dress, supporters of simplified dress differed over the design of the new costume. Conservative Mrs. L. Abell thought that dresses should not drag in the mud and that skirts should hang from shoulder suspenders to relieve pressure on hips and back. But she was vehemently opposed to the bloomer dress, citing God's command in Deuteronomy that the sexes ought not wear each other's clothing: "The Bible is against bloomers." Catharine Beecher's stand was more moderate and calculating. "As for striving to make women dress 'out of the fashion,' in order to be healthy," she wrote, "the effort would be folly and a failure. The wiser way is to circumvent Madame Fashion by ... paying her all demanded deference, and yet conforming to the rules of health and decency." Beecher herself designed a reform dress involving the replacement of heavy petticoats by a single petticoat held out by whalebone. Her conception resembled nothing so much as the hoop skirt that French designers introduced several years later.[25]

Godey's Lady's Book remained silent about the bloomer dress. In 1854, however, the magazine published a story, "A Bloomer Among Us," that made its objections clear. The story centered around a bloomers-wearing heroine who was persuaded to give up the costume on pragmatic grounds. Most people, according to *Godey's*, were comfortable in their regular dress and had no desire to change the style of their attire. Moreover, the majority viewed bloomers as a typically radical product of western New Yorkers, infused with the energy of Puritan forebears but lacking their sense of limits. Asked *Godey's*, "Does it make any sense to sacrifice not only your social enjoyments but also your usefulness, for the purpose of making an ineffectual attempt to change a fashion under which so many people have lived in health and comfort that it would be difficult to persuade them it is injurious?"[26]

Indeed, in the years after its appearance the bloomer dress became popularly identified not only with woman's rights advocates, but also with other radicalisms. Particularly noticeable were the free-love advocates, who wore variations of it not only at Oneida, whose members kept to themselves, but also at the small, activist communities around New York City. Free love, with its overtones of sexual promiscuity, was among the most reviled ideologies in Victorian America, and newspapers like the antifeminist *New York Herald* regularly identified free love with feminism, particularly since free-love advocates often appeared on woman's rights platforms to proselytize for their cause. The identification was furthered by the embarrassing disclosure that prostitutes inside New York brothels often wore a costume resembling bloomer dress.[27]

The critics of the bloomer costume were especially outraged by the trousers that were part of it. The dress that covered the upper part of the body was of a standard simple design, shortened to midcalf. The trousers, however, were a striking departure from customary women's costume. The belief that trousers were meant only for male attire had been strong in Western culture for centuries, and its venerable nature was underscored by the Biblical prohibition in Deuteronomy against women wearing trousers. By the nineteenth century the doctrine of separate sexual spheres lent additional authority to the canon, strengthened by trousers' symbolic role in establishing masculine identity and dresses in establishing female identity. "We believe in the petticoat as an institution older and more sacred than the Magna Carta," declared *Harper's Magazine* in an 1857 article that decried women's subservient economic position and advocated moderate woman's rights goals. But rather than fearing the bloomer as a badge of radicalism, *Harper's* was concerned that women would lose their influence over men if they wore it. "Man loses the only authority that can effectually tame him when woman loses the delicacy of mind and costume that marks her as his counterpart and not as his rival."[28]

In addition to old ideas about separate sexual spheres, cultural conventions associated with childrearing also lent a mark of radicalism to women's assumption of male attire. Until the twentieth century, infant boys, like infant girls, wore long dresses, and not until the age of five did boys wear trousers. Before then they were part of a female community, divided by dress from the adult male community. "Breeches represent, to the small boy in frocks, the first step to manliness," wrote one commentator. Such attitudes persisted into maturity. Strong-minded wives who persistently disagreed with their husbands were accused of trying to "wear the breeches." According to Amelia Bloomer, a standard means for one man to express contempt for another was to present him with a petticoat, a "badge of cowardice and inferiority." Cady Stanton's father, mortified at her adoption of bloomer dress, wrote that she had made a "guy" of herself. The *New York Herald* found the attempt to introduce pantaloons for women so outrageous that it predicted the bloomer women would soon "end their career in the lunatic asylum, or perchance in the state prison."[29]

"Pants are allied to power," asserted dress reformer Mary Tillotson. So strong was the identification of trousers with masculinity that not until the early nineteenth century had women worn divided undergarments, in the form of "drawers," as they were called. Long pantaloons as undergarments had had a brief vogue in the first decade of the century, but the opposition to them on the grounds of their resemblance to male trousers was so strong that they had disappeared by the 1820s, surviving only as attire among dancers and prostitutes and in the form of the pantalettes that young girls continued to wear as a way of covering legs under short dresses. Thus pantaloons were highly suspect, and even drawers were not universally accepted. Catharine Beecher, for one, remembered that in her youth in the 1810s and 1820s she had worn nothing but petticoats under her outer garments. One dress reformer speculated that the major problem with the bloomer was that it brought into plain view a garment women had only recently begun to wear as underclothing.[30]

Yet perhaps what doomed the bloomer dress more than anything else was that none of the bloomerites thought the costume particularly attractive and most were happy to abandon it. Sarah Grimké wrote to Cady Stanton that she found the bloomer dress difficult to make and unpleasant to wear. Elizabeth Smith Miller thought that the wearer looked presentable when she was walking or standing, but her appearance when seated was awkward. In general, Miller confessed, "it was a perpetual violation of the art of the beautiful." Cady Stanton thought the dress was "not artistic" and that it required "a perfection of form, limb, and feet, such as few possessed." Amelia Bloomer continued to wear it after Cady Stanton had given it up. But when she moved to the Midwest in 1853, she found that the winds there played havoc with the costume by blowing the short dress that accompanied the trousers over her head. When the hoop skirt was introduced in 1856, she adopted it with enthusiasm because it was "light and pleasant to wear."[31]

For a time Cady Stanton sought to find a compromise costume that would avoid the radical threat of the bloomers while preserving its benefits. In 1853 she attempted to introduce a modified reform garb in the form of a shortened dress worn with high boots rather than trousers. She wrote to Elizabeth Smith Miller that although she found the dress less comfortable than the bloomer costume, it was more attractive and drew less public attention. Yet the adverse reaction to dress reform had apparently gone too far, and within a few months she abandoned the outfit. From that point on, Cady Stanton refused to endorse any stance on dress reform, although in 1854 she speculated that the dress reform issue might be a means of drawing to their cause women writers opposed to radical reforms but critical of fashion. In 1869 she refused a specific request to endorse the bloomer from water-cure advocates who had formed a dress reform league. She responded to them that women might just as well wear masculine attire as any modification of regular dress.[32]

The failure of the bloomer agitation had substantial consequences for the whole woman's rights movement. For Susan Anthony, its failure seemed to teach the lesson that woman's rights forces ought to pursue one goal at a time—a path she later followed in suffrage agitation. Cady Stanton, on the other hand, continued to work for a variety of objectives, but she was careful to clothe her radical doctrines about divorce and birth control in an aura of respectability, particularly through wearing attractive dress that initially disarmed the opposition. How far she and her fellow feminists may have gone with such conciliatory gestures is indicated by the charge of one writer that the feminists "appear never to be done with their efforts to convince the public that they are as faithful to fashion as the prettiest imbecile of Fifth Avenue."[33]

Besides, by the late 1850s significant changes—of which Cady Stanton was aware—had occurred in both women's dress and their behavior. The hoop skirt, introduced in the mid-1850s, was regarded by many, including Amelia Bloomer, as an important reform in dress, for it eliminated the heavy petticoats women had previously worn. By the 1850s Queen Victoria began to wear shortened skirts, blouses, and sturdy boots on her Scottish family vacations, and the dress was widely publicized. Marion Harland remembered that young women in the 1850s wore a blouse, or "spencer," of thin, dotted muslin belted above a silk skirt. It was, she thought, the direct predecessor of the shirtwaist.[34]

Dressmakers throughout the nineteenth century turned directly to male costume for inspiration in designing women's fashions like the pelisse and the redingote. In the late 1850s, jackets, like the polka and the monkey, which New York City's elite assailed, became popular. For the most part, these jackets were patterned after military attire, particularly after the uniforms worn in the Crimean War. Along with blouses, they were important precursors of suits for women. Moreover, drawing inspiration from the attire of washerwomen who tucked their skirts above their petticoats for greater freedom of movement, the eminent French designer Charles Worth attempted as early as 1862 to give women more freedom in dress by introducing a short skirt for walking at summer resorts.[35]

During the 1860s the increasing number of women in the work force and women's participation in the Civil War stimulated further reforms in women's dress. Nurses under Dorothea Dix, for example, were required to wear sober, unadorned dresses without hoops. By 1863 women went about their war work in New York City wearing a "Fifth Avenue Walking Dress" with a hunting jacket cut deep in back and square in front. Waterproof cloaks and rubber boots, first introduced in the 1830s, finally became fashionable "in recognition that women go out of their homes to work." In the mid-1860s the mannish suit—with dark jacket, matching shortened skirt, and plain blouse—also appeared. Both *Demorest's Monthly* and *Godey's Lady's Book* contended that earlier experimentation with the bloomer costume had made possible the adoption, however limited, of such attire. Argued a *Godey's* writer, the bloomer had "an unconsciously educational effect on the minds of women at large."[36]

Such Civil War reforms made Cady Stanton enthusiastic that significant progress was being made. "The short suit has triumphed over enormities of trimming and immense shapes, noted the *Revolution* in 1871. The 1869 founding in New York City of Sorosis, the nation's first women's club, also encouraged Cady Stanton. It was headed by Jane Croly, the editor of *Demorest's Monthly* and a vocal dress reform advocate. Although Cady Stanton found the feminist program of Sorosis too moderate for her taste, she praised its advocacy of the suit with a skirt that cleared the ground, sympathized with Croly's attempts to persuade working women to wear simplified dress, and gave credit to Ellen Demorest for her attempts at moderate dress reforms—including walking suits, health corsets, braces to hang skirts from the shoulders, and special exercise dress. Cady Stanton also praised Demorest and E. L. Butterick for introducing standardized paper dress patterns and did not agree with critics who accused the two innovators of extending the dominance of French fashion over American women. Neither entrepreneur had any interest, she argued, in "wasp waists" or "dressing to kill." Their patterns were designed by women "who choose nothing because it is French and reject nothing because it is American." The *Revolution,* which often rejected advertising as exploitative of women, carried advertisements for Demorest's store and for her products.[37]

Cady Stanton observed with enthusiasm the growing popularity of exercise and rational dress among women. One experience in 1869 especially impressed her. Deciding to take the feminist message deep into enemy territory, the woman's rights forces held their 1869 convention in Newport, Rhode Island, the watering place of wealthy New Yorkers and a main setting of fashionable display among the American elites. In contrast to Marian Gouverneur some thirty years earlier, however, Cady Stanton was impressed not by a woman of fashion. Rather, Ida Lewis, the daughter of Newport's lighthouse keeper, caught her attention and that of the national press for rowing alone, during a severe storm, into the rough waters of the bay to rescue passengers from a sinking ship. "Just now Ida Lewis is the fashion," wrote Cady Stanton in the *Revolution.* "No one thinks of visiting Newport without seeing her." Cady Stanton recorded her impressions of the younger woman. She was a "frail-looking girl, seemingly with little force or endurance." Yet she told Cady Stanton that she loved rowing in the ocean and that "she liked best battling the ocean in a storm." They talked of recent rowing races at Newport between the "Harvards and the Oxfords"; they spoke hopefully "of the time when girls, too, should enter the lists in the prizes of life."[38]

As usual, Cady Stanton was sensitive to changes in behavior and attentive to future trends. At times she was optimistic about the new kind of American woman and argued that the hope of the future belonged to the strong, self-reliant young women who, like Ida Lewis, were growing up without the disabilities of Cady Stanton's own generation; who, by the 1850s, were being permitted to attend college and being encouraged to exercise; who were refusing to appear demure on city streets. They might, she hoped, bring into being the woman's rights goals for which her own generation had struggled with mixed results. Yet, though she called women's new direction a "revolution," she wondered where the revolution was going. In the final analysis, she feared, it was a revolution without real substance.[39]

Fashion might be threatened, but it could fight back on many fronts. Laws could be changed and attitudes amended, but whether or not the femi-

nists could radically alter basic social attitudes about women's nature remained to be seen. Cady Stanton refused to make an attack against fashion
her main concern because she believed other obstacles to be more serious;
yet she may have underestimated fashion's power and failed to realize the
extent to which it underlay the entire constellation of discriminations
against women. Standards of beauty might change and work for unmarried
women might become respectable, but women continued to define themselves by their physical appearance and their ability to attract men. The attainment of such qualities was a central goal of the rearing of young
women, and Cady Stanton was only too aware of this situation. She traced
what she called the "revolt" of the young to the end of puritanical methods
of childrearing and the substitution of child-centered, sentimentalized techniques, which produced young adults who were fixated on themselves and
had little respect for their elders. That they would become rebellious was, to
Cady Stanton, not surprising. The problem was the direction in which their
rebellion was headed, and here Cady Stanton found their sense of change
immediate and narcissistic. They were interested only in increasing their
possibilities for freer movement, for interaction with men, for fashionable
display. With the decline of Puritanism and the failure to develop a creed to
replace it, young women were growing up with no sense of the spiritual,
the uplifting side of life. The new women created by permissive standards
and the consequent youth rebellion were intent on personal beauty and
their appeal to men. Sensuality was their mode; marriage, their goal.[40]

Such was the conviction of many observers. One of them, Elisabeth
Finley Thomas, penned a striking portrait of this new woman in the person
of her Aunt Lily. Writing of her own childhood in New Haven, Connecticut, in the 1870s, Thomas claimed that what most impressed her about Lily
was that "pots of face creams, boxes of powder, and even rouge littered her
daintily draped dressing-table. She spent long hours applying ice packs to
her lovely throat and bosom; brushing to lacquered brightness her black
hair, and even doing calisthenics each morning." Lily's mother, Great Aunt
Agatha, of an older, Puritan generation, thought her daughter's attention
to her appearance bordered on the "immoral." But Lily went even further.
While Great Aunt Agatha kept her elbows close to her sides and never
leaned back in her chair, Aunt Lily went to the shocking length of crossing
her knees, which, with her freer gestures, many condemned as unladylike.
Nevertheless, according to Thomas, Aunt Lily possessed that characteristic
known as "charm," which by the 1920s would be called "sex appeal."
Young men with "spanking" horses continually appeared to take her to
drive. According to Thomas, "she brought a whiff of the outside world into
the old house." She was "distinctly modern."[41]

III

"Her very earliest observations and intuitions teach her this fact," wrote Ella Fletcher in her popular beauty manual, "that Beauty's path through life is a sort of rose-bordered one, a royal progress; for to Beauty the world, big and little, high and low, pays homage. As the girl ripens into the woman, every experience in life teaches her that her share of its successes and pleasures will be in proportion to her own ability to win favor, to please, and that the first and most potent influence is physical beauty."[42]

Above all, the power of fashion ultimately rested on the way American women were raised. Behind the seeming lack of parents' control over their daughters' behavior, subtle pressures operated to instill within the American girl a devotion not only to domesticity, but also to her physical appearance. It is these controls that explain the paradox that Alexis de Tocqueville and other commentators found in the behavior of American women, the paradox that independent, carefree girls could turn into docile, retiring wives. Young women's internalization of these controls also explains the failure of the revolution that Elizabeth Cady Stanton and others observed.

The pressures were in operation from a girl's earliest years. The dolls that girls played with, for example, were dressed in high style. "I have often thought," wrote Eliza Farrar, "that the very bad taste, in which dolls are usually dressed, may have something to do with this love of finery." In addition, young girls were often dressed in clothing that imitated their mothers' attire. Bemoaned one observer, "If mama opens the spring with silk and orange buds, ditto Anna Maria Wilhelmina; if mama blooms in summer with pink satin and flowers, ditto Anna Maria Wilhelmina." Moreover, clothes were a constant topic of conversation. "In every step of growing up," wrote Mrs. L. Abell, "little shoes and bonnets and dresses and her corals and ribbons are constantly being discussed in her presence."[43]

Some families permitted young girls to run and play during their early years, and the appellation "tomboy" was never entirely opprobrious. But the "laughing, spirited" girl of ten, according to advice writer William Alcott, too soon turned into the young lady of thirteen, "demure, dignified, and unwilling to run or play for fear of being called a 'romp.'" And, as was the case with most important events in a woman's life, clothes were a crucial part of this passage from childhood to maturity. The newly proclaimed young woman lengthened her skirts, put up her hair, and often donned a corset. According to Cady Stanton, she was "put through a system of intense restraint, of both body and soul," in order to make her "genteelly quiet and subdued." Above all, she was corseted, so that she would not "grow too large, or be too hoydenish in her manner."[44]

The term "adolescence" and the dimensions of this stage of life did not begin to receive precise definition until late in the nineteenth century. But earlier Americans were aware of the "storm and stress" nature of the teenage years. Early maturity is a time of "awkwardness, indolence, and capriciousness," as one analyst described it, with "boisterous spirits" one moment and depression the next. During the teens, according to Lydia Maria Child, "the imagination is then all alive, and the affections in full vigor, while the judgment is unstrengthened by observation, and enthusiasm has never learned moderation of experience." Above all, it was a time of fixation on a self undergoing rapid physiological change, a time therefore when dress and personal appearance also assumed overwhelming importance—at least for girls. "Young women, of course, are inclined to set a high value on beauty of form and feature, as well as to dread, more than most people, what they regard as deformity," wrote one analyst. "The glamour of fashion in the eyes of young girls is *complete,*" asserted Harriet Beecher Stowe. Many commentators noted that young women—more than older women—followed extreme Parisian styles. *Demorest's Monthly* deplored the fact that they "flaunted down village streets, dragging long gored and trained dresses in the mud." "The great portion of young persons' lives," wrote Catharine Sedgwick, "is spent in dressing and preparing their dresses."[45]

Well-to-do young women often spent their early maturity at boarding schools, where peer pressure about dress and physical appearance was powerful. From her classmates, wrote one author, the young woman learned about "the omnipotence of fashionable dress." According to another observer, once the notion of tightlacing became popular in a school, "it spread like measles." Beauty writer Susan Power Dunning remembered that the fashionable mother of a fellow student at her boarding school ordered that her daughter eat nothing but brown bread and syrup—a diet devised to enhance the complexion. In this case, none of her classmates had sufficient fortitude to follow such a regimen, but the girl's "carmine lips" were the envy of her classmates.[46]

Graduation from school was followed by a formal introduction into adult society, usually at the age of sixteen or seventeen. "To come out is the first thought of opening womanhood," contended *Harper's Magazine.* For the well-to-do, a ball was often the setting of the presentation; and once again appearing in the correct fashion was a central part of the experience. "The dress for the first ball," author Caroline Gilman apostrophized. "Who shall describe its infinite importance? How admiringly we gazed; how we folded every plait in the silky gauze, smoothed every wrinkle in the glossy satin, and measured the little slipper. . . ." A life of parties, balls, dinners, visiting, shopping, carriage rides, and vacations at summer spas followed this debut into society and formed the life of the young society woman as she continued her indoctrination within the world of fashion. Finally, she married—an event to which, once again, dress was particularly important, both in the wedding gown and in the increasingly popular trousseau, or wardrobe, which for the family of limited means could entail months of sewing.[47]

Behind the emphasis on dress and beauty in young women's socialization lay one preeminent motive: the securing of a husband. Nineteenth-century American opinion, typical of Western views generally, regarded marriage as the only legitimate goal for women; the spinster, an accepted figure in preindustrial societies where she served a useful role as laborer within the household economy, was ridiculed. Yet contemporaries commented extensively on what they observed as a decline in the incidence of marriage, and they traced the phenomenon directly to the behavior of men. Striving for success in the world of work, confronted with a consumption ethic that decreed ever more lavish household expenditures, advised by many physicians that sexual activity was not important to their well-being, many young men hesitated to marry. Elizabeth Cady Stanton traced the "frivolity, furbelows, and false pretenses" of young women in New York society to the fact that their main purpose in life was to win over these reluctant males. Mrs. A. J. Graves also noted throngs of young, indolent, fashionable women in the cities, trying to find husbands. French visitor Duvergier de Hauranne thought that men were absorbed in business from an early age and consequently were not often present at the kinds of activities conducive to romance.[48]

Of course, most nineteenth-century women eventually secured husbands. According to demographers, fully 90 percent of American women would marry at some point in their lives. Yet what is important is that contemporaries thought that husbands were difficult to find and that women believed they had to work to secure them. What this meant, in a society that denigrated female intelligence and assertiveness, was that women were increasingly drawn into attempts to improve their appearance as a means of sexual attraction. "It never entered into the heart of Catherine that men could be enslaved by any other charm but beauty," wrote novelist Caroline Lee Hentz, describing what must have been the common sentiment of women of that age. "From a child every instruction she had received seemed to have for the ultimate object, external attraction. She was excluded from the sun and air. . . . Her hands were imprisoned in gloves. . . . She was not permitted to read or study by candlelight, lest she should dim the starry brightness of her eyes, or to take long walks, lest her feet should become enlarged by too much exercise. 'Katy, my dear, don't run, it will make your complexion red. Katy, my love, don't eat too much, it will make your complexion coarse.' " But even to be a model steel-engraving lady was not deemed sufficient to be certain of securing a husband. Wrote author Elizabeth Stuart Phelps, "The same girl trained to a sense of modest demeanor is taught to express a shameful forwardness," to display her body through tightlacing and padding and her sensuality through flirting and thus to use sexuality to attract men.[49]

The fixation with fashion and the increasing fear that, if trends continued, young men might not marry at all, combined to create the century's most powerful model of beauty for women: the belle or the beauty, the young woman whom her immediate society—whether in city or town— proclaimed as the possessor of an outstanding physical appearance. General agreement on the "election" of a belle was sometimes reached by individual reactions that, passed by word of mouth, became general sentiment. Often, and increasingly as the century progressed, newspaper reporters gleaned information from conversations and observations and made the designation of the reigning beauty.

Generally the belle was a woman of the social elite. But she could just as easily be a middle- or working-class woman, although the newspaper space devoted to her would be limited. Still, the type of woman who later became known as a professional beauty and who is identified with the Edwardian period in England and the circles around the sybaritic Prince of Wales was in striking evidence in the United States throughout the nineteenth century. In the 1830s, for example, the beauty of Sallie Ward of Cincinnati was renowned "from the sources of the Ohio to the Gulf of Mexico," her reputation spread by steamboat captains and other riverboat travellers on the Mississippi River. In 1840 Mrs. Winfield Scott, wife of the famed army commander, became friendly with dancer Fanny Elssler when the two of them travelled on the same ship from France to the United States. Mrs. Scott reminisced about her past, when as Maria Mayo of Virginia, she was known not only throughout her state but also nationally as a "reigning belle." She remembered that whenever she travelled as a young unmarried woman, she had been followed by a retinue of enthusiastic swains who hoped to capture in marriage the hand of the celebrated beauty. Every city and village in the South has a "noted Belle," wrote Rebecca Harding Davis. "I was once in a southern town when one of these famous beauties passed through on her way to Virginia Springs. She remained all day with her escort in the little village inn, and all day a closely packed mass of men waited patiently outside to see her."[50]

In the antebellum years, the belle was described in terms otherwise applied to persons of genius or outstanding success. She was "celebrated" or "brilliant." Writers on beauty often succumbed to romantic hyperbole in describing their subjects. The beauty was a "queen," a "star." She had "subjects" and "attendants." Even Abigail Adams, a republican intellectual contemptuous of fashion, used a term common in the beauty literature of that period when she referred to a group of women in Washington as a "constellation" of beauties. Often a group of beautiful women at a ball or a party was called a "congress of beauty."[51]

The symbol of the belle vastly increased the power of the world of fashion and the commercial beauty business. Her impact operated on a variety of levels. Women tried to look like her; they copied her style of behavior. "The loveliness of a rival eats into a girl's heart like corrosion. . . . Every grace of outline is traced like lines of fire on the mind of the plainer one, and reproduced with microscopic fidelity." The public discussion of beautiful women increased the tendency of newspaper writers and other disseminators of public information to discuss all women in terms of the clothes they wore and the way they looked.[52]

"A private woman," wrote one 1858 critic of the cult of the beauty, "is altogether too sacred an object to have her charms and graces discussed in the newspapers, like the points of a racehorse or the lines of a yacht." But this criticism invariably went unheard. In 1842 the *New York Herald* covered in detail the New York City parade that celebrated the opening of the long-awaited and much-celebrated Croton reservoir. Following common practice, the *Herald* described the women spectators along the parade route in terms of their physical appearance. The city streets were jammed with women "who disremembered the delicacy of their sex to catch . . . a passing glimpse of the procession." But after this ritual Victorian invocation of prudery, the *Herald*'s report continued with a bold tribute to beauty. All along the Bowery, "the galaxy of beauty was bewitching." But the "crowning scene" was East Broadway. "Here the loveliness of the ladies surpassed belief, and the elegance and neatness of dress, beauty of form and feature of the belles of East Broadway will long be remembered by those who saw them." Whether this male writer was more concerned to reflect the views of his own sex or the values of the women he described would be hard to say. In effect, he was doing both and, in the process, capturing the essence of Victorian America's conventions of fashion and desire.[53]

6

The Voluptuous Woman

From Bouguereau to the
British Blondes

To be thin is no longer the acme of feminine desires," novelist and etiquette authority Marion Harland declared in 1880. The next year Harriet Hubbard Ayer noticed that "plumpness" was fashionable. One English visitor was surprised by "the number of fine buxom matronly women," another by young American women's fear of being too thin. "They are constantly having themselves weighed," he wrote, "and every ounce of increase is hailed with delight, and talked about with the most dreadful plainness of speech. When I asked a beautiful Connecticut girl how she liked the change, 'Oh! immensely!' she said, 'I have gained eighteen pounds in flesh since last April.' "[1]

"Plumpness . . . is beautiful," declared an etiquette writer of the period. "Great thinness, or as it is called *scragginess* . . . is no longer esteemed lovely." In his seminal work on what he called "nervousness" in Americans, neurologist George Beard, adding professional authority to passing observation, concluded that most of the American women he saw at the 1876 Philadelphia Bicentennial Exhibition were hearty and buxom and that the thin and pale women characteristic of the antebellum years were evident only among women from rural areas. "The women in all our great centres of population are yearly becoming more plump and more beautiful," stated Beard.[2]

In effect, by the 1860s the frail, thin, steel-engraving ideal of women's beauty was being challenged by a number of alternative prototypes, each of which presented a more vigorous, hearty model. First there was the natural woman of the exercise advocates, with her "large waist and strong arms," as Elizabeth Cady Stanton described her. Then there was the large-bosomed and -hipped, curvaceous and heavy model of beauty, the "voluptuous woman," as I call her. Before the 1850s she could have been found among English visitors and German immigrants as well as among actresses and prostitutes. Her size and contours were also apparent in important pieces of sculpture like Hiram Powers's Greek Slave or the German paintings exhibited on Broadway. By the 1860s such older influences combined with new ones to enhance her appeal. Popular medical theorists posited that fat promoted health. European artists who painted sturdy, voluptuous figures became better known in the United States. In addition, her vogue was especially promoted by a number of popular French *opéra bouffe* and British burlesque troupes whose members were built according to her dimensions and who came to the United States in the immediate postwar years.[3]

As early as 1859 Thomas Grattan, British consul in Boston and an acute observer of the American scene, noted to his surprise that the women he saw on city streets suddenly seemed plump. They seemed somehow to be rearranging what he thought was the draping of their dresses into "the semblance of embonpoint." Grattan was understandably confused about what had occurred, but the sudden change in women's figures he observed was probably produced by their use of padding to accentuate bosoms and hips. Grattan suggested that the major source for this new appearance lay in the works of European artists, whose rounded figures were finally beginning to influence styles of appearance in the United States.[4]

Evidence suggests that there may have been some truth to Grattan's observation. Before the 1850s, cultural nationalism had resulted in a decided American preference for the works of American artists, even on the part of wealthy collectors. But by the 1850s the growth in wealth and cultural sophistication had broadened the appeal of foreigners' works, and by 1870 the market for their art had become substantial. By then, travel in Europe had convinced influential Americans of the superior esthetic value of art identified with European masters, while a generation of Americans who had been financially enriched by the Civil War took up art collecting as a leisure-time activity of high status.[5]

For a variety of reasons, wealthy Americans came to prefer paintings by representatives of French academic (or "salon") art, particularly the works of its leading representatives, Adolphe William Bouguereau, Jean Louis Meissenier, Jean-Léon Gérôme, and Alexandre Cabanel. The English pre-Raphaelites were never especially popular in the United States, although a native American school did emerge in the 1860s, and in later decades Lord Leighton and members of the English esthetic school gained acclaim. In matters of style, however, Americans had long deferred to the French. Thus when they began to purchase art abroad, they followed this established pattern. And by the 1860s most American artists who studied abroad gravitated to Paris. The French link existed because of early revolutionary ties, because the great French artists of early century—David and Ingres—eclipsed contemporaries in other countries, because the bohemianism associated with the Left Bank and the Latin Quarter exerted a special fascination, and because the official art establishment—the French Academy—in its Atelier Julian had effectively organized local resources so that large numbers of foreigners could be assured of receiving some instruction from eminent artists. Moreover, the 1860s' French Second Empire seemed the world's stylistic and business leader, and its artists filled huge canvases with epic scenes that attracted American business entrepreneurs, individuals who easily confused size and splendor with artistic achievement and whose interest in profits did not diminish when the purchase of art was involved. French art seemed a guaranteed risk; Bouguereau and the others won most of the official art world's plaudits, while American artists trained in France advised wealthy Americans on art purchases and favored the French masters with whom they had studied.[6]

In contrast to French fashion designers, French artists' agents were aggressive in promoting French art in the United States. The French firm of Goupil, Vibert, and Co. by the late 1840s had established a successful branch in New York City. In 1872 *Appleton's Journal* noted that the Goupil Gallery was importing, showing, and selling a great number of French works, especially those by Bouguereau. The Art Gallery at the Philadelphia Centennial of 1876, which contained over three thousand paintings and six hundred sculptures and which was the first experience of high art for many of the millions of Americans who attended the exposition, amply documented the dominance of the French school and of academic traditionalism in general. A romanticized realism was the mode, and size was what counted. Not until art critic William Morris Hunt began in the 1880s to exert a formidable influence over American artistic taste did Americans turn from French salon art to buy British painters and some of the more innovative French artists.[7]

Arguing that high art could be an important force in moralizing populations and publicizing national greatness, artists in both England and France in the eighteenth century had successfully organized under government patronage associations whose annual shows of works, chosen competitively, established an official canon of artistic taste. Through these organizations, which also drew on guild traditions dating back to medieval times, artists enhanced their status. But by the mid-nineteenth century, at least in France, a rigidity came to dominate the Académie des Beaux Arts, whose highest honors went to artists like Bouguereau and Cabanel. The artistic

canon prevailing today is critical of the work of these esteemed mid-nine-
teenth-century painters. Major museum collections generally disregard
them, and their works are overlooked in histories of nineteenth-century art.
Only recently have shows of their works been mounted and the esthetic theory behind their painting explored. As such neglect suggests, their work,
technically well executed, was derivative, drawing on the techniques and
conceptions of Ingres and David. Like most academic artists of the last century, they romanticized reality and aimed at pleasing patrons rather than
striking out in new directions.[8]

Bouguereau in particular was a traditionalist. He was appalled by the
abstract art of the early impressionists and by the realists' interest in ugliness
and corruption. He thought that art ought to ennoble by showing "poetic
beauty"; and he liked to use classical and Christian symbolism and settings
in his work. Yet Americans called Bouguereau and the other French salon
painters "modern" and thereby signalled their pride in collecting what was
represented to them as the day's most up-to-date and respected style. The
most famous late-century private room in the United States was the ballroom of New York City social arbiter Caroline Astor. Its capacity of 400
persons supposedly defined the composition of New York high society,
often denominated "the 400." Like the Metropolitan Museum of Art and
other such institutions founded in the 1870s, the walls of Mrs. Astor's ballroom were covered from floor to ceiling with pictures of the nineteenth-
century French school, "New York's last word in European culture," as a
member of her social set put it.[9]

To describe the kind of women these artists painted is difficult, for a
number of types are represented in their work. One can perhaps best begin
by describing the kinds of women they did not paint. In the first instance,
they rejected the steel-engraving model of beauty; the submissive, small-
featured woman of the early century is not found in their work. The tall,
gaunt, bushy-haired model of beauty that the pre-Raphaelites painted also
did not interest them. In 1876 art critic Justin McCarthy noted that the
"gaunt, lank, and long-limbed damosel" of the pre-Raphaelites was "to be
found everywhere in certain circles of London society." But such was not
the case in the United States. Moreover, soon thereafter even in England the
classical models featured by Frederick Leighton and the esthetic painters of
the 1880s took precedence. Bouguereau, for one, found Botticelli's women
neurotic, and one assumes that he had the same reaction to their descendants in pre-Raphaelite works of art. Rather, his women, like those of most
of the other French salon painters, were drawn from a classical model or,
being buxom of figure, represented no other type so much as the voluptuous woman.[10]

The publicity generated by both the early nineteenth-century Romantics and the midcentury pre-Raphaelites has obscured the fact that the most important and continuing influence on European art of the nineteenth century, particularly in the area of figure painting, was not the medieval, but the classical model. It was not Botticelli's famous Venus that had striking influence on nineteenth-century artists, but rather the Venuses sculpted by artists of the classical era. Many artists used classical themes and models to cloak sensual subjects with respectability, since the classical style was viewed as grand and asexual. Few artists rejected the accepted maxim that in their sculpture the Greeks had achieved an unparalleled beauty of face and form. It was part of the general veneration for the ancient world that a classical education instilled in the elites and that was a strong part of their own republican tradition. Moreover, just as the excavations at Pompeii and Herculaneum had sparked the eighteenth-century classical vogue, similar discoveries in the nineteenth century had an impact in maintaining the ongoing influence of the classical model. For example, study of the statues from the Parthenon that Lord Elgin brought to the British Museum in the 1830s became *de rigueur* for British painters. And the enormous popularity of the Greek war for independence in the 1830s also played a role in maintaining the appeal of the classical mode.[11]

As classical models of female beauty, two female sculptures were preeminent: the so-called Venuses de Medici and de Milo. Few female sculpted figures survive from ancient Greece, partly because the male figure, not the female, represented that culture's beauty ideal. Among the existing Venus figures, art critics consider the Venus de Medici and the Venus de Milo to be unsurpassed. The first came into the possession of the Medici family in the sixteenth century and is to be found today in Florence. The second was found by a Greek peasant in his fields on the island of Milos in 1820 and was bought by the Louvre Museum in the 1830s. Praise for their appearance runs like a leitmotif throughout the beauty literature of the nineteenth century. Even when extolling the steel-engraving lady, who bore slight resemblance to the classical model, writers slipped into their prose encomiums to the Venus de Medici or de Milo, as though the convention of their preeminence in beauty was so well established that it could be used to bolster any argument about physical appearance, especially when ordinary people were probably unclear as to exactly how they looked.[12]

But what was important about these two figures was that they were broad-shouldered, large-waisted, and athletic-looking. Dating from the Hellenistic period of Greek women's increasing independence, they drew on Spartan notions that women's bodies, like men's, should reflect health and vigor. By the late nineteenth century, beauty reformers regularly described the physiology of these two figures in detail and gave their body dimensions as a way of persuading women to abandon artificial styles and standards of beauty, just as exercise proponents pursued in detail old analogies between American and Greek democracy and pointed out the importance of exercise in the civilizations of the latter. The classical female model was a precursor of the natural woman of late century; the voluptuous woman, fleshy, rounded, with large bosom and hips and small waist, was an outgrowth of other impulses and other sources.

Like contemporary British painters, the French salon artists of late century were influenced by the classical ideal—an influence readily apparent in the female figures they painted. Yet as often as Bouguereau painted women of a classical mould, he also painted fleshy, voluptuous women. Generally his madonnas and idealized peasant women were of the classical sort, and his nudes were voluptuous. Here, he found inspiration in the robust, heavy women of Ingres and of Raphael—Ingres's own inspiration for models of female beauty.

Whatever popular reputation Bouguereau retains today rests on his fleshy female nudes. Nineteenth-century Americans found them highly erotic. In particular, his canvas entitled *Nymphs and Satyr* gained him a protracted reputation as a painter of high-class pornography. In 1887 Edward Stokes, notorious as the slayer of speculator James Fisk after a sordid love triangle, bought the painting from the estate of Manhattan socialite Catharine Lorillard Wolfe. Stokes installed it over the bar of the Hoffman House, a popular New York hostelry of which he was part owner and which became noted as a gathering place for male celebrities. The painting became a national sensation. Working-class saloons and especially the concert saloons, which catered to a cross section of American males, had long adorned their walls with pictures of naked, voluptuous women. Now a respectable hotel with middle-class pretensions was following the practice. So great was the curiosity among women to see the painting that one day a week was designated ladies' day at the all-male bar, and a steady stream of women visitors passed before it. A special brand of Hoffman House cigars with a reproduction of Bouguereau's painting on the cover sold well throughout the nation, and it, too, publicized the voluptuous woman as an image of beauty. Soon hotel bars nationwide began displaying voluptuous nudes on their walls.[13]

Bouguereau was not the only nineteenth-century painter to include voluptuous women among his ideals of female beauty. Gérôme, for example, spent time in the Middle East and was influenced in his own work by the heavy, voluptuous model of beauty prevalent in that region. Dante Gabriel Rossetti, the primary pre-Raphaelite painter of women, often used as his model Fanny Cornforth, a former prostitute who was large, plump, and blonde. With regard to her, he wrote of "the marvelous fleshiness of the flesh." Franz Xavier Winterhalter, the foremost painter of royalty and of the aristocracy of his day, generally portrayed his female subjects as plump and buxom; one thinks of his famed portrait of the Empress Eugénie, a style setter for the Western world in the 1850s and 1860s, seated in the midst of her ladies-in-waiting. As a society painter intent on pleasing wealthy patrons, Winterhalter undoubtedly romanticized the physical appearance of his subjects according to the most popular prevailing type. Thus it is particularly indicative of popular standards of beauty that he stressed a fleshy, rounded look and not a thin, ethereal appearance or a healthy athleticism.[14]

Throughout the nineteenth century, the classical style also continued as a predominant influence in sculpture. Yet according to the most recent analyst of the subject, sculpted female bodies after the Civil War became heavier and heavier, and their breasts became larger. Mammoth female statuary, like the Statue of Liberty "large-boned, massively-curved," also came into vogue, a fitting representative of the period's nationalism and of the nouveau riche fascination with size. Perhaps, too, the new trends in female body type, with the emphasis on bosom and hips, represented an attempt to glorify motherhood in the post–Civil War age when song and story enshrined the national yearning for home, symbolized by loving mothers. Such an interpretation is possible, although little contemporary testimony supports it. Assuredly the voluptuous woman as an ideal of beauty looked older than the steel-engraving lady before her or the Gibson girl after her, but the maturity of her figure was sophisticated and sensual, not maternal. It was Venus, after all, the goddess of sexual love, on whom even the nineteenth-century classical model of woman was based. The voluptuous woman was a sensual model, appropriate to an age exploring new models of sensuality.[15]

II

Before the Civil War the voluptuous woman had arisen as a model of beauty in two sources: in lower-class and immigrant cultures that associated bulk with success and in the subculture of sensuality that was associated with the theater world, prostitution, and sectors of the upper and working classes. By the 1850s and 1860s both these groups—financially successful immigrants and the participants in the subculture of sensuality—were assuming new prominence both in Europe and in the United States. The man of the early-century ideal, following Byron and the Romantic poets, had been thin. By midcentury he was heavy and solid, even fat, a reflection in physique of the success for which American men strove. Presented with the large meals favored by the newly wealthy, women, too, began to accept the luxury of eating what they wanted and allowed their figures to swell.

Moreover, by the 1870s important sectors of the medical profession were beginning to recommend that plumpness was a sign of health and that both men and women should try to keep their weight up. Chief among the proponents of plumpness were George Beard and S. Weir Mitchell, the two most eminent neurologists of the age. Mitchell provided the physiological argument for their advice. He believed that the production of a large number of fat cells was crucial to a well-balanced personality and that thin people, lacking a sufficient number of such cells, were invariably querulous and discontented. It was for this reason, for example, that Mitchell's famed rest treatment for neurotic disorders, which many prominent women of the age underwent, involved the consumption of large quantities of food. Furthermore, drawing on the old belief that the severity of the American climate was responsible for the thinness of American women and the widespread incidence of nervous disorders among them, Mitchell further argued that American women in particular ought to increase the amount of their food. Other doctors expanded on Mitchell's advice. Natalie Dana of New York City remembered that during pregnancy doctors advised women to eat enough for two and that after her first child a woman was expected to "part with her figure."[16]

That fat women are cheerful women is an old convention, dating to the days of Chaucer's wife of Bath and to the contented, jolly prostitute of legend. She was "ample to a cheerful degree," wrote a dramatic critic in describing one of the day's variety actresses. In recommending plumpness as women's ideal, beauty adviser Harriet Hubbard Ayer cited the old axiom that "a sweet temper and a bony woman never dwell under the same roof." Yet even more important than health or emotional buoyancy in the definition of voluptuousness was sensuality, expressed particularly through a large bosom and hips. *Harper's Bazar* editor Robert Tomes, who in the late 1860s prefigured Mitchell's position, contended that the desire to gain weight was particularly strong among those women "destitute of that fullness essential to the female form." He declared that "most men, whose estimate of the female sex is entirely of a sensual kind, prefer a well-developed form to the finest countenance."[17]

"Opulent curves," wrote one analyst, were the mode. Or as chronicler Henry Collins Brown put it more crudely: "We liked our women with plenty of meat on them in those days." "No one counted calories," reported Helen Doyle, who had worked in a Connecticut corset factory. Hips and busts were proudly exhibited by their fortunate possessors, she remembered, and corsets were called "beau catchers." Henry Collins Brown thought that a thirty-six-inch bust was the ideal, although Harriet Hubbard Ayer remembered that her cousin had proudly displayed a forty-four-inch bust. Actress Eileen Karl, whose photographs were a popular item in the stock of Napoleon Sarony, the most outstanding theatrical photographer of the day, had a forty-inch bust and thighs that were thirty-five inches round. "I have heard women exulting at their hugely developed calves," wrote beauty authority Annie Wolf. "I have known women to pit the dimensions of their calves, one against another, as an evidence of health and natural charm."[18]

The genesis of the new voluptuous ideal has been traced to the immense popularity of actress Eugénie Doche when in 1852 she played the doomed heroine of Alexandre Dumas's *La Dame aux camélias* (popularly called *Camille*). The famed courtesan, Marie DuPlessis, on whom Dumas's heroine was based, had been dark and consumptive, but Eugénie Doche was blonde, plump, and curvaceous. Whether by design or by accident, Doche was followed on the French legitimate stage by a number of other actresses who were buxom and large of girth. Chief among these was Madame Ristori, acknowledged as the greatest actress of the legitimate stage in France from the 1850s to the 1870s, before Sarah Bernhardt superseded her. Ristori's well-proportioned body contrasted with the physical frailty of Rachel, her predecessor in greatness on the French stage. Important, too, in the genesis of the new standard of beauty was the fact that the Empress Eugénie herself was buxom, famed for her large bust as well as shapely neck and shoulders. Like Victoria of England, she had a natural predisposition toward plumpness and, as she grew older, apparently did not attempt to remain thin.[19]

The Empress Eugénie and actresses on the legitimate stage were only partially responsible for the spread of this new ideal, which had also been germinating for some time in the popular theater. Evidence suggests that heavy, voluptuous women had long been popular there. Photographs of Adah Isaacs Menken, an actress renowned in the 1860s for having a beautiful body and for displaying it on the stage, reveal a woman heavy by modern standards. Hortense Schneider, the most important French café-chanteuse of the Second Empire and a star of *opéra bouffe,* was, according to contemporary reports, "Rubenesque" in proportion. The buxom and rotund women whom Lydia Thompson gathered together in 1868 to form the astoundingly popular burlesque troupe known as the British Blondes had been known on the British music hall stage for some time.[20]

However, the popularity of size and voluptuousness in midcentury actresses should not be overemphasized. Throughout the nineteenth century, a variety of models of beauty could be found. Emile Zola's *Nana,* a realistic novel centered on the *opéra bouffe* stage and the world of the demimonde, offers an insightful portrayal of this milieu and the women in it. The novel opens with a careful physical description of the two women, both *opéra bouffe* stars, who will be the story's protagonists. Rose Mignon, popular for some time previously, is modelled on an older type of beauty that would, in later periods, once again come into its own. She is "small and dark, and of the adorable type of ugliness peculiar to a Parisian street child." Nana, the new star, is tall and plump, with "rounded shoulders, Amazonian bosom, wide hips." She represents a new, voluptuous type of beauty whose origins lie, Zola implies, in the street society from which she has risen through sagacious use of her body with men.[21]

The increasing popularity of the music hall in Great Britain and of the *opéra bouffe* in France was indicative of a new wave of sensual expression in both nations. The French Second Empire was a period of extravagance and amorality, when men of wealth kept mistresses and the demimonde was influential and popular. In 1861, after several decades in eclipse, high-class London courtesans once again began publicly to travel the fashionable avenues in their carriages as a way of attaining the public reputations they relished. In 1869 in England the Prince of Wales came to public attention as corespondent in the Mordaunt divorce trial in the first indication of his later career as philanderer, bon vivant, and leader of the rebellion against the standards of prudery that his mother exemplified.[22]

Such evidences of the public flouting of repressive moral codes were not absent from the United States—even in the 1850s. The young nation also had its courtesans; but their behavior was discreet, they were not publicly known, and their identities are difficult to uncover today. Yet the girl of the period, who was directly affected in dress and behavior by the erotic influences in French fashion, was symbolic of a new demand for body freedom. In addition, some important new trends appeared in the theater. Stimulated by the Panic of 1857, which devastated New York theater attendance, impresarios looked to sensuality as a way of attracting patrons. In New York City, Laura Keene, a noted Shakespearean actress who had received her initial theatrical training at the famed London burlesque house of Madame Vestris, copied her mentor by opening the Varieties Theatre and managed to stay afloat by staging elaborate spectaculars involving choruses of women in tights and ballet costumes who danced and sang. In 1857 the perennially popular minstrel shows, which for several decades had avoided offending Victorian morality by including only men in their casts, began to add women performers.[23]

That same year, in a shockingly realistic production of Dumas's *Camille*, American actress Matilda Heron introduced to the United States a new style of "emotional acting," centered around a passionate display of personality. Heron was not the first actress to play Camille on the American stage. But in previous productions the play had been rewritten to make the central character a flirt, not a prostitute; or a scene was added, set in heaven, where Camille repented all her previous sins and received God's absolution. Heron's style of acting would dominate the American theater for the next several decades and reach its apogee in Sarah Bernhardt. Generally young and beautiful, the emotional actresses expressed the utmost emotionalism in their characterizations, using face and body in ways that emphasized physicality. Camille was their favorite role. Yet so respected was the presumed genius of these actresses that none of them were prosecuted for their realistic portrayals of fallen women, until Olga Nethersole in the 1890s fell afoul of Anthony Comstock because of her passionate love scenes.[24]

These trends in the American theater of the 1850s became even more significant during the era of the Civil War and Reconstruction. Periods of war and their peacetime aftermaths are often characterized by freer behavior; one thinks of the hedonism of the 1920s. The destruction of the Civil War and the exhaustion of the postwar period produced a desire for fantasy and escape. "What the world wanted was not moral, not instruction, not wit, not poetry, not pathos," wrote one commentator; it wanted carefree entertainment. In 1858 the manager of the Academy of Music, a concert hall favored by the New York elite, tried to raise money for the hall by holding public masked balls, which journalist Hiram Fuller called "French entertainments." By the end of the 1860s these balls, with liquor flowing freely and women exhibiting extreme décolletage, were regularly held at a variety of places.[25]

In 1860 Adah Isaacs Menken burst on the American scene and subsequently scored an international theatrical success when she played the male hero in the popular equestrian drama *Mazeppa,* an adaptation from the poem by Byron about a Polish military hero. Her performance introduced a show-stopping scene in which, dressed in flesh-colored tights and top and apparently nude, she was strapped on the back of a horse that cantered on a ramp over the audience and across the stage. Actresses on the legitimate stage had long played male roles as a test of their acting ability, but female transvestism for erotic effect had heretofore been confined to the burlesque and variety stage. Indeed, so powerful was the erotic appeal of the horse and the bound woman playing a man that scores of Menken imitators appeared, both in legitimate and variety theaters, and sometimes they simply played the horse scene without the benefit of the rest of the production.[26]

The Civil War itself seemed to provide an excuse for actresses to portray soldiers and to display their legs in a transvestite setting. The year 1861, for example, witnessed a revival of *The Naiad Queen,* a drama that had been first performed some twenty years before and that included scenes in which numerous scantily clad women posed as water nymphs and marched in tights and tops as Amazon warriors. It thereby linked legs to the military and established a convention that later became standard in American popular musicals. From the 1870s to the 1890s hardly a production failed to include a scene with marching women in tights garbed as soldiers.[27]

During the war, New York City was a central dispatching area for northern troops going south, and there were sizable encampments of young men around the city. New concert saloons and variety theaters sprang up throughout the city, and in many cases the old family-oriented minstrel theaters were now reconverted into concert saloons. The incidence of prostitution and venereal disease increased substantially during the war. In New York, shop windows displayed colored pictures of the Parisian demimonde; cigar stores flourished as minimally concealed places of prostitution. On Broadway, in the midst of the upper-class shopping area, stores selling merchandise priced at a dollar came into being and were patronized largely by men waited on by young, pretty female clerks. In one of the last wars to include large groups of camp followers prostitutes regularly followed the troops, and from men under General Hooker's command came the term "hooker."[28]

For four years young men throughout the North left home and families to join the all-male army culture and participate in what must have been an intense experience of male bonding. One wonders to what extent the rise of the Woman's Christian Temperance Union in the early 1870s may have been motivated by women's determination to regain control over men's behavior after the loosening of behavior in war. During the war, whiskey was part of the regular rations, and "camp fire comradeship," as one commentator put it, encouraged smoking and drinking. Drinking and gambling became the common respite from battle. Wrote author John William De Forest: "If homicide is habitually indulged in, it leads to immorality."[29]

This lack of concern for convention spread beyond the men who fought the war. Foreign travellers noted that aphrodisiacs and birth control devices were regularly advertised in the newspapers and, according to Briton Lord Russell, "slang in its worst Americanized form is freely used in sensational headings and leaders." Wartime prosperity and fortunes made in army supply brought lavish displays of wealth, and outraged New Yorkers formed a Women's Patriotic Society for Diminishing the Use of Imported Luxuries. A kindred society appeared in Washington, D.C. Yet nothing seemed to stem the extravagance or to reinforce adherence to strict moral codes. According to observers, respectable young women did not hesitate to attend popular masked balls, and commentator Maria Daly discerned relaxed standards even in formal elite activities. Changes in the standard figures in the cotillion, the stylized dance that was the high point of society balls from the 1850s to the 1920s, seemed to her intensely symbolic. In these elaborate exercises, men and women exchanged partners at the signal of the cotillion leader, giving each old partner a gift and performing whatever dances or exercises the leader designated. Daly contended that new routines introduced in the late 1860s simulated gentlemen driving coaches in races, married women dining at Delmonico's without their husbands, and young society women acting in a "rompish" manner. There was, she contended, "a clique of fast young married women in New York City very much loosening the reins of good and decorous manners."[30]

Following the war, there was a sudden outbreak of domestic murders and divorce scandals, exemplified by the 1870 New York City trial of Albert McFarland for the murder of James Richardson, a *New York Tribune* reporter who had become involved with McFarland's wife, Abby Sage. Before the trial ended, salacious charges of sexual intimacy lodged against Sage and Richardson and of alcoholism and wife-beating lodged against McFarland had been widely circulated by the press. In what seemed the freer sexual environment of the 1870s, Harriet Beecher Stowe was willing to reveal the story of Byron's incestuous behavior; Tennessee Claflin and Victoria Woodhull received major publicity for their small, but vocal free-love movement; some let it be known that, in their view, the Greek poetess Sappho, whose writings were popular throughout the nineteenth century, had been a lesbian (and Thomas Wentworth Higginson attempted to refute them). And finally, Elizabeth Tilton and Henry Ward Beecher fell into a relationship that by 1876 came to public view in the greatest sex scandal of the century, when Theodore Tilton sued Beecher for the alienation of his wife's affections. By 1873 chronicler Elizabeth Ellet wrote that to be fast "was modish in New York, Newport, and Saratoga," and *Harper's Bazar* thought the attitude was widespread elsewhere. "The fast girl is now the girl of fashion," commented one of its writers. "In this exhausted age, the piquancy of sin" is predominant.[31]

Paralleling such trends in private behavior, corruption seemed endemic in government, exemplified by the Crédit Mobilier scandal, frauds like the Whiskey Ring in the internal revenue department, and corruption in the administrations of southern Reconstruction governments and northern municipal administrations, like Tweed's in New York. Wrote police officer John H. Warren, "The extravagance born of abundant resources, war, and success in all directions has so corrupted every portion of our national life, that the moral tone of the nation is no longer what it once was, but has reached a depth so low as to be shocking even to ourselves." Contemporary historian Don Seitz called the era "the dreadful decade," and in an oft-cited statement Walt Whitman echoed these sentiments: "The official services of America, national, state and municipal, are saturated in corruption, bribery, falsehood, maladministration; and the judiciary is tainted. The great cities reek with respectable as much as non-respectable robbery and scoundrelism. In fashionable life, flippancy, tepid amours, weak infidelism, small aims, or no aims at all." Living in New York City, Elizabeth Cady Stanton was appalled by rising statistics relating to prostitution, vice, and crime, particularly the crime of rape. With children to raise, she moved with husband and family to the suburbs.[32]

Changes in fashion seemed also to suggest the international decline of Victorianism. Dress styles in 1867, which had been shifting away from the crinoline for a number of years, deflated into a clinging, body-revealing line culminating in a bustle at the rear. The next year, in what was the most erotic style of the century, the "Grecian bend" came into vogue. The phrase itself indicated the widespread influence of classical style in the nineteenth century, but the Grecian bend itself bore no relationship to any Attic precedent. Rather, it involved the combination of a corset laced as tightly as possible with shoes having the highest possible heels in order to thrust the body both backward and forward so that bosoms and buttocks would protrude as much as possible. According to historian Herbert Asbury, the style was often so exaggerated that women could not sit upright in carriages, but rather had to lean forward and rest their hands on cushions on the floor.[33]

Cosmetics were suddenly widely popular. Altman's department store introduced a "making-up" department, and fashionable women began to carry a "Lady's Pocket Companion, or Portable Complection," containing rouge, powder, puffs, an eyebrow pencil, a brush, and a bottle of India ink to use as eyeshadow. One specialty New York cosmetic shop offered thirteen varieties of powder, twenty-three kinds of face washes and lotions, and twenty types of rouge. Enamelling also came into vogue. Introduced in 1868 by a chiropodist on lower Broadway and first employed by actresses, enamelling involved the coating of face and neck with plastic enamel, built around an arsenic or lead base, in order to attain a smooth, light complexion. Generally it was lightly applied, so the subject could move her facial muscles. If the coating was too heavy, however, the slightest movement was likely to produce cracks in the surface.[34]

The corseted, high-heeled, and heavily made-up woman of fashion of 1868 was popularly dubbed a Dolly Varden. The name was derived from the flirtatious, working-class heroine of Charles Dickens's *Barnaby Rudge,* first published in 1841. The appellation "dolly" well suited the doll-like quality of the women of Grecian-bend style, who wore, as Susan Anthony pointed out, long trains that picked up the filth of the street and skirts tied back so tightly that they could hardly move. But the central point about the Dolly Varden of the story was that she was plump and buxom; and, with no conscious effort on her part, most of the men in the story at some point sought to possess her. In contrast, the upper-class heroine—tall, thin, and pallid—interested only the patrician partner for whom Dickens designated her. But Dolly was a flirt by nature, "a plump, roguish, comely, bright-eyed, enticing, bewitching, captivating, maddening little puss." She was poor in patrimony, but rich in physical attributes, and women on all sides of the Atlantic for a time wanted to be like her.[35]

III

During the Reconstruction era, eroticism and extravaganza continued to be major trends on the American stage. In 1867 *The Black Crook,* perhaps the most famous production in the history of the American musical stage, was first performed. It was a melodrama based loosely on the Faust legend, lasting for five and one-half hours, introducing the most lavish scenic effects yet, and featuring a ballet troupe of several hundred women in scanty costumes as well as a solo troupe dressed in fleshings and apparently nude. Brilliant publicity engineered by the production's press agent gave it the false reputation of having pioneered in this particular form of spectacular theater when in fact it was simply a grander version of *The Naiad Queen* and other spectacles of earlier decades. Yet *The Black Crook,* more than any other event, symbolized in striking fashion a liberalization of American moral behavior, most specifically in New York City.

The Black Crook was followed in quick succession by a Parisian *opéra bouffe* company featuring Offenbach's operettas and then by a number of burlesque troupes, drawn especially from English music halls and burlesque houses. To them the United States seemed a mecca. The official British censor—the Lord High Chamberlain—had begun to outlaw displays of flesh on the stage and to increase restrictions on suggestive gestures or poses. No such official censorship existed in the United States. In 1849, so-called living picture productions (in which actors and actresses dressed in fleshings had reproduced famous nude Biblical and classical paintings) were raided by the police only when proprietors of concert saloons had produced them. Those in respectable theaters initially were not bothered, until the tawdry nature of the concert-hall variety drew a public outcry against all the productions, and the police closed them all down. Yet neither Adah Menken nor *The Black Crook* choruses were prosecuted for indecent exposure. Apparently, as long as body exposure was connected with a theater deemed respectable and the production was not too salacious, the authorities did not intervene. Octogenarian Frederick Van Wyck remembered that before the New York City authorities would permit Lydia Thompson and her burlesque troupe to perform, they required a private presentation and then ruled that the women of the troupe had to lower their skirts by two inches, but that was the only intervention.[36]

It should be remembered that the burlesque and variety stage had become popular in the United States well before the Civil War. Burlesque was not then the prurient, male entertainment it is today. Rather, it grew out of a respected form of theater dating back to the comedies of Aristophanes. Burlesque featured beautiful women and comic men who combined topical jokes and satire with song and dance. Frequently set in ancient Greece, burlesques were written in rhymed couplets. British burlesque troupes had regularly toured the United States in the antebellum era, and William Mitchell's New York Olympic Theatre, which featured burlesques, was famed throughout the nation in the 1830s and 1840s. In addition, by the 1850s most cities contained several theaters that specialized in variety entertainments, and all classes of the population frequented them.[37]

These favorable conditions prompted Lydia Thompson, a noted performer on the British music hall stage, to assemble a burlesque troupe to bring to the United States. Thompson had already won individual acclaim for her dancing in European tours. Unfortunately, the sources on Thompson are slim, but what emerges is a picture of a shrewd, ambitious, and talented woman who realized the potential financial prospects in the large American market. Her troupe, which arrived in New York City in 1868, became the most famed of all such British imports. "When we went through the United States in 1869 and again in 1872, it was like a triumphant march," Thompson told an interviewer. "The entire male citizenry of your republic rose up and threw open their arms everywhere to us in a welcoming embrace." For the next three decades Lydia Thompson troupes repeatedly toured the United States, and several of her protégés, including Pauline Markham and Eliza Weathersby, became stars of the comic opera stage.[38]

The Thompson troupe offered the American public a striking example of the voluptuous model of beauty. In addition, they displayed a vigorous, unconventional style of behavior. In one of the sharpest and most enigmatic style shifts of the century, they all peroxided their hair and became blonde. For half a century, brown hair had been the favored color. Now light blonde hair became the vogue.[39]

Regarding *The Black Crook*, novelist Mark Twain wrote: "The scenery and the legs are everything. Girls—nothing but a wilderness of girls . . . dressed with a meagerness that would make a parasol blush." Twain's comment was representative of the shocked response that *The Black Crook* elicited. However, the British Blondes, as they were called, drew mixed reactions. William Dean Howells saw the troupe in Boston and found the production indecent. Their dances were "wanton excesses"; there was "nothing of innocent intent" in any of their productions. According to actress Olive Logan, they sang "coarse" songs, in contrast to burlesque troupes that had preceded them, and their dialogue was filled with slang and double entendres, accompanied by the "wink, the wriggle, and the grimace." On the other hand, theater critic Richard Grant White found nothing offensive about their performances except for the high kicking in the cancan, which he exonerated on the grounds that women did it at private parties and there it was accepted as part of "the manners of the day."[40]

There was similar disagreement over the propriety of the costumes that the British Blondes wore. Howells compared their dress to that of "circus riders of the opposite sex," and he noted that they had eliminated the "volumned gauze" of the traditional ballet dancer's skirts, which had lent some respectability to that enterprise. On the other hand, Lydia Thompson contended that their costumes were no more revealing than what women wore in playing male parts in Shakespeare and in grand opera, and Richard Grant White pointed out that even the hoop skirts worn by respectable women regularly tilted upward when they danced, fully revealing legs and undergarments.[41]

Yet despite what seemed to many commentators to be the erotic nature of the British Blondes' performances, all remarked on the respectable appearance of their audiences. White had expected to find the audience at the performance he attended coarse and flashy, but, on the contrary, "it was notable, in the main, for simple and almost homely respectability." It was composed of "comfortable, middle-aged women from the suburbs and from the remoter country, their daughters, groups of children, a few professional men ... some sober, farmer-looking folk, a clergyman or two." Howells noted that even in Boston the audience included "a most fair appearance of honest-looking, handsomely dressed men and women." Both the *Spirit of the Times,* a dramatic journal, and Lydia Thompson separately noted that the audiences for the performances of the troupe contained many women.[42]

In contrast to the audiences for the British Blondes, those for *The Black Crook* had been almost exclusively male, despite the fact that both productions had been staged at Niblo's Garden, normally a place of respectable, family-oriented entertainment. It is possible that New York's censors may have discovered a truth that Commodore Tooker, press agent for *The Black Crook,* seemed to have conclusively proved: attacks on a production as immoral served only to increase its popularity. Thus ministers and moralists may have avoided attacking the British Blondes. It is also possible that the long controversy over *The Black Crook* had so tired New York Puritans that they left the Blondes alone. In her revealing memoir of New York City life, Mabel Osgood Wright contended that the resistance to attending the production had eventually been broken because the manager was related by marriage to influential New Yorkers, while several of the dancers in it married New York society men and became popular in their new milieu. After all, as Wright explained, New York high society remembered that Adah Isaacs Menken, "the Mazeppa against whom sermons were preached and virtuous eyes veiled," had become, after she moved to Europe, the intellectual comrade of such esteemed literary figures as Dickens, Swinburne, and the elder Dumas.[43]

The British Blondes themselves used a series of devices to legitimize their entertainments. "Even our blonde burlesquers make a *pretense* of respecting public opinion," wrote Olive Logan, "and offer 'appeals to the public' in defense of their nude 'innocent amusements.'" Drawing on traditions associated in the United States with minstrelsy, the comedy that was part of their production defused their sensuality. The satire they presented drew on the American democratic strain, "the disposition to criticize and to derogate from all high pretensions," as Richard Grant White put it in explaining their success. To justify wearing tights, the women all played male roles. Moreover, as several critics pointed out, they all spoke in impeccable, upper-class British accents.[44]

All this lent an aura of respectability, and women went to see them. After all, here was an opportunity to view women associated with new European standards of beauty and behavior. Existing photographs of the British Blondes show sturdy, buxom women. Henry Collins Brown thought that they looked like "the daughters of sturdy Norsemen," but possessed the "curves, undulations, and sinuosities" that were "the coveted outlines of the day." In a remark that subsequently became famous, Richard Grant White wrote that Pauline Markham, with whom he became romantically involved, had found "the long lost arms of the Venus de Milo." A Cincinnati newspaper contended that "the modern French school of painting never created an ideal fairer."[45]

Even William Dean Howells, as much as he disliked their performance, could not repress his admiration of the new buxom image of beauty they represented. The summer before the British Blondes appeared in Boston, he witnessed the performance of a minor burlesque troupe. Most of its members repelled him, for their figures were characterized by a "sad variety of boniness and flabbiness" and they did not have "countenances that consorted with impropriety." In other words, they did not have a sensual appearance. "It seemed an absurdity and an injustice to refer to them in any way the disclosures of the ruthlessly scant drapery." One of them, however, was a young woman "of a powerful physical expression" and a well-rounded body. "On the stage she visibly tyrannized over the invalid sisterhood with her full-blown fascinations."[46]

The blonde hair of the British Blondes was also fascinating to Americans. Indications are that audience demand prompted several members of the troupe with darkish hair to dye theirs the light color or to wear a blonde wig. Moreover, the appellation of British Blondes was actually bestowed by the newspapers; the burlesquers had called themselves simply the Lydia Thompson Troupe. Pauline Markham thought the hair fascination was due to the small number of blondes in the United States, but other commentators do not bear out her observation. There is no question that, by the 1860s, blonde hair was generally in vogue—at least in Europe. Eugénie Doche, the actress who first played Camille, had blonde hair, as did Zola's Nana and the chorus girls in the American *Black Crook.* Among the aristocracy, the Empress Eugénie was also famed for her blonde hair, which she sprinkled with real gold dust, thereby establishing one of the most frivolous and expensive fashions of the era. Huge masses of yellow hair came into vogue, noted a writer in *Harper's Bazar* in 1878, who held burlesque and variety actresses accountable. "The thing grew, and reached such proportions presently that life seemed to have become a vaudeville and the stage to have emptied into the parlor."[47]

Some say that the hair-bleaching properties of hydrogen peroxide had only recently been discovered and that actresses, alert to these trends, were the first to know about it. Earlier in the century dark hair had been popular partly because blonde hair, according to the theory of the physiognomists, indicated an uninteresting personality. But once the new trends toward open sensual expression began to permeate the transatlantic world, blonde hair was seen in a different way. Its old associations with innocence now became both a way of legitimizing the new sensuality and of heightening it by combining both purity and voluptuousness. The *Spirit of the Times* described the hair of the British Blondes as "golden clouds which envelop all imperfections"; it was also, by the canons of the time, enormously erotic.[48]

In the twentieth century, voluptuousness of figure and blonde hair have come to be associated with a kind of carnality revolving around an intense femininity. One thinks of the childlike Marilyn Monroe, the apogee of the "dumb blonde" figure who haunted American culture from the 1930s to the 1960s and who contributed powerfully to the modern misapprehension that a woman who is beautiful cannot be intelligent. The idea, too, was equally current a century ago, enshrined in the belief that intellectual women were invariably "bluestockings," that they were incapable of keeping their houses and personal appearances in order, that beauty was an attribute they could never possess.

The sensuality of the British Blondes, however, rested only partly on their femininity. William Dean Howells found their masculinity more than anything else shocking and intriguing. The women in *The Black Crook* had been fairies and goblins; the British Blondes were soldiers, vagabonds, pirates, and kings. They had conquered "all the easy attitudes of young men," in Howells's words; they were "radiant" as "young gentlemen" and ill at ease when they wore dresses on stage. They seemed to him "creatures of a kind of alien sex." One of their best-known scenes involved a parody of the fashionable Grecian bend; another spoofed the girl of the period, whose life was directed toward securing a husband.[49]

The assumption of masculinity permeated their performances. Borrowing from minstrel tradition, they did clog dances and played banjos and trumpets, and Olive Logan found their playing of instruments normally associated with men to be "queer." In a scene from *The Forty Thieves,* in which they portrayed bandits and poked fun at young men trying to shock their elders, they all smoked cigarettes. It was done wearing tights and performed in a comic vein, but there was more to it than the desire simply to provoke laughter—or to vamp men. As much as the British Blondes were showing women in their audiences a new kind of physical form, they were also demonstrating a new kind of behavior—one that was free, assertive, self-reliant.[50]

In doing so, they were borrowing from and extending the old and continuing convention of behavior typical of the standard female character of both the legitimate and the popular stage known as the soubrette. Originally a stock figure in French farce, the soubrette, whose traditional stage occupation had been domestic service, was designed to express both lower-class sensuality and droll criticism of her upper-class employers. In nineteenth-century drama, she became a type as common as the ingenue heroine, to whose passivity she posed a striking contrast. Although by then not always a servant or member of the working class, she was small, tough, daring, and determined. She often appeared as a young boy, thereby further legitimizing her rowdy stage behavior, seizing the opportunity to display her body in tight pants and shirt, and titillating audiences with a hint of sexual transvestism. By midcentury, stock companies as often contained a woman designated to play soubrette parts as they did a leading man or a leading lady, and the soubrettes were as popular as the other stars.[51]

The most important soubrette of the nineteenth century was Lotta Crabtree, a performer who began her career as an adolescent in San Francisco concert saloons and who took the nation by storm in the post–Civil War years with her combination of sly sensuality, vigorous singing and dancing, and burlesques of contemporary mores. Small, with a round childish face and a boyish figure, she was the forerunner of later soubrettes who would attain national prominence: one thinks of Maude Adams on the legitimate stage, of Eva Tanguay in vaudeville, and, of course, of Mary Pickford. At the very least, the soubrette destroyed the identification of smallness with aristocracy and paved the way for the late-century identification of height with elite status, a quality evident in the tall women of George Du Maurier and Charles Dana Gibson.[52]

In 1885 the *Police Gazette* incorrectly traced the origins of the soubrette in the United States to Lydia Thompson, but the attribution pointed to an important part of the British Blondes' appeal. Not only was their body build intended to attract men, but, combined with their behavior, it also represented a rebellion against the steel-engraving lady model of beauty and activity. Off the stage, too, their well-publicized private behavior was free and easy. They could regularly be seen in the afternoons on Broadway and in the summer at fashionable resorts. They associated with wealthy young men, who were dazzled by their glamour and sent them flowers and jewels and vied for their attention. They brought the "stage-door Johnny" into full view. In Chicago, Lydia Thompson supposedly horsewhipped an editor who accused her troupe of salacious behavior, and the incident was widely reported in the press. In New Orleans her visit during Mardi Gras and her supposed affair with a visiting Russian archduke made her a public celebrity and produced a song featuring her that is still sung during Mardi Gras.[53]

With extreme slimness in vogue in the late twentieth century, it is difficult for us to visualize the popularity of these women of ample girth. Yet more than their frame endeared them to the men who pursued them and the women who watched their exploits. The theatrical community comprised a separate subculture in the nineteenth century, one whose practitioners kept to themselves. Theater people were free and easy, constantly touring and travelling, taking on new roles. Victorian conventionalism was largely irrelevant to them, and in their world the regular social classes were all confused, with crude stagehands and set builders assuming a fraternity with chorus girls and dramatic actresses alike. In her biographical novel of theatrical life, *Mimic World,* Anna Cora Mowatt describes how the newly hired ingenue blushed furiously when a stagehand used the familiar term "my dear" to her, but she soon learned that its constant use among theater people had taken all familiarity out of it. A decade later, recording her experiences as a member of the chorus of Augustin Daly's famed post–Civil War repertory company, New York socialite Dora Ranous revealed how theatrical life had eroded her conventional mores to the point that while on tour, without hesitating, she went for a drive and to dinner with a man she met by accident.[54]

Among the women who survived the difficult road to theatrical success, participation in the world of the theater produced a special type, one who was skilled in all the ways of attracting a man, according to Richard Grant White. Yet at the same time, these women had "a certain freedom of restraint that makes intercourse with them easier than it is with purely domestic women. A clever and successful actress is generally a charming woman, with her womanhood slightly dashed with the open-hearted freedom of a good fellow, and the ease and repose of a man of the world." By the 1860s some American women had been experimenting with freer modes of dress and behavior for some time. In the 1870s and 1880s actresses would not only serve as models to maintain the knowledge of these modes in decades when they would come under attack, but they also would constitute a vanguard group to point the way to the re-emergence of freer modes on an even broader scale in the 1890s.[55]

By the 1870s the voluptuous woman had come into her own. She was apparent in popular art, particularly in French academic paintings. Her vogue was further spread by medical theorists who associated plumpness with health, by the physical appearance of the Empress Eugénie and other European style setters, by the tendency of the newly wealthy to associate size with prosperity, and particularly by the popularity of burlesque performers. Above all, she was a lower-class model of beauty that sectors of the middle and upper classes accepted as their own. Her vogue is a striking illustration of the fact that the elites do not always determine fashion and that behind the drive to demonstrate status and to eliminate vestiges of lower-class roots may lurk envy of a group whose behavior is perceived as free from the responsibilities of maintaining propriety and accumulating possessions. As the British Blondes portrayed the voluptuous woman, she was as energetic and emancipated as she was erotic—and thus an appealing figure on many levels. In many ways she was the forerunner of both the new woman of the 1890s and the flapper of the 1910s and 1920s.

7

The Voluptuous Woman in Eclipse

Lillian Russell, Lillie Langtry, and the Advance of Naturalness

D espite the importance of the voluptuous woman as a measure of beauty among American women, she never completely carried the day. Both the steel-engraving lady and the natural woman were also popular in the late nineteenth century. In 1874, touring British burlesque artist Emily Soldene (built along the hefty lines of Lydia Thompson) noted that she and the members of her company were called "beefy" by the New York press, even though impresario Robert Grau remembered that "it is questionable whether at any time in the writer's recollection such a collective band of beauty was ever organized." Yet women in fashion magazine illustrations continued to look thin and pale for most of the century, as did many American women. In these years the athletic, natural look was also becoming popular, encouraged by effective proponents of exercise and athletics, by the continuing classical vogue, and by the popularity of actresses like Lillie Langtry, who embodied its ideals.[1]

With respect to standards of women's physical appearance, the post–Civil War years were a confusing period, when varying types of beauty vied with each other before the natural look became predominant in the early twentieth century. The confusion can be seen, for example, in the differing American attitudes toward dieting. Even though it was not until 1885 that Natalie Dana's well-to-do New York circle adopted the voluptuous model, the eminent British dress designer Lucile remembered that the great beauties of the Edwardian era, whose initial prominence dated from earlier years, were all "big girls," weighing over 150 pounds. Robert Tomes of *Harper's Bazar* was a proponent of greater weight among women, but he had to admit in 1868 that many women still dieted to become thin. In contrast, as late as 1895 the *Phrenological Journal of Science and Health* asserted that Elizabeth Cady Stanton's figure (which to our eyes appears decidedly fat) had "that plumpness which indicates superb health, and it would be difficult to find a more perfect sign of digestion than is shown in the fullness of her cheeks." Actress Fanny Davenport was frequently cited as an important model of the voluptuous woman, but by the late 1880s she felt that her popularity was slipping because of her weight, and she began to diet.[2]

Indeed, dieting, which by 1900 would become something of a craze, was popular throughout the post–Civil War period, as evidenced in the substantial sales of a small book written by Englishman William Banting. A lifetime dieter, he had suffered from extreme obesity to such an extent that he avoided going out in public because of the stares he drew. He consulted doctors to no avail; their diet and exercise regimens simply did not work. Then, at the age of sixty-six, he encountered eminent surgeon William Harvey, whose studies of diabetes had shown that abstinence from starch and sugar not only helped a diabetic condition, but also produced weight loss. Harvey put Banting on a starch- and sugar-free diet, and he lost a pound a week for thirty-five weeks.[3]

The popularity of Banting's work, which went through twelve editions between 1863 and 1902, may simply prove that Americans like personal testimonials that report extraordinary individual perseverance in overcoming great difficulties. Nonetheless, Banting's volume provided news of major scientific findings about the factors that cause weight gain and loss. On the subject of nutrition, previous writers like Sylvester Graham had based their dietary advice on their own observations; Harvey pointed the way to the scientific study of nutrition, which health researchers and home economists would take up by the late nineteenth century. So well known did Banting become that dieting was called "banting" for many years.[4]

Even as thinness and athleticism were coming into vogue, voluptuousness was under attack from another quarter. Despite the fact that Lillian Russell's elegance and respectability eventually lent legitimacy to what was sometimes called the hourglass look, its association with the theater and the working-class culture from which it had emerged remained strong. In his insightful memoir of the behavior of the New York elites, Rodman Barnett declared that "the Lillian Russell type of good looks left Newport [women] cold," perhaps because the Newport men so thoroughly liked Bouguereau's voluptuous nudes. By the late 1870s, with the exception of dress, the American elites had switched their allegiance in matters of style from France to England, where the exciting Prince of Wales and his beautiful Princess Alexandra ruled society. In their circle the esthetic, classical look predominated, symbolic of their rebellion against Victorian rigidity and more in keeping with their sophisticated Marlboro House circle, which included artists and writers. Both Queen Victoria and the Empress Eugénie had been short and plump. In contrast, Alexandra was tall and spare. In body type she resembled Lillie Langtry and looked as though she belonged in a painting by Millais or Lord Leighton.[5]

Not all American elites followed the English in the new style of appearance. In the early 1870s New York society painter Giuseppi Fagnani painted the "nine reigning belles of New York society" in nine portraits depicting them as the Nine Muses of Classical Mythology to hang in the entrance hall of the newly opened Metropolitan Museum of Art. The figures, dressed in classical garb, are buxom and fleshy. Natalie Dana, daughter of the pastor of an elite New York City Episcopal church, averred in her autobiography that the voluptuous style did not even emerge in her circle until the 1880s, when plumpness came to be viewed as healthy. And in 1895, when socialite Irene Langhorne married Charles Dana Gibson, she padded her hips to make them look heavier.[6]

That many New York society women, however, did take up the leaner line is apparent in their portraits. Contemporary art historian Edward Strahan described Cabanel's 1876 portrait of art collector Catharine Lorillard Wolfe as showing "highly-bred refinement, attenuated elegance, such as will be found in their highest manifestation in one of our select American types. The pose is full of flexibility and pliant, willowy grace." In 1887 painter John Singer Sargent, then living in London, was approached by a number of wealthy Americans to paint portraits of members of their families. Although his career seemed in eclipse in Europe, where he had been born and raised, Americans had learned of his work through paintings that French dealers sent for sale in the United States. Primarily a portraitist, Sargent soon became the favorite painter of New York society. His portraits are individualized, yet his subjects all are tall and commanding, with long arms and fingers and small waists. They look like Gibson girls incarnate—some time before Gibson drew his ideal model.[7]

Styles of appearance have an independent life; they respond to the human desire for change as do fashions in dress and in a variety of other objects and activities. But they also change in response to social trends. By the 1870s, sectors of the upper and middle classes—acting independently of each other—began to oppose the sensual outbreak of the Civil War period. As they did so, the voluptuous model became increasingly suspect. It remained in force partly because of its association with health and partly because of the popularity of Lillian Russell, whose reputation for gentility obscured the connection of voluptuousness with sensuality. But by the 1900s, with the rise of naturalness as the nation's ideal, the voluptuous woman would retreat to the working-class culture from which she had emerged and once again become the furtive, if widespread, subject of pornographic pictures for men.

II

The success of the British Blondes had a striking impact on the American theater. "Theatres all seem to have vanished," wrote one impresario, "and we have Academies of Music, Olympics, Varieties, Gaieties, Opera Houses." "Negro Minstrelsy itself," he continued, "has had a hard time maintaining its own ground." According to Olive Logan, scores of foreign burlesque troupes travelled to the United States seeking, like Lydia Thompson's group, to tap the lucrative American market. Actresses won roles not for talent, but because of their physical appearance and their willingness to wear scanty attire. "It became a question with actresses seeking a situation not whether they were good actresses," wrote Logan, "but whether they were pretty and were willing to exhibit their persons, and do as the burlesque women did."[8]

Such a situation perhaps inevitably elicited a negative reaction. The British Blondes had preserved some degree of decorum; many of the new burlesque troupes and variety theater entertainers made no such attempt. By 1872 no less than five theaters "supposedly of a reputable class" featured productions with dancers doing the high-kicking, skirt-flinging cancan, according to producer Robert Grau. The police raided these theaters periodically, but still they remained in operation.[9]

Outside the theater, the free and easy behavior of the 1860s and 1870s provoked a powerful social purity movement in response. Remembering those years, Arthur Train called the appearance of social purity activities a "Third Great Awakening," occasioned by "the blatant masculine profligacy of the later 60s." In 1872 Anthony Comstock became concerned about the pornography circulating among the clerks with whom he worked in New York City. Shortly thereafter, under the aegis of the YMCA and his own New York Society for the Suppression of Vice, he mounted a single-minded crusade against what he viewed as immorality. In 1873 he successfully lobbied Congress for a law that prohibited the dissemination of pornography and birth control information. In addition to Comstock's initiative, vice societies were formed throughout the nation, while a major purpose of the Woman's Christian Temperance Union was the reassertion of traditional morality. In state after state, coalitions of medical doctors and vice reformers achieved the passage of antiabortion legislation; and vice reformers, often working with woman's rights advocates, were able to stop the campaigns of municipal leaders and other doctors for the legalization of prostitution. Coalitions of conservative reformers were also able to obtain tighter requirements for divorce in many states. Even in New York City, contemporaries observed changes, notably the end of street walking on middle-class avenues. "Not that there is a higher tone of morality in New York than in London," wrote one British observer, but "impure associations are very sedulously banished from the sight of the pure."[10]

The social purity campaign had other, less recognized participants. Caroline Astor, a descendant of the old Dutch aristocracy and the wife of one of New York's wealthiest men, decided to create a social hierarchy under her control, as she surveyed the many newly wealthy families attempting to gain admittance to New York high society after the Civil War and became aware of the private libertine behavior of the men of her own circle. Her campaign to assume the leadership of New York society has generally been interpreted as motivated by her frustrations in an unhappy marriage. But there was much more at play than the drive to assert a damaged ego. She worried that the absence of traditional morality would influence her daughter, to whom she was devoted, and she wanted to be certain of the character of her daughter's friends. With the help of her confidant, Ward McAllister, whose social sense seemed unerring, she came to have a firm hand over who would enter the coveted inner circles of New York's elite, the 400 individuals who presumably could fit into her ballroom.[11]

Other mothers and fathers, well placed and upwardly mobile, intent on good marriages for their daughters, and concerned to enforce propriety, also initiated new social forms. Thus the formal debut became a regularized mechanism of introduction into the elite world. By the 1880s chaperonage was reintroduced with more success than before. The straightjacket regimen of calling cards and strict rules of visiting appeared, and society women spent their days leaving their cards at the homes of others and receiving the cards of those who visited them. According to Arthur Schlesinger, the emphasis on sophisticated manners led to "exhaustive specifications of what to do in every conceivable situation." Thus society was formalized and freedom of behavior restricted.[12]

Among older society women fashion became increasingly elaborate, as women changed their gowns many times a day to suit each activity and thus more than ever spent their time involved with clothes. Moreover, the décolletage in vogue during the Civil War era was banished for daytime wear; before the evening all garb was high-collared. Street behavior, too, was rigidified. In 1870 Julia Newberry had noted that young New York society women roamed the city streets with impunity, but by the end of that decade the streets they could travel unescorted were limited. May King Van Rensselaer remembered such restrictions in her New York girlhood; several decades later, Clarence Day noted that "ladies lived and walked in a long, narrow strip between Sixth Avenue and Lexington."[13]

In literature, Malcolm Cowley tells us, the genteel tradition emerged even more strongly after the Civil War than before, and a generation of writers, magazine editors, and book publishers dedicated themselves to protecting the middle-class home "and its presiding spirit, the young girl," from all taint of immorality. In *Indian Summer,* William Dean Howells, a leader among this group, described the new social conservatism and its genesis in the concerns of the older generation about younger people. Despite the fact that Mrs. Bowen's girlhood in a western city had been "untrammeled," she rigidly limited her daughter's activities. "For her daughter there were to be no buggy rides, no concerts, or dances at the invitation of young men . . . no sitting at the steps at dusk with callers who never dreamed of asking her mother . . . nothing of that wild sweet liberty which once made American girlhood a long rapture." "Well, perhaps it will come right in the next generation," mused an acquaintance critical of Mrs. Bowen's policies; "then she will let her daughter have the freedom she hadn't." Mrs. Bowen replied: "Not if I am alive to prevent it."[14]

The new social conservatism was apparent in the ban on cosmetics that also came into force. In the 1860s fashionable women wore cosmetics; by the mid-1870s most did not. In 1874 reporter Arthur Pember searched for the enamelling studios in evidence in New York City in the late 1860s and found none. He did uncover a professional painter who advertised his services as an enameller for women who suffered from severe skin imperfections. The artist told Pember that only one other painter in the city provided such a service, although nearly all the large drug stores employed assistants who could paint out black eyes for men. The prohibition against cosmetics continued in force for some time; turn-of-the-century memoirs once again repeat the old belief that the use of cosmetics identified the wearer as a prostitute. Fashionable women like Elisabeth Thomas's Aunt Lily still might spend hours at their toilettes, but whatever lip cream or rouge they wore had to be subtly applied.[15]

The relationship between the social purity campaign and the theater has never been explored, but indications are that the new social conservatism had a substantial impact there as elsewhere. Available evidence suggests that the respectable audiences who came to see the British Blondes did not long frequent this kind of entertainment. Olive Logan perceived a swift change in public opinion in the 1870s. "In a time so brief that as I look back upon it now it seems almost marvelous," wrote Logan, "the theaters turned the burlesque women adrift." "It was public opinion," she contended, "that did this." Perhaps the novelty of seeing these productions wore off with the steady stream of imitators who followed them. In his vivid memoir of life in New York City in the 1870s, Henry L. Ford argued that the depression of 1873 played a major role in reducing the luxury spending of the middle classes and sparking a religious revival. Impresario Rudolph Aaronson, Lillian Russell's producer, thought that ministerial attacks on the burlesque theater had initially increased attendance at these performances, but that ultimately the public had come to support the ministers and boycott the productions. Perhaps the revival that Ford mentioned played a role. In effect, the theater lost a potentially large patronage before producers had had a chance to exploit it.[16]

The history of the popular musical theater in the late nineteenth century is the complex story of an art form evolving in the period of its greatest creativity. In these years, burlesque, spectacle, variety, the minstrel show, opéra bouffe, and the operetta all were combined to create the most indigenous American form of popular musical theater: the musical comedy. One of the major themes of its development was the search for a form of theater that would be both sensually stimulating and yet respectable.

Part of the solution to the search seemed to lie in devising a new formula that would downplay erotic dancing and emphasize some other element. Several American writers attempted new directions, but the major innovators were European. First, Hungarian brothers Imre, Bolossy, and Arnold Kiralfy returned to the tradition of extravaganza exemplified by The Black Crook, but eliminated suggestive scenes and used classical choreography. Moreover, they employed ballerinas who were not notable for physical beauty and who did not attract the stage-door Johnny set. In addition, Englishmen William Gilbert and Arthur Sullivan combined elements of burlesque with operetta, downplayed suggestiveness, but retained beautiful women as principals, and elevated music and lyrics over dance. Their H.M.S. Pinafore, first produced on the New York stage in 1878, was an enormous success. With the lack of an international copyright law, no fewer than five companies performed it simultaneously in New York City, and ninety national touring companies appeared.[17]

Despite the increased respectability of the popular musical theater, the voluptuous kind of female beauty that burlesque had initially publicized among American women did not disappear from the stage. Rather, actresses on the new, respectable musical stage and even within the legitimate theater continued its popularity, while burlesque itself developed into a salacious form of entertainment for men. The voluptuous actresses on the legitimate stage included Fanny Davenport, the star of director Augustin Daly's repertory theater, which the New York elites frequented. Burlesque star Emily

Soldene thought Davenport was the most "talked of" beauty on the stage, and celebrity photographer Napoleon Sarony was "overwhelmed" by the public demand for photographs of Davenport.[18]

The most important late-century exemplar of the voluptuous woman was Lillian Russell. Of midwestern origin, Russell was brought to New York City by her mother in 1877 to study for a career in opera. But she soon rebelled to pursue first an unhappy marriage and then a career on the popular musical stage, where she quickly rose to stardom because of her beauty and her considerable singing ability. Audiences appreciated her pluck and her fortitude; they admired her rejection of opera, an art form some considered effete and aristocratic. In her personal life she was well known for her generosity, her tough spirit, her humorous, laconic attitude. Rather than condemning Russell for three unsuccessful marriages, her public praised her for having survived. Her respectable, rural background, including a convent education, seemed to legitimize actions of hers that were condemned in other actresses. Too, she successfully appropriated for herself the term "prima donna," which, when accorded to opera stars, gave claim to a position of eminence with exemption from regular canons of behavior. According to Russell's friend, actress Marie Dressler, the press loved to refer to the musical comedy star as "every inch a prima donna."[19]

The most important factor in her appeal, however, was her appearance. Because of her blonde hair and luminous, white skin, innocence was the major ingredient of her beauty. According to drama critic Lewis Strang, she was "a golden-haired goddess with big rounded cheeks, soft and dimpled like a baby's." She had, Strang contended, "the most perfect doll's face on the American stage." "Her pink and white freshness appealed to the sentimentality of young manhood," a biographer has written. In her early career she was known as "airy, fairy Lillian." She played both ingenue and soubrette roles and, in her later career, society women or aristocrats. But in all cases, she romanticized sensuality. She was, according to journalist Dorothy Dix, "an edition deluxe of femininity." And she cultivated an image of propriety; in a celebrated incident at the height of her career in the 1880s she refused any longer to wear tights on the stage and successfully won a court decision upholding her stance.[20]

As Russell grew older, her originally lithe figure grew heavier, as though she felt herself obliged to modify her appearance to conform to a standard that the British Blondes, among others, had originally established. More than this, she loved to eat; and through the well-publicized stories of her gargantuan meals a generation of American women were able to justify their own relief at not having to diet. "There was nothing wraithlike about Lillian Russell," wrote Clarence Day, reminiscing about his experience in the 1880s as a super in one of her performances at New Haven when he was a Yale college student. "She was a voluptuous beauty, and there was plenty of her to see. We liked that. Our tastes were not thin or ethereal." Her beauty was "challenging, fleshly arresting," wrote journalist Beatrice Fairfax. She always dressed in elaborate style, and women came to her performances to see what she was wearing. She was always "royally gowned," noted the *New York World,* with "all the undulations of the prima donna's figure moulded graciously in ripples that were so many sonnets of motions." Edna Ferber compared her figure to a roller coaster.[21]

To several generations of American women Russell was the epitome of female beauty. "The American Beauty," she was often called. "You are no Lillian Russell, yourself" was a common retort to a slighting remark about appearance. For two decades she was the most photographed woman in America, and people went to her plays to see her more than the productions. She incarnated the voluptuous woman and brought elegance to the ideal.[22]

The most admired flower of the day—the deep-toned, full-blown, red American Beauty rose, the pride of American rose growers—was named after Russell by those who had developed the new strain through a complex grafting process. The symbolism of flowers was a component of nineteenth-century sentimentality, important to an age only recently removed from rural roots. Many beauty and etiquette manuals contain charts of the meanings of flowers. The rose signified deep affection—affection being a circumlocution for the flower's classic connection with sexuality. Feminist celebrations banked the stages with American Beauty roses; no society ball was complete without them. In his famous justification of the Standard Oil trust, John D. Rockefeller used the American Beauty rose as comparison. The flower symbolized whatever freedom Lillian Russell represented to American women and whatever voluptuous overtones they preserved from her image by late century.[23]

III

No less than the voluptuous woman, the natural woman as the ideal of beauty advanced in popularity only with difficulty over the course of the late nineteenth century. This is apparent in the ambivalent American reaction to Lillie Langtry, the British actress and one-time mistress of the Prince of Wales who, perhaps more than any other individual at the time, exemplified ideals of the natural woman—particularly as that figure was represented by the classical vogue among transatlantic artists.

The origin of Langtry's popularity is directly traceable to the efforts of the loosely linked group of British painters known as the esthetic school, a group that included John Everett Millais and James McNeill Whistler and for whom Oscar Wilde served as an occasional publicist. It was they who "discovered" Langtry at an evening soirée at the home of one of those late-century London hostesses whose guest list combined figures from high society, the theater, and the arts. At that point Langtry was the wife of an obscure country gentleman, and her own aristocratic family connections had brought the evening's invitation. Without the portraits that Millais and the others painted of her and the public adulation that Wilde heaped on her, however, it is doubtful Langtry would have risen so quickly into public prominence as a "professional" beauty and thus come to attract the attention of the Prince of Wales, whose involvement with her solidified her international reputation for beauty.[24]

What the esthetic painters found attractive in Langtry was her striking resemblance to the classical model of beauty that was their ideal. "She had a pure Greek profile," Oscar Wilde said of her. Moreover, she was tall (five feet eight inches), with a large bosom and hips. She was broad-shouldered, and her frame reflected years of exercise, beginning as a child on the Isle of Jersey, where her parents allowed her freely to play and roam with her five brothers, and continuing into adulthood, when she exercised every day and walked several miles before breakfast. Like the pre-Raphaelites before them, the esthetic painters developed their ideal of female beauty and then (whether consciously or not) chose a woman who resembled that ideal to promote it.[25]

After the end of her liaison with the Prince of Wales, Langtry's faltering finances prompted her to take to the stage. In 1882 she embarked on the first of many tours of the United States. She was a shrewd, ambitious woman. Like Lydia Thompson, she realized the financial potential of the American theatrical market and the value of publicity. With unerring accuracy she titillated the American taste for scandal, playing on her reputation as a courtesan, openly flaunting her affair with New York man-about-town Frederick Gebhard. Onstage, she was a lady, playing roles that allowed her to display her upper-class style, her impeccable diction and manners, and her sizable wardrobe. Offstage, she played a different part.

Whether or not Langtry could act was always open to question, but such was her notoriety that her performances always sold out. English feminist Emily Faithfull was astonished, when visiting the United States in 1882, to witness the furor Langtry aroused. The newspapers, she wrote, "publish every item of scandal which could be gathered from attendants at her hotels, car conductors of trains she travelled in, dressers at theatres where she played." In its pages the *Police Gazette* usually paid no attention to the major stars of the legitimate stage, focusing rather on the chorus girls and soubrettes of vaudeville and comic opera. Yet the journal covered Langtry's tour in detail and presented as the ultimate evidence of her popularity the story that a chambermaid at the hotel where she stayed in New York City had stolen her nightgown and sold it in small pieces to New York's "young bloods."[26]

Yet despite Langtry's reputation as England's most beautiful woman, many Americans did not find her attractive. Drama critic Amy Leslie thought that Langtry's appearance captured "all the gimp, reliance, and charm of the American belle, combined with British stateliness." But to others, her height, her muscular body, and her large nose and mouth all stood in the way of beauty. A Chicago newspaper noted that England may have sent the United States its most beautiful woman, but "she could not compare with scores of American ladies in every city where she is on exhibition." In New York the manager of Peale's, the city's most popular dime museum, held a beauty contest to find the most beautiful woman to challenge Langtry. The problem Langtry presented for Americans was partly a natural Anglo-American rivalry, well suited for the purposes of publicity; but the detailed analyses of her appearance in the press also reflected a more complex debate. No one disagreed about the fairness of her complexion or the "satiny texture" of her skin (which produced a radiance that her friend, the dress designer Lucile, contended she "had never seen in any other woman)." But beyond the complexion, there was no consensus.[27]

Again and again the press noted her resemblance to the Venus de Medici and Venus de Milo, but even that was not enough to convince Americans of her beauty. Despite their rhetorical praise of the classical type of beauty, Americans did not really favor long, large noses and large lips in their women. Both of these features are characteristic of the classical type, and Langtry possessed both, as is apparent from photos of her. Drama critic Frederick Fyles noted what her detractors called the "irregularity of her features." The cupid-bow mouth and retroussé nose that characterized Lillian Russell and echoed the features of the steel-engraving lady were not hers.[28]

Ultimately the long nose captured public favor, as is apparent in the fashion illustrations of the day. The change from the small to the long nose, for example, can be seen to occur abruptly in Godey's Lady's Book in 1887, although the newer feature is apparent earlier in Harper's Bazar. In 1877 Robert Tomes, Harper's Bazar editor, wrote that the Grecian nose was generally accepted as the most beautiful, but that some people still preferred the retroussé. But the large mouth still created problems, as Vogue fashion writer Edna Woolman Chase discovered in her adolescence in the 1890s, when her mother cautioned her always to put her hand over her mouth when she smiled, for it was much too large and "ungenteel."[29]

Her figure, too, was at issue. Theater historian George Odell noted the "divided opinion as to her beauty," but he found Langtry's form "exquisitely symmetrical." Other critics found her frame lacking in "roundness of limb." The problem, according to many, was the well-publicized fact that she exercised and dieted to keep her figure trim and thereby looked as much athletic as voluptuous. Early exercise, according to one commentator, had strengthened her body rather than rounding it, and "the taste of the public does not so much ask for a healthy grown woman on the stage, as for one that can charm by roundness of figure."[30]

Indeed, the vogue of the voluptuous woman suggests that the public preferred roundness of figure off the stage as well as on it. Yet by the 1880s Lillie Langtry's kind of appearance was established among the New York elites, who took their cues about behavior partly from the upper-class English social world she represented in American eyes. But elsewhere in the population, there were reservations about the way she looked, and even the elites did not immediately follow the English vogue of exercise to which both Lillie Langtry and Princess Alexandra were devoted and which had been characteristic of English women for some time.

IV

By 1882, the year of Lillie Langtry's first tour of the United States, whatever vogue for exercise and athletics had been sparked by Dio Lewis and Catharine Beecher had not gained universal popularity. Among educators, it is true, a significant physical education movement had continued after the Civil War. It was led by Dudley Sargent, whose impeccable credentials included a Yale medical degree and the directorship of the Harvard gymnasium, a post he assumed in 1879. From this position he bombarded the nation with exercise propaganda and trained many physical education teachers, especially at his Harvard Summer School for Physical Education. Together with Mary Hemenway, a Boston philanthropist who donated the money for the Harvard gymnasium that still bears her name, Sargent was key to the creation of professional institutions designed to raise the status of the physical education occupation and to provide organized advocacy for it. In 1885 the American Association for the Advancement of Physical Education was founded. Such progress enabled William Anderson, head of the Brooklyn Normal School of Gymnastics and author of a major textbook on calisthenics, to assert in 1889 that "it is now generally admitted by educators that pupils need physical education," although the extent to which such programs were introduced on any widespread basis is debatable.[31]

Despite the exercise advocacy of such individuals, most adult women were ambivalent on the subject. *Outing,* the journal of the burgeoning sports movement, reported in 1885 that, aside from school gymnasiums, almost no such facilities existed generally for women. The expense of building them, according to the magazine, was more than "private enterprise is willing to invest in anything so uncertain as the amount of use they might receive."[32]

Women's lack of enthusiasm for exercise is, in retrospect, not surprising. Existing women's reform groups, for example, by and large did not propagandize the exercise message. When it came to women's health, the focus of the Woman's Christian Temperance Union, of women's clubs, and of the American Woman Suffrage Association (Lucy Stone's organization) was on dress reform. There is some indication that, in fact, they did not share the goals of exercise reformers. In 1890 the *Union Standard,* the official organ of the WCTU, criticized vigorous athletics because they were not ladylike. "A girl must, simply because she is a girl, refrain from taking part in certain healthy recreations," noted one of the journal's contributors. "They must not forget they are young ladies."[33]

The major difficulty for advocates of women's exercise was the belief that strenuous activity produced muscular bodies and destroyed the rounded curves that were the day's desiderata of voluptuous female beauty. Strenuous exercise, it was held, burned an excessive amount of fat and not only made a woman thin, but also substantially reduced the size of her calves, bosom, and arms. "Women do not aim for an athlete's prodigious strength," proclaimed an advertisement for physical exercise in 1904, "but for the development of each muscle of the body to uniform strength and symmetry, giving those curves and lines of beauty which have made the feminine figure the model for all sculptors and painters." Harriet Hubbard Ayer criticized the well-developed muscles that she thought extensive exercise produced, writing that the beautiful arm should be round, white, and plump. Many critics of rigorous exercise for women realized the need for some sort of regular physical activity, but they thought that walking or calisthenics was sufficient.[34]

Women's interest in physical activity, along with their ambivalence toward vigorous exercise, culminated in the vogue for the exercise system of François Delsarte. A French theater personality, Delsarte had perfected a series of body movements initially designed to improve acting technique. Using a combination of mime, dance, and exercise, Delsarte claimed to have discovered the body poses that best expressed every possible emotional state. But his system went beyond such explanation: like many exercise proponents, Delsarte drew on the widespread belief in a reciprocal relationship between mind and body to argue that faithful repetition of his exercises could actually permanently alter mental states of being.

Playwright Steele MacKaye brought the Delsarte system from France to the United States in 1871 and publicized it through writings and lecture tours. Well-to-do women in particular took up Delsarte, perhaps because the French founder had numbered among his pupils eminent actresses and aristocrats. Among elite Washingtonians in the early 1890s, old notions of female delicacy were still current, but all the society women spent a good deal of time "doing Delsarte."[35]

Delsarte's importance lay in two directions. In the first place, his exercises were not strenuous. More than anything else, they were designed to enhance physical grace and control; according to reporter Anne O'Hagan, their real end was relaxation. They allowed women to have a sense of organized physical expression without violating mores dictating physical inactivity. On the other hand, the Delsarte system can be seen as an important episode in the development of what might be called the physical rhythm movement—a movement that reached its apogee in the early twentieth century in the vogue of Isadora Duncan and the so-called dance craze. Delsarte broke down old attitudes about the immorality of unstructured dancing and accustomed many women to moving their bodies with some freedom.[36]

Not only was women's commitment to exercise limited in the post–Civil War years, but their reaction to athletics was also ambiguous. Enthusiasm for a particular sport, generally first played in England, periodically swept the United States. Contemporary observers disagreed widely on the extent to which women participated in these enthusiasms and on the vigor they brought to the enterprise. In the 1870s and 1880s women took up croquet, archery, and tennis in turn. But while participating in each, they wore their regular, confining clothing, including tightlaced corsets. After all, playing sports early became part of the ritual of courtship, to which fashionable dress, with its emphasis on bosom and hips, was central. Moreover, by still prevailing genteel standards, sweat was considered "indelicate." In croquet it was considered improper for women to put mallets between their legs—a prohibition that leads one to wonder how women played the game effectively. Watching Newport women at archery, Edith Wharton wrote of "the lovely archeresses in floating silks or muslins, with their wide leghorn hats, and heavy veils flung back at the moment of aiming." Even *Godey's Lady's Book* in the 1880s, under the editorship of exercise advocate Jane Croly, agreed that archery and tennis were "tame diversions."[37]

Needless to say, women did not take part in the new, vigorous male sports like baseball and football. When the athletic instructor at Vassar College organized the women students into baseball teams, their mothers protested and the activity was ended. Since the bowling alley and the horseback riding ring introduced at the time of Vassar's opening had been aban-

doned because of lack of use, for some time the only exercise activities for
Vassar women were calisthenics and walking.[38]

Women's slow entrance into sports was particularly evident at Newport, the summer home of the New York elites, presumed national fashion
leaders. In the 1870s Caroline Astor set the fashions for Newport as well as
New York. With the exception of informal picnics that Ward McAllister
arranged, the same elaborate entertaining, formal visiting, and constant
changing of clothes characterized both places. May King Van Rensselaer remembered that the only exercise indulged in was gentle rocking on a
"joggle board," a seesawlike contraption with chair backs affixed to the two
ends of a plank placed over a sawhorse. Among this generation, wrote another participant, efforts to strengthen the body were considered "vulgar."
While husbands and brothers made Newport synonymous with sports like
polo, squash, and tennis, women's major daylight activity was being driven
in their coaches back and forth along oceanfront Bellevue Avenue in a daily
parade that came to characterize elite Newport just as much as the sports or
the palaces its summer residents erected there.[39]

It was in the mid-1880s that attitudes began to change on a variety of
fronts. When tennis was first introduced in the 1870s, it had been a tame
sport. But the growth of competition among men, particularly with the
formation of the United States Lawn Tennis Association in 1883 and the
holding of an annual national tournament at Newport, had brought over-
head strokes, the hard serve, and rushing the net. By the end of the 1880s
women were also beginning to use these techniques. In addition, women
tennis players began to wear the bloomer attire previously confined to gymnasiums, or they donned a modified version of male attire, involving a shirt
and skirt. Such changing trends in sports were apparent not only in tennis.
In 1889 the first public gymnasium for women opened in New York City,
and by 1901 in that city alone there were six private ones and numerous
others run by charitable organizations.[40]

In this same period, the eastern women's colleges introduced rigorous
athletics into their curriculum. By then their goals had become closely
linked with physical education as a means of maintaining women's health
to disprove the critics of rigorous academic work for women. This time, in
contrast to Vassar's experience in the 1870s, no major objections were
raised. According to reporter Anne O'Hagan, the calisthenics courses that
earlier had been the core of physical education programs now became subsidiary to outdoor athletics. Each college developed its sports specialty.
Wellesley women were expert in rowing, Bryn Mawr students in basketball,
Vassar women in tennis. "The young woman who wins a championship . . .
is a lionized creature."[41]

By the late 1880s the arguments of the physical exercise advocates were beginning to carry the day. It must not be forgotten that, in contrast to Catharine Beecher and Dio Lewis earlier in the century, many of these practitioners were regularly credentialed physicians. They kept careful records of their students in order to demonstrate that exercise improved physique and health. Dudley Sargent, a brilliant propagandist in these matters, mounted a display at the 1893 Chicago World's Fair of his measurements of twenty thousand college students; and his ongoing study of youthful physiques, which yearly involved thousands of measurements, had enough of a ballyhoo quality to it that even the popular press regularly covered him. Moreover, exercise advocates linked their positive evaluations of their programs to every possibly relevant physiological theory. Mary Taylor Bissell, a prominent New York physician, addressed the prevailing concern over American "nervousness" by arguing that exercise would invariably reduce tensions, for the muscles were "the natural outlet for excessive nervous energy." And, drawing on current physiological theory that posited the interrelationship of mind and body, Bissell predicted that individuals who did not exercise ran the risk of having areas of the brain connected to the nonexercised muscles atrophy and produce mental retardation. So confident was Sargent of his position that he took on the accepted social Darwinian theories of women's inferiority, arguing that any inferiority was the result not of innate factors, but of women's restrictive clothing and their lack of exercise and that women, society's only leisured group, alone had the time for the intellectualism and physical exercise that were the key to effecting the "higher evolution of mind and body" that Darwinists anticipated.[42]

Exercise advocates also insisted that athletic women could be just as voluptuous as any of their languid peers. Acknowledging the late-century preference for plump arms, sports enthusiast Margaret Bisland wrote that, despite vigorous arm motions in the game of bowling, "by some happy provision of kind nature, no matter if a woman's biceps grow as hard as iron and her wrists as firm as steel, the member remains so softly rounded, so tenderly curved, as though no greater strain than the weight of jewelled ornaments had been placed on them." And to counter the assumption that exercise destroyed body curves, it was probably not accidental that published reports of the improved physique of women who exercised almost always featured the increased size of the "chest." Characteristically outspoken, Sargent went so far as to argue that no woman could be beautiful without exercise: "It is the symmetrical and proportionate development of parts, with adipose enough to cover the angles and hollows, that constitutes true beauty. This is the style of development that is likely to accompany the active gyrations of the *première danseuse,* the skater, and the lady fencer. It may be attained by such exercises as running, walking, rowing, swimming, tennis, or gymnastics."[43]

The triumph of the exercise movement among women was the result of a number of factors. The growth and professionalization of the field of physical education and the authority of the arguments of its leaders played an important role. The renown and sense of mission of eastern women's college graduates were also important. After graduation they did not lose the interest in physical education that had been, for many, a crucial part of their undergraduate curriculum. When they came to New York and other cities to live, they sought out gymnasiums and sports clubs; when they married and moved to the suburbs, they founded country clubs. When they became reformers, as many did in this progressive era, they lobbied for exercise programs for working-class women. The first gymnasium in New York City, opened in 1889, was built for profit, but most of those in the years following grew out of the reform impulse and were to be found in settlement houses, at YMCA buildings, on the premises of progressive churches and schools, and at the working-girl clubhouses that Grace Hoadley Dodge was influential in establishing in the 1880s.[44]

Perhaps the most important event in the triumph of the physical fitness movement was the sudden, overwhelming popularity of the bicycle, a vehicle that attracted a mass constituency. In 1886 there were 50,000 riders, mostly male, nationwide. In 1890 there were 150,000 and by 1893 close to a million, a figure that included a sizable number of women. Observer after observer linked to the bicycle women's final abandonment of older ideas about fragility and their new allegiance to physical activity.[45]

Women rode bicycles partly for the same reasons men did. Bicycling was recreational; physicians, albeit grudgingly, came to endorse it; and it was a striking symbol of the technology Americans extolled and of their simultaneous desire to escape it by flight to nature. Enormous advertising campaigns and improvements in construction made bicycles more appealing to women, who previously had ridden tricycles, three-wheeled vehicles of the sort that children ride today. But for many women, riding a bicycle had additional meaning. Sports and gymnastics were private activities, confined to courts and fields and not open to general observation. Women on bicycles, who rode on public streets, immediately put themselves on public display; whether they wanted to or not, they made a public statement about what they thought a woman ought to be.

From available sources we can document the pattern of women's adoption of the bicycle. In many instances the first women in a given area to take up the bicycle were the sisters and wives of bicycle enthusiasts—as was true, for example, in both Buffalo and Syracuse, centers of bicycling, where male clubs and competitions had been in existence for some time. In other areas, working women saw it as a cheap, efficient means of transportation. In Boston a venturesome firm sold its machines on an installment plan. In her autobiography, novelist Mary Roberts Rinehart noted that she was the second girl in the city of Allegheny, Pennsylvania, to have a bicycle. Her parents, she explained, were "advanced."[46]

The word "advanced" is an important one, for bicycling implied not just exercise, but a whole philosophy about women, one that suggested they could leave the home—for work and pleasure. And women rode astride their bicycles, pedalling just as men did, violating a prohibition that had been in force for generations of women horseback riders. Only the most advanced horsewomen rode with their legs around their mount; most still rode sidesaddle. Moreover, the bicycle required some kind of loosened clothing. The shirtwaist blouses hidden in the 1880s on tennis courts now began to appear on city streets, and women even donned bifurcated skirts, descendants of the bloomers that were now called "knickerbockers" to give them an aristocratic cachet—even though society women were relatively late in taking up the bicycle.

Riding a bicycle was a feminist statement, and women who rode declared their approval of the new opportunities for women in a variety of areas. Nor did men always accept with ease women's assumption of a prerogative that gave them increased mobility and freedom. *Vogue* magazine reported that the first women cyclists in New York City in 1889 always rode with male companions for fear that rowdy male riders would force them off the road. By the mid-1890s, the woman bicycle rider would become sentimentalized into a comfortable figure of romance—a "daisy" riding on "a bicycle built for two," as the popular song had it. But by then American society had come to accept the educated woman, the working woman, the "new woman," as they called her. Henry James's Daisy Miller, a woman condemned for her sins against propriety, had become Daisy, the cheery bicycle rider. And the name "Daisy," with its older implications of outgoing, flirtatious behavior, had become a general term of male approval of women. "What a daisy," they would say.[47]

Had the bicycle not appeared, women eventually would have taken up sports and exercise anyway. By the 1890s the general cultural pressures for women to be active were too great to be avoided. Women sports figures like Eleanora Sears, who excelled in a variety of sports, began to appear; and newspapers fully reported their careers. They made public women's previously private athletic participation and paved the way for other women to follow. The bicycle simply broke through the resistance to such activities more quickly and became the vehicle by which more women at one time were forced to admit that freedom was preferable to dependence and physical activity to lethargy.

In the adoption of the bicycle, society women played a secondary role. As if to prove the democratic nature of the vehicle, contemporary sources carefully note that the elites of Newport and New York City did not begin riding the bicycle until several years after its vogue had begun. As with the introduction of vigorous sports, they were followers, not leaders. Their role was one of dissemination, not of innovation: they lent their cachet to the movement once it had already begun.[48]

One can trace with precision the involvement of Newport and New York elite women in the physical activity movement. Every group contains individuals who define themselves as innovators, those who either reject group standards entirely or attempt to modify those standards in a freer direction. Among the late nineteenth-century elites, as is often the case, the innovators were drawn generally from among the younger generation. Even in the days of Caroline Astor's hegemony, some Newport women had ridden horses, and in the 1870s some of them—known as "whips"—began to drive their own coaches in the afternoon parade. By the 1880s others were playing tennis. And in 1893 there occurred an event that was crucial to changing sports behavior among elite women. In that year Caroline Astor's daughter-in-law, Ava Willing Astor, directly challenged her mother-in-law's code by playing a vigorous tennis match dressed in bloomers at the Newport Casino—a center of male sports activity for the entire nation.

So arresting was the informal event that *Vogue* magazine devoted special coverage to it. Socialite Elizabeth Drexel Lehr called Ava Astor and the group she led "the moderns," thereby indicating their role as innovators among the elites. To the general population, however, they were transmitters of the sports vogue, women who lent their public visibility to sports for women. And it was they who were the models for Charles Dana Gibson's Gibson girl, thereby increasing their position as fashion disseminators.[49]

The triumph of the exercise movement ultimately signalled the downfall of the voluptuous woman as a standard of beauty for American women. By 1900 all sources acclaimed Lillie Langtry's beauty and forgot the time when Americans had disliked her classic features and her athletic frame. The natural woman had come to the fore, the product of the successful campaigns of exercise advocates, the determination of college women, the popularity of young aristocrats like Ava Astor and rebellious actresses like Lillie Langtry, the power of women joining the professions and claiming the prerogatives of husbands and fathers—women who were called with suspicion "advanced" in the 1880s and with enthusiasm "new" in the 1890s.

V

In the late nineteenth century, dress reform, like exercise reform, had influential advocates and a committed constituency. And it made substantial progress during those years. Yet the commercial culture of fashion also remained authoritative, both by borrowing from reform design and by challenging it directly. As early dress reformers learned to their dismay—and as we have seen in the 1980s' vogue for "designer" jeans—any style, no matter how reformist in origin, can easily be taken over by the commercial fashion world.

The failure of the bloomer campaign of the 1850s did not result in the demise of organized dress reform. Rather, more conservative groups, like the postwar women's clubs, the American Woman Suffrage Association, and the WCTU, took it over. Influenced by Catharine Beecher, they advocated minor modifications in women's dress, including the elimination of tight corsets, bustles, and trailing skirts, and, following Beecher, suggested the hanging of skirts by suspenders from the shoulders to relieve pressure on waists and hips. Stung by the virulent reaction to the bloomer movement, these dress reformers emphasized moderation and consistently stressed the similarities between their reformed garb and regular attire.

They were joined in their endeavor by a variety of other groups. The English esthetic movement, with its emphasis on the natural, persuaded some women on both sides of the Atlantic to give up their corsets and take up long, flowing garb. "Apostles of costume aesthetics," reported *Vogue* magazine, "draw crowds in private dining rooms and public halls." In addition, followers of Delsarte often wore some form of loose, flowing garb, in line with the reformist, semimystical stance that many assumed. Some actresses of international reputation, like Sarah Bernhardt and Lillie Langtry, also wore types of artistic dress—both as a way of underscoring their identification with artistic genius that rose above the commonality and as a means of gaining publicity. Langtry usually wore fashionable clothes, but she was credited with having introduced the jersey, the tight-fitting sweater designed for comfort and named after the island on which she had grown up. In addition to actresses and esthetes, certain women took up dress reform as a major pursuit. Chief among them was Annie Jenness Miller, a moderate who edited a dress reform magazine and lectured widely. Too, there were radical dress reformers, often descendants of the antebellum water-cure reformers. Their impact, however, was minimal. Their best-known representative was Mary Walker, a physician who wore male pants and coats and was consistently lampooned in the press as an example of feminism's presumed vagaries.[50]

The actual impact of these dress reformers is difficult to measure. Yet all sources agree that women in the 1870s and 1880s continued to wear the skirts, blouses, and jackets that many had adopted for work and street wear during the Civil War. In 1875 *Harper's Bazar* reported that department stores like Stewart's and Arnold Constable's were selling ready-made suits at reasonable prices. By the 1880s the ready-made suit industry was a major part of the apparel business. By then, prestigious British tailoring houses, like Redfern, invaded the American high-priced market for women's suits, claiming that male tailors were able to fit suits and coats better than female dressmakers. In 1893 *Harper's Weekly* noted that the "evolution of sensible dress" had kept pace with women's expanded participation in colleges, in the professions, and in the work force. The magazine defined sensible dress as the "blazer suit," consisting of a narrow skirt, what it called a "shirt-front" blouse, and a comfortable jacket.[51]

The most famous article of women's new attire was the shirtwaist blouse, which appeared on the market soon after 1890. The name itself indicates its derivation: it was modelled after a man's shirt (although the buttons on the woman's variation remained in the back, rather than the front). Exactly who first designed it remains unclear. As early as the 1850s a blouselike top, worn with a skirt, had come into fashion and during the subsequent decades had waxed and waned in popularity. In the 1850s it was known as a spencer; in the 1860s, as a garibaldi. In the 1880s serious sportswomen began to wear a new variation, based directly on men's shirts; subsequently, it seems, manufacturers marketed it in mass volume for the growing market of sportswomen and working women. The shirtwaist was an American invention, and contemporaries perceived it—in addition to suits—as a significant rebellion against French fashion. In 1884, *Godey's Lady's Book* noted that there were two kinds of prevailing styles: the newer "tailor-made" fashions and the older "couturier-made" apparel.[52]

By the 1890s proponents of dress reform claimed victory, although rather than sparking the movement toward simplified dress they may have ridden the crest of a wave created by economic necessity and women's growing independence. Still, Swedish traveller Alexandra Gripenberg noted in 1888 that "in almost every large city there are health, or so-called reform, dress seamstresses, and large associations with hundreds of members are spreading information on the subject through lectures, brochures, and exhibitions by models." Dress reform patterns were available in popular Butterick patterns, and many cities had dress reform stores. In 1890 author Elizabeth Stuart Phelps, whom some authorities claimed had sparked the post–Civil War dress reform movement with a rousing speech in 1873, exulted in the success of dress reform. She triumphantly quoted the manager of a large dress reform store: "When ten years ago we had only strong-minded women for our patrons, . . . we now have orders from fashionable ladies, ten to one."[53]

However, dress reform still encountered difficulties. For a few years women wore knickerbockers when riding bicycles and then, in the face of vigorous opposition, gave them up for loose skirts. And despite the comfort of bicycle costume, shortened skirts on city streets caused considerable problems for their wearers, as the case of New Yorker Daisy Miller (a real woman, not Henry James's heroine) demonstrated. An otherwise unexceptional young woman, Daisy Miller in the mid-1890s became exasperated at wearing dresses trailing on the ground in rainy weather, and she began to wear ankle-length skirts. According to the *Woman's Journal,* women riding bicycles or walking and climbing at summer resorts had previously shortened their skirts and, since no opposition to these innovations developed, the time seemed appropriate to bring the shortened dress to city streets. Here, however, the opposition was vociferous. Wrote Henry Collins Brown, "I would need the pen of a Carlyle to describe adequately the sensation caused by the young lady who first trod the streets of New York in a skirt . . . that was actually three inches from the ground. Crowds followed her, shrieking with loud and derisive laughter." Even after beauty columnist Harriet Hubbard Ayer supported Miller and other working women in forming a "rainy day club," their campaign was not easily pursued. When they wore shortened skirts on days without rain, they elicited "whistles, cat-calls, and even an over-ripe vegetable aimed at their shockingly-visible ankles." Yet by 1905 the Sears catalogue featured walking skirts that it counselled should be worn at least two inches above the ground.[54]

Even though reformed dress seemed to be making inroads among American women, the fashion industry continued to create clothes that were frilly and oppressive and to co-opt dress reform styles by introducing seasonal changes in them. From 1867, when the bustle replaced the crinoline, to at least 1900 the same silhouette remained in vogue. Straight through the waist and abdomen, it involved drawing the folds of the garment to the back around a bustle whose position and size shifted throughout those years. The focus of this style was on a small waist and moulded figure, and only an intricate corset could achieve the desired effect. Just at the point at which the renewed dress reform movement came into being, the corset industry was becoming more influential, for it was nearly impossible to make the fashionable corset at home. And, by the 1890s agitation against the damaging effects of tightlacing had seemingly had only limited impact. Although corset makers were marketing reform corsets, designed to obviate tightlacing and preserve body proportions, an extraordinary S-curve was the favored shape of the 1890s. Harking back to the Grecian bend in its redistribution of the natural body, it featured a huge bosom extending nearly from chin to waist, which could be achieved only by tightlacing.[55]

"Our waists were laced in, our collars were high, and our skirts swept the ground," wrote Natalie Dana. "Long steel pins and tight veils kept our large hats in place. Though we held up our skirts in correct folds with our right hands and tried to keep them from touching the streets, my legs were always black to the knee when I dressed for dinner." Dana's description of her attire could have referred to the furbelowed creations of the Parisian couture or the mannish suit. Even reform dress could be modified in accordance with the prevailing mode. The shirtwaist, too, became prey to the vagaries of fashion. In 1901 the *New York World* noted that when first introduced, the shirtwaist had been bought "direct from the counter." But within a few years it had developed extraordinarily shaped sleeves and confining collars and often needed special tailoring.[56]

By the first decade of the twentieth century, the bustle silhouette had remained in vogue for many decades, and designers, tired of the form, began to experiment with a loosened style that resembled the Empire mode. Paul Poiret, celebrated like Worth as the most brilliant designer of his age, by 1908 firmly established this line as the dominant style, and the small waist dominant for nearly a century was banished seemingly at a designer's whim.[57]

Yet Poiret's design was related to the dominant beauty themes of the age: the decline of the voluptuous woman as the model of beauty in favor of the natural woman; the impact of feminism, which permeated social institutions and destroyed the appeal of the ornamental woman; the rise of athleticism, which brought health and exercise permanently into vogue. In her history of German and Scandinavian feminism, Katharine Anthony contended that German dress reformers had been the predominant influence on Poiret. Nor was American dress reform without influence—on Poiret and more generally. The shirtwaist blouse, an American innovation, was key to the freedom of the natural woman. And dress reformers were an important part of the broad feminist coalition that existed by the 1890s and offered major psychological support for women not only to enter the work force or to pursue higher degrees, but also to wear suits and shirtwaists or to ride bicycles on city streets. Dress reformers did not always support the goals of exercise advocates, yet they played a considerable role in the emergence of the natural woman as the dominant kind of American beauty.[58]

VI

The change in standards of physical appearance in the late nineteenth century from fat to thin, from heavy to athletic, was slow in coming. Natalie Dana's circle did not begin dieting until 1895, and women in Appleton, Wisconsin, remained heavy as late as 1902, according to Edna Ferber. Margaret Sanger recalled that the schoolgirls in Corning, New York, in the late 1890s surreptitiously compared their body proportions with the plump, well-rounded actresses on cigarette cards.[59]

Yet the pressures to reduce were by then already strong. Actress Fanny Davenport began dieting in 1889. Lillian Russell, who first resisted, began a career of dieting in 1896 when reviews comparing her to a white elephant appeared. For the next decade or so her diet regimen was as much publicized by the press as any other detail of her life. Overnight, it seemed, Lillie Langtry became beautiful, and Sarah Bernhardt, regularly described as ugly in early visits to the United States because of her thinness, by 1900 was considered beautiful, too.

Yet the tradition of voluptuous heaviness lingered on the popular musical stage. Even after American entertainment entrepreneurs had combined the sophistication of European operetta with the pageant of the spectacle and the vitality of native forms like the minstrel show to produce the rudiments of musical comedy, they still included a chorus of hefty women in tights in every production. As late as 1895 the *Metropolitan Magazine* noted that the "regulation chorus girl type" had "thick ankles, ponderous calves, and a waist laced so tight that the lines of the hips and bust were distorted into balloon-like curves."[60]

Anxious to avoid offending social purity reformers, producers played down the role of the choruses in their productions, and chorus women did little singing and dancing. But the erotic appeal of women performers remained important to men, and before the 1900s men had still not lost their taste for heavy, voluptuous women. The chorus women featured on the pages of the *Police Gazette* are all decidedly fat (by our present-day standards), as were women on the burlesque stage and the actresses and chorus girls featured on cigarette cards, the major mass form of erotic art in the 1880s and 1890s.

Sometime during the 1890s, however, the appearance of chorus girls changed. To our modern eyes, the change is difficult to see, but observers witnessed it clearly. According to the *Metropolitan Magazine,* a major source on these matters, the change came with the 1894 vogue of living picture entertainments, in which actors reproduced scenes from famous paintings, scenes frequently involving nudity, which they simulated by wearing flesh-colored tights and tops. These shows were produced not only on the variety stage, but also in legitimate Broadway theaters. Since the late 1840s, when a burst of living picture productions had resulted in police prosecution, producers had avoided them. But by the 1890s the climate had changed. The physical fitness movement had generated a widespread interest in the human body, and the vice societies had been defeated in several nudity cases involving art works on the grounds that artistic merit legitimized nudity. In these popular living picture productions, according to the *Metropolitan Magazine,* producers at first cast the regular chorus-girl type. But faced with entertainments that focused entirely on women's large breasts, hips, and thighs, audiences laughed at them, and directors had to look elsewhere for their models.[61]

Unfortunately the *Metropolitan Magazine* does not describe where they went to find alternative types, although its writers do mention that, in a time of economic depression in the 1890s, the producers were besieged by applicants. Yet for some time critics of the popular musical stage had viewed the chorus-girl type as grotesque: "amazons" and "bovine mammals" were some of the terms of opprobrium used in print. Moreover, a renaissance and redirection of the chorus girl were already under way, sparked by Briton John Hollingshead's success in his London Gaiety Theatre, opened in the late 1880s, in avoiding censorship by clothing his dancers in long skirts that they kicked aside from time to time to reveal legs in tights. Producers, too, were concerned about attracting the continuing patronage of women who wanted to view the latest styles in dress and body style on the stage. By the 1890s Hollingshead and some American imitators had introduced a new kind of chorus girl, the so-called show girl, who neither sang nor danced, but was included to "show" the latest styles of fashion and beauty.

Still, it must be made clear that the 1900 model of beauty, by present-day standards, continued to be plump. Take the case of Frankie Bailey, a variety performer who gained fame for having what were touted as the most beautiful legs in the United States. "Critics, sculptors, and the general public went into ecstasy over her legs," one press report declared, for they were considered to be perfectly "symmetrical." "What Miss Bailey's limbs are," went another account, "is as much a known fact as the Brooklyn Bridge, and almost as famous." Just as the name "Lillian Russell" became a synonym for female beauty in general, "Frankie Bailey" became synonymous with beautiful legs. That Victorian prudery had declined to the point that legs could not only be shown on stage but also be discussed in public tells us much about the sensual attitudes of turn-of-the-century America. Yet what is important to note is that by current standards Bailey's legs appear unexceptionable, even pudgy and ill proportioned.[62]

Still by 1900 the voluptuous woman of the 1870s had retreated to the lower-class subculture of sensuality from which she had emerged. In *Susan Lenox: Her Fall and Rise,* a novel about women and the stage, David Graham Phillips presented the new, critical attitude toward the voluptuous woman. At the novel's outset, Susan Lenox joins a travelling variety troupe while fleeing from the man she has been forced to marry. Lenox, by Phillips's description, is "sensuous, graceful, slender—the figure of girlhood in its perfection and of perfect womanhood, too." She is shocked by her first view of the naked body of one of her fellow variety actresses. "It was sheer horror that held Susan's gaze upon Violet's incredible hips and thighs, violently obtruded by the close-reefed corset." Noting her stare, the variety actresses in the room discuss their appearance. They explain that the men in their audiences don't care for thinness in women. "Not the clodhoppers and roustabouts that come to see us," retorts Mabel. "The more a woman looks like a cow or a sow the better they like it."[63]

Such attitudes may have been extreme, but they appeared in American culture on many levels in the first decades of the twentieth century. In 1912, visiting backstage at the theater where her mother was performing, Miriam Young noticed a life-sized portrait of a large-bosomed woman in a fancy gown and a plumed hat. "Who is that fat lady?" she asked. The actors present looked at her in shocked amazement. "Why, baby!" her mother said in a low, shocked voice, "that's Lillian Russell."[64]

8

The Gibson Girl

Between 1895 and World War I, the Gibson girl came to dominate standards of beauty in women. She was the creation of artist Charles Dana Gibson, whose drawings first appeared in 1890 in *Life* magazine, and she was a national sensation by 1894, when the first folio edition of Gibson's work was published. In appearance she was tall and commanding, with thick, dark hair swept upward in the prevailing pompadour style. Her figure was thinner than that of the voluptuous woman, but she remained large of bosom and hips. Her mouth was small and her nose snub, although Gibson sometimes drew it in a longer, Roman style.[1]

From the mid-1890s on, plays featured the Gibson girl, and commercial advertisers exploited her image. Clothing and dances were named after her. Popular magazines and newspapers repeatedly pictured and analyzed her. Living pictures of Gibson drawings became favorite entertainments at charity bazaars and church suppers. Observers noted that women on the streets all seemed to look like Gibson girls. "Fifth avenue," wrote Mark Sullivan, "is like a procession of Gibsons." Her vogue cut across class, age, and regional lines. "The Gibson girl," Sullivan remarked, "is to be found in homes, in college rooms, in rude mining cabins in the Klondike." Gibson himself inspired many imitators who drew beautiful women under their own signatures. Some of them, like James Montgomery Flagg, Howard Chandler Christy, and Henry Hutt, came to rival Gibson in reputation.[2]

Why did the creation of a graphic artist—rather than that of a painter or sculptor—assume such importance? Why not a "Whistler woman"? Or, given Renoir's many idealized portraits of women, why was there not a vogue for Renoir's robust image of female beauty?

Well before Gibson, and in fact until recently, most of the dominant models of female beauty in the United States have been the creations of lithographers. Prior to the Gibson girl there was the steel-engraving lady.

After the vogue of the Gibson girl had ended, the Held girl, created by John F. Held, Jr., dominated the 1920s. The process of lithography, it might be argued, idealizes human types more than other art forms and, because of the ease of reproduction, is easily mass marketed. One of the reasons that the voluptuous woman never completely carried the day as a model of beauty may have been that there was no popular, idealized portrait of her available. People collected photographs of Lillian Russell and Fanny Davenport. They saw Bouguereau's *Nymphs and Satyr* on the boxes of Hoffman House cigars and the plump women on cigarette cards. But no graphic artist drew a general representation of this physical type that took on a general symbolism, as did Gibson's drawings. On the other hand, the voluptuous woman was never as powerful a model of beauty as the steel-engraving lady before her or the natural woman later. Many of Thomas Nast's political cartoons in the 1870s, for example, featured a tall and plump Columbia with a classic profile—Nast's symbol of reform in the midst of corruption—but this figure did not gain widespread popularity.[3]

The popularity of the Gibson girl was related to the fact that Gibson often drew her in satiric situations. By the 1890s the caricature had become a popular American art form. *Life* editor John Mitchell dated its American origins to the popularity of Thomas Nast's satiric drawings of Boss Tweed and his henchmen in *Harper's Weekly* in the 1870s. *Life* itself specialized in a blend of witty social commentary and sophisticated graphic humor. It was a descendant of the British *Punch* and a forerunner of the *New Yorker* of our own day. From the eighteenth-century age of Hogarth, lithography has often achieved its greatest critical acclaim when its practitioners have turned to social criticism.[4]

In the nineteenth century, graphic artists, like novelists, found an apt target in the extravagances of the world of fashion, especially of fashionable women. John Mitchell of *Life* believed that Henry McVickar in 1882 had been the first American graphic artist to caricature society through the woman of fashion, but in fact the tradition originated earlier. Noted graphic artists of midcentury, like Felix Darley and Thomas Nast, had drawn illustrations of beautiful women for the purpose of social satire. The beautiful women drawn by John Leech and George Du Maurier in *Punch* were known in the United States, and the Gibson girl bore a striking resemblance to Du Maurier's women.[5]

Female beauty as a subject is entrenched in the comic tradition of Western culture. Modern stock characters like the "little wife" or the "dumb blonde" persist. On the nineteenth-century stage English and French innovators drew on the ancient dramatic satire of burlesque and introduced scantily clad women to create new forms of theatrical entertainment, like modern burlesque and musical comedy. On the vaudeville stage beautiful women like Lillian Russell were characteristically paired not with romantic leading men, but rather with comics whose ugliness downplayed the women's sexuality and invoked the myth of beauty taming the beast, of innocence mastering sexuality.

In the 1890s Charles Dana Gibson was not the only illustrator to draw beautiful women in satiric situations. Harry McVickar, a regular *Life* contributor, also sketched them, as did Grey-Parker and S. W. Van Schaik. Indeed, it is apparent from the pages of *Life* that most of the publication's graphic artists regularly drew cartoons that criticized high society and focused on beautiful women. Why then did Gibson's women, and not those by McVickar or Grey-Parker, win acclaim? The alliterative appeal of the title of Gibson girl initially played some role. Publicists of the ballyhoo era of early modern advertising favored rhythm and simplicity. In 1890 the editors of *Century* refused to allow the use of the Gibson girl title to describe the heroine of one of their stories, even though Gibson drew the illustrations for it. For Gibson was then relatively unknown and the appellation "Gibson girl" to describe ideal beauty had only recently appeared. Tellingly, however, they devised a similarly alliterative name, the Goodrich girl, as an alternative title for their heroine.[6]

Yet Gibson was a fine lithographer, regarded by many as superior to *Life*'s other illustrators, and one reason for the popularity of his drawings was clearly his skill. Ultimately, Gibson came to hate the Gibson girl, to sense that the repetition of variations on a single theme hampered the development of his talent. He wanted to be a Howard Pyle or an Arthur Rackham, not a practitioner of "pretty girl art," as Norman Rockwell contemptuously described him. Yet according to the most recent student of his generation of illustrators, "without question, no American artist before or since could wield the pen as skillfully."[7]

Like many powerful cultural models, the Gibson girl seemed to represent a variety of styles. Contemporary feminists often saw her as a prototype of the "new woman." The blouses and skirts she wore for casual wear seemed in line with the goals of dress reformers, and the many scenes in which she was pictured at sports seemed to validate the aims of the advocates of exercise and athletics. In contrast to the typical woman of the day, wrote Charlotte Perkins Gilman, the Gibson girl was "braver, stronger, more healthful and skillful and able and free, more human in all ways." Indisputably tall, with long arms and legs, her body was clearly that of the natural and not the voluptuous woman. It was Lillie Langtry she resembled, not Lillian Russell.[8]

Yet the Gibson girl was only partly a reform figure. She was rarely portrayed as a working or college woman. Gibson never showed her as a settlement house or social worker. The important involvement of the day's women in reform, their search for self-expression, and their new roles as workers and professionals only occasionally found expression through Gibson's pen. Nor was Gibson sympathetic to organized feminism, for he had misgivings that involvement in politics would make women coarser and more masculine. In many ways the independence of the Gibson girl did not go much beyond playing sports, wearing comfortable clothing, and looking self-reliant.

Yet even when drawing the Gibson girl at sports, Gibson had difficulty rendering her as fully natural. Gibson would not draw women bicyclists in bloomers, for example, because he thought the attire unbecoming. The real Gibson prototype, wrote New York socialite and Gibson model Caresse Crosby, was her mother and aunts, who wore shirtwaist blouses to play the new sports, but who modified them to meet the restrictive demands of fashion. Moreover, in drawings depicting the Gibson girl in sports attire, her waist is often so small that tightlacing is clearly indicated, as it also is when she invariably dons fashionable garb for evenings.[9]

Illustrator Harrison Fisher, one of Gibson's imitators, pointed out that Gibson had abandoned "the little, dimpled chin, the low forehead, the tiny mouth" that had characterized the steel-engraving lady. But there were still similarities, particularly in the continued "cupid's bow shape for the mouth." The *New York Herald* thought the Gibson girl was always a lady, "possessing a wholesome athletic air that does not smack too much of athletics." Journalist Richard Harding Davis, Gibson's close friend and frequent model for Gibson's men, thought that the prototypical girl was characterized more than anything else by innocence, but that there were overtones of cynicism in her. Helena Rubinstein, founder of one of the twentieth-century's major cosmetic empires, discerned neither cynicism nor sensuality: "Her creed was modesty, and to the average American male she was an aloof dream girl."[10]

Many analysts thought of the Gibson girl as innocent; others called her worldly wise, a "tomboy," "slangy," "self-assured," with no sense of modesty. Actress Cora Potter thought that the Gibson girl had "curves deeper and bolder than those usually seen" and that she represented "a type of exaggerated feminity." Others emphasized the eroticism of her figure and pose. Musical comedy performer Belle Livingstone called her "a full-bosomed type of feminine beauty." Critic Winfield Scott Moody thought that she was "a perfectly pagan thing." In contrast, popular advice columnist Dorothy Dix thought that the Gibson girl looked like a "telephone pole," and Evelyn Benedict Ayres, professor of physical education at the University of Syracuse, was widely quoted as believing that throwing the shoulders back in the Gibson girl manner would unduly strain back and shoulder muscles and ultimately damage them. Along the same line, Madame Fine, "Modiste and Corsetière" of San Francisco, thought that the Gibson girl seemed overweight and worried that individuals using her as a model might decide that they need not wear corsets.[11]

Many analysts identified the Gibson girl as a representative of the aristocracy with which Gibson was personally associated. Indeed, many of the drawings and the captions beneath them identify her as at elite activities: at balls, the opera, or the Madison Square Garden Horse Show that opened the New York social season; in huge, elegant drawing and dining rooms; on ocean liners; at the Royal Court in London. "Perfectly dressed," according to a writer in the Denver Post, "her dress, her shoes, her hair, her complexion, her hands, all exhibit such exquisite care and cultivation" as only a New York society woman could achieve. Another analyst thought that her lack of both "self-consciousness" and "engaging simplicity" indicated that she was, at heart, a patrician.[12]

But the working classes also claimed her as their own. Throughout the torrent of print on the meaning of the Gibson girl, one question repeatedly haunted reporters: who had been the original model for the figure? This generated as much controversy as the question of what kind of American woman she personified. Journalists repeatedly pointed out that the common belief that the aristocratic Irene Langhorne Gibson had been the original model for her husband's ideal woman was inaccurate, since he had not met her until 1893, some time after his original drawings had appeared. The New York socialites who often sat for him also became his models only after the Gibson girl had become famous. Gibson himself never gave his publicists a definitive answer, nor did they really want one from him. Unflagging in their zeal, reporters were determined to find the original model among the working classes, to demonstrate that the wealthy were not the sole possessors of beauty, that beauty, in the end, was democratic.

The press finally fixed on two candidates. The first was Minnie Clark, a well-known professional model whose Irish working-class background was featured in all the stories about her. The second candidate was a woman who worked as a personal maid for Loie Fuller, a dancer renowned for her flamboyant use of long scarves and colorful lights and who was a precursor of Isadora Duncan. Journalists were particularly interested in Fuller's maid, for she was the daughter of a French father and a Cuban mother and in their view an ideally representative American. A hybrid in nationality, she seemed living proof that the American melting pot could work, that from the intermixture of racial nationalities could come the perfection of form and features that the entire nation could copy.[13]

In the final analysis, Gibson's contemporaries disagreed on the meaning of the woman he drew. Writing in 1903, on the occasion of retaining Gibson as a regular contributor to Collier's magazine, editor Robert Grant distinguished what he thought were seven types of Gibson girls: the professional beauty, the tomboy, the flirt, the sentimental maiden, the woman of determination, the ambitious woman, and the woman best characterized as "well-rounded in personality." Sometimes a drawing represented one type of woman, according to Grant, and sometimes another. Thus lithographs featuring the Gibson girl as professional beauty focused on her height and her contours. When she was a tomboy, she wore tailored dresses or shirtwaists and skirts. Grant thought that Gibson's own favorite was the well-rounded woman, for she was a happy combination of all the others. She participated in sports; she might have gone to college; she might work as a stenographer if financially pressed. Marriage was her goal in life, but she was an independent person and a companion to a man rather than his dependent.[14]

Grant's analysis captured the multifaceted nature of the Gibson girl. But he failed to penetrate other levels of her meaning. Why, for example, were Gibson and the other illustrators of his age so drawn to women as their subjects? Why was the American public so fascinated by their productions? What did Gibson himself think he meant when he drew his Gibson girl?

II

For the most part Gibson remained aloof from the controversy over the woman he had created. In a 1900 interview in the *New York World* he claimed that he had never intended his ideal woman to represent any particular type of woman, that he had used scores of models of a variety of types and social backgrounds, and that some tried to use the experience to further their careers by contending that they had been his original model. "There is no Gibson girl, there never was," he asserted. Pressed by his interviewer to admit responsibility for having created the nation's model of beauty in women, Gibson at first denied the assertion and then refused to talk further about the matter.[15]

Yet significant clues to the meaning of the Gibson girl can be found in Gibson's own biography. The descendant of prominent New Englanders, he was raised in modest circumstances in Flushing, New York, the son of a business salesman. His mother and father were devoted to one another, and the family—which included an older brother and three younger sisters—was close, his home life a seeming version of the happy family environment celebrated in nineteenth-century lore. Flushing, a New York suburb, offered many opportunities for sports, and Gibson, tall and muscular, became a star performer for the Flushing Athletic Club.

Gibson was early impressed with the importance of enterprise, an importance rendered personal to him by his family's example of early wealth and position, by his own need to support his mother and sisters after his father's death, and by his success at competitive athletics—itself a preparation for the larger world of competition that marked American enterprise and the nation's professional life. He never rebelled against his parents' traditional social arrangements, nor did he visualize perfection in human relationships beyond the love his mother and father had shared. Both parents had strongly influenced him; even when he frequented the world of the wealthy, he never really lost their values.

Limited family finances and his own inclination to pursue a career in art, for which he showed talent at an early age, kept Gibson from seeking a formal college education. Thus for several years he studied at the Art Students League in New York City. Apparently his instructors there did not single him out for praise, and that disappointment, plus the demand for magazine illustrators, led him to a career in graphic art. In his creation of an ideal female type, the several months he spent studying in Paris in 1888 were particularly important. Motivated by the still current notion that the Parisian experience was important for fledgling American artists, he studied in the Atelier Julian, where Bouguereau and other eminent *salonniers* taught. But the Parisian experience was more negative than positive: apparently he spent a good deal of time studying the Dutch masters and concluded that he did not like their heavy, voluptuous women. When he returned to the United States, he told his sister that he was "determined to sell the American way."[16]

In many respects the high point of his European trip was the visit he made on the way to Paris to see George Du Maurier at the latter's home near London. Du Maurier was considered the day's preeminent lithographer, and Gibson's early technique was derived from him. Du Maurier offered an interesting model to Gibson, both in his art and in his personal life. Du Maurier had been one of the original members of the pre-Raphaelite brotherhood, the group of young artists in the late 1840s who had rebelled against the rigidity of official English art by adopting medievalism in their artistic work and communalism in their personal lives. After this brush with bohemianism, however, Du Maurier married, turned to lithography, and became *Punch*'s leading illustrator. He adopted a bourgeois lifestyle, living comfortably outside London with his wife and daughters, whom he used as his models. If anything remained of his pre-Raphaelite past, it was the beautiful women who dominated his drawings. Yet in contrast to the thin, neurasthenic pre-Raphaelite women, his were well built and modelled in the classical mode.

Not only did Gibson's ideal woman resemble Du Maurier's prototype, but also the example of Du Maurier's fame and his comfortable life could hardly have been lost on Gibson, who later briefly participated in Parisian student life and then in the New York night-life world known as the Lobster Palace Society before himself settling into a comfortable marriage and a regular family life. Gibson told his sister that many of the women on London streets looked as though they had stepped out of a Du Maurier drawing. He liked that. He mused that he, too, would like to have all the world look like the women in his family. Interestingly, while in London he lived in the studio of John Singer Sargent, whose female figures resembled those Gibson later drew.[17]

In 1890 Gibson illustrated Constance Cary Harrison's *Anglomaniacs,* a novel that criticized wealthy Americans for spurning their rural, democratic roots and aping the British aristocracy, which she considered effete and immoral. Harrison claimed that her collaboration with Gibson had a major impact on his choice of subject matter, that "drawing these society types has opened a new vein to him which he greatly enjoys." At the same time, Gibson himself began moving in elite New York society, perhaps introduced by Harrison, who herself had entrée, or perhaps because of his striking good looks and impeccable bearing. New York hostesses were always on the lookout for agreeable young men whom they could commandeer to adorn their entertainments, since husbands and sons, busy at work and often involved with clubs and night-life, were not always available. Moreover, young New York society women craved publicity through which they might be denominated reigning beauties and thus might rule their social set. To pose for a Gibson girl illustration became a way of asserting such a claim, and chaperoned debutantes flocked to Gibson's studio. Gibson, the son of a family with wealthy, colonial roots, did not decline the attention.[18]

Gibson's drawings themselves may have fostered his acceptance by the elites. His satire was gentle and easily could be seen as drawing off harsher public criticism. The drawings, wrote one analyst, put the viewer "in a wonderful land where all is 'swell,' where beauty and luxury reign, a sort of enchanted isle." His presentation of elite material indulgence glorified as much as criticized it. What seemed to bother him most about the consumption of the rich was not their conspicuous display of mansions, yachts, and elaborate dress, but rather their practice of marrying for money and especially of marrying daughters to impecunious European noblemen—a practice that violated his sense of nationalism and romance. Yet it hardly constituted a major item in elite sins against democracy. In fact, his ideal woman, glorified because of her beauty, could be interpreted as justifying the existence of the upper class that had produced her. Women of the New

York elites encouraged publicity; it was a crucial part of their power as public personalities. In his function as illustrator of their foibles and glamorizer of their daughters, Gibson was important to them.[19]

Besides, by the mid-1890s Gibson had become as famous as the women he drew. He lived in New York City, where he was easily photographed. His own athletic good looks and his participation in the world of the wealthy were not lost on admirers of the Gibson girl, who often read about him in the papers. According to a contemporary analysis of his vogue, the newspapers pictured him as spending his mornings in outdoor recreations, his afternoons at receptions where he studied the women who flocked around him, and his evenings at dinners and dances. This popular impression of his life was inaccurate, since Gibson spent much of his time at work in his studio. He was, according to his nephew, "phlegmatic" and disliked pretensions. Still, he became what we would call a cult figure, especially among young women and male undergraduates, who hounded him for his autograph and sent him fan mail. In this respect, his renown signified a general shift in the esteem of artists. After decades of disregard, artists in the 1890s became individuals of interest to Americans, partly because of the increasing popularity of art but also because their bohemian lifestyle piqued the interest of Americans increasingly drawn to the unconventional. Popular magazines featured stories about artists, and etiquette books contained sections on proper ways for women to visit artists in their studios. According to Henry Collins Brown, illustrators like Gibson were as well known as movie stars later would be.[20]

There was, however, an additional reason for Gibson's personal popularity. He himself resembled the romantic young men he drew, the companions in athleticism to his ideal young women. Like the matinée idols of the contemporary stage, these men seemed possessed by love. Rarely were they shown in work-related situations; they appeared uncaring of the commercial and competitive spirit that was the official American emblem of masculinity. Gibson, like the Byronic heroes of women's gothic fiction or the romantic tenors of the minstrel shows or John Barrymore and other matinée idols, provided the romance that some women perhaps craved in their own lives.

Furthermore, whatever criticism Gibson's connection with popular magazines drew from the elites was muted by his 1895 marriage to Irene Langhorne, a Virginia socialite who had a national reputation for beauty and was known as one of the "Four Southern Graces." In 1893 Ward McAllister had chosen her to lead the grand march with him at the Patriarch's Ball. It was the highest honor a young society beauty could be accorded. Gibson and his wife were even included in the social set of Caroline Astor, still an acknowledged leader of New York society.[21]

Whether or not Gibson realized it, his choice to focus his drawings on New York high society played an important role in their popularity. In an age when our celebrities are drawn from sports, the screen, politics, and the world of fashion; when the old society pages in the newspapers have become women's pages, featuring professionals and homemakers as much as the wealthy and leisured; when the wealthy have spread throughout the country and disappeared into suburban retreats; when tax laws have made kingly extravagance less possible, it is hard for us to realize the fascination that the wealthy—and particularly the wealthy of New York City—had for Americans in the 1890s. There was, wrote Henry Collins Brown, "an insatiable public curiosity for news of high society." Wrote author Charles Belmont Davis, Richard Harding Davis's brother, "It matters little whether they are of it, or above it, or beneath it. It is unquestionably this one clique whose doings are forever interesting to the masses." Newspaper stories of high society, commented another contemporary, provided "a lively subject for family discussion among adults, and intense conversation in barber shops, restaurants, and neighborhood groceries."[22]

On Sundays and holidays, upper Fifth Avenue, where the palaces of the wealthy were located, was thronged with crowds trying to catch a glimpse of the American aristocracy. When a major society wedding took place, the police had to be called to keep order among the curious outside the church. The annual Madison Square Garden Horse Show in late October drew so many spectators that the boxes of the wealthy were often all but mobbed. Newspaper reports of the doings of America's plutocracy were even more important. Technological innovations and the commercial genius of newspapermen like Joseph Pulitzer and William Randolph Hearst had brought the advent of cheap metropolitan dailies, the huge circulations of which were built on exploiting the public craving for sensationalism and knowledge of celebrities. Sex, violence, the theater, and New York society were their stock in trade—features that were particularly apparent in the Sunday supplements, lavishly illustrated weekend magazines that were among the most popular entertainment publications of their day.[23]

James Gordon Bennett, considered the pioneer in American popular journalism, in 1835 introduced into his *New York Herald* a section devoted to the doings of the wealthy. By the 1890s what had been a modest enterprise became a large undertaking as reporters disguised themselves to gain entry into society events and bribed servants for inside information. Society leaders, themselves interested in publicity to cement their claims to preeminence, began to hire publicists and press agents. In any case, the rise of the American plutocracy after the Civil War was a fascinating story in and of itself, involving the conquest of the resources of a continent by industrial buccaneers who built palaces in Newport and New York, where they could be observed easily, and furnished them with European treasures. These men seemed proof of the nation's strength and vitality; and although we now know that the majority of them did not come from humble beginnings, the widely reported fact that some of them—like Carnegie or Rockefeller—had modest origins seemed to give reality to the widespread belief in the rags-to-riches mythology.

But men of great wealth were not the focus of the popular press. By the time of the emergence of the tabloids, their days of entrepreneurial abandon had ended. To understand their complex businesses required the analytic skill of an Ida Tarbell, unravelling the doings of Standard Oil in a muckraking journal. Absorbed in the details of the intricate corporate structures they had created, they left the balls, parties, and other leisure-time activities of high society up to their wives.

Indeed, in the pages of the popular press it was the wives—and especially the daughters—of the wealthy who were featured. Early in the century the beauty had emerged as a role to which women, especially of the upper classes, aspired. By the 1890s the popularity of the role had vastly expanded, and the coverage accorded the reigning New York beauty approached that given to public figures in politics or the arts. Foreign traveller Paul Bourget commented extensively on the American fascination with beautiful young women, noting that every city boasted two or three such aspirants to fame. "Their supremacy is so well recognized," wrote Bourget, "that you are continually receiving invitations to, for example, tea with Miss———, the Richmond beauty." Once the beauty was recognized, Bourget continued, she began a sort of official existence. Her name was constantly mentioned in the social gossip columns, and she was expected to represent her city in Newport, New York, and other places where, "as on a stage," American society displayed itself. "If one were to accept the oracles sent forth by certain newspaper correspondents writing from New York," wrote Constance Cary Harrison, "our debutantes might be ranked with athletic champions in training for boxing matches. What these young women are supposed to eat and drink, details of their bran baths, alcohol baths, massage treatment [are all reported]. Next, we hear of how many cotillions a week the young lady dances; how many luncheons and dinners she attends. . . ."[24]

Although Gibson had entrée into the New York elites, by and large he did not socialize with Caroline Astor's set. His close friends were drawn from among fellow illustrators or authors like Richard Harding Davis and Constance Cary Harrison, whose books he illustrated. His wedding to Irene Langhorne occurred in Richmond, Virginia, the day after Consuelo Vanderbilt's wedding to the duke of Marlborough; and the close scheduling did not allow time to attend the New York event, even though it was among the most important social affairs of the decade. Tellingly, the *Denver Post* once observed that, although the Gibson girl was an aristocrat in bearing, she was not of the highest aristocracy. The distinction was subtle, but important. For what the Gibson girl represented were those young women of the elite who were rebelling against the rigidities of Caroline Astor's generation, who were beginning to assert a greater freedom in personal style. It was Ava Willing Astor, not Consuelo Vanderbilt, whom the Gibson girl was meant to personify.[25]

The differences between the two women were important. Vanderbilt was raised in a traditional manner, hedged in by restrictions on her physical activity and personal behavior. She was supposed to become a conventional lady. In physical type she was tall, but exceedingly frail. She was not permitted to exercise; "she looked as though a wind might break her in two," wrote an acquaintance. Alva Vanderbilt, her mother, forced her to marry a man she did not love.[26]

Ava Astor was different. She was unconventional; she delighted in shocking the world of Caroline Astor, her mother-in-law. Describing Ava Astor's appearance in her 1893 tennis match at the Newport Casino, *Vogue* magazine focused on her athletic body. In *Vogue*'s estimation, she put to rest the old belief that American women were delicate by nature. She was part of an important group among American society women who in the 1890s were seeking individual expression in their own lives, who wanted "to excel in some individual attainment," in sports, in literature, in reform.[27]

Such subtleties in the meaning of the Gibson girl elude us today. But for contemporaries, who followed the doings of high society, they were apparent. Ava Willing Astor was known to the readers of the day's newspapers, as was Consuelo Vanderbilt. And contemporaries realized that Gibson was providing them with a positive model of the new woman, a kind of woman who had previously emerged among the working classes and the middle classes.

Reflecting on what Gibson intended his fictionalized woman to represent, his sister, Josephine Gibson Knowlton, once remarked: "My brother wanted to portray a totally American type. The Gibson Girl was symbolic of a wholesome, healthy, utterly American girl. She liked sports, was a little ahead of her time, definitely athletic, and certainly did not smoke or drink—then. Importantly, she carved a new kind of femininity suggestive of emancipation." The Gibson girl may have been wholesome and healthy, Knowlton implied, but emancipation could have worrisome consequences. Although Ava Willing Astor may have begun her public career as a sportswoman, in the 1900s she divorced her husband and began to be seen on the fringes of Lobster Palace Society as the companion of a group of New York clubmen known as the "Knickerbocker Dudes." Again, while in the 1890s the Gibson girl was identified with physical emancipation through sports, exercise, and dress, by the 1900s the group of elite innovators with whom she was connected was demanding more freedom in areas of personal behavior and sensual expression.[28]

In some ways the Gibson model, as Knowlton suggested, could accommodate changing mores. Characteristically elusive on the subject of why he had initially drawn the Gibson girl, Charles Dana Gibson once told a reporter that he had done so because he had been a young man, and young men are always preoccupied with thoughts of beautiful women. Gibson thus hinted at the sensual intent behind his Gibson girl, a symbol suited to an age exploring new modes of sensuality, but still infused with Victorian sentimentality and rectitude. One analyst of the image of women in turn-of-the-century art has argued that the typical female figure of the period was dignified and withdrawn, without sensuality, "an epitome of true womanhood," "a frozen goddess." The Gibson girl was clearly not such a figure.[29]

Yet the extent to which Gibson ultimately could modify his model of beauty to accommodate changing behavior was limited. By 1902 the *New York Herald* noted that the women in Gibson's drawings seemed shorter, with rounder cheeks and fuller lips, while their appearance seemed less aristocratic, more in keeping with a new model of beauty that was even then beginning the emerge. Yet in 1912 the *New York World* still described the women Gibson drew as tall and aristocratic, and although they continued to dominate standards of beauty, their vogue was waning. Within a year, the *World* reported that the model of beauty had completely changed. By 1913 the tall aristocrat was out and the flapper—"hipless, waistless, boneless"—was in vogue. The appearance of the flapper marked the fruition of a sensual revolution among American women that had begun in the 1890s and that the Gibson girl image could only partly accommodate. The Gibson girl—the exemplar of an earlier age of emancipation for women—now became a period piece, out of date and out of style.[30]

III

Behind the genesis of the Gibson girl lay a general American fascination with young women. Since the days of Cooper, Hawthorne, and Poe, American writers had used young women as symbols of the American character, as representing the conflicts between purity and sensuality, between traditional society and the future. Artists, reinforced by the pre-Raphaelites, identified women as objects of beauty in an ugly industrial world. Placing women on pedestals was characteristic of the legendary American chivalry, and nineteenth-century culture generally had spiritualized women and viewed them as representatives of morality. And the obverse side of the focus on spirituality was a fascination with physicality, with the shape of women's bodies in a culture in which they were supposed to be concealed.[31]

In the 1850s French traveller and astute observer Oscar Comettant had identified what he thought was a "cult of women" in the United States, exemplified by the images of women he saw everywhere. Barrooms and male clubs, he noted, were decorated with Venuses, nymphs, and even bathing beauties. Streetcars in cities displayed pictures of women on their doors. It was even in vogue, he observed, for men to sport daguerreotypes of women in the brims of their hats. If such was true in the 1850s, it was even more so in the 1890s. By then what we call the pin-up had become a major American phenomenon, whether in the form of cigarette cards, or pornographic *cartes de visites,* or on the pages of the *Police Gazette,* the *Playboy* of its day, which barbershops and saloons regularly carried. According to contemporary accounts, the most important figure in the circus was the female bareback rider; in early museums, the waxwork sleeping beauty; in their dime museum successors, the Circassian lady; in the parades put on by travelling *Uncle Tom's Cabin* theater troupes, Little Eva. A whole genre of musical theater developed around scantily clad women formed into a chorus line.[32]

Moreover, by late century the beauty had become a major public personality. Even the managers of the Women's Building at the 1895 Atlanta Cotton States and International Exposition put together a calendar featuring twelve beautiful southern women in order to raise funds. Newspapers regularly held beauty contests, and cities and states held competitions to find beautiful women to be models for civic sculptures or pieces to be sent to the era's many expositions and centennials. A colossal figure of Columbia atop the art building towered over the Philadelphia 1876 Centennial; in the central hall of the main building the nation was personified by an amazon holding a spear and a sword—"the aboriginal earth goddess" incarnate, according to one reviewer. The Chicago Columbian Centennial of 1893, the American World's Fair of the century, was dominated by statues of classical female goddesses.[33]

Such ubiquitous use of women as symbolic personification was not unrelated to venerable usages of women as symbols of nations and institutions, or as mastheads on ships, or as "daughters of the regiment"—company mascots whom premodern army units chose from among women followers; the practice was, in fact, widespread among Civil War troops. Yet the figures seen as especially symbolic of the nation varied over time. In the eighteenth century a young female Columbia—often represented by an Indian maiden—personified the virgin and abundant qualities of the New World. In the early nineteenth century she was replaced by a Greek goddess and then by Uncle Sam, a wizened yet sprightly grandfather who combined the levelling style of frontier homespun with the venerable appeal of the founding fathers. By late century the national pantheon had come to include another female figure: the goddess Minerva of the Statue of Liberty. She was a symbol that drew on visions of American might and on the massive classical statuary in vogue in the nineteenth-century age of national expansion.[34]

Yet although in eclipse, Columbia had not disappeared. In a more modern guise the young, virginal woman haunted American writers like Howells and James, who in characters like Lydia Blood and Daisy Miller penned their own representations of the American character, as did the popular lithographers of the period. In the introduction to his collection of drawings of young American women, illustrator Alexander Black acknowledged the broad cultural currents that motivated his work. Whether the young woman "illustrated the social and political changes which have taken place [during the century] or actually indicates why they have taken place," he wrote, "she presents a spectacle of peculiar interest . . . which has piqued the analytic spirit of the age." She was Columbia reincarnated, the United States as young once again, the new imperial nation in contrast to Old World cultures. She was "Miss America"—the title that illustrators of beautiful women often used to refer to the young women they drew and that the founders of the nation's most famous beauty contest borrowed when they inaugurated that event in Atlantic City in 1921.[35]

As the most powerful late-century representative of Miss America, the Gibson girl was symbolic of the hopeful changes of the age: the new movement of women into the work force, the new freedom of behavior between men and women, the new vogue of athletics promising healthier bodies. The restrictive etiquette that Caroline Astor and others had introduced in the 1870s to curb the behavior of young American women had never completely succeeded. Throughout the 1870s and 1880s, observers noted that in mixed social situations chaperones were not always present, that young girls still flirted, and that street behavior was not always restrained. As an indication of continuing strains of independence, post–Civil War fiction dealing with the West had produced a new heroine, the so-called Girl of the Golden West, who was independent in mind and body and was exemplified in heroines of fiction like Calamity Jane and on the stage by Lotta Crabtree, who combined the western influence with the tradition of the soubrette.[36]

Strains of western freedom as well as eastern independence were apparent in the Gibson girl. Like many critics of the day, Winfield Scott Moody compared the Gibson girl to Henry James's Daisy Miller. Yet the two, Moody thought, were only superficially similar. Daisy Miller had transgressed social mores out of ignorance, for she was the product of a provincial society in which the restrictive etiquette of the Astor circle had not fully developed. But the Gibson girl, whose world was that of the New York elite, willingly chose to break convention. Moody was critical of the choice, but on balance he preferred the new woman that he thought the Gibson girl represented to her more conservative predecessors. The Gibson girl had "eaten of the Tree of Knowledge," but she was nonetheless a "beautiful, brilliant, lovable girl."[37]

Yet as much as she represented the new realities of women's lives, on another level the Gibson girl was a fantasy figure in whom the problem of poverty, immigration, and labor strife were denied and through whom people could identify with a world of glamour. The 1890s was a troubled age, dominated by economic depression, labor turmoil, and the arrival of streams of immigrants whose appearance and mores differed substantially from those of the groups that had preceded them. Unemployed workers marched on Washington; the national guard was called out to quell industrial violence; the federal government declared the frontier, traditionally perceived as the safety valve for urban discontent, closed. In her guise as a figure of fantasy, the Gibson girl was representative of the romantic escapism of the 1890s—a mood that made the historical romances of novelists like Gibson's friend Richard Harding Davis great popular successes. It is significant that before the 1890s American novelists did not take up the historical romance as a major genre, even though the type was important in English popular fiction throughout the century. And although Gibson did not place his women in historical settings, overtones of medievalism echoed throughout the work of Richard Harding Davis, who, even when writing about contemporary times, saw his heroes as knights and his heroines as objects of chivalric adoration, people who constituted an aristocracy as secure as the medieval one had ever been.

When Lew Wallace wrote *Ben Hur* in 1880 and inaugurated what would be in the 1890s an avalanche of historical romances, he uncovered a cultural yearning for the security that the past seemed to provide. On one level the people of the 1890s called their era "gay," a time of the bicycle, Viennese operettas, and John Philip Sousa's band music, of electric lights and improved sanitation, of Phineas Fogg's trip around the world in eighty days and Nellie Bly's recapitulation of it in seventy-nine days. But on another level they also experienced it as a time of ennui and despair, of decadence, even of disorder.[38]

The Gibson girl was not, and was not meant to be, a radical figure—either in politics or in personal style. Had she been, she would not have gained and held such extraordinary popularity. The point becomes clearer if we compare her with another popular figure of the age who preceded her and whose popularity she, to a large degree, incorporated into her own.

That figure was Trilby, the heroine of George Du Maurier's novel of the same name, which, published in 1894, became an immediate sensation in the United States. Dozens of editions of the book were issued; thousands of volumes were sold. Public libraries bought scores of copies, but still had long waiting lists of readers. Theatrical adaptations toured the country to huge audiences. Invited to lecture in a New York City suburb, Richard Harding Davis began his talk by reciting the first eight lines of Trilby. He was greeted by a moment of silence and then by thunderous applause and laughter as the audience realized the trick he had played on them by reciting a passage they all knew by heart. Trilby fashions came into vogue. Wrote a contemporary, we wore "Trilby hats, Trilby coats, Trilby slippers, ate Trilby chocolates, played Trilby waltzes." What is more, the century-long fascination with small feet ended because Trilby, by Du Maurier's description, had feet that were "neither large nor small." Through Trilby's influence large mouths gained a new popularity.[39]

Conservatives tried to find a moral lesson in Trilby's story, but she was, in personal style, about as emancipated as a woman could be. She was an orphan who lived in Paris with a ragpicker and his wife and who made her money ironing clothes and modelling for artists. She smoked cigarettes, dressed like a man, posed in the nude with no sense of shame, enjoyed the bohemian comradeship of the Latin Quarter, delighted in dancing the can-can, and was promiscuous in her sexual relationships. The sense of guilt for her conduct that the love of a virtuous man instilled in her served only to oppress her and to doom her to possession by the devil in the form of the music teacher, Svengali. At the same time, the strictures of middle-class society, which finally kept Trilby's lover from her, psychologically emasculated him as well by making it impossible for him to love any woman. The moral of the story was the stupidity and insidiousness of Victorian propriety.

At the very least, Trilby's promiscuity and her working-class background were at variance with the Gibson girl's milieu. Nor did the two figures look like one another. By Du Maurier's description, Trilby was as masculine as she was feminine, with a large chin and mouth and a general appearance "that would have made a singularly handsome boy." More appropriate representations of the Gibson girl in fiction can be found in the works of those novelists who, like David Graham Phillips, Winston Churchill, and Booth Tarkington, focused on social reform as their special message and are often grouped together as the "Progressive" school. The minor luminaries of this school include popular writers like Richard Davis and Constance Cary Harrison, friends of Gibson who echoed in their fiction reform themes that found more vigorous expression in writers like Phillips and Churchill.[40]

In the fiction of all Progressive writers, women play a key role, both as villains and as heroes. On the one hand they are depicted as women of fashion, as interested only in display and self-indulgence, as parasitic representatives of the worst strains of American consumerism and materialism. Usually married, these women are the descendants of the belles and beauties who had earlier posed a threat to republican virtue in the works of antebellum women novelists. But the late-century women of fashion are even more dangerous than their fictional ancestors, for, in contrast to the latter, they are usually not unattached women, but rather wives and mothers with direct power over husbands and children. In addition to these villainous women, however, Progressive novelists also limn women of grace, strength, and intelligence whose heroic qualities and happy lives stand in contrast to the grasping women of fashion. These late-century heroines were the descendants of the natural women of the antebellum women novelists.

Various Progressive authors treated these women in various ways. Constance Cary Harrison liked to write about natural women who were drawn to stylish behavior in opposition to their true natures, but who, through a chain of events generally involving the love of a strong, honest man, realized their destiny in a simple, shared life, revolving around home and family. Booth Tarkington, like other Progressive novelists, reversed the pattern, writing about men with flawed characters whose basic nobility was rescued by strong women. Winston Churchill had still another variation: he typically contrasted virtuous heroines with materialistic, businessman fathers. In the writings of Richard Harding Davis, character development was not a major focus, and his novels centered on identifying the men and women who were the true natural nobility and then bringing them together romantically.

Nineteenth-century American reformers characteristically stressed individual example and self-reformation as the basic means of social redemption, and so did the novelists of the Progressive era, no matter their differing presentations of women. With views rooted firmly in the past, they envisioned the appearance of a moral elite, the clear superiority of whose lives would inspire self-reformation among all. The Gibson girl was their representative in the pictorial sphere. Strong and independent, at her best she was a companion to men, not a dependent. Her moral code was not always strict: sometimes, as in the works of David Graham Phillips, it was indicated that she was not averse to sex and that, although she might preserve her virginity until marriage, she did not avoid other sorts of physical relations. Yet, it must be reiterated, in none of these novels was she a Trilby. Even Susan Lenox, who takes to prostitution in Phillips's *Susan Lenox: Her Fall and Rise,* is driven to do so out of financial desperation and self-hatred, not out of the lack of a middle-class moral code. Some of the best Progressive novels deal with the conflicts of career women, and many of the writers exhibit sympathy toward women's drives for self-fulfillment outside the home. Yet true fulfillment for the women in the novels by Churchill, Phillips, Tarkington, Harrison, and Davis always lies within home and family. At a time of increasing divorce, alarming to contemporaries, these reformist novelists saw redemption in the reconstitution of the family around traditional values—a vision made appealing to a modern, urban society by the fact that the heroic men and women who held them were vital, not humble; ethical, not pious; and, above all, physically strong, athletic, and beautiful to look at.

These themes are clearly presented in Richard Harding Davis's 1896 novel, *Soldier of Fortune,* one of the most popular novels of the epoch and one that he dedicated to Charles and Irene Gibson. Gibson himself illustrated the novel, which deals with the successful attempts of a mining engineer and sometime soldier of fortune, Robert Clay, to thwart a coup in the South American country where he is attempting to establish a mining operation. His success is threatened by the country's villainous political opposition, as is the future of democracy in the nation. Two sisters, the daughters of a multimillionaire mine owner who is backing the South American project, play a major role in the novel. Alice Langham, a New York beauty who is acclaimed in the press and whom Clay has worshipped from afar, initially seems to be the novel's heroine. But as the story progresses, it becomes clear that participation in New York high society has ruined her, that she has lost her spontaneity of action and now moves according to "rules and precedents, like a queen in a game of chess," that money and leisure and participation in a society of "golf sticks and salted almonds" have lost her the claim to being a natural woman rather than a fashionable one.[41]

Indeed, it is Alice's sister, Hope, who emerges in the course of the story as the true natural woman. She is young enough that she has not yet been formally presented to New York society; there is hope for her future nobility. Nor has the natural tomboy behavior of the adolescent girl yet been drummed out of her by society's demands that she become a lady. She rides like a man, participates coolly in armed action, and in the final scenes of the story rescues Clay, now her intended lover, from certain death by ambush. Yet, as Clay makes clear, she also fulfills women's traditional role, not of fostering domesticity, but of representing "the sweetness, and grace, and nobleness of civilization." In his past Clay has been a cowboy, a rough sailor, a soldier for hire (so long as the cause was just). In his rise from the depths of poverty to success, "I've fought on the mud floor of a Mexican shack, with a naked knife in my hand, for my last dollar." Davis glorifies such male violence, but is also appalled by it. Hope Langham accepts it and ironically provides its justification: to secure civilization, which she represents, may require roughness and force.[42]

Above all, Hope realizes Clay's natural nobility. When he repairs a motor on the boat in which they all are travelling, Alice is repelled by his ability at a manual task that she thinks the servants should perform. Hope, on the other hand, finds his action thrilling, an expression both of his ability to move in a variety of worlds and of a mechanical genius that has not only enabled him to build bridges, roads, mines, and railroad lines, but also has made him the confidant of kings. Clay eventually realizes that she represents the way her sister must have been before she became a participant in high society, "before the little world she lived in had crippled and narrowed her." As the novel ends, Clay and Hope are planning to marry, and he has decided to become a consultant to mining engineers, rather than working directly in the field. The two of them intend that she will accompany him and, since she has become knowledgeable about his work, will offer him private advice.[43]

Like other Progressive novelists, Davis had difficulty in dealing with relationships between men and women once they married. The natural nobility he depicted was one of youth, not of age, and in one sense it represented his generation's rejection of what seemed the compromises of its elders, particularly in the area of sex roles. Davis's natural woman was athletic; he wished women to be companions of men and not dependents, and he implied that society could be perfected when this goal was reached. Yet exactly how his emancipated women would adjust to the strictures of the marriages he intended for them he never discussed, just as he never explained how the independent Hope could possibly enjoy a lifetime of private consultations and public silence.

Gibson, too, had difficulties with the later lives of his Gibson girls. Older women in Gibson's drawings are almost always shown as fat and frumpy or as scrawny and querulous, and discontent between older married couples and their attempts to manipulate younger people unfairly are among the central themes of his work. Perhaps he assumed that the athletic, physically superior people he drew would retain this quality in later life, that somehow they would sustain, as their elders had not, the romance that in his drawings seemed to be the central purpose of life. Still, in his 1903 series of drawings entitled *The Widow,* he showed a beautiful young woman in a variety of settings, attempting to overcome her grief, pursued by a flock of eager men. In the last drawings she has become a nun.

The notion that a moral elite can, by example, bring social reformation seems quaint to modern minds, an outgrowth of an older heroic tradition transmogrified in the popular melodramatic story into the idea that moral character is clear-cut, that there are such people as heroes and heroines better than the rest of us. The problem with Richard Harding Davis's novels is that they read like the romantic stories to be found in any of the day's popular magazines. They are escapist fiction, written to a formula, about a world that does not exist and people whose characters are not complex. And so is Gibson's world. It is no wonder that he came to hate the ideal woman he drew, bathed as she is in the false light of romance, often even pictured with fat little cupids, like a Valentine's Day card, surrounded by a false sentimentality that even Davis's novels avoided.

The problem is not the figure itself, but rather the story that Gibson's drawings implies and the setting in which his figures were placed. When E. L. Godkin offered his famous criticism of American society as a "chromo" civilization, he meant many things: that Americans would accept the shoddy rather than the genuine, that they too easily did what their neighbors did instead of forging their own way, that they accepted a brightly colored, sentimentalized version of reality rather than recognizing the corruption developing alongside the new industrial order and the complacency of the post–Civil War world. Godkin's "chromo" reference was to the chromolithograph, realized primarily in works that focused on scenes of everyday life, generally in a nostalgic or sentimentalized manner to make them appear soft, appealing, idealized. He might as well have included Gibson's drawings in his indictment, for they, too, were sentimentalized and fantasized scenes of life. His women are too beautiful, his men too handsome; his satire is not biting, but sweet. Even in his occasional scenes of New York City street life, his ragpickers and bums do not look desolate and defeated, but rather seem the forebears of Norman Rockwell's simple types, men and women who have accepted their lot and, as the traditional mythology has it, found satisfaction in the challenges of poverty. No Gibson drawing would ever stir anyone to take arms against the wealthy or change personal behavior—except to exercise or to take up sports to look more like Gibson's ideal women and men.

Yet it was no inconsiderable achievement to have provided a pictorial justification for women's new physical freedom. No less a personage than Charlotte Perkins Gilman, a dedicated proponent of physical exercise, saw the Gibson girl as symbolic of the important changes for women that had occurred over the course of the nineteenth century. The Gibson girl, in comparison to all beauty ideals that had preceded her, was "braver, stronger, more healthful and skillful and able and free, more human in all ways." Neither entirely radical nor conservative, reflecting in her image a complex combination of artistic, literary, and sociological strains, the Gibson girl was popular precisely because of her ambiguity.[44]

9

The New Order

By 1895 the new woman had made her appearance in American society. She was visible in education, in athletics, in reform, in the work force. The Gibson girl exemplified her independence, though Gibson's creation was a moderate figure, mirroring the artist's devotion to romance and marriage. Yet there were other models of beauty and free behavior. Du Maurier's Trilby was one; actresses were another.

The popularity of these two models indicates that Victorian prudery had been challenged long before the 1920s. By the 1890s, standards of propriety predominant in the 1870s and 1880s were eroding, as was conventional behavior in women's sports and exercise. By then commercialization and the pleasure ethic were making inroads in all aspects of American life. Their importance is apparent in the numbers of urban and suburban amusement parks, in state fairs and city festivals, in the growth of urban dance halls, and in the emergence of new music like ragtime and "coon" songs.

As with sports, it was not elite women who introduced new kinds of sensual behavior. Rather, other groups were seminal. First were actresses, who had long been attuned to new styles of liberated expression. Second was a group of society men who were attracted by the subculture of sensuality and who visited the haunts frequented by actresses and the demimonde. The connection of actresses and society men became strikingly visible in the 1890s with the emergence of Lobster Palace Society—the highly publicized crowd that frequented the new, large, and elaborate Broadway restaurants for after-theater dining. The third originators of freer standards of sensuality were young, unmarried working-class men and women who thronged amusement parks, dance halls, nickelodeons, and, by the 1900s, movies. The vanguard position of working-class women is evidenced by the fact that the most popular actress in the United States at the turn of the century was the chorus girl, a figure who personified the hopes of working-class women and whose free behavior both reflected and stimulated their own.

It was these diverse groups, more than 1920s middle-class youths, who were responsible for changes in the sensual behavior of Americans in the early twentieth century. Their diverse influences came together before World War I to spark the dance craze of 1912. By 1911, cabarets that offered entertainment and dancing had come to replace the Lobster Palaces as the arenas of New York night-life; in them were introduced a series of erotic and frenzied dances—the bunny hug, the turkey trot, the tango—which had originated in black and lower-class dance halls and on the vaudeville stage. Stimulated by the examples of famed professional dance couples like Vernon and Irene Castle and Florence and Maurice Walton, enthusiasm for cabarets and the new dances swept the nation.

Moreover, as new kinds of behavior developed, a new style of appearance came to accompany them: a small, flirtatious, sometimes boyish, sometimes voluptuous model of beauty—a lower-class competitor to the aristocratic Gibson girl. With roots in the tradition of Lotta Crabtree and the soubrette, the new style was first personified by Anna Held and the Florodora girls; then by vaudeville performer Eva Tanguay; and finally by Irene Castle, Mary Pickford, and Clara Bow. By 1913 the *New York World* identified the flapper as the preeminent model of female appearance and noted the demise of the Gibson girl.[1]

Moreover, red hair, reprobated for centuries as emblematic of deviance and evil and popularly believed to indicate a troublesome, passionate personality, now came into vogue. Fashionable ingenues in musical comedies commonly had Titian-colored tresses; society women, it was alleged, went to Rome for a sophisticated shade that Italian hairdressers had discovered. Whatever the source, the new color, whose popularity dated from the 1890s, symbolized the new sensuality of the end-of-the-century era.

From the days of *The Black Crook* and the British Blondes, actresses gained an increasingly powerful hold over the popular imagination. To the historian their vogue is not readily apparent, for the evidence is contained in sources often overlooked: theater collections, popular magazines, and the metropolitan dailies launched in the 1890s. The Sunday supplements to these newspapers express the popularity of comic opera and vaudeville actresses, a vanguard group in presenting new styles of behavior and appearance to American women.

In organs like *Harper's* or the *Atlantic Monthly,* the leaders of high culture ignored the popularity of these stage personalities. Whatever fascination the British Blondes had held for William Dean Howells in the 1870s he forgot by the 1890s when their descendants were the rage. Among the Progressive novelists, David Graham Phillips characterized the typical comic opera as a "loathsome mess" with "rotten music" and "dubious-looking people" and held that the star of such a spectacle, by pandering to the "low public taste" of the tired businessman and his "laced-wife," was little better than a prostitute. Richard Harding Davis, who later married a musical comedy performer, in an early story implied that immorality was inevitably characteristic of women of the theater.[2]

Yet such conservative moulders of public opinion represented a minority point of view. In their time as in ours, the public's attention was drawn to stage performers. Their popularity stemmed, in the first instance, from advances in photography. Within several decades of the invention of daguerreotype photography in the 1830s, publicity photos had eventuated in a vogue for collecting small celebrity photographs—the so-called *cartes de visites* marketed by clever photographers. Mathew Brady brought American photographic art to early maturity with photographs of presidents and battles, but his most celebrated successor in the second half of the century was Napoleon Sarony, a photographer of theatrical personalities. Among Sarony's first customers in the 1850s had been Adah Isaacs Menken, often credited with being the first American performer to realize the publicity potential of photos and of their display in saloons and shop windows. According to Henry Collins Brown, the names of the great theatrical photographers—Sarony, Falk, Mora—became "household words." In the 1880s, cigarette companies began to promote their products through the distribution of cards bearing photos of actresses and sports personalities. A decade later, new developments in photography allowed the reproduction of celebrity photographs in newspapers. Shop windows displayed enlarged versions of the cigarette pictures of actresses. By then, too, the Sunday editions of the newspapers were filled with theater news and gossip.[3]

Press agentry and merchandising methods also boosted the visibility of stage women. From the days of Fanny Elssler and Jenny Lind, actresses had employed press agents to publicize them. They soon began to set fashions in dress, particularly after Josephine Shaw in the mid-1850s married wealthy John Hooey and could afford the latest fashions for her stage roles. By the end of the century the demand to see the stylish actresses' taste in clothes was so great that even historical dramas were played in modern garb. Actresses with major public appeal could be confident that manufacturers, dress designers, and perfumers would appropriate their names for products and thus boost their appeal.[4]

The popularity of the theater itself enhanced the popularity of actresses. Even in the early nineteenth century, all major eastern cities had theaters, although they were sometimes called museums in deference to moral conservatives. Before the Civil War, the opening each season of Wallack's Theatre was a major event for New York society; after the war, Augustin Daly's repertory theater came to occupy a similar position. By midcentury, New York City hotels stressed in their advertising their proximity to the theater district; and by the mid-1870s Daly installed a telegraph wire in his box office so that tickets for performances could be purchased at local telegraph offices.[5]

By the 1870s an opera house was a common symbol of community pride and modernity in the burgeoning towns and cities of the industrializing nation. The completion of the transcontinental railroad in 1869 made theatrical touring immeasurably easier, and large booking agencies appeared in New York City to bring Broadway plays, operettas, and variety shows to communities throughout the United States. They built upon the pioneering efforts of antebellum travelling companies that had penetrated the frontier in response to a craving for entertainment and a desire, strong even then, to see a favorite "star"—the exalted term already in common use—despite the presumed déclassé status of actors.

Theatrical news and gossip, attuned to people's melodramatic instincts and their desire to identify with the lives of celebrities, became a major feature of the new journalism of the 1880s and 1890s. "A newspaper would lose its circulation if it excluded dramatic gossip," contended drama critic Alan Dale. "Actors and actresses are children of the public, nourished at the breast of the public." According to Mary Elizabeth Coolidge, echoing a score of commentators, the American people possessed a "never-ceasing curiosity regarding the lives of stage people."[6]

Theater reporters were ubiquitous, and visiting performers from Europe invariably found that their first sight in New York harbor after the Statue of Liberty was a boatload of reporters coming to interview them before they even stepped off the boat. "The importunities of the reporters did not give me a moment's repose," remembered Sarah Bernhardt. "Many times I looked to right and left, under the tables and in the closets, to see if a reporter was hidden anywhere. And one day I caught a young woman reporter in my bathroom, smelling the soap to see if it was scented." Reporters were not the only Americans determined to win personal attention from visiting theatrical celebrities. On his tour of the United States in 1876, Jacques Offenbach wrote of his astonishment at the "mania" of Americans for autographs. "They carry their passion to the very limits of indiscretion. I received, during my stay in the United States, at least ten requests a day from all parts of the American territory. I was accosted, followed, and pursued in the restaurants, the public gardens, in the theatres, and even in the streets."[7]

"Stage fever is more prevalent and dangerous than it is generally supposed to be," declared Elizabeth Cady Stanton and Susan B. Anthony's *Revo-*

lution in 1869. Indeed, by the 1870s, the theater's powerful attraction was evident in the emotional involvement of its audiences. Celebrities created fans, who in turn created celebrities. Chief among the devotees of the theater were the matinée girls, young women who attended afternoon performances, which producers devised in the 1850s as a way of increasing audiences. By the 1890s matinée girls were major characters of stories and songs. On Saturday afternoons in New York, according to *Munsey's Magazine,* they were found "crowding the thoroughfares, filling the lobbies of the theaters, and overflowing the cable cars." The *Dramatic Mirror* even had a gossip column entitled "The Matinée Girl." Sometimes the favorite was an actress: Sarah Truax noted that the teenage girls at matinées had given her hundreds of handmade handkerchiefs. According to an observer, Maude Adams's extraordinary popularity was due to her favor among matinée girls.[8]

Most often, however, matinée girls fixed their attention on male actors. "A handsome actor appears on the stage," wrote the *Galaxy,* "and they write him tender letters, send him flowers, and seek to make appointments with him. They even form a society of admiration in his honor, not on account of the excellence of his art, but of the graces of his person." Hundreds of women regularly gathered outside the stage door when Henry Montague was playing, and Charles Rignold received love notes. One French tenor declared that he would not return to New York unless there was some way he could avoid the "gauntlet of adoring eyes" from the theater to his hotel. In 1897 *Munsey's* reported that the latest fad of matinée girls was a "Hero Book," containing play programs, newspaper clippings, and photographs of their idols. In 1899 the *Ladies' Home Journal* began a regular series entitled "The Theatre and Its People" because of its worry about young girls' fascination with actors.[9]

But not only actors affected audiences of women. Strongmen like Eugene Sandow and artists like pianist Ignace Jan Paderewski had an impact on women of all ages. Florenz Ziegfeld cleverly exhibited Sandow at the Chicago World's Fair of 1893 without the lion skin that strongmen normally wore, and he persuaded Mrs. Potter Palmer and several other Chicago society leaders to come backstage after a performance to examine Sandow's muscles. Foreign visitor Paul Bourget reported that photographs of Sandow were widely sold and that women at Newport displayed them in their sitting rooms. Paderewski provoked an even more sensational response. When he played, according to advice columnist Beatrice Fairfax, "the women would leave their seats, and press forward like a besieging army. They'd tear off their corsage bouquets, and fling them, hundreds of bunches of violets, on the stage." Paderewski treated these admirers with an "unvarying cool courtesy that somewhat soothed these bacchantes of the gay 90s, these well-fed, well-dressed lion chasers who loved to take little holidays from their Victorianism."[10]

Men also responded fervently to their stage favorites. The stage-door Johnny who attempted to form liaisons with beautiful actresses was a familiar type, as were the college men who wined and dined actresses on tour or formed a cohort of distant admirers. If the popular press and actresses' memoirs are to be believed, Harvard students were particularly prone to this form of heroine worship. The *Cincinnati Evening Star* reported in 1887 that many Harvard men crossed the Charles River into Boston every night to see burlesque actress Eliza Weathersby, one of the original British Blondes. Vaudeville stars Billie Burke and Elsie Janis both claimed to have attracted a regular entourage of Harvard men. According to Janis, the group of blue-blood New York Harvard men who squired her around Boston when she played there was known as "Elsie's Husbands' Club."[11]

As individuals, actresses presented a variety of types with whom their fans could identify. Mary Anderson, popularly revered as "Our Mary," was renowned for her virtue and piety, both in her personal life and in her interpretation of dramatic roles. In contrast, several divorced society women, like Cora Potter, exploited their scandalous situations to attain major stage success. Sarah Bernhardt cultivated a reputation as an eccentric voluptuary; Lillie Langtry portrayed herself as both a lady and an independent woman. Both Bernhardt and Langtry were known to favor exercise and reformed dress for women. Their immense salaries, their glamorous lives, the adulation of dramatic critics, and the careful publicity planted by press agents brought these actresses enormous public attention.

But more than any other figure on the American stage at the turn of the century, it was the chorus girl who fascinated the American public. So common were the stories about her, so numerous the newspaper columns devoted to her that the *Denver Post* contended that she was more talked about than the president. Her predecessors were the young women who danced in the choruses of antebellum classical ballet troupes and popular spectacles and whose social standing was depreciated because of suspicions about their way of life. But the British Blondes had turned immorality into glamour when they created the legend that beautiful women on the stage received large sums of money and jewelry from admirers who competed for their attention. In the 1880s their popularity had declined—a probable casualty of the heightened moral sensitivity of that decade. Then in the 1890s a group of enterprising producers and choreographers—notably Rudolph Aaronson, George Lederer, and Julian Mitchell—demonstrated again that a chorus of beautiful women could be the chief ingredient in the success of a musical show. Long before Florenz Ziegfeld introduced his Follies in 1907,

[1]   1808

[2]   1829

[3]   1836

[4]   Late 1850s

[5] 1869

[6] 1874

[7] 1892

[8] Amelia Bloomer in the dress that bears her name.

[9]   Stewart's, 1850; New York's fashion emporium and a view of Broadway looking north.

[10]   Fanny Elssler in the Shadow Dance. The ballerina: the essence of the
steel-engraving lady.

[11]   Adah Isaacs Menken, 1860; the voluptuous woman, American style; the famous variety
stage star whose "nude" Mazeppa shocked and delighted two continents.

[12] *Nymphs and Satyr,*
Adolphe William Bouguereau, 1873.

[13] *The Empress Eugénie and her Ladies-in-Waiting,* Franz Xavier Winterhalter, 1867.

[14] ABOVE
Lydia Thompson, founder and leader of
the British Blondes, exemplars of
the voluptuous woman.

[15] BELOW
Lotta Crabtree, a great star of
the variety stage, the very model of the
soubrette to post–Civil War Americans.

[16] LEFT
Thalia: Miss Nellie Smythe; one of the paintings
in the series "American Beauty Personified as Nine Muses,"
Giuseppi Fagnani, c. 1873.

[17] BELOW
Portrait of Catharine Lorillard Wolfe by
Alexandre Cabanel, 1876, which shows the "highly-bred
refinement" and "attenuated elegance" associated with
her type of beauty.

[18] Fanny Davenport, star of Augustin Daly's repertory theater and one of the most photographed women of the late-nineteenth-century stage when the ideal of beauty was the voluptuous woman.

[19] Lillian Russell, 1889; uncorseted; at the height of her *avoirdupois*.

[20] Lillie Langtry. The looks of the woman considered by the English to be their greatest beauty perplexed Americans in the 1880s.

[21]   Princess Alexandra, wife of Edward, Prince of Wales. She represented an athletic
slenderness among the European aristocracy.

[22]   Gibson girl

[23]   Frankie Bailey, variety actress.
She had the most beautiful legs
in America.

[24]   George Du Maurier's drawing
of Trilby. She would have made
"a singularly handsome boy."

[25] LEFT
Consuelo Vanderbilt, an elite beauty whose style did not
become a popular ideal. "She looked as though a
strong wind might break her in two."

[26] BELOW
Anna Held, 1897; the sultry soubrette; Florenz Ziegfeld's
major contribution to American standards of beauty
before he introduced the Ziegfeld girl.

[27] The Florodora sextette. The most courted women in town, they made the chorus girl respectable.

[28] A tailor's advertising circular. The wasp-waisted man, companion to the steel-engraving lady in the 1830s.

[29] Paul Poiret's empire style, as interpreted by Butterick Patterns, 1908.

[31] Della Carson, secretary to the Dean of the Chicago Divinity School, winner in 1905 of a national beauty contest that drew 40,000 entrants.

,0] Susan B. Anthony (*left*), whose appearance was criticized; Elizabeth Cady Stanton (*right*), the ideal image of the elderly nineteenth-century woman.

[32] Richard Harding Davis, 1905, America's turn-of-the-century model of masculinity.

[33] LEFT
The Flapper, by John Held, Jr.

[34] BELOW
Miss America, 1921, Margaret Gorman
of Washington, D.C.

[35] LEFT
Dior's "New Look," 1947,
as interpreted by Vogue Patterns.

[36] BELOW
"Fire and Ice," the 1952 advertisement
that set a new standard for sexuality in
cosmetic promotion.

[37] Joan Crawford

[38] Greta Garbo

[39] Marilyn Monroe

choreographers Lederer and Mitchell carefully chose their chorus girls for beauty and made them central to their productions. Those who performed in the chorus line at Aaronson's Casino were collectively known as "Casino Girls"; those whom Julian Mitchell trained at the Weber and Fields theater were known as "Weber and Fields Girls." As the voluptuous woman had been eliminated, the chorus girls now were chosen with the Gibson girl in mind, or with the smaller model of beauty associated with Ziegfeld protégée Anna Held.[12]

What particularly dominated all discussions of the chorus girl was the world of glamour in which she lived. According to press agent Nellie Revell, "The words 'chorus girl' evoke in the average mind outside the profession visions of limousines, diamonds, gorgeous furs, champagne parties, and wealthy admirers." In 1895 one analyst claimed that every popular chorus girl in the space of a year received "flowers enough to pay a Fifth Avenue florist a fine profit for a year; enough letters to exhaust the output of a Ballston paper mill for six months; enough dinners to buy out Delmonico's." Such claims may have been a case of press agent exaggeration, but the extraordinary experiences of a group of women from the musical comedy *Florodora,* first produced at the Casino Theatre in 1900, made the mythology of chorus girl success a stunning reality.[13]

The plot of the musical involved a beautiful heiress swindled out of her inheritance, and it was set on a mythical island in the Philippines named Florodora. What created *Florodora*'s popularity was a scene in which six young women, fashionably dressed and carrying parasols, glided around the stage, each partnered by a handsome man singing the still well-known refrain: "Tell me, pretty maiden, are there any more at home like you?" *Florodora*'s lavish production had been particularly costly, but the initial reviews were all exceedingly negative. What saved the show, according to most accounts, was the extraordinary response of a group of Yale students to the sextette.

As the story went, these young men had seen *Florodora* in tryouts in New Haven. When they heard of its difficulties in New York, they travelled to the city to greet the sextette with standing ovations during their scene. In fact, according to one account, they regularly sang along with the men who danced with the sextette. Casino choreographer George Lederer hinted that the Yale involvement was the work of a clever press agent. But whatever its motivation, the ploy worked. Broadway men-about-town like Diamond Jim Brady, Stanford White, and Frederick Gebhard ordered standing tickets to the show, and the sextette was on its way to its singular success. Indeed, it was said that Stanford White once sat through *Florodora* for forty consecutive nights.[14]

In time-honored fashion, the six chorus girls were inundated nightly with bouquets containing money and jewels. Wealthy men lined the corridors outside their dressing rooms to take them to after-show suppers, particularly to Rector's, the most famous of the Lobster Palaces and the one that catered particularly to the theatrical community. There they could count on the presence of reporters and photographers to note their every move. Most important, however, all six of the original sextette married millionaires, and most did so shortly after the opening. Indeed, even Freddy Gebhard, who in his youth had been the notorious lover of Lillie Langtry during her 1883 tour, married a member of the sextette. Such fame and fortune seemed so easily available to the Florodora girls that there was a continual turnover in the sextette's personnel, as individuals left for marriage or for better stage opportunities. According to one reporter, they were "goddesses, the first of their class to immortalize the chorus girl."[15]

The Florodora sextette was unquestionably glamorous. Yet none of its members had any particular acting or singing ability. During the sextette number they sang only one line. The men sang and danced while the women moved around the stage in uncomplicated patterns. Nor did they participate in the singing and dancing of the regular chorus. They were chosen for their beauty and their approximation to a type: brunette hair, a height of five feet four inches, and a weight of 130 pounds. They were often linked in their own day to the Gibson girl, but in fact their modest height, contrasted to Gibson's statuesque model, portended the emergence of a new model of beauty among American women. The point is, however, that attractiveness governed acceptance into the sextette; only beauty, not talent, was required. The sextette, whose members came primarily from working backgrounds, embodied a powerful American Cinderella myth—a belief system that was for women the analogue of the "self-made man" myth for men. Just as there were supposedly few limits to the success a man could achieve through hard work, there were no obstacles to the heights a beautiful woman could attain, particularly the financially successful marriages she could make. Americans found in the chorus girl proof that high attainment was possible for women: "Now, Mrs. Langtry," went a typical reporter's question, "tell me the date of your rise from the chorus." As Lillian Russell pointed out, although not more than one of every hundred chorus girls advanced beyond the chorus, every star had once been a chorus girl.[16]

That the chorus girl was basically a working woman was central to all the publicity about her. The emphasis was intended partly to counter the criticism of her supposedly libertine lifestyle—a charge that might inhibit attendance at her performances. But it also reflected the kind of woman the chorus girl was. All commentaries about her stressed her independence, self-assurance, even toughness. She was "slangy and happy-go-lucky." Humorist Ray McCardell, in his widely published comic drawings, pictured her as empty-headed and jolly, the predecessor to the showgirls Anita Loos wrote about in *Gentlemen Prefer Blondes* and to those immortalized in the character of Lorelei Lee in *Guys and Dolls*. More accurate was the judgment of actress and former chorus girl Belle Livingstone, who argued that her former compatriots were hard-working, cautious, and careful always to go out on the town with a crowd, for what they wanted was not romance, but publicity.[17]

The working-class background of most chorus girls, according to one observer, made them "street wise" before they ever entered the profession. Even if such was not the case, the nature of the occupation fostered self-reliance and independence. The *Ladies' Home Journal* was always concerned to discourage young women from entering the theater, and its exposés clearly showed the difficulties for young women performers that only a great drive to succeed could overcome. Although women in musical comedies received higher remuneration than other kinds of working women, the work was hard to find. In 1904 there were ten thousand unemployed chorus girls in New York City, and the *New York World* that same year gave even a gloomier estimate: for each opening, they contended, sixty thousand women applied. "Girls who can stand in line and look pretty are as numerous as labourers who can swing a pick," wrote Theodore Dreiser in *Sister Carrie,* the story of a woman's rise from the chorus to stardom.[18]

Moreover, it was commonly believed that business managers and music directors expected free sex; "stage door Johnnies and the bald-headed lotharios in the front row primarily wanted a short term consort," asserted the *Ladies' Home Journal.* Indeed, ambitious young chorus women constantly competed for the attention of the manager and the audience in the hopes of landing leading roles. Some probably used sexual relations with directors and managers to advance their careers.[19]

There were, however, other and equally calculating avenues to success, should a special talent for singing or dancing not immediately draw notice. One was through the columns of the newspapers, by creating a sensation that would draw public attention. Thus many chorus girls were "fond of doing and saying, especially doing, unconventional things." At times they even attempted "adventures that rightly belonged only to the leading lady—such as losing her diamonds or horsewhipping an overardent admirer."[20]

Such activities had long been characteristic of members of the acting profession. What was new was that essentially minor performers, the members of the chorus, were staking a claim to public fame and were succeeding. In the process they were broadening even further what had long been the importance of the actress as a moulder of women's values. And essentially what the actress—and the chorus girl—represented was a new, modern concept of womanhood, one that involved independence, sexual freedom, and an enterprising, realistic attitude toward a career. Actresses showed American women a new sexual and personal style. They parlayed their popularity into salaries greater than those of most male actors and even of business executives and professionals. They inhabited a world of sensuality and pleasure, where men and women were not afraid to indulge themselves in the latest dances, the latest songs, the latest fashions. They played a central role in Lobster Palace Society.

Sexuality was hidden in this world, and scandalous liaisons were only hinted at in the press, which otherwise eagerly covered the doings of a publicity-conscious group fascinating to the public. Yet its sexual underside occasionally emerged into plain view in such events as the 1903 bachelor dinner, which was attended by many scions of New York wealth and which the police raided amidst reports that an infamous burlesque dancer, Little Egypt, was supposed to have emerged naked from a pie. And in 1906 the trial of Cleveland millionaire Harry Thaw for the murder of Stanford White, famed New York architect and Lobster Palace regular, revealed the sexual proclivities of its participants, including Thaw's sadomasochism and White's sexual penchant for young, beautiful women. Evelyn Thaw, Harry Thaw's wife and a former *Florodora* chorus girl, whose supposed rape by White many years before had been the motive for the killing, detailed their doings in her trial testimony. By implication, White was not unusual among the denizens of the Lobster Palace world.

The appearance of Lobster Palace Society signified the ritualization of pleasure among the theatrical elites in a lavish setting familiar to Americans in department stores, hotels, and vaudeville theaters. The open connection between the theater and men of wealth lent legitimacy to the setting and to the group's public activities: dining, being seen, listening to orchestra music. In addition, its popularity, plus that of the chorus girl, indicated the coming of a new wave of sensual expression, particularly apparent in the theater. It was perhaps the natural accompaniment of what John Higham has called the new virility of the 1890s, the reassertion of masculine force in that decade. Ragtime and its accompanying dance, the two-step, appear tame today, but in their own time they were shocking. They were the first wave of the cultural rebellion before World War I that dealt Victorian prudery the most substantial blow it had yet sustained. And if ragtime and its syncopated beat seem an expression more of Higham's principle of virility than of a new sensuality, the so-called coon songs that entertainers began to sing in the 1890s, like the torch songs of balladeers of a later age, focused, in contrast to the era's sentimental songs, on the sensual relations between men and women.[21]

"Whoever christened the 90s the Mauve Decade and presented it as a prunes and prisms era is mistaken," wrote popular musical comedy performer Jefferson DeAngelis. "In New York City you could do anything, get anything, be anything you pleased." By the 1890s the emotional actresses, who had first appeared in the late 1850s with new, realistic versions of *Camille,* more and more expressed themselves sensually. Bent on securing fame through press coverage, Olga Nethersole became notorious for her torrid love scenes with her leading men. When in the play *Sappho* the hero carried her to an offstage bedroom, Anthony Comstock arrested her on the grounds of indecent exposure. Yet Nethersole, with the backing of feminists and the press, won the case on the grounds of artistic merit. Moreover, the most popular feature of the Chicago World's Fair of 1893 was the midway, where belly dancer Little Egypt was the star performer, her name synonymous with the fair itself. Within a year no fewer than twenty-two Little Egypts were dancing at Coney Island. The original dancer performed widely on the vaudeville stage, doing her pelvic gyrations, or *danse du ventre,* as they called it.[22]

Such public displays of sensuality became a major characteristic of the American stage in the 1890s. The first French farce—with its standard theme of husbands and wives deceiving one another—played on the New York stage in 1895. Shortly thereafter, living picture entertainments began to be produced on stage. In them, actors and actresses dressed in fleshings and, apparently nude, reproduced scenes from famous paintings. Such tableaux (without the nudity) had long been popular entertainments at private parties, but when producers had mounted them on the New York stage in the 1850s, the apparent nudity of the productions had caused considerable scandal, and the police had closed them down. In the 1890s they reappeared with no obvious opposition. Moreover, a host of plays about prostitutes—*The Degenerates, Sappho, Zaza, Mrs. Tanqueray*—became popular. Noted the *Denver Post* in 1900, discussing current trends on the stage, "At present, we are deluged with the vampire kind of woman Kipling described."[23]

Desiring to expand audiences and responding to the social purity movement, in earlier decades producers of variety theater had devised vaudeville. What distinguished vaudeville from variety was its dedication to wholesome family entertainment, needing no outside censorship. Now, a new kind of entertainment emerged on the variety stage, forcing vaudeville managers to reconsider their principles. Central to the new stage style were female French singers who for decades had sung sophisticated, sensual laments and ribald ballads at Parisian *cafés-concerts*—the French version of the British music halls. In 1885 the *Police Gazette* noted that a Madame Judic from the Parisian cafés had scored a success by singing smutty songs in such a clever, covert manner that Anthony Comstock had decided it would be futile to prosecute her. She was followed by Yvette Guilbert, the greatest of the *café-concert* performers, whom William Hammerstein brought from the Moulin Rouge in 1893 to promote his new Olympic Theater, billed as the world's largest music hall. In contrast to Madame Judic, Guilbert did not tone down the eroticism of her songs. One reviewer in the *New York World* wrote about her performance: "The fiction of American prudishness has been killed; the word 'shocking' has been eliminated from the dictionary. . . . Yvette has sung her songs 'verbatim et literatim,' with their Rabelaisian wit and their Zolaesque naturalism, and they have been applauded and encored."[24]

Guilbert turned out to be a temporary phenomenon, brought to the United States for limited periods of time. Such was not the case with Anna Held, whom Florenz Ziegfeld brought to the United States in 1896 as a permanent beachhead of the French music hall world in the United States. Ziegfeld had many talents, not the least of which was an acute sensitivity to the popular theatrical trends of his time. He had introduced strongman Eugene Sandow to the American public at the Chicago World's Fair in 1893. In 1895, he discovered his new star, a French singer of minor repute, whom he determined to make a star in the United States.[25]

In an age of ballyhoo, Anna Held's career was the greatest triumph of press-agentry. According to the *New York World,* she was the most advertised actress ever to have appeared in the United States. "Photographs were broadcast everywhere, columns were written about her eyes, her complexion, her mouth." Reports were sent to the press cataloguing the rare jewels that her admirers supposedly sent daily with floral offerings; the expensive items she purchased were similarly documented. Ziegfeld, who married Held, bought Lillie Langtry's old railroad car and refurbished it to carry them around the United States on tour; he devised a constant series of stunts for her that left the press-agent world gasping.[26]

The first and most famous was the milk-bath incident, designed to introduce Held to the American public. For several days after her arrival in New York City the ubiquitous American reporters following her noticed a milkman from New Jersey carrying gallon after gallon of milk up to Held's hotel suite. For days they speculated on its meaning. Finally, Ziegfeld invited them in, and they found Held cavorting in a bathtub filled with milk. Daily milk baths, she claimed, were the secret to her beauty. Under the guise of an innocent activity, immersed in a substance that was connected with maternity and children and that concealed her nudity, Held permitted the photographers briefly to photograph her in her bath. Such a shocking act was a new and clever assault on conventional morality. At the same time Held was the forerunner of the many actresses for whom the bubble bath performance would become an almost obligatory scene of titillating sensuality.

Anna Held played an additional role in the history of physical appearance in the United States. Lillian Russell, her occasional rival, incorrectly argued that Held was responsible for the vogue of thinness in the 1890s—a vogue that had diverse roots. On the other hand, Held was a direct precursor of the short, boyish female with a doll-like face who would come to dominate standards of physical appearance in the 1920s. When Ziegfeld first saw Held, he must have realized how different she looked from the Gibson girl and how much she resembled the French gamine—a model of appearance that Emile Zola had described in the figure of Rose Mignon in *Nana* and one that drew on the tradition of the soubrette, personified by Lotta Crabtree. Held was a "petite, winsome, fairy-like creature," reported *Vogue,* "having all the artlessness of a child combined with great cleverness." The linkage between Held and the soubrette, however, should not be carried too far. Held was a sultry singer, not a sexual dynamo, and she conveyed by innuendo what the soubrette traditionally suggested by brazen activity. Moreover, she had a voluptuous, hourglass figure, and the rumor was that she had had her lower ribs removed to achieve by tightlacing the smallest possible waist.[27]

Still, the resemblance to the 1920s style is there, a resemblance found also in the Florodora girls and in Eva Tanguay, celebrated as the greatest female star of the vaudeville stage before World War I. Small, but "vulgar, vital, wistful with a Peter Pan quality," Tanguay was energetic and carefree and freely used her body in sensual, flamboyant dances. In the 1850s the voluptuous British Blondes, figures associated with the lower-class theater, had heralded new ways of expressing sensuality. Anna Held and Eva Tanguay—vaudeville stars of indeterminate social origin whose appearances differed as much from the Gibson girl as from Lillian Russell—represented the expression in physical appearance of another rebellion against prevailing Victorian strictures, and they did so well before the decade of the 1920s.[28]

II

The new woman included a variety of types drawn from the spectrum of the American class structure. She could be found among athletes, college students, reformers, and businesswomen. What characterized her was a new self-assertion and vigor and a new sensual behavior, a desire for pleasure that flew in the face of Victorian canons of duty and submissiveness. Throughout American society, women began to respond to new sensual themes expressed on the stage and in popular music and newspapers.

Given the numbers and types of women involved, no single set of qualities characterized the new woman. Traditional attitudes were apparent among women of all classes. Recent immigrant women preserved the traditional values of European peasant cultures, and these values remained strong even among young native-born contemporaries who, generally living at home even when they held employment outside it, were still enmeshed in traditional family arrangements and influenced by conservative religious and family values. Among the middle classes a new interest in domesticity and childrearing appeared, spearheaded by the emergent home economics and child study movements. New magazines like *Good Housekeeping,* geared to this interest, gained wide circulations. In her trenchant 1910 analysis of American women, Katherine Busbey was struck by the fascination that babies held for middle-class women. Breast-feeding was universal among them, she claimed; and even when they shopped, they took their infants with them. Traditional standards could be found even among career women living alone in cities—a group often identified by contemporaries as most typical of the new woman. Despite the popular belief that these women lived gay and irresponsible lives, one 1896 analyst claimed that the typical career woman, "motivated by the home-building instincts of her sex," spent her spare time in domestic tasks in her room.[29]

Nevertheless, what is especially striking is the extent to which new possibilities for personal pleasure and sensual gratification had a wide appeal across class lines. As much as American women deferred to traditional values, they also sought to enjoy themselves. No less than men, women were influenced by the new gospel of leisure that was undermining the work ethic, offering support to new concepts like annual vacations and shorter working hours and creating new patronage for places of commercial entertainment. The nouveau riche wife who made no pretense of real activity, wrote Lydia Commander in her popular analysis of American society, was as much a new woman as the reformer or the professional.[30]

The most elusive group in any analysis of turn-of-the-century American women remains the middle class. In contrast to upper-class women, they did not leave extensive memoirs. Nor did social welfare agencies study them as they studied working-class women. Yet middle-class women—and men—are key to understanding changes in behavior in this period, if for no reason other than the vast changes in composition that this group underwent. In these years new industrial technology and managerial needs created a huge number of new jobs whose holders could claim middle-class status. Robert Wiebe has written compellingly about the new sorts of urbane lawyers, educators, and executives. But there were also middle-level plant executives, insurance underwriters, and travelling salesmen who adopted the "white collar" as the symbol of emancipation from manual labor and as the badge of their claim to genteel status. In 1910 they numbered about five million people and had increased eightfold between 1870 and 1910.[31]

We know little about this group and even less about their wives and daughters. In his classic analysis C. Wright Mills wrote that "they have not emerged on a single level but have been shuffled out simultaneously on the several levels of modern society. . . . Types of white collar men and women range from almost the top to the bottom of modern society." We do not know if their change in status resulted in the adoption of new values and mores or in a revitalization of old ones. Insofar as analysts like Lydia Commander and Katherine Busbey are correct, both a retreat into the comforting traditionalism of domesticity and a movement toward participation in the new institutions of pleasure could be observed among these women. It is revealing of the values of these people that some of the most penetrating—albeit brief—analyses of them have been written by historians of entertainment, who have encountered them as audiences at vaudeville houses and as vacationers at seaside resorts and amusement parks. Analysts of the rising divorce rate commonly found its primary cause in the growth of a new pleasure ethic under which women in particular would no longer tolerate unsatisfactory relationships.[32]

Surveying the "new middle class," one commentator noted that a wide range of women, whose husbands' incomes ranged from $6,000 a year to several million, constituted a new leisure class. They spent their time, she contended, at shops, manicurists, hairdressers, and theater matinées. Divorce analyst Anna Rogers described what she called the "fashionable young matron of today," characterized by "youthful attire, an 'assisted' complexion, slang, cocktails, and cigarettes." Living in Tenafly, New Jersey, a New York suburb in which the new middle class clustered, Elizabeth Cady Stanton worried about similar behavior she witnessed among young wives. In his trenchant analysis of the vaudeville theater, Albert MacClean has written that the tastes of the new white-collar group differed from genteel tastes. "They were faddish and volatile; they sought sensation; they supported yellow journalism."[33]

The Progressive novelists scorned these new middle-class women, describing them in pejorative terms before moving on to their preferred upper-class protagonists. Richard Harding Davis felt the exemplars of bad taste, for example, were the women from Harlem (then a white middle-class district) who "like bargain counters, and who eat chocolate meringue for lunch, and then stop in at a continuous [vaudeville] performance." Constance Cary Harrison was even more scathing. These middle-class women, she wrote, were of the class "that flood the shopping-streets of a fine afternoon, that perfume themselves with cheap scents, struggle over bargain-counters, and indoors read 'society columns,' dreaming of an El Dorado wherein their husbands or fathers may, by some lucky fluke, lift them up to be a part of this coveted social whirl."[34]

In addition to middle-class women supported by husbands and fathers, numbers of urban career women living on their own salaries also exhibited indulgent, pleasure-seeking behavior. Many analysts reported that young career women in New York City travelled freely around the city, even after dark, and that they went alone with beaux to fashionable restaurants after the theater. In line with such then unconventional behavior, these career women were popularly called "bachelor girls." It was a complimentary term, reflecting society's acknowledgment that single women were not simply spinsters, but could, like single men, live irresponsible, pleasure-filled lives. With regard to the bachelor girl, wrote one reporter, "all the freedom and gaiety of the great city seemed to shine through her novel slang, her audacious opinions, her tales of lively suppers where the glasses were supplemented by tooth mugs and one spoon did for three."[35]

Yet despite the seeming freedom of middle-class women and especially of the bachelor girl, there were limitations on their behavior. Much middle-class indulgence either was private, like reading society columns, or, when public, was conducted in a community of women, at department stores or vaudeville matinées, for example. There is little evidence before about 1910 that many married women went to public dance halls or cabarets or even to movie houses—places at the vanguard of the emergence of freer and more public sensuality in the early twentieth century. Even bachelor girl behavior was limited. The restaurants to which a young man could take a "respectable" bachelor girl were limited, and sometimes the women themselves would respect convention by demanding that escorts hire chaperones to accompany them. In fact, there were agencies in New York City where such women were available. And, according to Albert Payson Terhune, despite the numbers of dance halls in New York City in the 1890s, there was none sufficiently respectable that a proper young woman could be taken to it.[36]

The emergence of a new system of values was neither simple nor straightforward. Some sectors of the middle classes embraced the new ethic of pleasure and individual expression wholeheartedly; others held back. Some middle-class women were willing to take up exercise and reform dress and even seek employment; yet they would never wear makeup or go to an after-theater dinner. Most stopped short at being Gibson girls; few were willing to become Trilbys.

III

The same mixture of restraint and rebellion observable among the middle class can be seen among the New York elite—a group that is particularly important because its behavior was so closely observed by the rest of the nation through the newspaper press. Until at least 1920 many social leaders patterned themselves according to Caroline Astor's rigid code. Grace Wilson Vanderbilt, for example, Caroline Astor's successor in the 1910s, was exclusive in her entertainments and scornful of innovations. Others, however, went in a different direction. Ava Willing Astor broke the barrier against women in sports, and Alva Vanderbilt, wife of the head of the Vanderbilt clan, scorned another convention by divorcing her husband in 1898 and marrying the equally wealthy August Belmont.

What Alva Vanderbilt thereby did was to shatter an elite moral taboo against divorce, which, seemingly successful, had not really worked at all. In their memoirs, members of New York high society protect their privacy, but their indignation makes them unanimous on one issue: the men of their class were not faithful to their wives. Caroline Astor's husband spent much of his time on his yacht entertaining chorus girls; Alva Vanderbilt, to shame her husband, divorced him in New York on the grounds of adultery so that his infidelity would be publicly known. Cornelius Vanderbilt remembered that his mother, Grace Wilson Vanderbilt, and her friends openly discussed the adulterous behavior of the men of their set. " 'Of course he has a mistress,' Aunt Belle remarked as matter-of-factly as though speaking of some gentleman's valet." In the 1880s Alva Vanderbilt had successfully forced Caroline Astor to grant her admission to the Astor circle. In the 1890s she had successfully married her daughter Consuelo to the duke of Marlborough, Europe's most eligible bachelor. Her charisma and authority forced her friends to recognize her divorce action, even though under New York's rigid moral code divorced women were supposed to be shunned. But Alva Vanderbilt successfully exposed what was in reality a silent acquiescence in oppression that, one suspects, none of them really liked. After her action others in her social group also divorced unfaithful husbands.[37]

In divorcing their husbands, elite women were no doubt influenced by the behavior of the men of their social circles—and of the actresses and chorus girls with whom their husbands and sons spent time. Although they might choose to ignore the Lobster Palace world, from which they were barred by propriety, society women could hardly be unaware of its existence. Not only was it reviewed in the popular press, but by the late 1890s society women were actually holding some of their own balls and parties in private dining areas and ballrooms located in several of the restaurants that drew an after-theater crowd.

There were other ways in which the separate culture of the males of their group met up with their own. Their dinner parties, for example, did not begin until 8:15 in order to accommodate husbands and sons who stopped off at private clubs or bars for the cocktails they could not consume at home or to visit the women they kept on the side. And so loudly do all sources on New York society lament the lack of men at balls and parties that one suspects not only hard work—but also exciting play—was luring them away.[38]

Rarely did the media of the day give any indication of the meeting of these two worlds: high society and Lobster Palace Society. Yet *Vogue* magazine, devoted to chronicling the doings of the New York elites, addressed the issue directly in a story in which a debutante lures her fiancé away from the influence of two chorus girls by appearing in a comic opera theater audience with two Bowery toughs and so alarming him that he reveals himself to her and thereby admits his behavior. But the message of the story is additionally revealing: even though exposed, he expects her to remain virtuous in her own world while assuming for himself the male prerogative of operating in both societies.[39]

The independent action of the heroine in *Vogue*'s story is indicative of a growing rebellion among New York society women, who gradually seized the privileges long held by the men of their circle. Clever commercial entrepreneurs, anxious to secure their patronage, helped ease the transition for them. The building of the Waldorf Hotel in 1892, erected with Astor money, and its expansion in 1896 into the Waldorf-Astoria, designed to embody the utmost elegance with its luxurious Palm Court for dining and its Peacock Alley for display, brought women into a public restaurant for dining. Ava Willing Astor, who divorced her husband in 1907, was caught out late at night after an evening spent in the company of her group of male admirers. She successfully challenged the prohibition against women's registering alone at a hotel by demanding and receiving a room for the night at the Waldorf. In 1907 she was a primary force behind the building of the New York City Colony Club, the first dining and sports club for elite women in a city that for decades had boasted innumerable exclusive men's clubs. Other society women in small, but nonetheless indicative, gestures smoked cigarettes in public or took out powder puffs and lip rouges and deliberately made up their faces.

Such public acts signified a change in private behavior as well. Many sources indicate that flirtations between older married women and younger men became common by the 1890s and that for an older woman to have a younger lover became a mark of achievement. By the early twentieth century memorialist Peter Cassill charged that a group of New York society women were violating convention "with complete indifference to press and public."[40]

Prominent among the flamboyant society women was Mamie Fish who, bored with elite society, began holding parties that parodied the entertainments of her stuffier peers. She assembled a throng to meet a visiting Spanish grandee and brought in a monkey; on another occasion her male accomplice, Harry Lehr, impersonated the tsar of Russia. She dispensed with the practice of separating men and women after dinner, invited theatrical celebrities to her parties, and limited the amount of time spent dining. Fish was probably faithful to her husband; at any rate Harry Lehr was homosexual. But Fish, restless and ambitious, was determined to be in the vanguard of modernity. By the 1910s she challenged the last bastion of elite conservatism: the graceful ball, with its waltzes and cotillions. She began giving dancing parties at Sherry's, with black bands playing ragtime and couples doing the new dances that were sweeping the nation. "Coon breakdowns," they were called.[41]

The three novels that Edith Wharton wrote about the world of New York wealth in which she was raised constitute a major record of elite behavior from the 1870s to the 1910s. *The Age of Innocence* focuses on the 1870s and details a rigid social hierarchy and regimented social rules. *The House of Mirth* deals with the 1890s and describes a growing split between public behavior, still decorous, and private behavior, now ruled by individuals who follow their own inclinations.

In *The Custom of the Country*, set during the first decades of the twentieth century, the old rules have broken down in the public sphere as well as the private one. In this novel old New York society is routed, defeated by its lack of spirit in the face of the superior vitality of the materialistic, amoral modern world. Undine Spragg, the shallow and self-centered heroine, symbolizes this new world. She is the Circe that American culture and the Cinderella mythology assume represents every woman's dream: the woman who is so beautiful that no man can resist her. She is, tellingly, the daughter of a millionaire who has made his fortune through a new process for curling women's hair. She rejects the men who love her until she meets a man whose crass materialism matches her own. As the wife of a new millionaire, she is unrepentant at the end of the book, even though her callousness has resulted in the suicide of her first husband, a member of the New York elite who cannot come to grips with the materialism and loosened morality that Undine embodies. But by then, in Wharton's view, the old codes of behavior have been shattered. Only among strict adherents of the old morality, for example, is it considered scandalous any longer for women to be seen alone with men in Lobster Palaces. "Almost everyone in

Ralph's set would agree that it was luck for a girl from Apex to be started by Peter van Degen at a Café Martin dinner." And "Ralph's set" was drawn from among the young of the most exclusive New York families.[42]

The breakdown of upper-class prudery was a slow process, involving the actions of innovators like Alva Vanderbilt and Mamie Fish, the example of errant husbands, the appeal of the huge fortunes of the newly wealthy whose values did not mesh with older ideals, the glare of publicity in which the elite lived and for which they came to vie. The radical departure of some artistic styles, such as the esthetic dancing of Isadora Duncan, also played a role, for she was popular among the New York elite. Among them Duncan's free movements were the natural successor to Delsarte's controlled ones, and her emancipated lifestyle did not go unnoticed.

Yet in the elite's adoption of new styles, there was always a certain hesitation. Grace Wilson Vanderbilt, as well as her aunt-in-law Alva, determined the values of this group. When a *danse du ventre* was added to the characterization of the title role in the opera *Salome* at the Metropolitan Opera House, a major scandal ensued, and Anthony Comstock aligned with the conservative elite to close down the production. Yet there was no attempt to suppress the scores of *Salome* imitators (Eva Tanguay being the most popular among them) who subsequently appeared on the vaudeville stage in a reincarnation of the Little Egypt fad of the 1890s. The Metropolitan Opera House represented elite culture, and innovations there were considered dangerous; vaudeville and variety were for the middle and lower classes, and incursions there on conservative standards were permitted. Nor did elite women take up public dancing until 1911, when the cabarets first appeared. And, although some young members of the elite went to the cabarets, Julia Hoyt, a well-publicized New York beauty, remembered the consternation she caused by going to see Florence and Maurice Walton dance, even though she was chaperoned, did not herself dance, and did not stay late. The New York elite remained protective of the young, beautiful women who represented it before the public.[43]

IV

In her autobiography, anthropologist Margaret Mead described how her well-to-do mother divided the world into three kinds of people: "fine people"; "people with some background"; and "ordinary people." Ordinary people were those who "let their children chew gum, read girls' and boys' books, drink ice cream sodas, and go to Coney Island or Willow Grove, where they mingled with the 'common herd.'" Although Mead's mother's

remark was infused with an elite bias, her perception about the differing behavior of American social classes was common in the hundreds of analyses
of working-class behavior written by Progressive reformers, even in those
analyses written by reformers who assumed working-class identities and
lived among their subjects. Dorothy Richardson, whose depiction of her life
as a working women in the early 1900s is among the most insightful, was
shocked by such differences between herself and her worker associates.
Where she paid careful attention to propriety, most of them had no such
concern. Where she planned for the future, they lived for the moment.
Richardson's perceptions indicate that the new kinds of free behavior that
would become characteristic of American mores in the 1920s were apparent
among sectors of American working women in the 1890s and 1900s.[44]

Middle-class families transmitted their values through home, church,
and school, monitored by parents, teachers, and the general community
concern for righteousness. But the crowded conditions of tenement life dictated that city streets and commercial institutions of pleasure often became
the places where young working-class working women spent their leisure
time, learning their values at soda fountains and saloons, at neighborhood
variety theaters or movie houses, at Coney Island and the amusement parks
at the end of trolley lines, at dance halls. "We see thousands of girls walking
up and down the streets on a pleasant evening," wrote Jane Addams, "with
no place to catch a sight of pleasure . . . save as these lurid places provide
it."[45]

The commercial mass culture that appealed to people's sensual instincts
and their desire to escape the difficult realities of their day-to-day lives permeated the city and occasioned the anger of reformers like Addams, who
realized the extent to which commercial entertainment had already captured
the mass working-class market before Progressive reformers launched their
campaigns for parks and playgrounds, for dances that would reflect ethnicity
and not eroticism, for movies that were wholesome and not, as the early variety, often lascivious. While Anthony Comstock and the other social purity reformers had concentrated on pornography and nudity, on halting the
regulation of prostitution and raising the age of consent laws, new forms of
commercial recreation of which they seemed hardly aware had arisen in and
around cities by the 1880s.

Some of these new places of amusement, like movie houses and amusement parks, have been analyzed in detail and their erotic content noted.
What bears emphasis are the extent and range of urban commercial entertainment that challenged prudery and advertised sensual pleasure. In New
York City, penny arcades showed pornographic pictures and seemed particularly to attract young people by their bright electric lights, what the *Ladies'
Home Journal* in 1907 called "the prodigality of their illumination," espe-

cially compelling in an age when electricity was new and its use limited. If lights dazzled youthful eyes, sound bombarded their ears to the beat of ragtime and the coon songs. Wrote Jane Addams, "The streets, the vaudeville shows, the five-cent theaters are full of the most blatant and vulgar songs." At popular music counters in department stores, demonstrators pounded out popular selections on pianos and young men picked up partners for "dates." By 1900 Tin-Pan Alley, the New York City location of the nation's major commercial music publishers (originally on Fourteenth Street near Broadway) had come into existence, and its entrepreneurs, carefully attuned to the public taste, exploited a desire for sensationalism and sensual expression while developing innumerable outlets for their music. "There'll Be a Hot Time in the Old Town Tonight" was representative of coon songs. Jane Addams described as typical lyrics a song in which a young man went through the city streets and then to nearby New York beaches looking for young women he could pick up.[46]

Prior to the existence of movie houses, the dance hall was the most popular institution of working-class recreation. It was also a place where observers witnessed striking evidence of new behavior. Its history gives ample evidence of the breakdown of Victorian prohibitions. In antebellum New York City, public dancing had taken place at Jones's Wood, an amusement park built in what previously had been picnic groves. Some of the beer gardens, too, had public dancing. Yet the public dance hall early came to be associated with immorality, as a place where prostitutes solicited customers. Members of elite society, for example, participated in public dancing at the hotels at summer resorts, but only infrequently did they do so in their regular urban surroundings. Elite young men went to Apollo Hall, but they did so surreptitiously and danced with the working-class women there. Even among the working classes, some hesitation about public dancing developed. Post–Civil War sources discuss the popularity of dancing among laboring people, but the dances seem most often to have been carried out under the sponsorship of an organization: police or fire departments or local political, fraternal, or immigrant associations.[47]

More than anything else, the tremendous popularity of the concert saloon in the post–Civil War period made public dancing suspect. Concert saloons were entertainment centers that catered to male tastes, and, although prostitution was not carried on there, the waitresses were available for assignations after hours. Even at Harry Hill's, which was the most elegant dance hall–concert saloon in New York City and was renowned for its boxing matches as well as the patronage of famed sporting figures and other men about town, any woman who entered the premises was considered a prostitute. Thus the private sponsorship of dancing preserved the distinction between what was morally legitimate and what was suspect.[48]

By the 1890s urban entertainment had become much more complex, and the vast increase in city size made the concert saloons much less visible and less suspect among new immigrant groups. Saloonkeepers realized the profits to be made by opening a room with a few musicians or a player piano; they did not even have to provide waitresses, as they had in the concert saloons. To lure women who might be hesitant about frequenting these places, women were admitted free. In addition, from the days of their rapid expansion in the 1880s as the terminal points of city streetcar lines, amusement parks always had had dance halls. Women generally came to them alone or with female friends, and the convention was that any man could ask any woman to dance. As the urban dance halls developed, pleasurable activities in suburban retreats moved to the city.[49]

Too, by the mid-1890s there appeared new, exciting songs and dances that, demonstrated on the variety and vaudeville stages, became popular among young Americans. The *New York World* reported that from the Casino productions had come the whirlwind and the dervish and the sandwich drag; other dances originated on the Weber and Fields variety stage. Inhibited by tradition and propriety, respectable folk at first danced them in private, if they danced them at all. Alice Roosevelt, President Theodore Roosevelt's fun-loving daughter, scandalized Newport society in the 1900s by dancing the hootchy-kootchy; yet she performed her outrageous act not in public, but in the privacy of Grace Vanderbilt's home. Such was not the case in working-class dance halls. In 1897 the *San Francisco Examiner* noted that partners in these places were dancing in "drag"; in 1901 a variation of what would later be the bunny hug appeared. In Chicago waltzes and two-steps were popular, as they were in New York, where one observer contended couples were doing swings and dips. In all dance halls couples held each other closely, dancing cheek to cheek. "They're spoons on each other," wrote one observer.[50]

If we can believe contemporary commentators, young women who worked long hours at boring occupations during the day did not collapse with fatigue at night, but rather desired nothing more than to forget themselves in activities like dancing. "She will work all day and dance all night," noted the *Ladies' Home Journal* of the "East Side Girl" in 1899. Aside from YWCA and settlement house gymnasiums, regular physical exercise in the form of athletics and sports was not available to working-class women. Perhaps, as Mary Simkhovitch surmised, that lack was partially responsible for the popularity of dancing among young working-class working women. Too, the dance hall was central to a culture in which young working women devoted a large proportion of their after-work hours to seeking men. It was not always a question of looking for a husband; sometimes the quest was simply for someone to pay for recreation that poorly paid working women could not afford or to bask in the "prestige" of being with a man. "No amusement is complete," wrote one analyst, "in which 'he' is not a factor."[51]

Thus, one suspects, working women were often forward in their behavior in trying to attract men. And, although many sources report that they did their looking in tandem with women friends, doubling up was as much for companionship as for protection. The conventions of working-class pairing could be complex. At Coney Island it was expected that women would pick up men who would pay for their entertainment, but that they would avoid having their new companions escort them home, for such companionship obligated the recipient to a physical relationship with her benefactor. "When a girl is both lucky and clever, she frees herself from her self-selected escort before home-going time, and finds a feminine companion in his place for the midnight ride in the trolley. When she is not clever, some one of her partners of the evening may exact tribute for 'standing treat.' Then the day's outing costs more than carfare."[52]

By the late nineteenth century, such unrestrained behavior was reflected in new words in common usage. By the 1880s the "masher," or the man who tried to attract single women on city streets or in theaters or dance halls, seemed so ubiquitous that the slang word was commonly used by all classes. By the early twentieth century, the term "to date" with its implication of a private, unsupervised experience in public places had come into existence; by then the term "pick up" was in widespread use among the working classes.[53]

The clothes that working women wore also reflected their assertion of the right to pleasure without conventional restraints. The shirtwaist and skirt had become their work uniform. But for parties and even street wear, young working-class working women donned their version of fashionable finery, their "Cinderella clothes," as Dorothy Richardson described it. And, like the antebellum Bowery G'Hirls, their dress often parodied elite styles while copying them. Their clothes were gaudy and extreme, according to middle-class observers. When Leo Tolstoy criticized Jane Addams for the size of her sleeves, her only retort to this exemplar of the natural life and champion of workers was that the sleeves of the working girls she served were even larger. By late century, developments in textile manufacturing, particularly the production of cheap fabrics resembling silk and satin, had, paradoxically, made the pursuit of fashion both easier and more difficult. Whereas early in the century working women had worn silk fabrics indistinguishable from those of the wealthy, by late century they bought cheap versions that sensitive observers could differentiate from the more expensive varieties. Yet, restrained as working women were during the day in dull shirts and skirts, their use of bright colors and costume jewelry at night was an assertion as much of independence as of a desire to copy the elites.[54]

Not all working-class working women followed such patterns in dress. Upwardly mobile working women were as anxious to lay claim to their era's version of respectability as they were to represent modernity, and dress became a major means of differentiating between the various orders of working women. Salesladies, by all accounts, copied the fashions of their customers and abandoned exaggerated working-class dress. Secretaries, another high-status group among working-class women, also took care that their dress appear discreet and expensive, for good appearance was regarded as a major avenue to promotion. Upward-striving working-class working women in other ways differentiated themselves from their working-class backgrounds. According to observers, they rarely went out in the evening, but rather went to technical schools to learn advanced skills. They also learned more appropriate middle-class behavior there. For instance, tuition-free telephone schools for training telephone operators required that successful applicants, even before being admitted to the schools, speak softly and grammatically and avoid slang. Moreover, better-paid secretaries and salesladies did not patronize the same entertainment places that attracted their less affluent peers. When they frequented the New York beaches, for example, they went to Far Rockaway and not to Coney Island. "They had the white collar feeling completely," wrote stenographer Helen Woodward, "and they thought themselves independent and ladies."[55]

Yet salesladies, secretaries, and telephone operators were a minority among working-class working women, a large proportion of whom found their values within the commercial pleasure culture. Writing about working-class life in 1910, journalist Hutchins Hapgood celebrated the adventurous sense of fun and frolic of young, urban working-class women, whose character collectively reminded him of "a rather wild young man of twenty-one." Using what he called East Side slang, he reported that these young women "rubbered" about at night looking for men. But, he contended, they were always careful to protect their virtue; thus their rubbering was always done in tandem with a friend. Others, however, were not so certain that the slang, the dancing, and the free and easy behavior were so innocent. The working women about whom Dorothy Richardson wrote, for example, were of many sorts. Some lived with families; some lived alone. Some preserved an ethnic identity; others were Americanized. Yet most of them, in Richardson's view, coped with the difficult lives they led through fantasy and bouts of pleasure. They read the lurid romances in the cheap, yellow-back storybooks written by Laura Jean Libbey and others—stories whose plots centered around the love of a wealthy man or around a powerful male figure who threatened the working-class heroine. They discarded their old names to take new, romantic names from the heroines of the storybooks. Their language was filled with slang words that Richardson did not understand; they exchanged off-color stories and jokes across the tables where they worked. Some, according to Richardson, took to prostitution. They did so, she thought, not only because their economic exploitation as unskilled laborers made the higher wages of prostitution seem preferable, but also because they wanted the money to participate in the glittering world of consumption they saw around them.[56]

Field investigators for the Massachusetts Vice Commission reported that in every Massachusetts city sizable numbers of young women loitered around cafés and dance halls, waiting to be picked up by men. "To the total stranger," the investigators reported, "they talked willingly about themselves, their desire to 'see life,' 'to get out of this dead hole,' 'to go to Boston or to New York.' " In Baltimore this group was known as "charity girls." Numerous turn-of-the-century biographies report that sexual liaisons with working-class young women were common for young middle-class men of the period; the relations between college men and actresses were a glamorous variation of this type of behavior. When press agent Bernard Sobel as a young boy transferred from a middle-class high school in Lafayette, Indiana, to one in a working-class area, he was astonished to find that sex was the chief interest in life of his new classmates. Margaret Mead noted a similar difference between the middle-class and working-class young men and women in the high school she attended in the 1910s in Pennsylvania. In his renowned memoir of his adolescence in Wilmington, Delaware, Henry Seidel Canby noted how he and his male friends visited the nearby amusement parks at night, looking for the girls they knew would be displaying themselves. James Montgomery Flagg, a famed illustrator of beautiful women, had the same experience in New York City, where as a young man he and his friends would saunter up Riverside Drive, picking up "chippies."[57]

Actresses and particularly chorus girls, who had characteristically risen out of working-class ranks, were important models for such behavior. Like their male counterparts, working-class women avidly read the metropolitan dailies, which were designed for a mass, ill-educated audience. The last pleasure a working girl would deny herself, wrote one analyst, was the Sunday supplement, where she could find a fantasy retreat into a world of glamour, where actresses from working-class background achieved fame and fortune, where chorus girls married millionaires and beauty contests gave hope to the ordinary woman that she, too, might be touched by such glamour. In the metropolitan newspapers working women learned in detail about Anna Held, about the chorus girls, about Evelyn Nesbit and the Thaw trial. Nor was the lesson forgotten. Jane Addams noted how, when all the daily newspapers were filled with the details of the Thaw trial, she saw young working girls in the streetcars leaning over newspapers and expressing to each other their admiration for Thaw's clothes, her beauty, and her "sorrowful expression." She was one of their own who, despite all, had succeeded, and they tried to dress and look like her.[58]

"It is one of the obsessions of the leisure class that they set the style for the rest of the country," wrote Alice Duer Miller in a striking essay on cultural change in the early twentieth century. Miller thought this obsession was inaccurate, because the working class, not the wealthy, had been the innovators. In the 1880s, according to Miller, a few philanthropists had decided that some sort of organized amusement ought to be provided for the working classes, while entertainment entrepreneurs had realized the commercial possibilities. The result was "Coney Island, Revere Beach in Boston (run by the state), moving-picture shows, five-cent theaters, music in the parks, recreation piers and playgrounds, and cheap magazines." From the working classes, the new ideas about entertainment and leisure had spread to the young of the middle classes, according to Miller, and there they had effected a complete revolution.[59]

In the 1860s a similar outbreak of sensual expression had emerged from the subculture of sensuality to influence the nation's mores. In the 1890s and 1900s a comparable process occurred. And, just as the voluptuous woman had heralded the changes of an earlier age, the flapper—as personified by Anna Held, Eva Tanguay, and the Florodora girls—signalled the renewed sensual expression of the new century and indicated its working-class roots.

10

The Culture of Beauty in the Early Twentieth Century

As the twentieth century opened, feminist standards of beauty continued to vie with fashionable ones for the attention of American women, and the authority of each was furthered by dominant trends of the period. Inventiveness and advancing technology lay behind the development of new kinds of cosmetics and new ways of curling and straightening hair. Increasingly sophisticated marketing and advertising methods brought greater sales for luxury items like cosmetics. The growth of consumption for pleasure, which underlay the era's new amusement parks and dance halls, also played a role in undermining Victorian strictures against the use of cosmetics and in legitimizing the most characteristic institution of the modern commercial beauty culture: the beauty parlor.

At the same time the reform mentality of the Progressive era heightened the appeal of naturalness. Just as muckrakers revealed corruption in business and politics, they also exposed the shoddy and sometimes dangerous practices of cosmeticians and beauty parlor operators. Reformers who pressed for the passage of the Pure Food and Drug Act of 1906 were concerned not only about adulterated food and harmful drugs, but also about toxic ingredients in cosmetics (although cosmetics did not come under federal supervision until the 1936 Food, Drug, and Cosmetics Act). Moreover, a health reform mentality found expression in the nearly universal argument that natural means, not artificial ones, were the best way to become beautiful. Exercise, proper diet, and natural techniques like steam baths and massages, it was said, were the ways to a pleasing appearance. Coincidentally, the straight-line dress that Parisian couturier Paul Poiret introduced in

1908 came to dominate high fashion in dress. During the Progressive era the natural woman of feminists and health reformers seemingly carried the day.[1]

In 1899 the *Denver Post* exclaimed that the leaders of New York society had discovered "the secret of youth." How had they done so? By paying attention to diet, by exercising, and by taking steam baths and massages. How had Leonora White, California's most beautiful model, maintained her beauty? Even more important, how had she created it? The answer was that she lived a temperate life, got plenty of sleep, exercised, and watched her diet. Indeed, in the innumerable analyses of beautiful women in the popular journals of the day—whether these women were actresses, society women, or beauty contest winners—the beauty advice was always the same: live right, eat right, exercise, and you will be beautiful.[2]

In no era of American history until recently has physical fitness been of such importance to Americans. Old exercise systems developed by Dio Lewis and calisthenics experts vied with new ones, like those of Delsarte and Dudley Sargent. Many were faddish and designed to exploit the national fitness vogue. In 1902, for example, the *Denver Post* featured a series of "football exercises" that had presumably been developed by an instructor in physical education at the University of Pennsylvania, and ten years later *Vogue* satirized the diet mania by advising its readers to "pirouette while you peel potatoes" in order to lose weight. Even the water-cure treatment again gained a certain popularity, and well-to-do Americans frequented the sanitarium of Doctor Kneipp in the Harz Mountains of Germany for fresh air, exercise, and cold baths. Lillian Russell in her later years kept her public image alive by interviews focusing on her epic battle to lose weight. She tried every possible diet and exercise system and diligently reported them (although her photographs during those years show only modest weight loss). The *New York World* in September 1909, gave feature coverage to her latest regimen, which involved rolling over 250 times in the morning and which—in a typical Russell drollery—she confided had been invented by Turkish harem women.[3]

Newspapers and beauty manuals regularly printed the measurements of ideal women. Although the figures represented were plumper than present-day standards, one can discern a reduction in the size of bosom and hips after 1890 and an increase in the size of the waist. Again and again writers dwelt on the ample size of the waist of the Venus de Milo. Harriet Hubbard Ayer identified it as twenty-seven inches, although most sources promoted a size of twenty-four, a dimension considerably larger than the eighteen inches of the tightlaced ideal.[4]

By the early twentieth century, proponents of the natural look ventured beyond diet and exercise in their beauty advice. By then they argued in overwhelming chorus that mental attitude was central to physical appearance; indeed, that individuals could alter the way they looked by mental effort. Sometimes the advice went no further than the reasonable assertion that self-confidence could help a shy, stooped person achieve a straight bearing or that a happy person radiated an attractive contentment. Some writers, however, argued that through mental exertion women could actually modify specific physiological features. "If You Want Beauty, Think Beauty" was the title of a typical beauty advice article of the period. "If you could keep from tension of any sort . . . your neck would not be scrawny, nor your skin peaked. . . . If life were perfectly free to act in every cell of your body with equal force . . . there would be no accumulation of fat. . . ." If your skin was filled with vitality, "there would be no open, idle pores . . . to fill with dirt." "Every beautiful thought leaves its impress" was a typical sentiment. In 1910 none other than Lillian Russell contended that she was such a firm believer in the ascendancy of mind over matter that she read Marcus Aurelius every day. Lillie Langtry asserted that the study of Buddhism had led her to believe in self-control, which she called "soul beauty."[5]

Such notions reflected ideals that had been current in American culture for some time. Phrenologists and physiognomists of the early nineteenth century had argued that mind and body were intimately related. It was a popular folk belief, elevated into systematic theory by early eugenicists like Elizabeth Cady Stanton, that the human fetus and the developing child could be profoundly influenced by the emotional state of the mother and father at the time of conception and the mother during pregnancy and lactation. Cesare Lombroso and other eugenicists of the early twentieth century, drawing on the theories of the physiognomists, believed that facial types reflected individual character—an idea embodied in Oscar Wilde's *Picture of Dorian Gray,* in which the evil that the handsome protagonist has perpetrated finally appears in his own face. The Delsarte system of exercise was based on the assumption of an integral relationship between mind and body, as was the Christian Science creed. Of particular influence on turn-of-the-century beauty writers was a school of businessmen-cum-ethical theorists, led by Ralph Trine, who proposed a doctrine known as New Thought, in which, it was argued, self-control could produce success in business as well as personal life. Such mind-over-matter theories were a logical—if extreme—outgrowth of basic American beliefs about the importance of hard work and regulation of self.

Popular culture, one easily forgets, reflects in its disparate and unsystematic manner the common concerns of a people at all levels. Thus the literature on physical appearance in the Progressive era resonates with sophisticated themes of higher culture, provides insight into how the common thinking was influenced by those themes, and lays bare the ideas that had an especially common currency. Reform was the most important of these ideas, as evidenced in the universal support for the natural woman in the beauty literature. Moreover, the millennial optimism that permeated reform thought was strikingly apparent in the common argument of popular writers on beauty that beauty was not a benefit conferred by nature on a select few, but rather that it was available to all, that any woman could be beautiful.

The scientific advances of the age, which underlay the millennial rhetoric, were drawn on to support this proposition. "We stand on the verge of such a scientific upheaval," wrote *Harper's Bazar* beauty expert Grace Peckham Murray, "that little will remain of the old natural philosophy and chemistry." In support of this view she cited improvements in sanitation and the discovery of vaccines for epidemic diseases, which had decreased infant mortality and increased life expectancy. With such revolutionary gains, Murray predicted, science would soon conquer the mystery of aging and the secret of beauty itself. Coincidentally, she identified the business of beauty as a scientific pursuit—a legitimizing theme common in the beauty culture of the period.[6]

Among popular scientific theories Darwinism in particular was enlisted on behalf of beauty. Some Darwinians argued that all human beings ultimately would be beautiful, as men and women chose beautiful people as mates and passed this beauty on to offspring, while ugly people, unchosen, had no progeny. Henry Finck, a well-known music critic and commentator on Darwin, tried to establish what he called a science of comparative esthetics, which seems to have involved collecting photographs of beautiful women from a variety of world regions and deciding from the photographs what the universal standard of beauty among them ought to be. Finck, a traditionalist who wanted women to remain in the home, chose the steel-engraving lady as his superior ideal.[7]

Henry Finck was not alone in his use of Darwinism grafted to the optimism of nineteenth-century thought. The combination permeated the culture. Figures as disparate as illustrator Alexander Black, one of Gibson's imitators, and dress reformer Annie Jenness Miller familiarly drew on Darwinian notions in predicting the triumph of dress reform and the appearance of ever more beautiful women. To Miller, "fixed and unchangeable laws" were bringing inevitable social improvement; to Black, the "process of natural selection" dictated that beauty among women would increase.[8]

There was a political as well as a scientific dimension to the notion that all women could be beautiful. Just as Progressive reformers viewed their reform work as advancing democracy, so did beauty specialists see their goal as a democratic demand. As one author stated the oft-expressed sentiment, beauty was a "natural right" of American women.[9]

Moreover, in line with assimilationist views of the day, writers on beauty characteristically viewed the ideal female as an amalgam of ethnic types, as proof that the American melting pot could work. The argument was apparent in the long controversy over who had been the original model for the Gibson girl and in reporters' triumphant claims that Minnie Clark, of Irish extraction, or Loie Fuller's maid, half French and half Cuban, had been Gibson's original inspiration. The rampant nativism of the period did not influence writers on beauty, who welcomed an amalgamation of racial types and argued that out of the mixture of many racial stocks would come a higher kind of beauty, truly unique, democratic, and American. "To speak of an American type," wrote a representative author, "would be an anomaly. From all races we have absorbed characteristics, mental and physical." Exulted illustrator Howard Chandler Christy, "Never before have the selected individuals from all the races of the world been brought together under such conditions as to come to the best of which they are capable."[10]

The democratic rhetoric of beauty experts in the early twentieth century was not without a feminist component. The belief in the moral superiority of women—an ideal central to pre–World War I feminism—was closely connected to democratic beauty ideals. Both feminists and beauty experts argued that spiritual qualities were more important to creating and maintaining the appearance of beauty than were physical attributes. Both argued that beauty was potentially available to any woman, if she followed the proper ethical path.

Indeed, physical appearance had long been of concern to organized feminism. Since the mid-nineteenth century, feminist leaders like Elizabeth Cady Stanton had called for the advent of a natural woman whose face and figure would be shaped not by fashion, but by vigorous exercise and healthy living. The need for proper diet and exercise was an important theme in the writings of Charlotte Perkins Gilman, who herself had used physical exercise as a way of overcoming depression. When Inez Milholland rode a white horse at the head of a 1912 New York suffrage march, it was a tribute not only to her leadership, but also to her recognized physical beauty. Dancer Isadora Duncan preached a gospel of simplicity, freedom, and return to a natural life—principles embodied in the white, flowing drapery she wore, the freedom of her dance movements, her bare feet and flowing hair, and the classical illusions woven into her dances and her settings. Indeed, the need for a return to the simple and healthful living of the ancient Greeks was a leitmotiv in all the writings on beauty during these years and underscores the reform thrust that pervaded the work even of conservative writers on women's affairs.

Yet during the early decades of the twentieth century, organized feminists did not directly agitate the issues of women's dress or physical appearance. From the 1870s to the 1890s, for example, the pages of the *Woman's Journal,* the official organ of the American Woman Suffrage Association and then of the unified National American Woman Suffrage Association (NAWSA), were filled with articles about dress reform. In 1901, however, the interest ended, and dress reform as an issue disappeared from the periodical. In subsequent years, NAWSA conventions made no mention of the reform. Intent on suffrage and social reform, feminists did not attach the same kind of urgency to issues involving dress and physical appearance. The exercise battle seemed won, and insofar as women regularly wore suits, skirts, and blouses, the dress reform battle also seemed to have scored a victory. Yet from the vantage of hindsight, feminists incorrectly saw a victory where the battle had been only partly engaged.[11]

There were, in the first instance, decided antifeminist themes in the beauty literature of the period. One of these was the notion that to prevent wrinkling and aging and to preserve a youthful appearance, women must remain calm and serene and avoid mental and emotional exertion. Another was the argument that beauty was important not as a measure of healthy living or of self-respect, but as a means to secure promotion in a job or to make certain that, with the onset of middle age, women did not lose their husbands to younger rivals. Harriet Hubbard Ayer, for example, took up her later career as beauty expert particularly to help secretaries and professional women; for so long as women were trying to succeed in a world of male employers, she said, looks were more important than ability in women's promotions. In her popular beauty manual, champion swimmer Annette Kellermann, who was also a well-known vaudeville and movie performer, spoke of woman's enslavement as man's "toy" and praised the growing simplicity of women's dress. Yet Kellermann thought that women needed to pay attention to their physical appearance especially so that they would not grow fat at forty or "shrivel up at fifty" and lose their husbands to younger women.[12]

Such attitudes, which accepted a male-dominated culture rather than challenging it, were damaging to the women's cause. Above all, the notion that every woman could be beautiful was a dangerous concept, just as easily adapted to the ends of business as of reform. Feminism had succeeded in the early twentieth century because it had galvanized the universal American belief in women's moral superiority to bring women out of the home and into reform work. A corollary of that success was the identification of beauty with the natural woman as well as the notion that every woman could be beautiful. With the demise of the moral superiority argument in the 1920s, such an identification was seriously undermined. But the possibility that every woman might be beautiful, once raised, did not disappear. With its powders and lotions, its cosmetics and hair dyes, the commercial culture of beauty then became the major claimant to the means of beauty for all women. When in the 1920s women no longer were seen as possessing a superior spirituality, their outward appearance could be viewed as more important than their inner character, and external means could become central to improving their looks.

Perhaps there was nothing that feminists could have done, for by 1910 women were already extensively using cosmetics. Moreover, not only were the sexual liberationist themes of the 1920s already apparent then, but also the commercial culture of beauty was already effectively using themes of moral uplift and scientific advance to it own ends. To our modern eyes, the moral superiority argument of early-century feminists appears outdated and, with its overtones of asexuality, counterproductive to the movement for full sexual expression. Yet it had raised an important barrier to the commercial exploitation of women in the area of physical appearance. With its demise, the modern commercial culture of beauty scored a significant triumph.

II

In order to delineate the development of the modern commercial beauty culture and especially of its most characteristic institution—the beauty parlor—it is necessary to return to the 1870s and to the fascination with hair that became so powerful among women in that decade and continued until World War I.

Sometime in the 1870s fashionable women abandoned cosmetics and, after a lapse of a decade or so, once again came to identify paint with promiscuity. Almost as if in compensation, hair then became enormously important in the general definition of beauty. No longer was it sufficient to have shiny or wavy or thick hair. Rather, the beautiful woman of fashion had to have masses of hair arranged in intricate displays. Ultimately the effect could be achieved only by the extensive use of false hair. In 1873 administrators at Ohio Wesleyan University tried to ban false hair because the women students were spending so much time fixing their hair that they were not doing any work. But the attempted ban did no good, remembered Julia Foraker, a student there at the time. Even Foraker's history teacher— "thin, prim, forty"—secretly asked to borrow Foraker's switch. "No woman under 95," wrote Foraker, "was free from hair vanity."[13]

Among the best-known women of the age were the fictional Seven Sutherland Sisters, invented by a hair tonic promoter to advertise his product. Their thick, luxuriant hair was the central feature of the advertising posters that they graced and that druggists displayed in their windows nationwide. As late as 1905 three pages in the Sears, Roebuck catalogue were devoted to false hair pieces. The importance and duration of this fascination with hair are underscored by the fact that two of the best-known scenes in American literature revolve around a woman selling her hair. In Louisa May Alcott's *Little Women,* published in 1868, Jo March sells her hair to pay for her mother's trip to nurse her father, wounded in the Civil War; in O. Henry's "Gift of the Magi," which saw print in 1902, the wife sells her hair to pay for a chain for her husband's watch.[14]

Some psychologists think that hair is a symbol of sexuality. Indeed, the connection between the two has venerable roots in Western culture. One thinks of the fairy tale princesses, imprisoned in towers, who let down their long hair so that the heroes can rescue them—thus symbolizing the female power to cure impotence. Or there is Lorelei, a darker image of female sexuality, the legendary siren who sits along the banks of the Rhine, combing her long hair to lure boatmen to their doom. Lorelei herself is a prototype of the mermaid, whose luxurious hair is a central part of her complex appeal, combining the beast with virginal purity, the terrors of drowning with the purifying force of water. Or a woman's hair can be wholly dangerous and symbolic of her frightening sexuality, as in the classic Medusa story. Catholic nuns coiffed their hair to indicate their denial of sexuality; married orthodox Jewish women traditionally cut their hair and wore a wig to indicate their reservation of sexuality for their husbands. Our own response to the importance of hair as sexual symbol may be indicated by the fact that the otherwise unexceptional scenes in Alcott's novel and O. Henry's story have become so renowned. Why do we all remember that Jo sold her hair? Is it because it seems the ultimate expression of her tomboy nature, her social deviance? Or is it because she seems to be selling her virginity through the sale of her hair?[15]

It is possible that the increased amount of hair women wore represented an increased sensuality on their part. Yet it must be remembered that adult women of that era did not wear their hair long and flowing, that putting one's hair atop one's head was a declaration of maturity as important as lengthening skirts. Hats, too, remained as popular as they had ever been. By the 1870s the confining bonnet was abandoned, to be replaced by broad-brimmed styles, often decorated with flowers and feathers, perched precariously atop pompadours and held on by hat pins.

Nor did women leave their hair loose for bed. As the inevitable scene in movie depictions of Victorian women shows, most women—even married ones—braided their hair before they went to bed after brushing it repeatedly to make it shine. Or they put it up in rags so that it would be curled in the morning. At least one contemporary participant in the "hair craze" thought it was an outgrowth of prudery, not its antithesis. In small-town New England where Bertha Damon grew up, hair was regarded as a "good thrifty crop like corn we had raised ourselves." It was also naturally unruly and needed to be subdued—a typical "Puritan" exercise, as she termed it.[16]

The extensive use of artificial hair may also have been the outgrowth of a real health problem. At least one analyst of its origins traced its genesis to the Empress Eugénie who, by this account, had begun to use false curls and falls when she began to suffer from hair loss. There is indication that this health problem was not uncommon among women generally. Nineteenth-century beauty manuals invariably include a section on how to stop hair loss, and journals of the day are filled with advertisements for restorative hair tonics—for women as well as for men. It is possible that women commonly suffered from this ailment, one symptom of nervous disorder, improper diet, mercury poisoning, or significant changes in the body, like pregnancy, not to mention the damage women may have been doing to their hair by using curling irons and acids.[17]

Finally, the false hair industry, an especially vigorous branch of the burgeoning beauty business, fueled the growth of the hair craze by its extensive advertising. Like the cosmeticians and perfumers of an earlier age, the individuals who composed the ads for false hair cleverly appealed to women's needs and desires. Mrs. C. Thompson, coiffeuse of New York City, guaranteed that her hair pieces would stay curled "through the hot days of summer and damp weather, when one's own hair will hang limp and crimpless." L. Shaw of New York City contended that his Victoria hair piece, an intricate arrangement of curls and waves that covered the front half of the head, was a potential key to social success: "By means of a Victoria a lady is always ready for the drawing room." On the other hand, Shaw's Camille hair piece—named after Dumas's popular heroine who had died of consumption—was meant for "ladies who have lost their hair."[18]

The elaborate styles of late century and the difficulty of blending false hair with real were a boon to the hairdresser, who played no small role in popularizing the new styles. Henry Collins Brown dated the growth of "hairdressing parlors" in New York City to the 1870s and thought that they had arisen in response to a definite need: the time-consuming physical labor needed in the care of a woman's hair. Moreover, by the 1870s advancing technology and the professionalization of domestic activities were reducing household tasks. Increasingly accustomed to goods and services produced outside the home, women were willing to ignore early-century strictures about the immorality of male hairdressers and to use their professional services.[19]

The speedy growth of women's hairdressing as a profession in the

1870s is evidenced by the appearance in 1878 of the *American Hairdresser,* the first national magazine for the trade, and in 1888 of the Hair Dealers' Association of the United States. The association initiated the practice of issuing fashion plates of voguish hair styles throughout the year and of distributing them to magazines, thus furthering the influence of hair stylists over the way American women wore their hair. As early as 1878 *McCall's Magazine* contended that hairdressers had complete control over fashionable hair styles and that it was they who kept the voluminous and costly hair styles in vogue.[20]

Hairdressing establishments were precursors to beauty parlors, but hairdressers were not solely responsible for the latter's development. Rather, their growth proceeded from entrepreneurial efforts in a number of fields. And, in this case, the entrepreneurs were not always men.

In the development of the beauty parlor—a place where a comprehensive variety of beauty services are available—the sellers of false hair were initially the most aggressive entrepreneurs, perhaps because they realized that they could bypass Victorian reservations about public hair styling since much of the hair they dealt with was already coiffed. Thus in 1880 F. Goering of Baltimore, who featured himself as an importer of human hair, also advertised that he had available on his premises a Ladies' Hairdressing Saloon. Green and Lewis of Springfield, Illinois, and L. Shaw of New York did the same. The "Elite Mme. S. Flanders of New York" advertised hairdressing, shampooing, hair dying and bleaching, manicuring, and bang cutting. The services of Mrs. L. H. George of Cape Island, a New Jersey seaside resort, included cutting and shampooing women's hair and fitting a variety of false hair pieces, including wigs, braids, frizettes, curls, waterfalls, and toupées. The Maison Française of New York City sold hair goods, dressed women's hair, and carried a full line of "French cosmetiques for the complexion and other articles of ladies' toilet." A. Suber and Company even had bathing and Turkish bath rooms.

The pictures of these establishments printed on advertising circulars and cards often show large buildings, resembling stores rather than the small salons characteristic of today's beauty parlors. Pursuing what seems an analogy to department stores (popular places of women's recreation), many of the early beauty shops that had grown out of hair importing businesses were called "bazaars," as some of the early department stores had been. And at some point before the turn of the century, department store owners themselves introduced hairdressing salons, usually, it seems, by expanding the ladies' parlor, where women had gone to rest and to try on dresses. Such innovations provide further proof of the complex borrowings among various types of businesses that characterized the commercial beauty entrepreneurs of the period.

As a business, hairdressing was long dominated by men, despite the challenge of assertive women like the "elite Mme. S. Flanders of New York" or Mrs. L. H. George of Cape Island. Yet in contrast to hairdressing, a new calling associated with personal beautification—manicuring—appeared in the 1870s, and women quickly made it their own. Nineteenth-century beauty writers traced its origins to France in the 1830s, when a M. Sitts, King Louis Philippe's pedicure, or foot doctor, removed a hangnail from the king's hand. Realizing the commercial possibilities of this service, as the story goes, Sitts subsequently developed a system of nail care that he claimed was a vast improvement over current home practice. Under the old system, metal instruments were used to clean the nails and a scissors and acid to loosen and cut the cuticle. In Sitts's system, which resembles present-day techniques, the manicurist used only an orangewood stick (adapted from a dental instrument) to clean the nails and to push back the cuticle after soaking the hand in soapy water.[21]

After Sitts's death his niece took over his practice, and her intervention was key to the feminization of the occupation. Beauty expert Harriet Hubbard Ayer visited her in Paris in the 1870s. Like many successful beauty practitioners, this new leader in the field of manicuring spoke familiarly about the lives of her aristocratic customers, and Ayer returned from her sessions with this self-styled "artiste of the hand" feeling as though she had associated with royalty. Although Virginia Penny reported in 1848 that a Mr. L., the first chiropodist in the nation, had a thriving business trimming, polishing, and tinting the nails of women customers, other chiropodists did not seem to have followed his example. According to one authority, a Mrs. Mary Cobb introduced the Sitts system into the United States, and its popularity rapidly spread. Although as late as 1874 there were no more than two or three professional manicurists in the nation, in 1884 Emily Faithfull remarked on the surprising number of manicurists she saw.[22]

Perhaps it was inevitable that manicurists would be women, and their early assumption of leadership in the field was not the primary factor in the occupation's feminization. Delicate, well-kept hands were important to nineteenth-century definitions of beauty in women, but having men hold women's hands while they shaped their nails may have been too directly sexual for Victorian culture, even though by the 1900s male barbershops often had women manicurists to serve male patrons. Nonetheless, the prohibition allowed women to excel at a craft that, according to one writer on beauty, was "in greater demand than any other operation of the beauty culture." In fact, some elite manicurists developed their own beauty parlors, where hairdressing and other beauty services were subsidiary to their central emphasis on hands. By the 1890s, for example, Riker's Manicure Parlor in New York City occupied several floors of a building and included separate departments for hairdressing, electric scalp treatment, facial massage, hair dying, chiropody, and manicuring. In *The Custom of the Country,* Edith Wharton provided a vivid picture of the potential power of manicurists. Mrs. Heeny, a manicurist, was regularly summoned by New York elite women to do their hands and hair, and she was an important source of advice and gossip for them.[23]

However important they were before World War I, manicurists became subsidiary to hairdressers during the 1920s, the major era of the expansion of beauty parlors. Such subordination, however, was not characteristic of women cosmetics entrepreneurs, who maintained positions of authority throughout the twentieth century. Because a profession of cosmetician, in contrast to that of hairdresser, had never developed, women were able to hold their own in an unstructured field. Ellen Demorest was an important cosmetic pioneer in the mid-nineteenth century. Her most eminent successor late in the century was Harriet Hubbard Ayer, a Chicago socialite impoverished by her husband's bankruptcy who built on her own reputation for beauty and the example of the self-made men she knew in Chicago to establish her own New York City firm. Because of emotional difficulties and the machinations of a vindictive male associate, she lost control of her company in the 1890s. Eventually she became a *New York World* columnist, supporting natural rather than artificial means to beauty and criticizing the kinds of products she once had marketed.[24]

The basis of Demorest's and Ayer's cosmetic businesses was the marketing of creams and lotions. They were followed, however, by a generation of businesswomen who, although they often developed their own lines of cosmetic products, centered their operations in shops where they applied their creams and lotions directly to the faces of their customers. In this function they were the descendants of the male enamellers of the eighteenth century and the 1860s. With the exception of Elizabeth Arden and Helena Rubinstein, limited data is available on these women. But their shrewd business sense is evidenced by the fact that they generally called themselves beauty culturists or specialists and claimed to be scientists, more than artists, in the rejuvenation of the skin. Often claiming training in physiology and chemistry, the new beauty specialists represented themselves as professionals deserving the high prices they charged for their services.

In doing so, they were also influenced by major developments in the field of dermatology and by the appearance of a new group of irregular physicians who set up "colleges," "schools," and "institutes" where they practiced new techniques in facial restructuring. Like dentists, they claimed to represent a new specialization within the medical profession. Their techniques involved, for example, face peeling, first developed in 1886. Face

peeling, or skinning, involved the application of acid and electricity to remove the upper layers of skin in order to eliminate scarring or simply to
give a youthful appearance. The injection of paraffin under the skin was
used to round out gaunt cheeks and sagging eyelids, and surgical techniques
were available to reshape noses and to perform rudimentary face lifts to
eliminate wrinkles. Most of the accounts of these dermatological institutes
come from muckrakers who considered the techniques dangerous and the
practitioners charlatans. Yet in full-page ads in the *Metropolitan Magazine,*
the John H. Woodbury Dermatological Institute, with its headquarters in
New York City and branches in Boston, Philadelphia, Chicago, and St.
Louis, announced that its doctors had treated many people, including President Grover Cleveland, for excess flesh. In addition, the institute personnel
could tie ears back, remove wrinkles, reshape noses, and tone down high
cheekbones. As many of the major actresses of the period reached middle
age, they underwent face skinning, which was especially popular.[25]

In the late nineteenth century, beauty as a business was in the process
of formation, and its various practitioners borrowed widely from one another as they vied for preeminence. Critics contended that many beauty parlor operators practiced face skinning and injected paraffin with even less
training than the "professors of dermatology." Whatever the truth of their
criticism, biographies of Helena Rubinstein and Elizabeth Arden, for example, make clear that they did not use toxic substances in their cosmetics nor
did they offer services for which their staffs were not trained. Before Rubinstein opened her London salon, she studied dermatology in Paris with a renowned dermatologist. Both Rubinstein and Arden were convinced that
they had dedicated their lives to the promotion of beauty—which they saw
as a worthy goal. And Rubinstein's medical studies were not necessarily unusual among beauty practitioners. Anna D. Adams, a specialist interviewed
by a popular journal entitled *Woman Beautiful,* began her career in the 1880s
as a surgeon. But she met such prejudice against women in medicine that
she became a professor of chemistry and took up the skin as her research
specialization. In 1888 she utilized her previous scientific training to set up a
beauty parlor.[26]

The services of beauty specialists were not necessarily ineffective. Their
creams contained oils and bleaches that could soften and whiten the skin to
attain the translucent quality that many women sought. By the 1880s elec-
trolysis, an effective technique for removing facial hair, had been developed.
Moreover, by the 1890s specialists had developed a system of facial massage
that was the most important part of their treatment and that drew on the
vogue for body massage first utilized by S. Weir Mitchell and widely recommended as part of diet and exercise regimens. Before the renewed popularity
of makeup, cosmeticians were limited in the number of services they could

offer; thus they added massage to make their beautification rituals more attractive to their clients. And the stimulation to skin and blood that massage provided was undeniably therapeutic.

The treatment at beauty culture establishments soon became complex. In 1908 *Woman Beautiful* described a new process for treating wrinkles. The technique began with a thorough cleansing of the face with distilled water. Then cream was smoothed in and wiped off, and a cooling lotion was applied. A careful massage of the face was followed by the application of wrinkle remover—a thick white paste painted on the neck and face and left to dry for half an hour. Once the wrinkle remover was taken off, face cream was again smoothed in, and the client sat for a time under a red light, to be certain the cream fully lubricated the skin. Another massage followed, and then the face was cleansed with astringent lotion. Finally, powder was dusted on. For the massage the operator used an electric vibrator—an example of the widespread use of electrical gadgets in these treatments as a way of further legitimation through identification with science and technology.[27]

As early as 1893 an observer in *Harper's Bazar* noted that "the culture of beauty has grown immensely during the past few years." The expansion, she thought, was largely due to the authority asserted by the new beauty specialists. "Public opinion, aided by masseuses, hairdressers, complexion specialists, and manicure and pedicure professors, has undergone a great change in the last few years." By the first decade of the twentieth century the beauty parlor in its modern form was in existence, and the familiar name was in widespread use. Sometimes manicurists were the pivotal figures in these shops; more often hairdressers and cosmeticians dominated. By then, although the arranging of false hair was still a substantial part of the services hairdressers provided, they had developed other techniques difficult for women to perform at home. One of these was marcelling, a process for producing waves in the hair with a curling iron that Frenchman Marcel Gateau had developed in the 1870s and that required a skilled operator for best results. In addition, Alexandre Godefrey had invented a hot-blast hair dryer that greatly reduced the time needed to dry the hair after shampooing. Expensive and bulky, it was not an item that women were likely to buy for the home. Finally, in 1906 Charles Nessler invented the permanent wave machine, but it did not come into widespread use until the 1920s, when artificial hair was no longer popular.[28]

In 1903 beauty writer Anne O'Hagan asserted that manicuring establishments were "almost as thick upon the city streets as the saloons." In 1909 the *American Magazine* contended that there were "thousands" of beauty parlors in American cities; Chicago alone had more than sixty beauty shops along several blocks of downtown State Street. Primarily staffed by women, they catered to women of all income levels. In them, wrote one ob-

server, there was a "professional hierarchy": "The royal favorites may touch
the face. The ladies-in-waiting may handle the hair; the maids of honor do
the nails." In this fictionalized description, however, a Mr. Spoots, "the artist who arranges coiffeurs," was brought in for special consultations. Other
observers reported that the hairdressers were male and mostly French in nationality, especially in expensive shops.[29]

Yet at the intermediate level women more and more were coming to
dominate the beauty business. In 1908 *Woman Beautiful* offered figures to
show that female hairdressers in most beauty parlors were swiftly replacing
"professors." By 1890 approximately 9,000 women hairdressers existed
throughout the nation; there were 18,000 by 1900 and 36,000 by 1907.
Woman Beautiful counted an additional 25,000 manicurists in 1907 and
30,000 specialists in face massage and skin culture. One beauty writer in
1910 recommended the beauty business as offering excellent careers for
women and contended that the salaries were significantly higher than in
many comparable occupations, including nursing.[30]

Shrewd beauty shop owners realized the psychology of the service they
performed. Their decors were often luxurious, with mirrors, dim lights, and
delicate scents in the air. Elizabeth Arden filled hers with antiques and used
the word "salon" rather than "parlor" or "shop" to give a high-class, foreign
tone to her enterprise. In some the decor was natural, with green carpets to
simulate grass and flowers and leaves as decorations. *Woman Beautiful* contended that beauty parlors generally had white, enamelled furniture to give
them the hygienic look of hospitals and to boost beauty operators' claims to
scientific expertise. All paid careful attention to customer relations. Clever
operators gave special attention to regular clients and made the occasional
visitor feel as though she was missing the excitement and authority of being
part of the powerful culture of beauty located within the beauty shop.
Beauty parlor operators, according to one analyst, called their patrons "clients" rather than "customers," referred to Cleopatra constantly, and on all
windows displayed "the sorcery of the word scientific."[31]

The popularity of the beauty parlor furthered the growing use of cosmetics—a development occasioned by women's new assertiveness, the
growth of the pleasure ethic, and the astuteness of commercial beauty entrepreneurs. In England, according to one fashion historian, cosmetics were
widely used in the 1890s in imitation of Queen Alexandra, who wore
makeup at night. In the United States, however, the return to paint lagged
by a decade. Yet by 1900 rouge was in sufficient demand that several brands
were advertised in the Sears catalogue. In 1908 one etiquette writer counselled that it was permissible for women to use rouge sticks and powder
puffs openly at the table when dining out at lunch, but not at dinner.[32]

From rouge sticks to lip glosses and finally to eye shadow the movement was speedy. In 1910 beauty writer Elizabeth Reid wrote that "the mania for make-up has spread from the theatrical profession up and down the line, from the aristocratic lady in her private car to the saleswoman and the factory girl." Every restaurant, hotel, and store of any importance, she asserted, kept a supply of cosmetics in their dressing rooms or bathrooms for the use of their female patrons. Most of the exclusive beauty shops manufactured and sold their own preparations, and most beauty parlors, even modest ones, employed a cosmetic specialist or "artiste" to demonstrate makeup techniques to patrons. Cosmetics manufacturers themselves spent sizable sums on advertising. Most handbags sold, she noted, had specially fitted sets of cosmetic accessories, with a powder puff, a rouge box, and an eyebrow pencil.[33]

In 1910 a *New York World* reporter sat at a café window at the Forty-second Street center of the theater district in New York City to investigate the extent to which women were indulging in new styles of appearance and behavior. Although she saw only one woman smoking, she was impressed by the amount of cosmetics women wore: "Eyelids can't be painted too blue nor lashes too heavily beaded." Nor did women wear the new cosmetics only when at leisure activities. Settlement house activist Lillian Wald noted that many of the young women who frequented her Henry Street Settlement wore makeup. They did so, Wald asserted, because they thought it an important asset at work. "As for the paint—many girls thought it wise to use it, for employers did not like to have jaded-looking girls working for them."[34]

Yet in 1910 most cosmetic advertisements stressed that their products would impart a natural look, and shades of rouge and lip gloss were pale and pink. When Helena Rubinstein established her first New York City salon in 1915, she contended with some justification that American women did not wear makeup at all. On the other hand, Rubinstein wanted to perpetuate the myth that she was responsible for the vogue of eye makeup, a particularly heavy version of which she designed for Theda Bara in a 1915 movie, *A Fool There Was.*[35]

No less than the advocates of the natural look, leaders of the commercial beauty culture profited from the age's fixation with beauty and its interest in advancing democracy and self-improvement. Throughout the prewar period, beauty parlor owners were careful to stress natural rather than artificial means to beauty and to use feminist and democratic rhetoric in their advertising. "The cult of the beauty specialist," contended *Woman Beautiful*, "is the cult of decent respect for oneself, of optimistic belief in one's heritage of beauty and a desire to come into one's own." Further, claimed one enthusiast, "the added longevity with which humanity is being blessed is due to the physical care in beauty shops."[36]

Even the use of cosmetics could be justified in such terms. Novelist David Graham Phillips was not particularly sympathetic to the prostitutes and pimps about whom he occasionally wrote, but in Mrs. Belloc of *The Price She Paid* he created a complex figure in whose character the reformist and commercial themes of the age were interestingly intertwined. A former whorehouse madam, at the beginning of the novel Mrs. Belloc seems crass and self-serving, but by the end of the book she has redeemed her past and offered a lesson in personal self-redemption to the heroine, wallowing in self-pity occasioned by difficult circumstances. What has Mrs. Belloc done? She has spent her time and money improving her personal appearance—having her hips reduced, her hair dyed, and false teeth implanted. "Yes, I think I've improved," she tells the heroine. "That's what we're all alive for—to improve—isn't it? Most women are too lazy to live. They'll only fix up to catch a man. I'm improving, mind and body, just to keep myself interested in life, to keep myself young and cheerful."[37]

Attention to personal appearance may be a sign of psychic health. But the line between appropriate behavior and behavior determined by the exploitative standards of a commercial culture is a thin one. And even before World War I, when the ideal of the natural woman was at its height, the commercial beauty culture was increasingly able to exploit this ideal to its own ends. For example, as women increasingly wore abbreviated sports clothing and as hems rose and sleeveless fashions were introduced, women began to shave their legs and underarms. As opera star Lina Cavalieri noted in her 1914 beauty manual, American women had always had a particular aversion to body hair: recipes for the removal of facial hair were standard in all nineteenth-century beauty manuals. However, the process of extending the practice to legs and arms was slow. For a time, according to an observer, "some removed the auxiliary hair and others did not." But by the end of the war the practice was nearly universal. In 1918 the *New York World* carried an advertisement for Delatone powder, designed to remove unwanted body hair, and the ad featured a model whose underarm hair had been removed.[38]

Writing of her experiences in the United States during this era, Elinor Glyn, renowned in the 1920s for her writings that set styles in sensuality, noted that every American woman, young or old, went regularly to beauty shops. "It is difficult to exaggerate the importance of the influence of the 'Beauty Parlour' on American life," she wrote. Glyn, whose sister was Lucile, the British dress designer, was herself a part of the new entrepreneurship of pleasure. Yet like Helena Rubinstein and the beauty practitioners generally, Glyn was not troubled by the fact that the modern beauty culture came to be based on the manipulation of women. She believed, in fact, that the beauty parlor had been a positive force among American women because, she argued, it had aroused and maintained "a greater feeling of self-respect and hope amongst all classes." The sentiments, if true, were admirable, but one wonders about the goals advocated and the methods employed.[39]

III

In the early twentieth century, both liberationist and exploitative themes within the beauty literature are especially apparent in changing attitudes toward old age. Older women in the nineteenth century occupied a special sphere in which their clothing, behavior, and physical appearance were supposed to set them distinctly apart from the young; by the twentieth century these special categories no longer applied. Older women became freer to dress and act as they wanted. They also became vulnerable to exploitation by the commercial culture of beauty.[40]

Throughout the nineteenth century older women had met contempt as much as veneration. American society revered the image of the saintly grandmother who presumably played a key role in family cohesion and governance. On an ideal level Martha Washington represented this type. The "republican grandmother," who acted according to the canons of women's supposed moral vocation to ensure virtue within the republican experiment, was a real personage. But there was also the matron excluded from social pleasures, the spinster seen as crabbed and superannuated, the older woman described as lank, bare-boned, and unattractive in much of the literature of the day. By contrast older men could be statesmen and politicians. Since businesses did not have mandatory retirement policies, older men could retain their employments as long as they desired. Uncle Sam, an aged man, became a prominent national symbol.

Older women occupied an ambiguous position in the early nineteenth century. Yet the negative appraisal of their role usually predominated. For example, women were considered to be old at ages much younger than men. In the antebellum era the word "youth" was used indiscriminately with regard to men and was applied even to men of thirty-five and forty. Such, however, was not the case with women. For them, marriage was the crucial dividing point in their passage through the stages of life. When a woman married, she was supposed to signal her commitment to domesticity by giving up social activities like dancing, and she was no longer regarded as young. With regard to judgments about her physical appearance, she entered a state of limbo. Beauty in a moral sense was still available to her, but as Nathaniel Parker Willis pointed out, most people simply disregarded her physical appearance.[41]

Married women by virtue of the marital state were eliminated from the category of "youth," and by their mid-thirties women were considered old. Often married by the age of eighteen or twenty, by their late thirties women could easily be grandmothers, and it was in the grandmotherly role that society cast them. By age thirty-five most women donned caps under which they tucked their hair as a mark of grandmother status, thus symbolically renouncing their sexuality. Whether they liked it or not, women who were single or widowed were expected to move in with grown children and serve the household. "Our grandmothers took to caps, false teeth, and knitting before they were forty," noted a 1907 commentator, "and more than half their allotted years were spent preparing for death instead of enjoying life." At a point when a man was still considered in the prime of his life, a woman was considered old. Noted a late-century observer, "It was a hoary fallacy that women grow older more quickly than men."[42]

In the 1890s women's magazines were filled with articles critical of previous attitudes toward old age. They provide a scathing indictment of blatant discrimination marked by the romantic image of the contented grandmother who, as Jane Addams sarcastically put it, was supposed willingly to don her cap and cheerfully to rock by the fireside, knitting. Undeniably, before modernity brought medical advances, women's lives were hard. If many women by the age of fifty had worn faces and possessed misshapen bodies, it was because being a wife and mother involved difficult burdens. "Only those who have experienced them know the terrible exactions of those relations," with the ever present fear of death in childbirth and of the onset of incurable gynecological problems. Yet society, according to this analyst, was not sympathetic. While husbands in their forties and fifties were social and professional leaders, honored for their accomplishments, most people denominated all women dull by age forty. A popular joke among men was that "any man would gladly exchange his wife of forty for two twenties."[43]

Yet there was not much women could do about the prejudices directed against old age. To be Martha Washington, the dutiful domestic devoted to husband and family, was a comforting, but hardly exciting, role, yet it was the best society had to offer to most women. In 1851 novelist Caroline Kirkland published an eloquent attack on negative attitudes toward old age in Nathaniel Parker Willis's *Home Journal*. Kirkland focused on society's refusal to allow older women to wear bright colors or youthful fashions, on the fact that dress indicated age as much as any other factor. Behind this limitation, Kirkland thought, lay the fear that the elderly might become sexual beings, that older women might try to attract older men. The result was that old women—and sometimes men—became crabbed and censorious, exhibiting the kind of behavior that was expected of them, but into which society's rigidities had actually forced them. "For one aged butterfly, we have a dozen prematurely old and morbidly grave people, who seem to think that goodness and attractiveness are incompatible and amusement a weak, if not sinful, indulgence." "Of all the castes yet devised for partitioning years," Kirkland concluded, "this is the most offensive." And perhaps, as Kirkland implied, Victorianism arose partly out of the disjunction between youth and age and the elderly's need to assert some authority.[44]

As the century progressed, young women became more and more interested in personal beauty, and this, too, must have deepened negative attitudes toward older women, particularly since the dominant model of female beauty, the steel-engraving lady, was youthful. Older women did what they could to enhance their physical appearance. Late-century writers noted with relief older women's abandonment of the false front of black curls that many had earlier tucked under their caps, as if to deny the whitening of their hair. According to these writers, the curls had looked ridiculous. Observers early in the century had noted that many older women had unpleasantly gaunt, angular figures—a body type that may have reflected an attempt to copy the slim outlines of youthful fashion. On the other hand, whatever attempts at beautification older women made were often partial and halting. *Vogue* magazine contended that, although dentists early in the century could "stop" (or cap) decayed teeth, women over thirty-five regularly had all their teeth pulled because their concern with personal beauty was not sufficient to justify the great expense of the stopping process. Nor did older women always wear false teeth after they had had their permanent ones removed—again because of a combination of expense and of the acceptance of imperfections in appearance in old age.[45]

Yet there were countervailing forces. Literate American women were aware, for example, of the authority and reputation for beauty into advanced ages of French women of the eighteenth-century salon; indeed, some must have known that French people generally found older women more attractive than younger ones and held that a woman did not reach her peak of attractiveness until the age of forty. Furthermore, American women must have remembered the white powdered wigs their grandmothers wore, a symbol in earlier centuries of the power of age. Widows of whatever age regularly remarried, and sometimes there must have been involved some physical attraction based on personal appearance. In 1833 Eliza Jumel, a legendary beauty, captivated the noted womanizer, Aaron Burr, and became his second wife. He was then seventy-seven and she was fifty-eight. The remarks of Nathaniel Parker Willis and others indicate that older women in New York society in the early nineteenth century allowed their daughters to dominate social arrangements. But in Ann Stephens's popular 1854 novel, *Fashion and Famine*, the central character is a woman of forty whose wealth makes her a powerful figure in New York society and whose beauty is still so great that she almost wins the hero of the novel away from the younger heroine.

Moreover, indications are that a specific standard of appearance for older women existed, at least among certain sectors of the population. Based on plumpness, it was a model at variance from the way in which younger women were supposed to look. Thus, although it preserved the differentiation between youth and age, it also allowed older women a measure of attractiveness. We know of its existence from the many sources that criticized the thin, wan look of older women and thought they should be plump. Contemporary analyses of its extent and significance are hard to come by. But feminist Margaret Fuller, generally silent on these matters, was sufficiently annoyed by plump, older women to make specific reference to this model of appearance. Let us look, she wrote, at "a common woman of forty," possessed of "matron beauty." Fuller described her as a "coarse, full-blown dahlia flower," as "fat, fair, and forty," showily dressed, and exhibiting manners as broad and full as her frills or satin cloak. People observe, " 'How well she is preserved!' 'She is a fine woman still,' they say."[46]

Fuller's analysis, published in 1845, seems to indicate that the voluptuous model of beauty in the post–Civil War period may have developed partly out of a specific age and class location—namely, among older women of the upwardly mobile nouveau riche. Yet other authorities refer to the plump model for older women in more general terms and seem to relate it to the notion that increased weight brings increased contentment. Assuredly, all societies are interested in finding a way that their members can grow old gracefully as they pass through the various stages of life. Thus in *Miss Ravenel's Conversion*, a popular novel of the post–Civil War period, John William De Forest wrote of the plump model of beauty in older women as a general standard. "Thin-lipped, hollow-cheeked, narrow-chested . . . such are too many of the Boston women when they reach that middle age which should be physically an era of adipose." One of the reasons for Elizabeth Cady Stanton's popularity in the late nineteenth century was that her heavy appearance approximated this model of beauty for older women. Newspaper after newspaper commented on her pleasing appearance, which they indicated as the way older women should look. On the other hand, the press found the thin, taut figure of Susan B. Anthony decidedly unattractive.[47]

In his perceptive analysis of old age in the United States, Andrew Achenbaum has convincingly argued that demographic data cannot explain changing American perceptions of old age. Before the twentieth century there was no appreciable change in the percentages of older people in the population. Rather, he argues, factors in the realm of ideas and attitudes must be sought to understand changing views. Using literary, medical, and scientific sources, Achenbaum argues that a negative attitude toward old age emerged in the post–Civil War period, the product of the rise of professionals, who usurped the elderly's reputation for wisdom; of a scientific community, that was influenced by evolutionary theory and viewed the elderly as afflicted with disorders and not able to keep pace with an evolving world; of a corporate structure, which had no use for old people; and of the emergence of a fixation with youth.

Yet in the popular literature of post–Civil War years—in the fashion magazines, the beauty advice books, and even in journals like *Harper's* and the *Atlantic*—a different picture emerges. Here what seems significant is that the elderly were no longer viewed as old, that women of whatever age were permitted and even encouraged to act as they liked and to look as young as they wanted. These new attitudes pertained especially to a woman's middle years: no longer were women of thirty and forty viewed as old. It was "the Renaissance of the Middle Aged," as one observer called it. Yet the new attitudes did not exclude women even in their fifties and sixties. The boundary between youth and age had totally disappeared, wrote one observer. In striking contrast to the early nineteenth century, when women of elite society had retreated in favor of younger ones, the most influential women of New York high society were now all older in years.[48]

Behind the changes in society's perception of older women lay the separate forces of feminism and the commercial beauty culture, which in this case were intertwined and directed toward a common goal. As older women left the home to participate in voluntary activities or to take up careers, their forcefulness brought in its wake a different social perception of all older women. Elizabeth Cady Stanton's *Revolution* discerned a change as early as 1870, when popular author Fanny Fern wrote that because of the woman's rights movement and women's increasing employment, the dependent and unpleasant old maid of legend had ceased to exist. Older women were independent; they dressed well; they did not care whether or not they married. By 1900, stories about the exciting, independent lives of urban "bachelor women" affected society's earlier perception of old age, since these women were not necessarily identified as beginning careerists in their twenties, but also could be established women of older ages. The woman of thirty-five, wrote one observer, is now considered the most interesting possible companion. In the 1890s and 1900s famed feminist leaders like Elizabeth Cady Stanton, Susan B. Anthony, and Frances Willard remained vigorous into their sixties. It was impossible to identify them with

previous notions of grandmotherly behavior. Mary Baker Eddy founded the
Christian Science Church when she was in her fifties and continued to lead
it until well into her seventies.[49]

Constantly in the public eye, these vigorous women created a new
model of behavior for elderly women, one that, among other things, dis-
proved older beliefs that menopause was an illness that reduced women to
chronic debility. Cady Stanton in fact argued that the onset of menopause
had been a liberating experience, lessening her emotional commitment to
home and family and allowing her to embark on an absorbing reform career
away from home.[50]

The career and reform involvements of older women in the post–Civil
War years established women's right to age definitions similar to those of
men. But it was a group of actresses who especially advanced the claims of
older women to beauty. As fortune would have it, many prominent nineteenth-century actresses not only lived long lives, but also remained active
on the stage until well into their sixties and seventies, building their later
reputations partly around their abilities to retain youthful, beautiful appearances. Lillie Langtry continued her tours of the United States into the
1900s; in the late 1890s Lillian Russell launched a new career in vaudeville
when her position as a star of comic opera seemed slipping; at eighty Sarah
Bernhardt was legendary for her ability to play convincingly the part of a
young boy. One of the most famed elderly performers was Adelina Patti,
the opera singer, who gave frequent interviews about her ability to retain
her youthful beauty. "No tragedy in life is so awful to a woman as the realization that her youth is gone," Patti told an interviewer, "and that in its
place are the wrinkles, the dull eyes, and the decrepit figure of age." But, as
the day's media pointed out, Patti had developed none of these presumed
disabilities. In her sixties her face was unlined, her figure trim, her step
firm.[51]

When Patti and the others discussed their beauty secrets, they usually
stressed proper diet, exercise, and rest, in line with notions of naturalness
that were a strong part even of the commercial beauty culture. Yet most of
them, given the financial gains involved, could not resist endorsing face
creams and powders. And, although they themselves may have planted the
stories to increase press coverage, debates over whether or not prominent
older actresses had had their faces skinned were consistent news items, sug-
gesting to older women generally that they themselves might employ such
methods to preserve their looks. Thus actresses' assertions of older women's
right to beauty had a feminist dimension to it; at the same time some
of their actions approved methods developed by the commercial beauty
culture.

On the one hand, the dropping of age barriers for women in the area of personal appearance was liberating, but on the other it created new restrictions and new penalties. For it was not that the normal physical attributes of old age—white hair, wrinkles, sagging muscles—were seen as beautiful, but rather that the cultural prohibitions against older women's attempting to look youthful were dropped. Now older women could diet to look thin and exercise to look healthy. At the same time, they could dye their hair to hide gray, wear corsets to conceal excess flesh, put on creams and makeup to conceal wrinkles, visit massage studios and beauty parlors and dermatological institutes, where their faces could be skinned and wrinkles surgically removed. The slogan for Dr. Dys's dermatological products, advertised in the day's newspapers, was, "Dys laughs at time." His products, he contended, could moisturize the skin into a youthful appearance in an age when "it is an open secret that there are no more middle-aged women."[52]

One suspects that the striking increase in the patronage of beauty parlors in the 1890s and 1900s was an outgrowth of the search for youth among older women with the money to indulge themselves and the desire to try whatever remedy seemed promising. The dimensions of this search even *Harper's Bazar* questioned in 1892. Why was it that innumerable products were marketed for women to stave off old age, but nothing was advertised for men? The truth of the matter was, as the magazine pointed out, that age was not a negative factor for older men, that they did not have to look young to be appreciated. They could be deemed "interesting, wise, magnetic, full of various learning and various resources" and be attractive at any age. Women might have these qualities, but on some level their physical appearance would be judged and their approximation to a youthful standard measured.[53]

American society had come to approve older women's participation in public affairs outside the home, but such participation had not brought a new respect for the physical appearance of old age. Perhaps Americans in the late nineteenth century had become contemptuous of old age; and their disdain provoked the generational, frantic urge to look young. In any event, the commercial beauty culture played a powerful role in standardizing the connection between beauty and youth. To have conceded that older women were intrinsically beautiful would have been to destroy a potentially immense market before the exploitation of it had ever begun.

11

Men

"T he distinction of sex," wrote liberal Congregational cleric Horace Bushnell in the 1850s, puts men and women "in different classes of being. One is the force principle, the other is the beauty principle." Lillian Russell echoed his sentiments some thirty years later: "It seems the intention of the creator that men should be strong and women beautiful." In the nineteenth century the term most frequently used to describe a pleasing appearance in a man was neither "handsome" nor "good-looking," but "manly," for beauty was a category of appearance reserved for women. "In the male sex," wrote a representative author, "beauty is a defect. A man can scarcely be beautiful without losing his manly characteristics."[1]

Such ideas indicate the nineteenth-century bifurcation of masculine and feminine roles. Yet in reality it took some time for a dominant model of masculinity to develop in American culture. Throughout the nineteenth century a number of alternative models existed, and they remained in force until at least the 1920s. It was not foreordained that aggressive masculinity would become the dominant American type.

One of the curiosities of nineteenth-century prints and fashion plates is that the steel-engraving lady is occasionally accompanied by a male companion whose small stature, diminutive waist, and tiny mouth match her own. Indeed, foreign visitors and native observers through the middle decades of the century consistently remarked that the American men they saw, particularly in New York and other northeastern cities, were nearly as pale and thin as the women they accompanied and that, like their wives and daughters, men paid little attention to exercise and health. *Harper's Weekly* noted "the dyspeptic men, the puny forms, and the bloodless cheeks." Visitor James Burn wrote of "the almost skeletal forms and sallow complexions of the male portion of the population." In 1858 Oliver Wendell Holmes delivered an oft-cited attack against the appearance of American men. "I am satisfied," wrote Holmes, "that such a set of black-coated, stiff-jointed, soft-muscled, paste-complexioned youth as we can boast in our Atlantic cities never before sprang from loins of Anglo-Saxon lineage."[2]

In explaining such physical characteristics, contemporary observers cited the extremity of the climate in the United States or the prolongation of Puritanism, which frowned upon organized sports. Most often, however, observers traced the appearance of American men to their fixation with business. According to *Harper's Weekly,* Americans abjured exercise because of their "commercial spirit." Charles Dickens thought that American men all looked alike because of the "prevailing serious air of business." Spending long hours in offices, neither merchants nor the thousands of young clerks who aspired to their positions took time for exercise. Our devoted attention to business, wrote Nathaniel Parker Willis, is "health-impairing."[3]

Yet contemporary Americans did not consider the prevailing thinness and wanness of American men necessarily unattractive. Francis Grund contended that "an American exquisite must not measure more than twenty-four inches round the chest; his face must be pale, thin, and long; and he must be spindle-shanked." The type resulted from women's predilections, Grund contended. "There is nothing our women dislike so much as corpulency; weak and refined are synonymous." Like others, William Burns noted that the clerks in New York stores were all good-looking young men, chosen to attract women shoppers. In describing their appearance, he called them pale and languishing. "A straight-back and well-carried chest," wrote Nathaniel Parker Willis, "always means a soldier or a foreigner." Willis, an advocate of exercise and robust physiques for men, complained that a man's size was not deemed important in judging his physical attractiveness. Those men with a reputation for being "the handsome men around town," he wrote, all are judged in terms of their "fine eyes and complexions and good features."[4]

Such conceptions of the ideal male appearance arose partly from the contemporary popularity of Byron, renowned for his leonine head, fair skin, regular features, and body that he regularly subjected to diet regimens. In 1882 Londoner George Sala remembered that when he was young, a popular type of male appearance consisted of "chiselled features, great fineness and silkiness of the hair, delicacy of the skin, tapering extremities." This model of appearance had been known as Byronic, and Sala was astonished to find many examples of the type among New York males.[5]

The Byronic hero—sensitive and passionate—was a prototype of masculinity in antebellum women's novels, a usage that attested to the appeal of the type among women. Yet the Byronic image of masculinity was not created solely by women's preferences. Young men of the 1830s and 1840s established their generation's mark as "young America" and responded to

Byron's rebelliousness by copying his dress and behavior. They turned down their shirt collars and grew whiskers. Among college men it became the fashion "to drink gin, wear collars à la mode de Byron, cultivate misanthropy of the system, and manifest the most concentrated horror of seeing women eat!"[6]

Many observers of male standards of physical appearance in the antebellum years were critical of them. Yet such standards constituted a set of requirements that meshed well with both the prevailing commercialism of American culture and its underlying revolutionary romanticism. The thin pallor of the clerk could be seen to represent either his attentiveness to his work or his esthetic sensitivity. Moreover, antebellum Americans viewed the short, thin man as just as masculine and manly as their descendants would regard the tall, muscular type. We might view the Byronic figure as effeminate; Sala described him as "virile." Napoleon Bonaparte had established the masculinity of the short man. Prince Albert, who came to govern Queen Victoria with a firm hand, himself was short and thin.[7]

Power and force are central to modern definitions of masculinity. Although the typical American man of the antebellum era did not explicitly display such qualities in his physical appearance, they were evident in dominant styles of male public behavior. Men of the time displayed their vigor through the speed with which they moved and the concentration they gave to tasks at hand. Constantly hurrying, American men seemed to observers never to sit still. They arose earlier in the morning than their European counterparts: "Stores are open and business is going on briskly before our shopkeepers are out of bed." They stood up at saloons. They bolted their food with such speed at hotels and boarding houses that foreign travellers never ceased to be amazed at their crudity and their disregard for digestion. When vacationing at resorts, asserted two visitors in 1860, American men seemed not to know what to do with themselves, so accustomed were they to constant work.[8]

Moreover, men also asserted vigor and physicality through the widespread practice of chewing and spitting tobacco—a practice that remained popular until at least the 1920s. Such behavior was not new. Many societies have accepted various kinds of smoking and chewing as means of calming nerves. Others have used smoking as a way of ritually affirming group cohesion, as did American Indians with their peace pipes. But the nineteenth-century habit of chewing tobacco was distinctive by its results, which women in particular found repellent. Innumerable sources repeated David Macrae's descriptions: "You see people chewing and spitting in the streets, in the stores, in the hotels ... and in every ferry boat, steamboat, and railway-car." Spittoons were everywhere. "They occupy an honoured place at the White House," wrote Macrae. "They cover the floors of both houses of Congress, and the floors of all the Legislative Halls throughout the country. They abound in steamboat saloons and cabins, in railway-cars, in stores, offices, private houses, colleges, and even in places of public worship." Not only was spitting ubiquitous, but men were also casual in their use of spittoons. "Even in New England you see the floors of railway-cars traversed with heavy splashes of tobacco-juice, which have been projected with inadequate force in the direction of some distant spittoon; and at other times filthy with puddles of the same fluid, gradually thickening and expanding between the feet of assiduous chewers."[9]

The chewing and spitting of tobacco were a public form of sex differentiation. They were also an assault against the nineteenth-century version of proper womanhood, for in all cultures spitting is a form of contempt. In New York City in the 1820s Charles Haswell remembered that malicious men hid where they could not be seen and expectorated on the skirts of unsuspecting women passersby. Their casual vindictiveness underscored men's underlying contempt for the notion of female purity. Women hated the habit, but could do little about it. In contrast to liquor, it did not create alcoholics; it did not even necessarily take men away from the home. Rather, in a society where domesticity as well as feminism had become militant and the purity of a woman's person was reflected in the cleanliness of her home, it allowed men to demonstrate a dominant masculinity by symbolically scorning what women had come to represent.[10]

II

Whatever Byronic or commercial models of masculinity existed in the early nineteenth century, by the 1830s the muscular man of height and physical prowess had appeared to challenge them. The new model was embodied by Andrew Jackson: soldier, frontiersman, and man of the people, whose tall, sinewy frame seemed to reflect years of action and valor. By the time he sought the presidency, Jackson's frontier fighting days were long past, and by then he was a gentleman farmer and slave holder. Yet he continued to represent the victory of the frontiersman over nature, the authority of the untutored, simple yeoman, and the success of the man of iron will who pursues his goal relentlessly. In 1840 William Henry Harrison handily defeated incumbent Martin Van Buren for the presidency by appropriating the democratic, masculine symbols of the coonskin cap and the whiskey barrel and by associating Van Buren, a small, slight man, with the "effete" Euro-

pean aristocracy because he wore cologne and had a chef in the White
House. A "man-milliner," Van Buren's opponents contemptuously called
him.[11]

Jackson and the frontier tradition he represented were not the only
sources of the muscular model of masculinity. English aristocrats and
southern gentlemen, who patterned their behavior upon a mixture of cava-
lier and frontier examples, valued the strenuous outdoor life, the martial
tradition, and competitive sports. German immigrants brought with them a
devotion to gymnastic exercise. The Irish prized the brawny man and the
boxer; and in Mose the Bowery B'Hoy, the legendary voluntary fireman of
massive fists and gigantic stature, they had a folk hero who rivalled in popularity frontier giants like Davy Crockett and Mike Fink. Even Lord Byron
liked sports, exercised regularly, and, in one notable passage, lionized Daniel
Boone as an example of the natural kind of nobleman.

By the 1840s the muscular male model strongly influenced American
ideals of men's appearance. By then the term "Yankee," of obscure derivation, but commonly applied to northern businessmen, had acquired a pejorative connotation. In the guise of a veteran farmer, the Yankee was sometimes applauded as a northern version of the natural rural nobleman, and
some commentators praised the Yankee for inventiveness and drive. Yet
this positive image was offset by a view of the Yankee as calculating and
bent only on personal gain. Yankees are "cold and cunning," Thomas Grattan charged. Their character is "reserved and calculating," their temper is
"stern and cold," their manners are "stiff and inelegant," wrote Theresa and
Francis Pulsky. According to Nathaniel Parker Willis, "A Yankee always
looks haggard and nervous, as though he was chasing a dollar." In folk mythology the Yankee was either a country bumpkin or a crafty trader, and "to
play a Yankee trick" was a common phrase to indicate the success of a de-
vious maneuver. Such negative meanings reflected a common concern about
the nation's mercantile proclivities, the intensity of which violated Christian modesty, aristocratic notions of the leisured life, and the egalitarian
view of democratic relations.[12]

In addition, the emergence of the Yankee as either fool or villain reflected the increasing importance of the frontiersman, the southern gentleman, and the robust brawler of the working classes as important symbols of
American masculinity. In his popular *Miss Ravenel's Conversion,* John William De Forest explored their various associations. The central theme of
the book is the relationship between a doomed Confederate officer, hard-
driving, hard-drinking, athletic, the epitome of muscular masculinity, and
a sensitive Bostonian who, through athletics, overcomes the inertia of the
New England type to become robust. In this case the Yankee, through ap-

plying his qualities of self-control and determination, is transformed into an athlete. De Forest admires both the southerner and his Yankee rival, but he has no respect for the wealthy, delicate Harvard students who also feature in the novel and who, in De Forest's presentation, lack any attractiveness of body or mind.

Commenting on the growing importance of a muscular ideal of appearance for American men, Nathaniel Parker Willis traced the new standard to two sources: first, to the "pugnacity" aroused by the successful prosecution of the Mexican War and, second, to the continued immigration of "broad-chested Germans and pugilistic English and Irish." In 1850 Emmeline Stuart-Wortley observed that American men were increasingly attracted by the military mode. There was a growing profusion of military societies, especially among New York City ethnic groups who had been, by her account, "at the forefront of the volunteers in Mexico." Even more, once American boys had fired off their pistols and miniature cannons at July Fourth celebrations, they wanted to be part of the adult military societies.[13]

In addition to a new militarism, the growing popularity of sports was important in shaping the new ideal of male appearance. As Willis suggested, early sports interest was centered in German, Irish, and English immigrants. And, aside from horse racing, boxing was the earliest competitive sport that aroused the attention of a sizable number of males. Of all sports, boxing requires aggressiveness, strength, and muscularity. It is a male sport par excellence and was particularly so in the days when protective gloves were not worn and safety rules were minimal. In New York City, a center of the sport, well-known pugilists led many of the city's gangs; in the South planters pitted slaves against each other. In 1858 when two fighters met for what was described as the "American championships," anxious crowds huddled around Western Union offices. Two years later Baron Salomon Rothschild contended that Americans were more interested in the fight between American John C. Heanan and Englishman Tom Sayers to establish international boxing supremacy than they were in the convention being held concurrently in Charleston to decide whether South Carolina should secede from the Union.[14]

In addition to boxing, baseball and college sports like gymnastics and rowing also existed before the Civil War, but it was not until the 1870s, after the experience of war and several decades of pro-sports propaganda on the part of health enthusiasts and sports promoters, that sports began to be an American passion. Indeed, in the 1860s another masculine type emerged to challenge both frail and muscular men: the portly, rotund man, partner of the plump, voluptuous female beauty. There had, of course, always been portly American males: George William Curtis described the leaders of

New York society and business in the 1820s as having an "amplitude of countenance and form." But the man of large girth was increasingly admired in post–Civil War America. He reflected the general desire to display a new maturity after the shattering experience of war and the interest of businessmen in displaying in their figures their new prosperity. The rotund man of midcentury appeared middle-aged, and, as if to underscore the point, he wore a full beard. His emergence as a distinct type coincided with a period of general social conservatism, just as the earlier age of reform was accompanied by the youthful image of masculinity.[15]

Moreover, this model of ample girth weakened the old association between the businessman and the Yankee, always pictured as thin and gaunt. It drew on venerable associations between plumpness and prosperity characteristic of immigrant, lower-class tradition and on the medical theories of S. Weir Mitchell and George Beard, which held that, no less for men than for women, a thin body frame was unhealthy. "A fat bank account tends to make a fat man," Beard wrote. "In all countries," he continued, "amid all stages of civilization and semi-barbarism, the wealthy classes have been larger and heavier than the poor. Wealth, indeed, if it be abundant and permanent, supplies all the external conditions possible to humanity that are friendly to those qualities of the physique—plumpness, roundness, size—that are rightly believed to indicate well-balanced health." As press agent Dexter Fellows put it: "A little paunch above the belt was something to be proud of." Even John L. Sullivan, the famed boxer and masculine model of late century, grew stouter as he grew older. "Men, drinking beer and eating huge piles of potatoes," wrote his biographer, "were expected to achieve their second chins soon after their wisdom teeth and, at thirty, their vests, copiously hung with watch chains, already were taut tents of great expanse."[16]

Yet there was more to this portly ideal of masculinity than status display. Among the group of writers, reporters, press agents, and cartoonists with whom Dexter Fellows fraternized, he thought that heavy eating was linked to conviviality, that it was a bond that held them together. Diamond Jim Brady, Lillian Russell, and John L. Sullivan became fat primarily because they loved to eat, and prevailing ideals of physical appearance allowed them freely to indulge this pleasure.

The portly gentleman of the late nineteenth century was ultimately no match for the athlete as an arbiter of male appearance. Yet for several decades he maintained his own. And traces of his continuing appeal are apparent in a cultural tradition that is still more leniently disposed toward amplitude in men than in women and in which the portly, middle-aged, successful businessman remains sexually attractive to young women although his female counterpart does not remain attractive to young men.

III

On the question of men's dress, some observers contended that American men did not follow fashions; others asserted that they did. "Black dress is the costume for men everywhere in the United States," noted Oscar Comettant in 1857, and Camille Feri-Pisani, writing five years later, agreed: "Everyone dresses the same way; the carriage driver, the porter, the merchant, the artisan, the banker and the lawyer all have the same appearance." Henryk Sienkiewicz thought that the elaborate dress of American women looked strange beside the clothing of the men who accompanied them, for the latter paid "no attention to clothes"—a lack of concern that Thomas Grattan, among others, thought was due to men's singular preoccupation with business. Yet democratic attitudes also may have played a role in American men's seeming indifference to fashion. William Marcy, Franklin Pierce's secretary of state, for example, decreed that all American diplomats, even ambassadors, were to wear black suits on all occasions to symbolize American democracy in contrast to the elaborate dress of European representatives of aristocratic regimes.[17]

Yet even though many American men were indifferent to fashion and though men's dress varied much less in decoration and style than women's, style was nonetheless important to some men. In every city tailors and ready-to-wear merchants attempted to control fabric selection and the cut and decoration of the finished product. Although in the nineteenth century there were no men's fashion magazines and women's fashion publications did not generally include men's clothes, New York City tailors displayed plates of the newest London fashions for men in their windows. Philadelphia men's ready-to-wear merchants, whose businesses dated from the 1840s, published a *Bulletin of Fashion,* which they furnished to distant retailers to promote their products. This innovation was copied by manufacturers in other cities. The paper patterns published and disseminated by Demorest's and Butterick's from the 1860s on included patterns for men's clothes, drawn by artists who used suits that fashionable New York tailors sent them as models.[18]

Stylish dress appears to have been particularly important among specific groups of men. Successful businessmen may have affected a nonchalance about their clothes, but for upwardly mobile young men how they looked was important, not only as a means of business advance, but also as a measure of self-esteem. "Over-dressing themselves is a serious evil among young men in America," wrote etiquette authority Charles Day. "They hope by such means to raise themselves in public estimation." Harriet Martineau noted that a new class of affluent mechanics in New York City strutted around Broadway "with sleek coats, glossy hats, gay watch-guards, and dove-skin gloves." On every street corner were barbershops, so-called hairdressing saloons, elegant tonsorial establishments that were mute testimony to the fact that, if display in clothing was downplayed, display in hair might take its place. George Sala noted that some of the best-outfitted American men he saw were hotel clerks, assistants in stores, and sleeping car conductors: "Every American who does not wish to be thought 'small potatoes' or a 'ham-fatter' or a 'corner-loafer' is carefully 'barbed' and fixed up in a hairdressing saloon every day." Such behavior, Sala wrote, was not characteristic of English clerks, who never dreamed of a "glorious future." Yet "young America rarely looks at himself in the glass, after he has been 'fixed' by the barber, without seeing reflected in the mirror the features of a future President of the United States or of a Minister Plenipotentiary or Judge of the Supreme Court, or a big hotel proprietor at the very least."[19]

In 1865 Harriet Beecher Stowe, comparing men's and women's dress, wrote that men's clothes "have as many fine, invisible points of fashion, and their fashions change quite as often; and they have as many knick-knacks with their studs and their sleeve-buttons and waistcoat buttons, their scarves and scarf-pins, their watch-chains and seals and sealrings." Indeed, black clothing for men did not become universally popular until the 1850s. Before then, bright colors were still in vogue as well as tight-fitting pants that resembled eighteenth-century breeches. In New York City in the 1820s, noted Charles Haswell, black clothing was never worn except by clergymen or for mourning.[20]

Yet a certain conservatism characterized men's clothes throughout the nineteenth century. The kind of leisured gentlemen who had dominated the nation's business and politics a hundred years before and had lavished time on sartorial display and personal adornment no longer existed, noted one authority. In a "modern" community, in which "time has a commercial value," what was needed was a simple costume that could easily be put on and off. The suit with shirt and tie fit such a purpose well, and so it had developed. Even the dandies—leisured individuals who expressed their individuality through their clothes—accepted the confines of the dark costume by the 1850s, when it came into full fashion.[21]

If we can believe the many observers who contended that American men devoted themselves maniacally to their work, the argument about the conservatism of men's dress because of commercial reasons becomes even more compelling. Referring to Chicago's wealthy after the Civil War, Harriet Hubbard Ayer wrote that they considered a man who paid attention to fashion either a ne'er-do-well or a fool. From this perspective the elegant dressing of well-paid young mechanics in New York City may have been designed not to impress their employers, but rather to differentiate them-selves from the thousands of young men who were flooding into American cities in the 1830s and 1840s, all looking for upward mobility through commerce and thereby creating an intensely competitive situation.[22]

Men may not have taken up black clothing until the 1850s, but in the 1830s they already wore the large black stovepipe hat that, ungainly and uncomfortable, was associated in the public mind, according to George William Curtis, with "punctuality in meeting pecuniary obligations" and that would remain in fashion for much of the rest of the century. A series of concerted efforts in the 1840s and 1850s to replace it with a soft, low-brimmed hat were not successful, despite the fact that soldiers in the Mexi-can War and miners in the California gold rush—popular figures in the East—took to wearing a Mexican sombrero version. In his triumphal tour through the United States in 1850, Hungarian revolutionary Louis Kossuth wore such a hat, as did a popular team of English cricketers who gave dem-onstration matches throughout the East that same year. Then sales began to soar, particularly after hatmakers removed all decorations from previous models, manufactured it in black, and advertised it as a combination of the stovepipe with the Kossuth hat. Even then fully 50 percent of the male pop-ulation remained faithful to the stovepipe, and within a few years the low-brimmed hat had largely disappeared, at least from the East.[23]

Even though most American men refused to accept the innovative, low-brimmed hat, facial hair—previously considered a sign of radicalism or of effeminacy—came overwhelmingly into vogue by midcentury. During the eighteenth century, clean-shaven faces had been in fashion. They are ap-parent, for example, in pictorial representations of eighteenth-century aris-tocrats as well as of the major American revolutionaries who patterned themselves after the clean-shaven legislators of classical Greece and Rome. Later, more rugged male models like Davy Crockett, Daniel Boone, and Mose the Bowery B'Hoy were also pictured in lithographs and drawings as clean-shaven. The first president to wear facial hair was Abraham Lincoln.[24]

Still it must be remembered that soldiers as well as men in frontier situ-ations generally grew beards because of the difficulty of shaving. The clean-shaven faces of frontiersmen Daniel Boone and Davy Crockett were ideal-ized images, still modelled on the revolutionary presentation of the ideal American as the natural nobleman, young, classic, and aristocratic. For men, beards can perform a number of symbolic functions. No less than for women, men's hair has sexual connotations, and the connotation has been one of virility and power: in the classic tale Samson shorn of his locks is powerless. At the same time a beard can also be a sign of maturity: wise old men, like Uncle Sam in his late-century representations, are rarely pictured without long beards.

A combination of the desire to demonstrate wisdom and potency lay behind the American vogue of beards. Young men in New York City who affected the latest European fashions first wore moustaches in the 1830s. They then became popular among soldiers during the Mexican-American War and among frontiersmen during the California gold rush. By 1851 Nathaniel Parker Willis wrote that men of all classes and ages in New York City were experimenting with facial hair. Varina Clay Clopton remembered that when her husband first entered the Senate in 1853, the senators were uniformly clean-shaven; when he left in 1861, almost all wore side and chin whiskers. By the mid-1860s, the fashion was ubiquitous. What had been considered radical and effeminate in the 1850s was now considered normal. So anxious were men to display this virility, according to a New York observer, that beards were overdone and resulted in walruslike appendages that "must either slop into the tea or coffee or be pushed away by a brace on the inside edge of the cup, which cup was overdecorated as if to call attention to its function."[25]

By the 1860s maturity was an important male ideal, and the portly ideal of masculinity was prominent. The smooth face is a youthful face; even the moustaches of the dandies of the 1830s had a youthful look to them. But men in the 1860s wanted to look solid and secure, and beards added to this effect. Abraham Lincoln, for example, grew a long, full beard because he wished to look wise. Men had rejected the soft-brimmed hat of the 1850s because, no matter its color or lack of decoration, it still looked youthful and radical. Beards, on the other hand, could be grown in such a manner as to deepen men's look of maturity.

Yet we must not forget the function of the beard in symbolizing virility and force. The Mexican War, the armed confrontations in Kansas and elsewhere in the 1850s, the violence of the frontier, and, above all, the Civil War had raised the martial spirit. It was no accident that one popular type of facial hair, namely short side whiskers, was named after Civil War general Ambrose Burnside. And even after the conflict had ended, the glorification of combat and aggressive masculinity continued. Ultimately these forces would aid in legitimizing competitive sports in the United States, which would in turn absorb aggression and the martial spirit to a certain degree. But they also remained present in an undiluted form in the combative physicality of cattle and mining frontiers and in the brutal, violent wars with the Indians.

For easterners, William L. Cody, known as Buffalo Bill, came to be an important model of masculinity in the 1880s. A former buffalo hunter and army scout, Cody became famous as a result of re-enacting his western experiences in Wild West shows, beginning in 1883 and continuing for the next twenty years. Why Buffalo Bill wore facial hair is important in understanding the underlying meaning of beards. As Cody told the story, his long moustache, goatee, and shoulder-length, straggling hair were a response to the conditions of Indian warfare. Indians regarded hair as a source of individual power. Thus they scalped opponents and proudly displayed their trophies, while they themselves wore long hair (although not beards). To grow a "respectable scalp-look," according to Cody, became the mode among Indian fighters. Beards and moustaches heightened the effect. "To cut the hair short," he continued, "was to be a coward; to let it grow was to display sportsmanship and proclaim defiance."[26]

Beards were the masculine equivalent of women's abundant hair in the late nineteenth century. Each mirrored the other, as the sexes often do in the area of physical appearance. But while women put their hair atop their head and concealed their hair's abundance, men's beards were visible for all to see, a proud display of martial might and of the wisdom presumably gained through warfare.

IV

Men played many roles in the nineteenth century. They were politicians, explorers, businessmen, frontiersmen, soldiers, and athletes. One of the most important and least understood was one catalogued under a pejorative slang term: the "dandy." Today we are familiar with the type through the revolutionary song, "Yankee Doodle Dandy," a satire of behavior associated with sectors of the English elites. In her insightful study of the type, Ellen Moers has contended that the dandy, who dressed elegantly and ostentatiously, stood for the aristocratic values of superiority, irresponsibility, and inactivity against the values of equality, commitment, and energy of the rising democratic majority. "Dandyism was a product of the revolutionary upheavals of the late eighteenth century," writes Moers. "When solid values like wealth and birth are upset, ephemera such as style and pose are called upon to justify the stratification of society."[27]

Dandies in the United States, like those in Europe, usually were sons of the wealthy with time to enjoy the leisured frivolities denied hard-working fathers. In 1837 satirist Asa Green contended that they were to be seen in every part of New York City, but primarily in public places—at the corners of streets, on the doorsteps of hotels, and in various public walks. Like many analysts of dandies, Green found them effeminate; according to him, they wore monocles and gold chains around their necks and carried canes with tassels, which they switched. "The truth is," wrote Green, "the race is not particularly admired."[28]

Yet it is too simple to dismiss the dandies as effete and unimportant. Nathaniel Parker Willis, recognized as the leader of New York dandies, was a fop, according to George Ticknor Curtis, but he was not a fool. In fact, he was an advocate of exercise and athletics and an important social critic of his day. Moreover, many sources indicate that the affectation of extreme fashionable dress to the point of parody was not confined to the wealthy, but also cut across class lines and became a visible symbol not of effeminacy and impotence, but of rowdy, rebellious attitudes and behavior.[29]

Among the elites, for example, dandyism was characteristic of the set of young men known as "fast." Charles Astor Bristed characterized their style as "showy" and thought that, along with the young women they escorted, they controlled society. But they were necessary to society because many of the older men of new wealth were rough and simple, unaware of proper social behavior and, according to George William Curtis, unable to dance. Many of the fast young men, Curtis noted, had been to Europe and had come back with an indolent, effete style, while they cultivated reputations for having been intimate with "uncertain women in Paris." Known as "blades" and "bloods," they thronged the theaters and wined and dined chorus girls and actresses, for whom they came to form the core of the stage-door Johnnies. Their numbers increased in the postbellum period of advancing wealth. Then, according to the *Ladies' Home Journal*, they came to constitute a "leisure class" of young men. Police officer John Warren remembered them as dashing youths who drove their carriages in Central Park in the afternoons and patronized the concert saloons at night. By the 1890s they came to be known as the "gilded youths of the fin-de-siècle," an oft-repeated term, particularly on the pages of the Sunday supplements, which loved to dwell on the real and fancied exploits of the type.[30]

As a phenomenon, dandyism was not limited to a select few among the elite. The pattern of behavior that the New York fast set exhibited was found widely on college campuses. Even Louisa Alcott, in *Little Women*, portrayed Laurie at college in a dandy period, with seventeen waistcoats and endless neckties. Alcott herself expressed the opinion that "young men must sow wild oats." The clothes that Harriet Martineau noted on New York City mechanics strutting down Broadway must have borne an air of exuberant extravagance. The clerks George Sala found in New York's hair saloons all wore their hair in "dandified fashion."[31]

By late century, too, members of occupations whose role was to attract and entertain the public—like circus barkers, vaudevillians, and saloonkeepers—affected loud, flamboyant clothing. So, too, did salesmen, strident and brash, the forerunners of commercial civilization whom Arthur Miller apotheosized as representative Americans in the overbearing, endless-talking, misogynist Willie Loman of *Death of a Salesman*. As early as 1841, Ned

Buntline noted that certain American men consistently overdressed: "Many of our readers may have noticed the almost professional look of a smart, showy stage-agent; or of an outside hotel-runner, or of some of our city merchant 'drummers.' "[32]

Abruptly in the 1880s, the word "dandy" (of French derivation) was replaced by the American slang word "dude" to refer to men of style. Although the new word reflected the fact that Edward, Prince of Wales, had become a new model of dress and behavior for men, its derivation came from the western United States and reflected the perplexity of westerners in the face of well-dressed easterners. Yet alongside the dude, an upper-class model, there also appeared a similar model among working-class men. According to commentator Edgar Fawcett, the dude "pauses decorously on the threshold of vice." Among the working classes, a similar individual appeared, one who by most accounts did not "pause decorously," but rather plunged into whatever situation was at hand. This new type was known as a "masher."[33]

Sometimes a cultural phenomenon is so striking that even contemporaries far removed from it cannot help commenting on it. Such was the reaction to the masher—a type who, suddenly appearing, seemed ubiquitous on city streets. The masher, according to a detailed contemporary analysis, "hovers everywhere, from the marketplace to the meetinghouse, and from the promenade to the theater." He was drawn from a variety of social groups: "He may come from the slums or be the son of a first-class preacher of the gospel." He could be young or old, "from the young man who negotiates with you over a counter for a paper of pins or a dozen shoe-strings, up to his employer." The term "masher" apparently originated in theatrical people's calling romantic fan letters "mash" notes, a word they derived from the gypsy verb "to love." And the origin of the masher as a type partly proceeded from the stage-door Johnnies—wealthy men who openly courted stage favorites. But he also partly conformed to a pattern of ostentatious behavior long current in concert saloons and among those elements of the theatrical and sporting worlds who had never paid attention to Puritan values: the old sporting crowd known as "the fancy," who kept relatively separate from women in their public events and who wore gaudy clothes, according to one participant, because women were not present to dress up these events.[34]

What apparently happened in the 1880s was that a kind of behavior previously confined to specific sectors of the male population became widespread. Numbers of men began to dress in a special way to announce their allegiance to a new style of behavior, one that was at base sexually assertive. The masher was a "barber-and-tailor-shop decoration, moved by a wild ambition to attract and hold feminine attention." Yet he could also be subtle in dress and style and thereby even more compelling. In *Sister Carrie,* Theodore Dreiser effectively described his appeal:

> Good clothes, of course, were the first essential, the things without which he was nothing. A strong physical nature, actuated by a keen desire for the feminine, was the next. A mind free of any consideration of the problems or forces of the world and actuated not by greed, but an insatiable love of variable pleasure. His method was always simple. Its principal element was daring, backed, of course, by an intense desire and admiration for the sex. Let him meet with a young woman twice and he would straighten her necktie for her and perhaps address her by her first name. In the great department stores he was at his ease. If he caught the attention of some young woman while waiting for the cash boy to come back with his change, he would find out her name, her favourite flower, where a note could reach her.[35]

As Dreiser characterized the masher, who in *Sister Carrie* was a "drummer" (a travelling salesman), his appeal was nearly irresistible. Dreiser's description rings true. Few other cultural phenomena of the age concerning men, women, and physical appearance elicited so much contemporary commentary as the masher. People were both frightened and intrigued by him. In addition to the actress, he represented the first sign of the breakdown of the Victorian synthesis regarding sensuality and the emergence of a new assertive attitude that would later appear so strikingly among working and society women. As much as the businessman and frontiersman, he was a major exemplar of male appearance and behavior in the late nineteenth century.

V

What Lewis Feuer has called "generational disequilibrium"—the tendency of each generation to differentiate itself from its elders—was an important force in nineteenth-century America. Before the Civil War, the prevailing model of masculinity was a youthful one, characterized by a clean-shaven face and a slim figure. The Civil War encouraged the appearance of the full-bearded portly man—the representative of a middle-aged conservative business civilization—although youthful variations existed throughout the post–Civil War years. By late century, however, the youthful type issued a striking challenge, as the vogue of athletics became preeminent and the beard went out of fashion.[36]

The new challenge of youth perhaps appeared first in the growing vogue of cigarette smoking, rather than tobacco chewing or cigar smoking. The cigar dated to the days of the colonial Dutch, who had cultivated tobacco in their East Indian plantations. In many ways it had become the symbol of the financial success of the portly gentleman. It was large, and the aroma was strong. A room filled with cigar smoke quickly drove out non-smoking women. Writing about Newport society in the 1880s, George Lathrop described the industrialist's library as the private "temple" of his religion of business. His immense desk was the "high Altar," and the "incense of a cigar" was a regular tribute to the "established cult." According to Henry Collins Brown, in the 1880s many banks and offices prohibited the smoking of cigarettes, which were considered "exotic": only cigars were allowed. Too, the cigar was a natural accompaniment to the day's after-dinner ritual, when men and women went to different rooms, the men for brandy and cigars and the freedom to talk about business and to tell bawdy stories. And in the corporation office and board room, where alcohol might befuddle brains and food require too much concentration, the cigar was an appropriate symbol of masculinity.[37]

Cigarettes had long been smoked in the Near East, and the habit was brought to England by British officers in the 1856 Crimean War. From them it spread to sophisticated aristocratic circles and to bohemian groups and finally to young men in American cities, probably the dudes and mashers who seized on such innovations as part of their social rebellion through style. In a famous scene of one of their burlesques, the British Blondes mocked young men by puffing on cigarettes. The adoption of cigarettes was in large part due to the widespread effectiveness of the advertising campaigns launched by the industry's leaders, particularly through advertising cards contained in cigarette packs. Carrying the likenesses of actresses and athletes, the cards linked cigarettes, sex, and youthful athletic prowess. Older men were appalled by the growth in their use. For a time the rumor spread that they were unclean and could damage the lungs; many people called them "coffin nails." By the 1890s, however, the popularity of cigarettes was demonstrated by the casualness with which young men in the novels by such popular writers as Richard Harding Davis and Constance Cary Harrison smoked them.[38]

A significant rebelliousness characterized the generation of the 1890s. Many of its members were disenchanted with the compromises of their parents; they wished new challenges, new possibilities. The Civil War had decimated and disillusioned a generation of young men; now their descendants forgot the cost and romanticized the glory. Numerous commentators have remarked on this generation's enthusiasm for war, which they saw as noble and heroic, and on the extent to which the Spanish-American War of

1898 was an outgrowth of this enthusiasm. "Impetuous youth," wrote Constance Cary Harrison, "was arrayed against experienced old age. No memories of the awful war between the States . . . could dissuade a younger generation eager for a new fray at arms." Yet the exuberance for war was only one part of a general enthusiasm for the active life, for play, for reform, for a new kind of nobility on the part of this generation.[39]

Among this generation of youth, sports particularly solidified its hold. In the 1870s, athletic clubs, as well as professional baseball teams, had appeared in many cities. In the 1880s clerks in many business houses in the major cities organized baseball and athletic leagues, and football gained its enormous importance in American colleges. In the 1890s the bicycle became popular; physical education became a key part of YMCA programs; and advocates of physical fitness, like weightlifter Eugene Sandow, made body building popular among men. Throughout New York City, remembered Henry Collins Brown, appeared "physical culture parlors where cadaverous clerks set to lifting weights."[40]

Coinciding with the national fixation with sports, college men gained a new stature within society. Their new popularity partly reflected the fact of rising college enrollments. Although in 1900 only a fraction of the eligible age group in the population attended institutions of higher education, a college education was increasingly becoming a major aspiration of American youths, as a degree increasingly became a necessary step to professional certification and employment in business management. At the same time, colleges themselves became administratively larger and more efficient, with a curriculum geared to contemporary life and with connections to the financial community that underwrote their efforts. Elite preparatory schools and colleges developed connections to the American aristocracy, and the link itself glamorized college attendance. Most important, however, the popular sport of football was located on college campuses, and the famous football players were college students. By the 1890s Saturday games assumed major importance as rituals of community cohesion. The sports pages of metropolitan dailies now regularly covered football games, and their reporting humanized the colleges and made them seem a part of American popular culture with which all Americans could identify.[41]

In the 1890s Charles Dana Gibson drew a composite portrait of the new image of youthful masculinity. His man was young, tall, athletic in build, clean-shaven—a complementary companion to his Gibson girl and one easily identifiable as the college athletic type. Within a few years his ideal man would become popularly known by the name of his close friend who had been an original model for the drawings: the Richard Harding Davis man. Davis, whose talent for self-publicity equalled his considerable journalistic skills, had been a college athlete of note whose later life embodied the values of the college community that had moulded him as it would mould a generation of young American men. Wrote Henry Seidel Canby in his insightful memoir of American college life at the turn of the century, "From these campuses came many, if not most, of the two generations of Americans who are now in executive charge of the country, and the greater part of the codes, ideas, manners, and ideals of living which dominate us."[42]

Key to the nature of the college man was the student culture in which he participated—a culture that by the 1890s in most colleges became a force as powerful as the faculty or the curriculum. Intensely competitive, the student culture revolved around clubs and extracurricular activities, and on many campuses it duplicated the frenzied, self-seeking nature of adult business and professional life and was itself exclusionary. Moreover, drinking and rowdyism became standard behavior at many colleges, particularly those that were exclusively male. Canby called his Yale classmates "romantic barbarians" and implied that visits to prostitutes were not uncommon. Lillian Russell detested playing college towns because of the rowdy behavior of the undergraduates; the experience was always like "being in a storm at sea." At Harvard a fast set spent its time drinking, playing cards, and romancing chorus girls.[43]

Yet there were countervailing forces. The widespread appeal of the YMCA on college campuses reinforced Christian, humanitarian ethics. The vogue of sports also effected a change in attitude. Involvement with physical activity and its emphasis upon stamina and strength substituted for liquor and women and allowed young men to expend their aggressiveness on the playing field. Rudolph Aaronson, Lillian Russell's producer, noted with amusement that all one needed to do to calm a college man was to tell him that his body looked like that of Eugene Sandow.[44]

Important in the popular image of the college man was his identification with eastern single-sex male colleges, particularly Harvard, Princeton, and Yale—institutions that had always held an elite position in American higher education and at which the major football teams were located. From their origins in the colonial era, these colleges had existed not only to educate, but also to shape values and attitudes. By the twentieth century this purpose had become even stronger. The colleges sought to create "Christian gentlemen" as representatives in the real world of the moral elite that Progressive novelists described in fictionalized form. The private preparatory schools from which many of the students at these colleges came also held to such ideals. Moreover, a large part of the late nineteenth-century literature written for children was permeated by the ideals of the powerful "genteel" group of publishers, writers, and editors that controlled the day's prestigious publishing firms and magazines. On the juvenile as well as the adult level, these authors wanted to create "gentlemen" whose life goals were self-discipline and service to others. Thus a powerful set of forces was in operation from his earliest years to influence the rebellious, idealistic young man of late century in the direction of reform.

On the other hand, the student culture of the late nineteenth-century college reinforced egotism and elitism. Too, football in particular was a violent sport, and it fed whatever glorification of masculine aggressiveness had come to exist in the early twentieth century. Attending an all-male school created an isolation between the sexes at an impressionable age, further reinforced the separate cultures of the sexes, encouraged male solidarity, and strengthened the male tendency to see woman as a chivalric object, as the "symbol of civilization," in Richard Harding Davis's words. But by the early twentieth century even male colleges contributed their share of Progressive reformers, and the moralism that was a central theme in Progressive thought was very much a product of the ethical emphasis of many American colleges.

VI

Recent scholarship on the subject of masculinity in American culture has contended that a significant crisis among American males occurred between the 1890s and World War I, that men, threatened by the women's movement and by a supposed decline in the opportunities for individual entrepreneurship, adopted a bellicose, ultra-aggressive character as a means of compensation. Many problems beset this interpretation. In the first place, although men exhibited hostility to women's suffrage, the majority of writers in the day's popular journals and newspapers were not hostile to women's education or to their participation in work and sports. By and large, men applauded the new woman. Like the heroine of the Progressive novelist, she was an interesting companion, not a dependent. Elizabeth Cady Stanton explained the attitude when she once wrote that men welcomed the appearance of the new woman because they could no longer stand the frailty and constant fainting of her predecessor.[45]

Moreover, although the growth of business in this period produced corporate structures in which men were employed by others, we do not yet know precisely what kinds of men entered the new white-collar world—whether they were of farming stock, of middle-class entrepreneurial backgrounds, or of an upwardly mobile working-class sector. Writings about their wives and daughters imply that they came from all these groups. C. Wright Mills described them as ranging "from almost the top to the bottom of modern society." Finally, the advice literature to young men in these years was not pervaded by a sense of young men's anxiety about their future. Although Albert J. Beveridge, for example, alluded to their worries, he was more concerned about young men's repeating their fathers' mistake of total concentration on business and, in working too hard, becoming prey to nervous disorders, which neurologists like George Beard identified as a pervasive problem for American males.[46]

Who were the influential male models of appearance and behavior in turn-of-the-century America? Sports figures like boxer John L. Sullivan were important, as were businessmen and industrialists. In addition, western cowboys were also admired. They had inherited the mantle of the frontiersmen and Indian fighters after Owen Wister apotheosized their lives as cattle raisers into a saga of gunslinging drama in his 1901 novel *The Virginian.* But there were others whose image was softer and whose aggressive masculinity was countered by sophistication and humor.

Cosmopolitan men of the theater, for example, were popular. This was the age, after all, when the Barrymores first rose to prominence. In the 1890s many stationery and jewelry stores displayed in their windows photos of Maurice Barrymore holding an elegant demitasse cup and saucer in his hand and garbed in full dress as in one of his famed portrayals. Men pictured as dudes were also popular. Humor magazines like *Life* were filled with illustrations of dudes, exemplars of high society. Series of cigarette cards also featured dudes: one series included Fifth Avenue, Hoffman House, and Bowery examples. Among the New York elites was a group of ten young men, known as the Knickerbocker dudes, with whom Ava Astor associated and who were fashion style setters. They were tall, broad-shouldered, and known for their athletic ability. Their doings were recorded by the press; according to New York socialite Margaret Chanler, "the Dudes" were talked about in western towns.[47]

Magazine illustrators like Charles Dana Gibson and James Montgomery Flagg were as famous as the women they drew, and newspapers liked to feature their supposedly dashing lives. Newspaper journalists also were people of fascination, and they offered an important model of masculinity. In the nineteenth century, the reporter had been a hired hack overshadowed by powerful publishers and editors like Horace Greeley and James Gordon Bennett. The old-style reporter had begun in the printing room and worked his way up from setting type, and the artisan roots of the occupation as well as the association of reporters with the suspect world of vice, about which many wrote, depreciated the status of the calling. Yet attracted by the growing numbers of newspapers in the 1890s and by the high wages that top reporters were receiving, aspiring college writers were drawn to newspaper work, both as a means of financial security and as a way of testing their mettle as writers. Moreover, just as Robert Woodward and Carl Bernstein's investigative reporting of the Watergate scandal in the 1970s lent an aura of romance to journalism, so Jacob Riis's investigation of poverty in New York City and William Stead's of child prostitution in London placed journalists in a new light.[48]

The profession of journalism had little hierarchy or direct oversight. Assertiveness and individualism were what counted in scooping a story or finding details missed by other reporters. Journalism had the excitement of public exposure, of living a life at the center of public events and in the shadow of the famous and notorious, of operating on the fringes of the fascinating and sordid side of sports, politics, and the theater. Richard Harding Davis wrote that newspaper work provided "the experiences of the lifetime of the ordinary young businessman, doctor, or lawyer, or man about town."[49]

Like Jacob Riis and William Stead, the reporter was often a detective, ferreting out the details of elusive news stories, even solving crimes in an age when police departments were often corrupt or inefficient. This part of the profession also appealed to young men who, by the 1880s, were reading not only stories of Indian scouts and desperadoes in their dime novels and cheap magazines, but also accounts of urban criminals and detectives, in which reporters often played featured roles. With the demise of the western frontier, it was no longer possible to become pathfinders or cowboys, but young men who wanted adventure and had some writing skill could still become journalists on the urban frontier. Thus many Progressive novelists, like David Graham Phillips and Stephen Crane, worked as reporters at some point in their careers.[50]

In journalism, young men could find a camaraderie enjoyed by practitioners of few other professions. Hours were irregular, and an intense solidarity grew up among young men who had little money and living space. They congregated at bars and cheap eating places, where they exchanged information and gossip and waited to launch the next round of adventures. Editor Malcolm Bingay called them "wild carefree Bohemians." Theater owners, hopeful of free publicity, gave them season passes; if they grew more affluent they frequented Lobster Palace Society. The reporter became, according to Hutchins Hapgood, a kind of "rounder"—an individual whom Hapgood described as a sophisticated man about town whose life was lived in theaters, in restaurants, and among the society of other rounders.[51]

Perhaps more than any other individual, Richard Harding Davis came to represent the journalist in the public eye. He had an uncanny ability to make himself prominent, and within a few years after his 1890 arrival in New York City he had become a star reporter, a writer of best-selling novels, a favorite of New York society women, and the model of the ideal American man drawn by Charles Dana Gibson. Recent biographers have not been kind to Davis. They have damned his histrionics, his love of elegance and fine clothes, his intense relationship with his mother, and his unsophisticated moralizing. Yet they have overlooked an equally important part of him. Like Gibson, his aspirations were shaped by a Protestant middle-class background, by a love of New York sophistication, and by the college world of competitive athletics in which he had enthusiastically participated. He was the product of the genteel drive to produce gentlemen and of the college culture as it had developed by the late nineteenth century. To a large extent he never grew up, and his wanderings around the world as a foreign correspondent had to them the aspect of a youth playing at cowboys and Indians or of a medieval crusader off to the wars. He was, according to Charles Dana Gibson, "a splendid, healthy, clean-minded, gifted boy at play."[52]

The heroes of Davis's novels were always successful because their brand of Anglo-Saxon morality and American virility simply was invincible. Gibson had shown young American men and women as a natural aristocracy in their native milieu; Davis pictured them in far-off lands and amid exotic settings, where they talked nostalgically about Delmonico's and lived the strenuous life. More than any individual of his age, Davis lived his life exactly as he wanted it to be—as a hero of romantic fiction—and in his writings and adventuring fulfilled the fantasy life of a generation of American boys. "Those were grand days for young men," wrote his friend Lionel Barrymore, "with everything in its proper place, no war or threat of war, and great men to admire."[53]

Davis's desire for fun, his wit, and his good humor were apparent in other, more aggressive models of the period. That the teddy bear was named after Theodore Roosevelt and that the cowboy was denominated a "boy" and not a "man" was not accidental. There was a playful side to both, a boyish quality, a level on which Roosevelt's blustering and the cowboy's controlled violence were the aggressiveness of boys playing at being soldiers and adventurers. The Virginian of Wister's story played practical jokes; he laughed with ease and found enjoyment in simple pleasures. In contrast to eastern businessmen, intent on success at any price, he knew how to relax. Too, there was an element of dandyism in the cowboy's decorated boots and shirts, and his code of honor and ritualized gun duels made him a gentleman of the chivalric sort.[54]

The male aggressiveness exhibited on the football field and the battlefield in these years, the violence that the tales of Tarzan and the cowboy implicitly condoned, was a part of male behavior. But we are unfaithful to the historical record not to realize that other models were also current, models both humorous and serious and appropriate to an age of reform that at its best moments was infused with the millennial vision that the nation might lead the world in righteousness, that all women might be beautiful and all men gentlemen, motivated by the highest standards of ethical conduct and of concern for others. The tall, athletic, clean-shaven figure of Richard Harding Davis exemplified this ideal.

12

The Pursuit of Beauty as Woman's Role

The Beauty Contest, 1800-1921

On September 5, 1921, the best-known beauty contest in the United States was inaugurated when Margaret Gorman of Washington, D.C., was chosen the winner of Atlantic City's first Miss America contest. The initial competition involved eight contestants, representing cities within easy access of Atlantic City. The next year representatives of fifty-eight cities took part. By 1927 seventy-five contestants entered, from as far away as California and Alaska. Reported by newspapers throughout the nation, the competition overnight became a major event that seemed to enshrine the "bathing beauty," with her proud display of a seminude body, as a central symbol of American women.[1]

The history of beauty contests tells us much about American attitudes toward physical appearance and women's expected roles. Rituals following set procedures, beauty contests have long existed to legitimize the Cinderella mythology for women, to make it seem that beauty is all a woman needs for success and, as a corollary, that beauty ought to be a major pursuit of all women. In addition, beauty contests also illuminate American attitudes toward sensuality and offer a gauge of the influence of Victorianism in American culture. They reveal the nature of community rites designed to further cultural homogeneity and to integrate social classes within the American democratic order. In the years of their development between 1800 and 1920, beauty contests were amalgams of elements originating both in high and in low culture. Their history demonstrates the ways in which the cultures of the elites and of the masses interacted and the avenues by which these interactions took place.

As an event, the beauty contest was not entirely American in origin. European festivals of venerable lineage often included a competition to choose the most beautiful woman participant. Each man attending the Viennese Annenfest was given a ticket that he, in turn, gave to the woman of his choice, and the woman who collected the most tickets was declared the winner. Parisian laundresses held a *Fête des Blanchisseuses,* which included the election of the most beautiful representative of the group. Local May Day celebrations for centuries involved the selection of queens. Although nineteenth-century English observers noted the disappearance of this traditional folk event, a casualty of industrialization, it staged a revival in Europe when Catholics appropriated it to celebrate the Virgin Mary by anointing her the May Day queen.[2]

In the United States, competitions for the gauge of beauty also first appeared at May Day celebrations. The day itself gained an early notoriety because of its association with Thomas Morton's Merrymount settlement, which the Massachusetts Bay colonists destroyed in 1630. The Puritans, who reprobated festivals, forbade May Day observance along with other colorful English holidays and replaced them with Thanksgiving.[3]

Yet like many premodern folk observances, May Day survived into the modern age as a ritual of childhood. According to Lydia Maria Child, girls in the nineteenth century in both England and the United States on the first of May crowned their favorite friend Queen of the May. Girls' schools both South and North held May Day ceremonies. In the antebellum South, novelist Caroline Lee Hentz reported, students at the school she headed demanded May Day festivities, even though her own "republican principles" made her suspicious of "these royal rites." May Day rituals at schools for young women survived into a later age in such practices as Vassar's daisy chain and spring celebrations at Wellesley, Bryn Mawr, Mount Holyoke, and Elmira.[4]

The special features of May Day celebrations—particularly their use of women as fertility symbols—were occasionally invoked on other occasions to pay special tribute to the nation's leaders. When George Washington journeyed from Mount Vernon to New York City in 1789 to assume the presidency, delegations of young women dressed in white strewed palm branches in front of his carriage in the cities along his route. When Lafayette triumphantly toured the nation in 1826, similar delegations of young women greeted him and spread flowers in his path. In Newark, New Jersey, a thirty-five-foot classical temple was built out of flowers and evergreen branches, its twenty-four arches representing the twenty-four existing states. In each of the arches, beautiful young women were positioned. In Washington, D.C., twenty-five young women representing the capital city and the twenty-four states officially welcomed Lafayette to the nation in the square in front of the Capitol. Gaining great esteem through their association with the national hero, these women for the remainder of their lives were known as "Lafayette girls."[5]

In addition to their central role at May Day celebrations, queens were also important at Twelfth Night parties, which were held twelve days after Christmas to celebrate the magi's gifts to the baby Jesus. At these parties, a ring and a bean were baked in separate cakes, and the man who found the ring and the woman who received the bean in their servings became king and queen of the evening. Of greater significance in the development of beauty contests, however, were tournaments, nineteenth-century recreations of medieval jousts. Held primarily, although not exclusively, in the South, tournaments were an outgrowth of the early-century romanticism that found inspiration in the medieval pageantry of kings, queens, and knights and that seemed particularly to appeal to the South, with its pretensions to aristocracy and its fondness for horsemanship and military ways. The tournament described in Sir Walter Scott's *Ivanhoe,* published in 1829 and numbered among the most popular books of the period, was influential in the vogue, as were tournaments held in England, particularly the one at Eglinton in 1839, which drew twenty thousand spectators and was widely reported by the American press.[6]

Before the Civil War and for some time after it, tournaments were regularly held in all the southern states. Usually they were scheduled on holidays—Christmas, May Day, the Fourth of July, or, most often, Washington's birthday. Sometimes the tournament was part of a broader program, such as a fair or a militia display; sometimes it was the sole event. The format of the tournament rarely varied. In the competition, three small rings were hung on a hook at the end of a wire fastened to a bar. Then horsemen, carrying long lances and riding at top speed, attempted to spear the rings off the hook. Sometimes a figure was painted on a board, and each horseman was required, while riding, to fire at the figure with a pistol and then to slash at the head with a saber. Whoever speared the most rings or most mangled the figure was the winner, and he had the privilege of naming the queen. Each runner-up named an attendant. A coronation ceremony and ball followed.

Upon occasion tournaments were held in the North as well as the South. Many sources detail the elaborate tournament that the Tory aristocracy sponsored in Philadelphia in 1778. One of the principal features of the annual meeting of the German *Turnvereine* in New York City in the 1850s was a tournament, although in this case the contestants were not mounted.

Tournaments involving the horse and the lance were held in Ohio, Pennsylvania, New Jersey, and New York both before and after the Civil War. Theatrical productions also often included tournaments—as did *Mazeppa,* the play that Adah Isaacs Menken made famous by her display of seeming nudity. In 1876 a tournament held at the Philadelphia Centennial Exposition drew two thousand aspirants for fifteen contestant places and featured the selection of a queen for the entire centennial. By this time tournaments seemed so popular that *Harper's Weekly* speculated that they might become the national sport, superseding even baseball in public favor.[7]

The selection of queens at May Day celebrations and tournaments took on a more familiar form in the many festivals that cities and states began to hold in the mid- and late-nineteenth century. Such festivals were most popular in the West, where Calvinist influences were weak and Catholic and Indian cultures, with their emphases on ceremony and display, were strong. In addition, young cities vied with one another to attract settlers. Up and down the California coast by the 1890s cities held yearly festivals: San Jose celebrated May Day; San Diego and Santa Cruz held water carnivals. Rose festivals were held in Santa Rosa, San Mateo, and Tulare, and they were designed through the use of flowers to display the balmy California climate to easterners. They reached their most popular and long-term manifestations in the Pasadena Tournament of Roses, first held in 1889, and in the Portland, Oregon, rose festival, first held in 1909.[8]

Cities in the central western states also held festivals. Omaha mounted an Ak-Sar-Ben festival (the name is Nebraska spelled backward); St. Louis, a Veiled Prophet's Ball; Denver, a Festival of Mountain and Plain. At the Denver festival the Greek myth in which Paris gives a golden apple to Venus, instead of to Juno or Minerva for superior beauty, and which is often cited as the first beauty contest in history, was re-enacted. The vogue for festivals also spread southward and eastward. In 1885, spurred by unfavorable comments in the eastern press about Minnesota's weather, St. Paul businessmen initiated their still existing winter carnival. In 1896 St. Petersburg, Florida, then little more than a town, initiated a parade of children which later became the sizable and still popular Festival of States.[9]

The common ancestor of all American festivals was the New Orleans Mardi Gras, first held in 1699, shortly after the founding of the city. In the literature of festivals the Mardi Gras is unique: even though festival promoters generally refuse to acknowledge rival festivals, they all trace their origins to the Mardi Gras. Its venerable age and nationwide reputation were important reasons for its popularity, plus the fact that it lasted for nearly a month each year. Its founders and major celebrants were aristocrats who dominated New Orleans life. Indeed, out of the Mardi Gras festivities evolved an elaborate system of exclusive clubs that formed the nucleus of New Orleans social life throughout the rest of the year. To all later festivals the Mardi Gras lent the glamour of social cachet. Its parades and balls, its costumes and bur-lesques, the selection of its queens—all established the conventions that later festivals would follow.[10]

What is most interesting in the long history of the selection of queens for May Day celebrations, tournaments, and festivals is how rarely there was any protest against an action that might have been seen as a violation of the Victorian prohibition against a woman displaying herself in public. Indeed, the only such protest on record occurred in New Orleans in 1871, when conservatives condemned the initial decision of the Mardi Gras managers to add a queen to their celebration. Yet this unusual protest may have reflected more the prudery of a high society in a city renowned for its sophisticated vice district than it did the general sentiments of conservative Americans. And the Mardi Gras organizers cleverly blunted the criticism by eliminating any features of their competition that might appear prurient. First, they re-stricted the candidates for their queen to married women. Second, they chose their ruler by following the old Twelfth Night custom of baking a bean in a cake and proclaiming the woman who drew the bean as their queen. They thus legitimized their suspect action by luck, fate, and demo-cratic selection in a democratic nation—precedents that other festival man-agers and beauty contest entrepreneurs followed in selecting their queens.

The very nature of the festivals and the function of queens within them also legitimized whatever suspicion might attach to women's assuming the public role of queens. In 1836, at a time when there were few American fes-tivals, the distinguished French analyst Michel Chevalier pointed out the need for festivals to invoke civic pride and affirm community values. They would complete the national character and "thrill the fibers of democracy." And once festivals began to appear, they fulfilled just this function. Even in those festivals established initially to enhance the commercial prospects of their cities, like the Portland Rose Festival and the Pasadena Rose Parade, all classes came together to perform a ritual of community solidarity. Al-though most festivals were organized by representatives of the community's elite and thus reinforced the hierarchical nature of American society, they gave momentary credence to the utopian hope that anyone could attain high status and public acclaim. The New Orleans Mardi Gras, for example, may have been integrally related to members of the New Orleans aristoc-racy, who were its organizers and major celebrants, but all citizens donned costumes and assumed new identities for the parades and street dancing. The lower classes had their clowns and burlesques that momentarily broke through the barriers of class surrounding their social superiors, but ulti-mately reinforced the strength of the traditional social order by dissipating hostility through laughter.[11]

For all the functions of festivals, queens were crucial. Since both con-servatives and feminists considered women the special guardians of Ameri-can morality, what better way was there to symbolize enduring community values and future utopian expectations than by choosing women as festival queens? Michel Chevalier indicated that festivals were incomplete without queens, who provided their real meaning as enduring symbols of commu-nity solidarity and fruitfulness. Take women away from tournaments, he wrote, "and these become nothing more than fencing bouts."[12]

Moreover, queens could usefully demonstrate the supposed existence of American social mobility. Over the years some of the Mardi Gras queens were chosen from among working-class women, and the community ballot-ing that was often used to select festival queens occasionally produced a winner from the working classes as well as from the elites. Balloting for the Sacramento festival queen in 1900, for example, resulted in the election of a Miss McAdam, a clerk in a department store, over Mrs. H. G. Smith, the "society leader." And Sacramento society displayed its democratic generosity and its ability to co-opt a potential critic when wealthy Mrs. E. W. Hale loaned the new queen her mansion in which to entertain in regal style dur-ing the celebration.[13]

Physical beauty was not always the overriding factor in the selection of festival queens. Sometimes they were chosen for outstanding civic leader-ship, in honor of a powerful male relative, or for their popularity in the community. The 1888 queen of the St. Paul Winter Carnival was the daughter of the mayor; the early queens of the Portland Rose Festival and the Ak-Sar-Ben celebrations were often community leaders. Thus, early competitions among women for symbolic community leadership rewarded endeavor as well as appearance; entitlement was gained for achievement or position as well as for beauty. Still, physical appearance counted in the se-lection of many May Day, tournament, and festival queens. As early as the antebellum era, the beauty was a recognized type, and public competitions offered a way to regularize the selection procedures and more forcefully to announce the way women were supposed to look. At the same time, public festivals reinforced the centrality of physical beauty in women's lives and made of beauty a matter of competition and elitism and not of democratic cooperation among women.

II

The participation of women as May Day, festival, and tournament queens in upper-class pageants that revolved around medieval and classical fantasies occasioned no particular opposition. Such was not the case when commercial entrepreneurs, realizing the powerful appeal of beautiful women to their audiences, introduced beauty contests into middle- and upper-class places of entertainment. So long as theatrical entrepreneurs and museum directors kept their contests at places frequented by working-class people among whom physical display was accepted, there was no public outcry. But when they attempted to broaden their appeal and to cross class lines, difficulties emerged.

Phineas T. Barnum encountered this barrier when in 1854 he conceived what might be called the first modern beauty contest, involving women's display of face and figure before judges. Normally sensitive to public moods, in this case Barnum underestimated the amount of moral opposition his contest would arouse. Yet for some time displays of physical beauty on the New York stage had drawn huge audiences, even in respectable theaters. In 1840 the passionate dancing of Fanny Elssler had been greeted with encomiums; a year later Charlotte Cushman, the most respected actress of her day, had starred in *The Naiad Queen,* a musical extravaganza featuring one hundred dancers in tights. In 1847, middle-class women had thronged the displays of Hiram Powers's Greek Slave, and in 1853 a group of New York showmen opened Franconi's Hippodrome, a theater whose spectacles and circuses rivalled Barnum's displays and in which tournaments with queens of love and beauty were featured.[14]

Barnum had cloaked Jenny Lind in a mantle of moral respectability when he managed her celebrated 1850 tour of the United States, but he may have been emboldened to abandon such subterfuges by the increasingly free and easy behavior of women on New York City streets, as well as by the regular newspaper accounts of noted beauties. Moreover, before his 1854 beauty contest, Barnum had held successful dog, bird, flower, and baby contests at his New York City American Museum. He had also long been president of the Fairfield, Connecticut, county agricultural society and organizer of six county fairs at which, according to several accounts, races among women horseback riders were the most popular entertainments.[15]

Yet despite the fact that Barnum offered lavish prizes—a diamond tiara if the winner were married, a dowry if she were single—the only women who initially submitted entries to his contest were "of questionable reputation," according to Oscar Comettant, whose memoir provides the only detailed account of the contest. The respectable women that Barnum hoped to attract did not apply. "No mother or husband—no matter how liberal—would allow a daughter or wife to thus appear in public," continued Co-mettant, hinting that, in fact, young women might have had more interest in the contest than their failure to submit applications indicated. Barnum, however, quickly rectified the error he had made and by a simple change in procedure gained approval. Rather than requiring that his contestants appear in person, he announced that they need only submit daguerreotypes for judging. The reason may have been that the studio of Mathew Brady, the nation's most distinguished antebellum photographer, was located across the street from Barnum's museum. Brady often photographed Barnum's performers; perhaps he suggested the photographic contest. In any case, by 1854 the popularity of the daguerreotype was so widespread that its use for these purposes cleansed the occasion of the taint of immorality otherwise thought inherent in public displays of women's figures.[16]

Moreover, Barnum enveloped his contest in a haze of soothing rhetoric. He advertised it both in *Humphrey's Journal,* the leading organ of daguerreotypists, and in a separate circular. He offered to pay the postage of the photos sent to him and suggested that the names of the women did not have to be included. He explained that he intended to have portraits painted of the photographs and to display them in a gallery, a so-called Congress of Beauty, in order to encourage "a more popular taste for the Fine Arts, stimulate to extra exertion the genius of our Painters, and laudably gratify the public curiosity." Over the period of a year all visitors to the portrait gallery were to vote for the one hundred most beautiful portraits and, from these, the ten most beautiful. All women involved would receive prizes, and the final ten would be included in a world book of beauty that a French publisher was presumably planning to issue. Appealing to American patriotism, Barnum contended that his winners would conclusively prove that American women were the most beautiful in the world. Finally, Barnum stated that he would not accept photographs from "disreputable persons." Barnum sold his museum before the photographs arrived, but the last report of the contest in *Humphrey's Journal* indicated that the new owners attempted to carry out his plan.[17]

So popular did the photographic beauty contest originated by Barnum prove to be that by late century newspapers throughout the country adopted it as a promotional device, particularly after the development of the halftone plate in the late 1880s permitted the reproduction of photographs in newspapers. In 1888 circus entrepreneur Adam Forepaugh accentuated the trend when he advertised in the nation's newspapers for photographs to find the nation's most beautiful woman. The winner was to receive $10,000 and to star in Forepaugh's production of a dramatization of Thomas

Moore's *Lallah Rookh,* a spectacle that would allow the circus entrepreneur to use scanty costumes and many elephants. More than eleven thousand women submitted photos, and the winner, actress Louise Montague (who had begun her career in the chorus of *The Black Crook*), was dubbed the Ten Thousand Dollar Beauty and became the spectacle's main attraction. The next year Barnum attempted a similar contest in connection with his own circus, but he cancelled it when he apparently could not secure funding for the prizes.[18]

Such beauty contests were especially popular among the mass circulation dailies that appeared in the 1890s and whose editors boldly utilized sex and violence as part of their appeal. In 1901 the *St. Louis Globe Democrat* conducted a competition throughout the old Louisiana Purchase territory in order to find the most beautiful woman to be featured at the Louisiana Purchase Exposition of 1902. In May 1904 the *Denver Post* announced a competition to find the most beautiful woman in Colorado, and in 1905 the *San Francisco Examiner* solicited photographs to discover the five most attractive California resort girls. In 1906 the *St. Louis Post Dispatch* searched for the most beautiful girl in St. Louis, as did the *Denver Post* for the six most beautiful in Denver. In 1912 the *San Francisco Examiner* again sought the most beautiful girl in the United States. A standard variation on these photographic newspaper contests were city and state competitions conducted through the newspapers to find beautiful women to be models for civic sculptures or for statues sent to the many expositions and centennials of the period.[19]

Perhaps the most elaborate of the newspaper beauty contests occurred in 1905, when promoters of that year's St. Louis Exposition contacted various newspapers to select city representatives to compete for a beauty title at the exposition. The newspaper editors saw the publicity potential. The *Chicago Tribune* began what developed into an extensive war of words by issuing a challenge to other cities to match the beauty of its contestant, Della Carson, whose position as secretary to the dean of the Chicago Divinity School implied a moral respectability that may have played a role in her selection. In March 1905 the *New York World* reported that the intense competition had extended to a dozen cities. According to one report, forty thousand entries were submitted. Della Carson, who won the contest, was widely featured in advertisements and general interest stories.[20]

So successful did the newspaper contests prove to be that even the *Ladies' Home Journal,* which catered to the middle class, began to employ them as promotional devices by 1911. In 1907 the *Journal* damned the many photographic beauty contests then being held. "It is inconceivable," the editor declared, "that any woman laying the least claim to be considered a woman should enter a photograph in a beauty contest." Yet four years later the *Journal* solicited its readers to submit photographs for competition to select from five regions of the country the five most beautiful young women in the United States. Each winner was to be brought to New York City, where Charles Dana Gibson would paint her portrait. Given the importance of the newspaper beauty contest, it is not surprising that the promoters of the first several Miss America contests themselves turned to newspaper editors to conduct the preliminary judging for the competitors in their final Atlantic City event.[21]

Despite Barnum's difficulty in holding a beauty contest involving the physical presence of the contestants, later in the century such events were frequent, particularly at dime museums, for these places were institutions of mass culture with only fleeting pretensions to respectability. Barnum's museum was located on fashionable Broadway, and his admission price was twenty-five cents. The New York dime museums charged a dime and were located mainly on the Bowery. Before the development of the movies, they were central institutions of American popular culture. Like Barnum's American Museum, the model for the rest, they included both eclectic displays of curiosities as well as stage entertainment. Their offerings were sufficiently salacious that women, by and large, did not frequent them. Yet, located in or near immigrant areas, they functioned as important avenues of acculturation, particularly since their customers did not have to know English to understand the displays. Their beauty contests were significant means of transmitting to immigrant men and women American standards of physical appearance.[22]

Critic Alexander Woollcott remembered that during the Trilby craze all the dime museums in New York City held contests in which patrons voted among a number of women for the perfect Trilby. Chicago dime museum proprietor George Middleton asserted that one contest he held in the 1890s became a standing joke in the city when the woman who was voted the winner turned out to be middle-aged and unattractive. The best known of the dime museum beauty contests was held at Bunnell's Museum in New York City in 1882 on the occasion of Lillie Langtry's first tour of the United States.[23]

The contest was a huge success. Wrote one observer, "It is the thing to drop in at the museum, cast a few extra votes for the favorites, and try to get a chance to talk with this or that Beauty—although the crowd is so great that conversation is almost impossible." The *Police Gazette* described the contestants as "true types of healthy, sensitive American girls with a well-balanced mixture of Yankee prudence and French vivacity." The *Spirit of the Times* reported that Bunnell's contest differed from the usual "Ladies' Show" by having "one or two really good-looking women among the competitors." One of the contestants, who attracted reporters because of her shyness, gained brief public acclaim as "the Bowery Lily."[24]

By the 1890s beauty contests were also held at carnivals. Carnivals, like midways, were descendants of dime museums taken on tour. All were related to the circus, which was the parent institution whose roots can be traced to medieval times. But circuses were the productions of the tightly knit, inward-looking world of circus performers, and they did not generally include audience participation. The midway developed to serve this entertainment need, although its core was always the display of freaks and curiosities. Carnivals, with their fanciful rides and their tossing and pitching games, were wholly centered around the participation of those who entered their gates.[25]

The growth of the carnival was related to the initiative of entertainment entrepreneurs who persuaded the organizers of the ubiquitous agricultural fairs in the post–Civil War period to include carnivals among their entertainment offerings. The Chicago Columbian Centennial of 1893, the most important American exposition of the century, provided an additional impetus to the growth of carnivals. The fair's organizers, drawn from Chicago's elite, sponsored an official "Midway Plaisance," following the example of a number of previous European expositions. Its inclusion indicated growing middle-class acceptance of popular entertainments, like the circus and the carnival, previously reprobated as immoral. For this 1893 midway the ferris wheel was developed, the belly dance was introduced, and, resonant of Barnum's original beauty contest, a large building housed a Congress of Beauty, composed of young women from various countries in the dress of their native lands sitting on a stage.[26]

The world's fair midway provided a model for later expositions. For example, the midway of the Atlanta International Cotton Exposition of 1895 rivalled the northern fair in extent. Acknowledging the popularity of displays of female beauty, its managers also included a beauty show among the midway attractions. In imitation of the earlier one in Chicago, the women on display represented a variety of foreign countries. One spectator contended that it was "the Mecca of the show" and that the manufacturing exhibits were neglected for the "galaxy of stars snatched from the sparkling North and the glowing tropics."[27]

The depression of 1893 brought the suspension of agricultural fairs for a number of years. Thus carnival promoters had to look elsewhere for patronage. Given the success of the midways at the Chicago and Atlanta expositions, town chambers of commerce and fraternal associations of businessmen now found carnivals attractive means to promote civic enterprise and business initiative. The sources for the history of the carnival are few, but evidence indicates that, as they developed, they began to incorporate certain features of the festivals; for example, they now began to employ beautiful women as queens of their events. But in keeping with the origins of the carnival in the world of midways and the dime museums, carnival operators did not hesitate to focus on women's physicality. For example, beautiful women and beauty contests were a central part of "The Elks' Mid-Summer Street Carnival, Art, and Industrial Exhibition," sponsored in 1898 by the combined Elks' Clubs of the Ohio cities of Akron, Zanesville, and Canton. On the first day of the fair a prize was awarded to the township sending the most attractive wagonload of women under the age of eighteen. The midway at the carnival had a "congress of beauty," and a contest was held to find the most beautiful woman among those attending the fair. On that day, all the guards, gatekeepers, and workers at the carnival were women.[28]

The success of the 1898 Ohio carnival, like the 1911 *Ladies' Home Journal* beauty contest, seemed to indicate that beauty competitions were becoming an accepted feature of American life. Yet difficulties still remained, particularly when women had to appear seminude or parade before judges. In 1903 famed physical culturist Bernarr Macfadden held a contest in New York City's Madison Square Garden to find the world's most perfectly formed man and woman. Contestants came from all the states and from foreign countries, and the audience was asked to vote for the final winners. Yet even though Macfadden's expressed purpose was to promote physical fitness "by showing living models," Anthony Comstock successfully secured an injunction to stop the presentation on the grounds of indecent exposure, for the women participants were wearing tights and jerseys without the shorts or tutus used even on the burlesque stage. Moreover, even though neither bathing suits nor the display of nudity was involved in the beauty contest at the St. Louis Exposition of 1905, its managers encountered widespread protest. The Reverend Thomas B. Gregory of Kansas City, Missouri, gained national publicity for his arrangement: "Imagine a really refined and innocent young girl sitting upon a platform at a great exposition to be gazed at and ogled and discussed and commented upon by the great mixed multitude. . . . No truly refined young girl would submit to such a thing. The mere thought of it would drive her mad."[29]

Although by 1905 the photographic beauty contest was an accepted feature of American life, and women regularly assumed the roles of queens at festivals and of beauty contest winners at dime museums and carnivals, there was still difficulty when it came to a question of presumably refined women publicly displaying themselves before judges or the public. This problem would not be completely overcome until the Miss America promoters successfully combined the features of lower-class carnivals with upper-class festivals and thereby fused energy with refinement in a natural and national setting that celebrated the young American woman as a symbol of national pride, power, and modernity.

III

One development paralleled the spread of beauty contests and played a role in legitimizing the latter events. The emergence of modelling as a respected career for women and the assumption on the part of the model of her present-day position as a primary source of beauty standards for women made all women's public displays of beauty acceptable, even envied.

In the nineteenth century, modelling was not a respectable occupation for women. Like actresses, models were suspected of being prostitutes on the side, particularly since some of them modelled for artists in the nude. Nude modelling could be lucrative: in the 1860s a clothed sitting paid $2 a day, while a sitting in the nude earned the model $25 to $30—figures that seem to indicate resistance on the part of women to such work. As late as 1894 one commentator contended that women who worked as artists' models kept their identities hidden and refused to allow artists to share their names with fellow artists. "Even the models who pose for the head," wrote this observer, "do not allow their names to be spoken out of the studios, as there is an association with the word 'model' which makes a woman looked at askance."[30]

Yet such attitudes were soon to change. Trilby's popularity made the artist's model seem a figure of romance, and the elite women who sat for Charles Dana Gibson made her seem glamorous. Some months after the publication of *Trilby,* sculptor Augustus Saint-Gaudens remarked that every woman he met wanted to be a model, and newspapers regularly began to interview the women who modelled for Gibson, James Montgomery Flagg, Howard Chandler Christy, and the other popular illustrators of the day. As with actresses and chorus girls, newspapers were sympathetic to models, whose image they played a considerable role in enhancing. In typical articles on modelling as an occupation for women, they stressed the occupation's hard work and the propriety of most models, or they noted that models came from respectable working-class backgrounds and middle-class families impoverished by unfortunate circumstances—like the southern women who came north for careers in entertainment or related occupations after the Civil War. Some of the best-known models, like Minnie Clark of New York and Leonora White of California, basked in newspaper publicity.[31]

By the 1890s, too, old prohibitions against the use of women in advertisements were beginning to fall. Advertisers could hardly fail to realize the success of cigarette advertising using cards with photos of buxom women on them. Early in the century perfume cards usually featured cherubic children; by the 1880s fashionable women had replaced them as subjects. Subsequently, popular magazines like *Cosmopolitan* began to use photographs of beautiful women as story illustrations, and a group of photographers began to specialize in this kind of portraiture. Finally, numerous commercial companies, particularly in liquor and patent medicines, decided that their copy in newspapers and magazines ought to be "brightened by pretty faces," and they began to use photographs of beautiful women for this purpose.[32]

In addition to their work for artists and advertisers, models were also employed to display clothing. Since the early nineteenth century, dressmakers had used their assistants to display their wares, as had elite stores when they introduced women's ready-to-wear. According to a contemporary source, clothing models were often required to have precise body measurements, and many, like their counterparts in later decades, had to diet rigorously to keep to the mark. By the early twentieth century, fashion shows became common. Dress designer Lucile remembered holding them as early as 1910 in New York City, the same year that the United Ladies' Tailor Association at its annual convention switched from displaying on wax dummies its standard exhibition of several hundred gowns to a fashion show featuring "fifty of the most beautiful women in New York City." To attract buyers from outlying regions as well as afternoon shoppers who might otherwise go to matinées, a number of New York department stores held regular fashion shows to introduce the latest Parisian fashions. The mood and timing of these shows removed the model from any association with the subculture of sensuality and made of her a svelte, elegant creature. Slowly she walked down the steps in front of the audience and across the stage with a "slow, proud motion, apparently oblivious of the audience." Within her disinterest lay a claim to recognition as a principal model of beauty in women.[33]

For this kind of work, predictability and professionalism on the part of models were important. At first, for example, the new art photographers used photos of young women they had taken surreptitiously or informally and submitted them as art or advertising copy. But they quickly turned exclusively to professional models after such casual practice resulted in several lawsuits for damages on the part of women who had not consented to have photos of themselves used commercially. Although young society women clamored to sit for Charles Dana Gibson, he preferred to use professional models, who were expert in assuming poses and sitting still. During the time she worked as a Greenwich Village artist, Elisabeth Finley Thomas found that New York models were hard-working and businesslike and that they belonged to associations of painters and models. This very professionalization helped models assert a claim to respectability.[34]

Yet as late as 1920 there were still inconsistencies in modelling organization. For example, when artists or department stores wanted models, they often advertised in newspapers, rather than dealing with established associations of models. John Robert Powers, an out-of-work actor, stepped into the void and organized the nation's first modelling agency. The Powers model eventually became as famous as the Ziegfeld girl had been before her. In fact, Powers completed the transformation of the model from an object of opprobrium to one of envy. So esteemed did the model become by the mid-1920s that Powers was able to employ New York debutantes—women who normally considered work degrading, but who now found modelling glamorous and in keeping with their own aspirations for social preferment.[35]

The rise of the model to a position of esteem coincided with the rise in popularity of the chorus girl. In fact, Powers contended that most of the early models were, in fact, chorus girls out of work. Their new position demonstrated once again the determination of a certain number of American working women to rise from the ordinary to popularity in one of the few democratic fields of women's employment, that of public entertainment. And the elevated status of the model and the chorus girl helped to legitimize the beauty contest. Like the chorus girl and the model, the beauty contestant displayed herself before the public. Like the chorus girl, she often wore abbreviated clothing; like the model, she neither danced nor sang, but rather walked before a panel of judges or put herself on display for the public to vote. The early Miss America contestants were judged in a number of different kinds of clothing, not just bathing suits, and they put on displays of attire like those in fashion shows.

In contrast to recent beauty contests, in which the prizes generally involve money, material goods, or college scholarships, beauty contests of the 1890s and the early years of the twentieth century often offered as prizes an opportunity in modelling or in the theater. And although then as now most beauty contest winners quickly faded into obscurity, some did achieve positions in Ziegfeld's choruses or became models for one of the "pretty girl" illustrators. The most famous of these early beauty contest winners was Clara Bow, born in extreme poverty, who parlayed a screen test won in a 1921 *Photoplay* magazine photographic contest into a major movie career. The limited data on other beauty contest winners also suggests that they viewed the experience as affording them potential social mobility and that, like the 1900 Sacramento Festival Queen, Miss McAdam, and the 1905 national beauty contest winner, Della Carson, most were secretaries or sales-

women—positions of prestige within the hierarchy of working women and
ones usually held by native-born women of some education.[36]

Yet although beauty contests, like the chorus and modelling professions, offered the possibility of social mobility to a few working-class
women, their primary purpose in the past, as in the present, was social discipline and not social advance. Queens of nineteenth-century festivals and
tournaments played a conservative role as symbols of community cohesion
and continuity. Twentieth-century beauty contest winners were no less conservative in their celebration of women's physical appearance and in their
application of the mode of competition. Men competed in sports, business,
and the professions; women competed with their faces and their bodies. Nor
must we forget that the majority of beauty contest winners, then as now,
achieved no tangible gains as a result of their triumph. In an insightful analysis of the psychology of beauty contests, former Miss America Jacque
Mercer has pointed out that the appearance of most Miss Americas, as well
as that of the winners of the hundreds of local contests that precede her selection, is wholesome and clean-cut, that neither their faces nor their figures
are really appropriate for fashion modelling or the movies. Most, as she
points out, become wives and mothers once their reign has ended, proof to
American women that the real end of beauty is to secure a husband.[37]

Just as the rhetoric surrounding beauty contest winners in the early
twentieth century was more career oriented than that of the later Miss
America contests, so the winners seem to have been chosen in line with
standards then appropriate for potential stage or modelling careers. The
early twentieth century was, after all, an age of some liberation for women.
But the differences between earlier and later contests can be carried too far.
It was never the future potential of the beauty contest winner that was
stressed, but rather her present reality: what she looked like, how she was
shaped. The turn-of-the-century sensual revolution eventually ended the old
associations between women and morality and made women vulnerable to
exploitation by the commercial beauty culture. A similar process can also be
seen at work in the beauty contest. As the beauty queen left her throne in
the tournament and festival, stepped out of the photograph, and shed her
clothes, donning a bathing suit so that more of her body could be seen,
women also shed their association with morality, masked their professional
skills, and became sex objects, competing in an arena where men were the
judges and the promoters. The rise to eminence of the model opened a new
career for women and dignified for them many sensual associations previously seen as suspect. On the other hand, the model brought with her an
emphasis on the body that was not liberating, but rather confining, and that
locked women into stereotypes in many ways more destructive than the old
ones.

IV

The Miss America contest drew from a rich background of beauty contests in festivals, dime museums, expositions, and carnivals and in the columns of newspapers. Curiously, seaside resorts were relatively late in holding them, although in the 1890s in Saratoga, Bar Harbor, and elsewhere floral parades featuring women in flower-covered carriages were popular. A beauty contest took place at Rehoboth Beach, Delaware, the largest resort on the state's Atlantic coast, as early as 1880. But it was not until the turn of the century that beach beauty contests appeared with any regularity. By all accounts these contests were casual affairs, although in 1920 an official queen of the five New York City beaches was chosen, and in 1921 the winner of this event became a contestant in the Miss America competition. Yet even Coney Island, Atlantic City's great rival, did not hold a beauty competition. Rather, its major activity was a festival—a so-called Coney Island Mardi Gras—that featured a king and queen chosen from among popular actors and prominent Long Island individuals. Whatever competition was involved did not include bathing beauties.[38]

Seaside resorts occupied an ambiguous place in the minds of Americans. They were places of anonymous meeting, outside the regular confines of American culture, away from "conventional restraints." They mixed together friends and strangers in new and novel combinations. They were close to nature and the relaxing forces of sun and fresh air, away from the accustomed circles that monitored behavior. At them conventional mores were easily loosened. By all accounts seaside resorts especially served a female clientele. Older women with children came to them to escape the heat of eastern summers, while their husbands, committed to work, stayed behind or commuted on weekends. For younger women, resorts were places of fashionable recreation or of the husband hunting for which the resorts were renowned. At them young women might freely engage in flirtations and liaisons.[39]

The "resort girl" or "summer girl" she was called in stories, songs, and newspaper descriptions that loved to feature her. Sometimes the characterization was complimentary and focused on her athleticism and sense of fun. Often it was pejorative and stressed the fashionable display evident on afternoon boardwalk promenades, at evening dances, or during the flirtations that indicated the underlying sensuality of the resort world. More than anything else, the reputed dangers of resorts became focused on the bathing suit, which became less and less voluminous as the century progressed. In 1910 many analysts found the scene at beaches alarming. "Young men in skin-tight, sleeveless, and neckless bathing garments, about a yard in length, and bare-armed girls with skirts and bloomers above the knee, loll together in a sort of abandon, or dive and bathe while screaming and clutching one another like contortionists," one noted. "Two lie side by side, toasting themselves to the popular russet tint. . . . In wilder moods they cover each other with sand which sculptures every outline of their bodies; they do cake-walks and skirt-dances." Municipalities in which beaches were located passed ordinances regulating the extent to which arms and legs had to be covered. In 1913 a woman at Atlantic City wearing a short bathing suit was assaulted by an outraged crowd.[40]

The 1913 incident at Atlantic City indicated the particular problem of repressive morality at that resort. Before the Civil War, the major resorts like Saratoga and Newport catered to a wealthy clientele. But the period after the Civil War witnessed the vast expansion of existing resorts and the creation of new ones, like Atlantic City and Coney Island. Atlantic City's patrons were drawn from across the spectrum of American society. The hotels on the boardwalk catered to the well-to-do, while hostelries and rooming houses back from the beach provided vacation quarters for the less affluent. Rehoboth Beach was able to hold its beauty contest in 1880 with impunity because the resort's clientele was drawn heavily from working-class people, while a convention of working women meeting at the resort conveniently provided contestants. Yet the situation at Atlantic City was more complex, and the extent to which its well-to-do vacationers would accept the beauty contest was problematic. On the one hand, the contest, held during the first two weeks in September, seemed a way of increasing tourism by extending the summer season past September first; on the other, a conservative protest might emerge against what was in effect the first major national occasion in which young middle-class women would expose themselves in bathing suits before a panel of judges.

To avoid conservative protest, the managers presented their contestants as natural and unsophisticated. Their publicity stressed that none of the entrants wore makeup or bobbed their hair—symbols of 1920s modernity that had already assumed a powerful influence in cultural styles. To underscore the contestants' youth and wholesomeness, they were carefully separated from "professional beauties," women who had already achieved some success on the stage or in modelling. In fact, representatives of the latter group competed in a special contest for trophies and modest cash prizes, although their contest was secondary to that of the amateurs. To add glamour to the occasion, the contest promoters persuaded some of the most important of the famed male illustrators of beautiful women to serve as judges. In 1921 Howard Chandler Christy alone performed this function; in 1922

James Montgomery Flagg, Cole Phillips, and Norman Rockwell joined him.

As additional legitimation of their contest, the Miss America promoters borrowed heavily from circumlocutions employed by filmmakers who previously had launched the bathing beauty as a successful cinema character. Subject to censorship through voluntary and public boards of review, movie makers had had to exercise caution in the expression of sensuality in film. A pioneer in this regard was Mack Sennett, famed for his slapstick comedies involving the Keystone Kops and Charlie Chaplin. Yet it must not be forgotten that Sennett also included beautiful women in bathing suits in his films and that he boasted of having thereby created the bathing beauty.[41]

Sennett's own premovie experience had been in the world of vaudeville and burlesque, in which beautiful women were characteristically paired not with romantic leading men, but with comics whose ugliness and childlike temperaments downplayed the women's sexuality while indirectly highlighting it by invoking the myth of beauty taming the beast, of innocence mastering sexuality. The Keystone Kops were the ostensible stars of Sennett's films, yet they also functioned as foils to the beautiful women who appeared with them, as a way of legitimizing through laughter the force of sexuality.

Sennett also drew on the contemporary vogue of athleticism among women. Thus the publicity for Sennett's actresses always emphasized their athletic ability and their swimming expertise, despite the fact that, with the exception of Mabel Normand, Sennett's most famous protégée and a champion swimmer, none of them had any such ability. But there was strong public acceptance of women sports figures, particularly in the case of swimming, in which famed Australian Annette Kellermann had established the precedent of linking beauty with physical ability. Struck by polio at an early age, Kellermann had taken up swimming for exercise and had become a champion swimmer, parlaying her athletic expertise and physical beauty into a successful career in American vaudeville and movies. Kellermann was the Esther Williams of her day, and her saga of triumph over tragedy through personal endeavor was bound to appeal to upward-striving Americans. Kellermann designed a one-piece bathing suit worn with tights rather than bloomers and, posing in it, she paid no attention to American prohibitions about seminudity, although in 1907 she was arrested on a Massachusetts beach for indecent exposure when she wore it during a promotion campaign to boost its sales. The sleeker the suit, she argued, the more effectively the swimmer could swim.[42]

The examples of Kellermann and Sennett were prominent in the events surrounding the Miss America contest. During the several days it was held, the Atlantic City police dressed like Keystone Kops. In addition, a special section of the parade that opened the event was reserved for individuals dressed as clowns. One commentator in 1922 remarked on the striking number of Chaplin imitators among them. "They set up Mack Sennett as a standard of customs and manners," complained a 1924 critic of the Atlantic City event. Moreover, the Miss America promoters included swimming exhibitions by the local Atlantic City women's swimming club as part of their entertainment. In 1922 a contingent of women from New York City arrived by seaplane, jumped in the ocean, and displayed their athletic ability by swimming to shore. As if to underscore their prowess, the plane fired several booming shots and released a banner proclaiming, "Hello, Atlantic City, here is New York." Marchers in the opening day parade who were not dressed as clowns all wore bathing suits; they included Atlantic City's mayor and members of its city council and chamber of commerce, which had been instrumental in managing the event. Many of the contestants and the women marchers wore Annette Kellermann bathing suits.[43]

Moreover, the beauty contest itself was surrounded by a week-long, elaborate festival that included staged spectaculars, sports events, automobile races, orchestra and dance competitions, nightly balls on the boardwalk, and the opening parade, which attracted an estimated 200,000 spectators by 1922. In addition to the comics and bathing suit marchers, the parade featured bands, floral floats, a King Neptune of the seas attended by mermaids, and the famed boardwalk rolling chairs decorated with flowers. By embedding their event in a festival that drew on venerable traditions of community cohesion, classical illusion, and elite distinction, the organizers of the Miss America contest—or pageant, as they came to call it—further obfuscated the sensual elements of their production.

The winners of the competition were carefully enveloped in a rhetoric that stressed their wholesome, natural qualities as well as their athleticism. The first, Margaret Gorman of Washington, D.C., bore a striking physical resemblance to Mary Pickford, and many commentators speculated that she had, in fact, been chosen the winner precisely because of this resemblance. Yet her choice more likely reflected the predilections of Howard Chandler Christy, the only judge, who had been drawing a Pickford type of woman for some time. Still, as "America's Sweetheart," Mary Pickford was the personification of innocence, mixed with a dose of adolescent independence and a certain skill at sports that was alluded to in her press releases. Neither a sex symbol nor a bathing beauty, her image was a perfect foil for any presumed celebration of sensuality behind the bathing beauty queen of the United States. Regarding Margaret Gorman, none other than Samuel Gompers, head of the American Federation of Labor, described her in *The*

New York Times: "She represents the type of womanhood America needs—strong, red-blooded, able to shoulder the responsibilities of home-making and motherhood. It is in her type that the hope of the country resides."[44]

Curiously, the 1922 winner, a young woman from Ohio, differed considerably in face and figure from Gorman. Yet she, too, was described in terms that dampened any aura of sensual display. Tall by the day's standards (five feet six inches), she had broad shoulders; and most descriptions of her revolved around her athletic build. Illustrator Cole Phillips, one of the contest's judges, asserted that she represented a new and dominant type of American woman, "rather tall, with straight lines, fairly athletic, with broad shoulders," and without the large bosom and hips that Phillips asserted had been definitive of beauty in American women for over a century. Confused by the differences in looks between the 1921 and 1922 Miss Americas, the *Atlantic City Daily Press* chided the judges for their "capriciousness" in deciding on the ideal type of American beauty. In actuality, the difference resulted from the fact that other illustrators, and not just Christy, were the judges in 1922. Still, giving the award over the years to several types of beautiful American women appealed to the democratic instincts of Americans, if nothing else. The Miss America contest organizers were intent throughout the competition on offending no one.[45]

Yet despite the attempts to legitimize the contest, its promoters could never entirely eliminate the overtones of salaciousness in their production. Their festival seemed to many much more like a lower-class carnival than a high-class production. Writing in 1922 about the pageant's parade, one commentator thought that it drew on "the splendors of the Orient, of jazz parlors, of bathing beaches, and even the circus. There were piquant jazz babies, who shook the meanest kind of shoulders; pink-skinned beauties of all types; tanned athletic girls; bejeweled favorites of the harem." Indeed, in 1928 the contest was cancelled, not to be revived again until 1935. The cancellation was apparently due to the objections of several influential hotel owners who catered to the middle class and argued that the contest was driving away business because their patrons found it immoral. Despite the protest of the president of the Atlantic City Realty Board, who argued that the resort's clientele came as much from the masses as from the elites, the argument of the hotel owners carried the day and, for a time, the contest ended.[46]

The Miss America pageant is a striking example both of the breakdown of Victorian prudery in the early twentieth century and the strength of Victorianism in a specific setting. Moreover, although the contest rhetoric, the composition of the parade, and the festival setting were all attempts to make a display of women's bodies respectable, they did not overshadow the fact that the contestants were being judged on how they looked in bathing suits. Even when later pageants added talent divisions and gave college scholarships as prizes, the review of the contestants in bathing suits was still the most important part of the competition. Despite pretensions to intellect and talent, physical beauty remained the overriding feature of the ideal American woman.

13

The History of Women
and Beauty Since 1921

B y 1921 the basic institutions of the American beauty culture had taken shape. The fashion and cosmetics industries existed. So, too, did beauty contests, the modelling profession, and the movies. All continued to expand during the following decades, building on increased affluence, the growth of the pleasure ethic, and the heightened sophistication of advertising. Shifts in the internal structures and external relationships of the beauty institutions did, of course, occur. Yet after about 1920 no new institutions concerned with the creation and dissemination of beauty appeared—with the exception perhaps of television. Moreover, the themes that had dominated the development of the beauty culture in the nineteenth and early twentieth centuries continued to do so. These included the conflicts between feminism and fashion and between social classes in asserting fashion leadership; the willingness of American women to identify with glamorous figures of stage, society, and especially screen; and the commercialization of the beauty culture and the concomitant emphasis on a youthful appearance as the desideratum of beauty.

Beauty continued to be big business. Even during the 1920s, when many women abandoned corsets, they took to wearing heavy makeup, as they would continue to do through the 1950s. In larger numbers than ever before, they frequented beauty parlors to have their hair shortened and curled. In 1920, when bobbed hair first became widely popular, five thousand beauty parlors existed nationwide. By 1925 their number had risen to twenty-five thousand. In 1927 the electric waving machine, which Charles Nessler had invented several decades before, became a sensation. Consequently, by 1930 beauty parlors numbered forty thousand, and the sales vol-

ume of American cosmetics companies was close to $180 million. Critics
pointed out—as they would consistently in the decades to follow—that
much greater sums of money were being allocated to self-adornment than to
education or social services.[1]

Neither the Great Depression nor World War II slowed the growth of
the cosmetics industry. Beauty treatments seemed to be important morale
boosters as well as a means of securing employment through personal
grooming. The 1930s gave birth to the Almay Company, specializing in
hypoallergenic products; Clairol, in tinted shampoos; Wella, in hair care
products; Maybelline, in eye makeup; and Germaine Monteil, in general cosmetics. Charles Revson shepherded Revlon to a major position by concentrating on colored nail polish, which major firms like Rubinstein and Arden
had largely overlooked. Max Factor built a national business on special
makeup he developed for Hollywood actors and actresses. In 1939 the nation's major mass marketer of cosmetics took shape when the old California
Perfume Company became Avon Products. Even during the war years, new
cosmetics lines—Tussy, DuBarry, and Tangee—appeared. In fact, the entire
cosmetics industry profited greatly from wartime scientific advances. Lano-
lin, the basis of modern skin creams, was a discovery of the early 1940s, as
was aerosol, which the Helene Curtis Industries put to use in the late 1940s
in the first hair spray, Spray Net.[2]

Postwar prosperity increased even further the demand for cosmetic
products and stimulated even greater competition among cosmetic companies. The most important innovator in the 1950s was Charles Revson,
who early in the decade began to employ explicit sexual motifs in Revlon
advertising. Cosmetic advertising of the 1920s and 1930s had downplayed
sexuality, perhaps because the connection between paint and promiscuity
was still strong enough in the public mind that cosmetic entrepreneurs hesitated to make the point too obviously. *Vogue* ads for Elizabeth Arden and
Helena Rubinstein in these years remained discreet. One-page spreads filled
with copy detailed the youthful, regenerative powers of their face creams in
black, formal letters with small, stylized portraits of faces of beautiful
women at the top. By 1942 Max Factor advertisements included endorse-
ments from Hollywood stars and photographs of them, although the poses
were not glamorous. In that same year, Tussy and DuBarry ads were dominated by full-face portraits of young women, although the faces were an-
gelic and the accompanying copy stressed—as did that for Rubinstein and
Arden—the potential of their products for recapturing youth, not for creating allure.

Revlon ads in the 1930s and 1940s were similarly discreet, although
Revson devised exotic names for his nail polishes and later his matching
lipsticks: "Bimi" and "Sudan" were some of the early ones. By 1952, sensing

the new sensuality of that decade, Revson threw off restraint. He named his new deep red lipstick and fingernail polish "Fire and Ice" and chose an advertisement for it that featured a sophisticated model in a silver, sequin-encrusted dress with a scarlet cape, accompanied by a questionnaire entitled "Are You Made for Fire and Ice?" As the look of the model and the title of the questionnaire implied, the questions themselves involved allusions to sensual behavior. Revson also promoted Fire and Ice through an extensive marketing campaign involving tie-ins with *Vogue,* special window displays in drug stores, and payments to department store salespeople to give special consideration to the product. Sales of Fire and Ice soared.[3]

Where Revlon pioneered, others followed. In 1955 advertising executive Shirley Polykoff invigorated a struggling Clairol Company by an intensive ad campaign for peroxided blonde hair. Sensing that most women regarded dyed blonde hair as too sexually suggestive, Polykoff's ads featured smiling blondes, often with children, looking "P.T.A.ish and ladylike," as Polykoff described them. Still Polykoff could not resist borrowing from Revson's sexual approach. The captions for her Clairol ads read, "Does she or doesn't she?" The question pointed to the supposed naturalness of Clairol hair dyes but also contained a clear allusion to sexual behavior. As the decade advanced, other companies successfully used a more open sexuality as a way of selling their products. Ads for undergarments, for example, became increasingly sexual and even exhibitionistic as the decade advanced, culminating in Maidenform's unclothed woman on city streets. The caption read, "I Dreamed I Stopped Traffic in My Maidenform Bra."[4]

Few other industries in the United States market a product as nonessential as cosmetics, and in few other industries has advertising played so crucial a role. As early as the 1920s cosmetics companies ranked second behind food companies in the amount of money spent on advertising. By the 1950s, when competition for the mass market became especially intense, cosmetics companies were spending up to 80 percent of their budgets on advertising. By then their promotional campaigns were extensive: with proper timing and the correct perception of the public mood, it seemed, they could sell almost anything. So successful had been the cosmetics industry's earlier manipulation of desires and insecurities that chemical underarm deodorants had found a major market in the 1920s. Hair sprays followed in the 1950s and, more recently, even vaginal deodorant sprays, clearly dangerous to health.[5]

Yet surveys estimate that only about 20 percent of cosmetic products marketed each year are successful. Chemist Hazel Bishop unsuccessfully launched several cosmetic products before she invented a lanolin-based smearproof lipstick successfully marketed after World War II. Yet Bishop could not survive the competition from Revlon and other major companies, which quickly brought out their own variations of her invention. One is reminded of the Farrah Fawcett line of cosmetics that was brought out with great fanfare several years ago and has failed to establish much of a market. American women are willing to spend sizable sums of money on cosmetics; what they will buy is often unpredictable.[6]

It nevertheless remains clear that, since the 1920s, to be beautiful has involved the adoption of artificial means, whether cosmetics, hair curling, hair coloring, or even plastic surgery. Obsessed with self in an individualistic, competitive society, some women are willing to display the marks of commercialism as part of their persons. Only occasionally have they returned to the late-nineteenth-century vision of beauty as a spiritual quality. Women briefly gave up dark red lipstick and nail polish in the 1960s and early 1970s, and for a time straight hair came into vogue. But the 1970s and 1980s brought back curls, permanents, and elaborate eye makeup, and for a decade cosmetics makers have been trying to bring women back to reddened lips and nails. In 1975 beauty shop receipts alone reached $4.7 billion; by 1980 they totalled $7.3 billion.[7]

And the question remains as to exactly how safe cosmetics are. In the 1930s the American Medical Association vigorously contended that some cosmetics manufacturers were fallaciously claiming health benefits from their products while using lead and arsenic in them. Under pressure the federal government in 1936 brought makeup under the regulations of the Food, Drug, and Cosmetics Act and forbade the use of harmful ingredients in cosmetics products or fraudulent claims in advertising. Yet although cosmetics firms test their products for toxicity and potential irritation to body tissue, even their staunchest defenders admit that some proportion of the population is allergic to almost every cosmetic ingredient. Still the public is not daunted. When the federal Food and Drug Administration announced several years ago that its tests showed that hair dyes could cause cancer, sales of the product fell by only 4 percent. The story may be apocryphal, but one elderly woman was reported to have said that she would rather have cancer than gray hair. So strong is the drive to be beautiful.[8]

II

Three themes have dominated the history of American women since the 1920s. The first has been the growth of what Betty Friedan brilliantly explored as the "feminine mystique," the twentieth-century version of nineteenth-century Victorianism that saw domesticity and motherhood as women's central roles and to them added sexual seductiveness. Triumphant in the 1950s, the feminine mystique had roots both in the early century growth of home economics and of mother's clubs and in the rejection in the 1920s of organized feminism for individual fulfillment. The legitimation of the use of cosmetics and their powerful hold over American women are a striking example of the dominance of the drive for femininity.

The second theme in the history of women has been the reality of women's continued discrimination, evident in their continued relegation to low-paying, low-level positions, and their still comparatively low rankings in business and the professions. Yet a third theme has been contradictory to the other two. Women have consistently protested against their situation, and this rebellion has led contemporaries in every decade since the 1920s to proclaim that women have attained equality and that feminist goals have been achieved. We know that these claims were and remain invalid and that they masked the true reality. Still, although the organized feminist movement became factionalized in the 1920s and was generally disregarded by women from the 1920s to the 1960s, certain strains of women's rebelliousness remained powerful and gave the impression of increased emancipation. The best known among these indicators of emancipation has been women's rejection of Victorian prohibitions on sensual expression. Equally important has been their continued demand for comfortable and healthy lives—a demand often expressed in dress and behavior.

Thus after World War I ready-made dresses cut along simple lines came into vogue. Most analysts have interpreted these dresses either as an expression of a sexual revolution in the 1920s or as an indication of the buying power of working women, who found them attractive in office situations. Yet they also represented the appeal of comfortable clothing to women—an appeal that was stimulated above all by the growing popularity of sports among women and the growing fame of female athletes. With their low-slung waists and lack of bust lines, these dresses were initially modelled after women's sports attire, itself designed to draw attention away from women's physical features and to allow them freedom of movement.[9]

Exactly who first designed the typical dress of the 1920s remains obscure. Most sources, however, credit French designer Gabrielle "Coco" Chanel with bringing the idea to its most representative early realization. Both athleticism and her lower-class background lay behind Chanel's initial inspiration. Chanel was determined to rise above her peasant origins, and while she was still a young woman, her wit and beauty brought her upper-class lovers. But eschewing any connection with the demimonde, with whom she might otherwise have been identified, she wore simple, severe dresses of her own design rather than the frilly frocks voguish among this group. All her early lovers were sportsmen; from them she gained a love of athletics and the out-of-doors. Her own biography meshed with the dominant cultural themes of her age: women of her generation were willing to share Chanel's rebellion through dress.[10]

Aside from film stars, the most prominent women in the United States in the 1920s and 1930s were sportswomen. Almost every sport had its women champions, and the public celebrated their successes. Tennis star Helen Wills was known as "our Helen" and "Queen Helen," and her 1924 match with French star Suzanne Lenglen created a national stir. When Gertrude Ederle in 1928 swam the English Channel and broke the world records of three previous male swimmers, she was welcomed back to New York with a ticker-tape parade down Broadway. Sonja Henie electrified the nation with her brilliant skating in the 1932 Winter Olympics and parlayed her popularity into a successful film career while launching the first commercial ice-skating shows. Sportswriter Paul Gallico contended that swimmer Eleanor Holm was much better known than any male counterpart. Esther Williams carried on in the tradition of swimmer Annette Kellermann, and Babe Didrikson, a golfer and all-round athlete, was nationally beloved.[11]

In addition to these athletic stars, lesser-known, but nonetheless able women competed in almost every sport except football and boxing. Metropolitan tabloids promoted women's swimming matches. Commercial firms employing women sponsored competitive basketball and baseball teams. So professional were these teams that potential Olympic competitors, like Didrikson, were recruited from them. Chambers of commerce fielded women's basketball and swimming teams to promote their towns, a practice especially common in Florida during the land boom of the 1920s when developers vied in attracting buyers.[12]

Many of these women athletes promoted freer dress. Tennis player Helen Wills consistently argued in the popular press that shortened skirts, sleeveless blouses, and bare legs were essential to an effective tennis game. Their arguments were seconded by film actresses, who became symbols of new sports fashion and behavior. Wearing slacks and casual clothes off the movie set, they displayed themselves in their Hollywood setting, a region of bounteous sun and geography that had never really lost its sense of frontier freedom. Continually dieting to maintain slim figures, they played tennis and went ocean swimming. Many of the major stars were tough, resilient individuals reminiscent of Lillian Russell and Lillie Langtry. Clara Bow, Joan Crawford, Marlene Dietrich, and Katharine Hepburn all displayed a rebellious, self-willed side that led them, off screen, to do, say, and wear what they wanted.[13]

The influence of athletes and actresses in promoting a vogue for simple, functional clothing became particularly powerful in the 1930s, the age of the democratization of American sports. More people than ever before personally participated in sports, and sports clothes became a major field of fashion design, associated everywhere with the United States. A vogue for dude ranches in 1930 induced the Levi Strauss company, founded in 1850 in California as a manufacturer of men's work clothes, to introduce Levi's for women. The 1932 Lake Placid Winter Olympics greatly increased popular interest in winter sports and stimulated the growth of several companies, like White Stag, which specialized in winter sportswear. Most important, however, was the impact of New Deal social programs, which brought the building of scores of public tennis courts, golf clubs, and swimming pools. The lessened work week, with an opportunity for increased leisure, and lowered incomes, which reduced the extent of holidays taken away from home, brought more people to these local facilities and accustomed them to wearing sports clothing, including shorts for women, previously reprobated as immoral away from home and beaches. But the example of sports figures and movie stars, plus mass participation in sports, legitimized the wearing of previously suspect attire.[14]

Tanned skin now also came completely into vogue. Since the 1890s and the beginnings of women's athletic interest, some women had favored a darker skin tone, associating it with sports and new sensual beach behavior and not with lowly peasant women working in fields. As the vogue of athleticism increased, so did the popularity of tans, particularly when it became apparent that women working in factories away from the sun had pale, not dark, skin. Finally, in the 1920s Coco Chanel was pictured in the tabloids with tanned skin, and her adoption of it gave the final imprimatur to a style in keeping with class, sensual, and physical-fitness motives.

Sportswear was significant in its own right. It also had a major impact on dress design more generally from the 1920s on. The 1920s shift offers a striking example of this impact, as do, in more recent years, wrap skirts, initially designed for golf. Today, sweat suits designed for jogging appear everywhere. The American public has demanded simple, comfortable clothing, in keeping with a relaxed, leisured style of life, and dress designers have responded.

Yet such attention to a kind of physical liberation has not meant that designers have been feminist in point of view; their own commercial interest has usually required that they attempt to ensure a continually shifting pattern of fashion. Nonetheless, most of the century's innovators in the direction of more liberating dress have been women, and this fact may indicate an underlying feminism on their part. These designers included in the 1920s, Chanel; in the 1930s, Vionnet and Schiaparelli, both of whom designed with comfort and convenience as well as glamour in mind. Finally, in the 1930s and 1940s, there was Claire McCardell, acclaimed as the first major American designer, whose revolutionary costumes, designed like sacks and tents, were consciously intended to offer women physical ease. In sharp contrast, it was a man, Christian Dior, who introduced the full-skirted, cinched-in-waist styles of the 1950s that recalled Victorian modes.

In the 1920s and 1930s, French couture ruled fashion design. Rarely was an American designer identified in clothing labels or in advertising. Department stores promoted their clothes as of the French mode, and American clothing manufacturers sent copyists to the French shows to re-produce Parisian lines rather than trusting to native talent for their designs. The American challenge to this monopoly emerged slowly, but its origins can be seen in the 1930s. First, Dorothy Shaver, president of Lord & Taylor, featured the clothes of several American women designers, including Claire McCardell, in her store promotions. Second, Hollywood studio designers began to be acclaimed for their movie clothes. Chief among them was Gilbert Adrian, responsible for the padded-shoulders look that predominated in fashion into the 1950s.

The 1940s and 1950s brought American dress design to commercial maturity. Sportswear continued to expand, and American design houses first created the concept of sizing and styling for particular age and size groups, such as juniors and petites. The Pratt Institute of Technology, the Parsons School of Design, and the Fashion Institute of Technology, where emerging talent could be identified, trained, and introduced to the wider fashion world, were founded in New York City. American designers, un-acknowledged in earlier decades, now came into their own. Along with cosmetic executives, they became important moulders of the ideals of physical appearance for women.

III

What have the ideals of physical appearance for women been since the 1920s? The most obvious has been a youthful appearance. An unlined face, hair neither gray nor white, a slim body with good muscle tone have been the signs of beauty achieved. Yet to conclude that youthful models of beauty have been unidimensional or that youthfulness has been the only standard of beauty for women during the past six decades is inaccurate. From the 1920s on, an older, sophisticated type has consistently challenged models of an adolescent variety. In the 1920s Theda Bara and Greta Garbo were her primary representative; in the 1930s most beauty models were so-phisticated and mature.

The most important 1920s model of physical appearance—the flapper—beamed a number of behavior messages. On the one hand, she indicated a new freedom in sensual expression by shortening her skirts and dis-
carding her corsets. On the other hand, she bound her breasts, ideally had a
small face and lips like the steel-engraving lady, and expressed her sensuality
not through eroticism, but through constant, vibrant movement. The athletic charleston, not the erotic tango, was her characteristic dance. Clara
Bow defined "It," the 1920s circumlocution for sex appeal, as vivacity and
fearlessness and a basic indifference to men. Armed with such attitudes,
screen flappers remained pure until marriage, which was their ultimate goal.
John Held, Jr.'s famous drawings of the flapper in *Life* magazine depicted
her not as sensual, but as comic: a stick figure with flying arms and legs. The
name "flapper" itself bore overtones of the ridiculous. Drawing from a style
of flapping galoshes popular among young women before the war, it con-
noted irrelevant movement and raised the specter of seals with black flapping paws.[15]

In contrast to the flapper, Theda Bara personified sophisticated eroticism. Yet, like Bow, she too had a comic side. She wore heavy makeup and
tried to look jaded, in keeping with her movie role as the vamp, the woman
who, like the legendary vampire, drained men of their masculinity and destroyed them. Bara, born Theodosia Goodman of Chicago, was, however, a
ridiculous figure—both in her overacting and in the outlandish stories
about her past made up by her press agent. She was the daughter, it was alleged, of an Algerian soldier and an Egyptian dancer; a band of Egyptian
cutthroats kidnapped and raised her; she possessed occult powers. Her name
was an anagram of the phrase, Arab Death. The aura of foolishness about
her became captured in the word "vamp," popularly extended to describe
Bara's sexual maneuverings. It quickly came to denote a comic seduction,
an attempt to arouse that had an exaggerated, ludicrous aspect to it.

An adolescent quality permeated the 1920s as Americans were first exposed in quantity to consumer goods like radios and automobiles destined
to change radically the nature of their lives. Advertising celebrated the leisured, consumption-oriented life. The flapper, with her frenetic dancing,
represented the vitality of these developments, with their promise of a new
life. Like the vamp, she indicated attempts to come to grips with the new
ethic of sensual expression. At the same time, the comic side of the flapper
represented something more. The film flapper (the most important representative of the type) was invariably a college student, a working woman,
secretary, or saleslady. The cultural focus on fashion and after hours activities in the lives of these women glamorized the working world for women
while trivializing it. The prewar secretary with her tailored, masculine at-

tire was replaced by the 1920s typist in a silk dress, anxious for a good time, but intent on securing a husband, and that goal was the ultimate message.

Americans could accept the sexuality of the flapper and the vamp because they could laugh at them, while the working woman became a fun figure, too. This familiarity paved the way for the acceptance of Greta Garbo, a figure of mature, earnest passion. With her long nose, masculine features, and broad-beamed body, Garbo bore little resemblance to Clara Bow, Theda Bara, or Gloria Swanson, for a time her predecessor in sophisticated sensuality on the American screen. Bow, Bara, and Swanson all had small noses and mouths and round faces. Garbo was mysterious, aloof, and foreign—in keeping with the convention that American women, like the nation itself, were more innocent and incorruptible than European women. Native to Sweden, a country with a reputation for liberal sexual attitudes, she was a fitting representative of an emerging freedom in sensual expression for women.

The glamour and maturity Garbo personified indicated a new standard of beauty and behavior for American women—a standard that became predominant in the 1930s, a time of economic distress in which Americans seemed to desire a more mature model of behavior and appearance. In 1929, hemlines came down, and waists and bosoms reappeared. Joan Crawford, the only 1920s screen flapper to make a successful transition to sound movies, completely changed her appearance from one decade to the next. During the 1920s she was a flapper with a flat body and round face, a small mouth, and the obligatory short, waved hairdo. By the 1930s, her shoulders and face were square, her figure buxom, her eyes and lips large, her hair shoulder-length and smoothly coiffed. "I'd been a flapper in an age of flappers," she explained, and then a "sophisticated lady in an era of sophistication." Her biographers trace her change in appearance to 1930 and identify Garbo as the original inspiration for the new look.[16]

Garbo's glamour was a predominant attribute of the ideal women of the 1930s. In addition, they acquired a look of assertive, self-confident masculinity. The assertiveness was especially apparent in the vogue for squared shoulders, achieved by padding, used not only in suits and sports attire, but also in evening wear. Adrian first designed the squared shoulders in 1932 for Joan Crawford, adapting a line which Schiaparelli had previously introduced. But, according to Adrian, it was Crawford's own demand for loose, unconfining clothing which, more than anything, led him to take up the new shoulder line. Because to meet Crawford's requirement with the tailored styles of the early 1930s required letting dresses out so much at the back that they drooped, Adrian hit on the expedient of shoulder padding, which permitted freedom of movement and eliminated the droop.[17]

Yet one suspects that the squared shoulders came to mean more than just physical freedom to Crawford and the others who wore them. The initial shoulder-padded dress that Adrian designed for Crawford was the much-copied one that she wore in the movie *Letty Lynton*. The dress is frilly and feminine, and the padding is hardly discernible. But as Crawford's career progressed, the padding became bolder, the look of masculine determination greater. And Crawford accentuated the look in other ways, by using makeup, for example, to enlarge the size of her mouth and eyes. By the late 1930s, whatever her role, she looks powerful, confident, and defiant—traits that are characteristic of other film actresses of the decade, like Katharine Hepburn, Bette Davis, Claudette Colbert, Myrna Loy, and Irene Dunne.

Assertiveness in dress matched the kind of roles these women played. The descendants of Garbo in mature sensuality, they drew on the tradition of the working-girl flapper in their most characteristic roles. In her 1920s films Garbo usually played sex-starved women consumed by the love for one man—a sacrificial theme that made heroic her passionate physicality. But the flappers during their daytime, nondancing hours were secretaries and salesladies. So were many of the women portrayed in the films of the 1930s, now often promoted to higher-status employment as journalists and business executives. Rarely were women during the latter decade shown as wives and mothers, unless in a sophisticated, upper-class setting. And when they were not career women, they were usually socialites, acting out fantasies about power and preferment that had been characteristic of American escape literature since at least the 1890s. But whether workers or society women, the women of the 1930s films were proud and self-reliant, imperious to servants and subordinates.

In the final frames of all 1930s films these women capitulated to the men who pursued them. No one in the film world was willing to question the cultural canon that marriage was the proper goal of a woman's life. On one level the message of these films was a perpetual "taming of the shrew," of men demonstrating to women that they were happiest in subordinate, domestic roles. Yet what would happen after Katharine Hepburn acceded to Cary Grant or Spencer Tracy was never made entirely clear: the vigorous independence of her character before marriage could lead her in a number of directions. And the independence of Hepburn, Crawford, and the rest was underscored by the fact that even the so-called sex goddesses of the 1930s were assertive women. A cool sophistication characterized Carole Lombard, while Marlene Dietrich, like Garbo, possessed a masculine force that showed through the whores and villains she usually portrayed. Jean Harlow, with a raspy voice, was tough-minded and wise-cracking, as were most of the gun molls and chorus girls who followed her.

Why America's most popular medium for the creation and dissemination of mass values displayed such a striking interest in independent women has never been adequately answered. The question becomes even more puzzling in light of the fact that the major studio executives who set policy for the film companies were antifeminist in point of view, although what screenwriters and directors thought about the roles they created and interpreted remains unknown. It is possible that independent women in films were intended, as one commentator has argued, to oppress women by encouraging the belief that job markets and career ladders were open to women when in fact they were not. It is also possible, in contrast, that working women, who constituted 24 percent of all women in 1930 and 28 percent in 1940, formed a substantial film audience and that many films were specifically directed toward them.[18]

Part of these films' attraction was undoubtedly that the women in them, whether they were socialites or working women, usually wore glamorous clothing and were displayed in glamorous settings, thus underscoring the romanticized, escapist version of life and work dramatized by their plots and characters. The imposition of the 1933 Production Code, which barred open sexuality in film, may also have encouraged producers to cloak physical romance even more fully in themes revolving around work, social preferment, and glamour. Still, the 1930s were a time of social chaos and economic despair. The nation seemed to need strong women, and that is how the movies depicted them.

Moreover, the personal independence of stars like Hepburn and Crawford who played the working women and socialite roles radiated through their screen personalities and formed an important part of their public personalities. In private they were proud, defiant women, and no matter whom they played, these characteristics showed through. Muncie, Indiana, carefully studied by sociologists Helen and Robert Lynd, provided an example of the effect of one of these film stars on local young people. Joan Crawford, they noted, was a model of behavior for adolescent girls. She "has her amateur counterparts in the high-school girls who stroll with brittle confidence in and out of 'Barney's' soft-drink parlor, 'clicking' with the drug-store cowboys at the tables; while the tongue-tied young male learns the art of the swift, confident comeback in the face of female confidence."[19]

The vogue of child actress Shirley Temple throws into sharp relief the independence of women in the films of the 1930s. Although Temple was probably the most popular film star of the decade, she was never presented as anything more than a child, and she never influenced adult fashions in dress and physical appearance. Her popularity was related to the pastoralism of many 1930s movies, designed to appeal to a generation stunned by the breakdown of the modern commercial order. Temple represented the uncorrupted child who, because of her lack of sophistication, could solve family and social problems that baffled adults. But what is important for the history of physical appearance is that Temple clarified the difference in the ideal physical appearance of female children and grown women. To look exceedingly young was not the ideal for women in the 1930s. In that decade women were to be competent and mature.

These qualities were extended and accentuated during World War II, when women entered industry in record numbers. "Rosie the Riveter," in her trousers and shirts, and Rosalind Russell, with her extreme man-tailored suits and her deep, masculine voice, became the feminine film ideals of the time. Such, however, would not continue to be the case.

IV

From the period of the movies' initial popularity in the 1910s, film stars had governed the definitions of ideal female beauty in the United States, and they continued to do so through World War II. Thus the history of models of physical appearance during those decades is virtually synonymous with the history of film, and this close relationship remained the case through the 1950s.

In that decade two models of physical appearance predominated. One was adolescent and childlike, the other voluptuous and earthy. Both resembled earlier types: the childlike figure, the flapper; the voluptuous model, the 1930s sensual woman. But where the flapper had been a working woman or a college student, the 1950s adolescent was usually a high school student. And where the sensual woman of the 1930s had been moderately curved and often upper-class in style, the voluptuous woman of the 1950s was huge-bosomed and, as portrayed by Ava Gardner or Jane Russell, of indeterminate, lower-class origin. "Mammary goddesses," one scholar has called them. Both ideals—the childlike model and the voluptuous one—reached their apogee in Marilyn Monroe.[20]

Betty Friedan and others have amply documented the postwar tensions that produced the resurgent Victorianism of the 1950s. In response to the reconversion to a peacetime economy, the tensions of the Cold War, and the popularity of antifeminist Freudianism, a "feminine mystique" enforcing domesticity, motherhood, and sexual suggestiveness subordinate to men came into being. This repressive view of women was embodied in the two principal models of beauty. As portrayed by Debbie Reynolds or Sandra Dee, the adolescent beauty was immature and intent primarily on securing a husband. Adult versions of adolescent actresses, portrayed by June Allyson or Doris Day, were as insipid and subordinate to men as the younger film actresses, whom they resembled in physical type. Housewives now were glorified; career women were pictured as dangerous or neurotic. In *Mildred Pierce,* Joan Crawford ruined lives and caused deaths because of her work. In *Lady in the Dark,* Ginger Rogers was able only through psychoanalysis to understand that her work denied her real femininity. Bette Davis and Joan Crawford portrayed shrews in romantic dramas and witches in horror films.

Alongside the adolescent, asexual models of beauty existed the voluptuous, earthy one. As Ava Gardner, Dorothy Lamour, and Hedy Lamarr portrayed them, their sensuality was so florid that their films were often set in foreign climes, where they could portray fallen women outside the bounds of society. Dominated by men or waiting for men to rescue them, they were rarely granted the independence displayed by their 1930s predecessors, like Carole Lombard or Jean Harlow. Moreover, the 1950s sirens were bigger in build than those of the 1930s, and their breasts were heavier. Designer Irene Sharaff wrote that every Hollywood actress knew exactly how much padding was needed "to bring her bust up to the ideal." Women were to be homemakers, yet they were to be sirens to boyfriends and husbands, concerned with attracting men through sexual display.[21]

The most important film representative of the 1950s voluptuous woman was Marilyn Monroe, who differed from the others by combining with sensuality strains of childishness reminiscent of the adolescent stars. She thereby created a powerful combination that encompassed the era. Technically unschooled and often intellectually vacuous in her film characterizations, she nevertheless possessed both the shrewdness of the classic chorus girl (a character she often portrayed in film roles) and the intuitive genius of a child, able to see more clearly to the heart of a matter than others more sophisticated around her. As a down-and-out member of a seedy female band in *Some Like It Hot,* she taught fleeing mobsters Tony Curtis and Jack Lemmon the meaning of friendship and love; as a chorus girl in *The Prince and the Showgirl,* she taught the same lesson to Laurence Olivier, the head of a fictional kingdom. Most of the other voluptuous film stars had dark hair, but Monroe's was peroxided a light blonde—a color that invoked traditional images of angels and virtuous women, reflected the light locks of the era's adolescent film stars, and both legitimized and heightened her sensuality.

Previous exemplars of female sensuality had also had blonde hair: one thinks of the British Blondes in the 1860s and Jean Harlow in the 1930s. But Monroe differed strikingly from the Lydia Thompson troupe and from Harlow. They were tough, wisecracking, even masculine in type. With a slight, lisping voice, a soft curvaceous body, and a seriousness about life, Monroe projected an intense femininity and an inner vulnerability. Her sensual posturings were reminiscent of Mae West, although with no hint of the parody that West intended. Monroe regarded her body with dead seriousness. Long before she was acclaimed as movie actress and sex queen, she had posed for the first nude centerfold in *Playboy* magazine, destined to become a trend-setter in liberalized sexuality and a showcase for the bodies of beautiful women.

Monroe's popularity ensured the triumph of the vogue of dyed blonde hair, which cosmetics companies had been promoting. Sales of hair coloring soared; platinum blondes seemed everywhere. The widespread dying of hair to be light blonde indicated women's acceptance of a model of looks and behavior that had them be feminine, sensual, and unintellectual. Women were to seem like children, expressing their adulthood primarily through their sexuality. The "dumb blonde" who had "more fun" and whom "gentlemen preferred" now became the dominant image of beauty for American women.

Fashions in clothing in the 1950s reflected the combination of social repression and sexual exploitation that characterized American attitudes toward women. More than anything else, fashions came to resemble those of the Victorian period. Skirts fell to midcalf length and became full, held out by starched crinoline petticoats. Alternatively they were exceedingly tight, sometimes making walking difficult. Waists were bound in, and women wore girdles, called minimizers, strengthened at the waistline. For evening, they wore boned corsets, called "merry widows," which they tightlaced. Young women exulted in the small size of their waistlines and compared their dimensions with their friends. Breasts were supported to appear as large as possible, and padding was commonly used to enlarge natural endowments. Most brassieres were wired or boned in such a manner that the breasts were held rigid and straight, coming to points that accentuated the nipples. Shoes came to sharp points that pinched toes and made walking difficult. The popular heel height was three inches.

The repressive features of the 1950s for women are particularly apparent in the area of women's sports—a field of endeavor that had been central to women's earlier movement toward personal emancipation. With few exceptions, the kind of acclaim accorded to individual women sports stars in the 1920s and 1930s no longer existed, and the commercial women's swimming and basketball teams popular in these earlier decades faded from view. The best-known woman tennis player of the era was Gussie Moran, a competitor of secondary rank who attracted front-page coverage because of the abbreviated skirts and lace-trimmed panties she wore in major tournaments. In high schools and colleges, women's athletics similarly came to occupy a modest position vis-à-vis men's sports. In the 1920s, interscholastic competition among women's sports teams had been eliminated due to the widespread opposition of physical education teachers, doctors, and civic leaders like Lou Hoover, Herbert Hoover's wife. Some of these opponents of women's competitive sports argued that women did not have the stamina for them; others were opposed to sports competition of any kind, whether it involved women or men. In a variation of the nineteenth-century argument about women's moral superiority, some contended that women should withdraw from sports competition in order to persuade men to do so.[22]

Whatever the argument, the results were the same: physical education programs for women were depreciated and underfunded. While male football and basketball players became heroes, their athletic counterparts among women were ridiculed. Instead, cheerleaders and pompon girls became the corresponding female cynosures, chosen not for physical or mental ability, but rather for the presumed beauty of their appearance.

V

By the 1960s films no longer exercised a dominating influence over definitions of physical beauty in American women. Television now issued a major challenge. Moreover, the radicalism of the 1960s and the emergence of the American fashion industry to worldwide importance became equally powerful influences in shaping canons of appearance.

The last female film star to have a direct, personal impact upon standards of physical appearance was the French film actress Brigitte Bardot, who starred in 1957 in *And God Created Woman,* the first film shown in neighborhood theaters to include a nude scene. Bardot was young, blonde, and voluptuous, and she embodied the ideal appearance of the 1950s. But her long hair, light lipstick, and nudity foreshadowed the rebellious fashions of the 1960s and the more liberal sexual attitudes of that era. As much as she represented the past, she also indicated the future.

The 1960s, however, should not be seen solely as an era of iconoclasm and new ways in fashion. The decade was characterized as much by a continuation of the consumer-oriented, self-involved culture of the 1950s as it was by a radicalism aimed at overturning those values. And commercial interests quickly exploited "liberated" fashions and captured them for their own. The "mod" youth culture, with its rock music, erotic dancing, and new clothing was pre-empted by traditional fashion sources—dress designers, fashion magazines, the media generally—who designed their products in accord with the new style and used the mod idioms to promote sales. And there were indications of traditional consumerism even at the heart of rebellion. Young rebels were the first to wear blue jeans and thrift shop clothes, but miniskirts and pants suits were invented by dress designers like Britain's Mary Quant. These designers were for the most part young and previously unknown, but they were inspired as much by commercial as design concerns.[23]

If anything, the sophistication of advertisers and the media in promoting consumerism increased during the 1960s. For decades the American fashion industry had unsuccessfully attempted to challenge the Parisian hegemony over fashion; in the 1960s American designers came into their own. Their success was due, on the one hand, to the appearance of an especially talented group of designers and, on the other, to the ability of these individuals and the fashion press to sell their designs and personalities to the American public. Designers like Bill Blass and Oscar de la Renta were as good at public relations as they were at designing clothes. They wooed the wealthy away from French designers by becoming their friends and confidants; appearing at elite parties and reported on by the press, they became known to the general public. Building on the American skill in mass marketing, they established tie-ins with clothing manufacturers and opened their own ready-to-wear departments. To mark their success, they inscribed designer logos and signatures on shoes, handbags, scarves, and eventually in the 1970s blue jeans, and women eagerly bought their emblazoned wares.

The success of the fashion industry was also aided by the growing market for new fashion magazines, like *Seventeen,* which catered to the burgeoning youth market, and the revitalization of older publications like *Vogue,* under the leadership of editors like Diana Vreeland, utterly devoted to the furtherance of fashion. Press agent Eleanor Lambert, who had been preparing publicity for dress designers since the 1930s with limited success, now came into her own. Buyers flocked to the shows she organized, and in 1965 she successfully lobbied to have fashion included as one of the arts under the initial funding for the National Endowment for the Arts.

A major indication of the increased power of the fashion industry was the emergence of individual models as style setters in their own right. The first model to gain national prominence was Suzy Parker, who posed for Revlon ads in the mid-1950s. She was followed by the likes of Jean Shrimpton, Twiggy, and Cheryl Tiegs. Some models, such as Suzy Parker, made a successful transition to television and films and thus increased the prestige of the modelling profession in general.

As a group, models were responsible for the vogue of extreme thinness that has remained in fashion since the early 1960s. Since the professionalization of fashion photography in the early century, it has been canonical that clothes are best displayed on lean bodies, which do not compete for viewer attention with the model's attire. By the 1960s this doctrine was extended further. As fashion photography became more sophisticated, the model, clothing, and setting were all supposed to blend into an artistic whole, in which line and angle were stressed. More than this, dieting became symbolic of the competitive nature of the modelling business, in which only those who fit the rigid photographic requirements could qualify. It was, as well, another way in which dominant cultural values have been trivialized for women. Americans have always responded to challenges that require hard work and self-control; dieting for women is comparable to sports expertise or professional success for men. The most commonly reported fact about models, aside from their supposedly glamorous lives, is their "starvation" diets.

The new popularity of models has been indicative of a tendency toward glorifying celebrities and creating popular culture heroes. While blacks and women marched in the streets and students barricaded college buildings, fashion designers, the wealthy, and consumer-oriented publications were creating a new group of international celebrities. Diana Vreeland called them "the beautiful people." But the name belied the fact that they were in reality a continuation of the "café society" of the 1930s and the "jet setters" of the 1950s, now become more prominent with the decline in popularity of the movies. High society and its celebrity compatriots often adopted the rebellious styles of the decade. They supported the avant-garde and frequented native designers; "radical chic" became the phrase to describe these tastes. Yet their standards of consumption and adornment remained constant. After all, despite the Vietnam War, the affluence of the 1950s continued into the 1960s.[24]

The acknowledged leader of the beautiful people was Jacqueline Kennedy, the president's wife whose celebrity status was unparalleled. To a certain degree her image worked to advance the position of women. She staked out a career of her own in elegant entertaining and White House redecorating; her intelligence and formality countered the mindless voluptuousness and domesticity of the 1950s ideal woman. But her contribution to the fashion industry and the consumerism of the 1960s was great. The large amounts of money she spent on clothing were widely publicized; her ties to fashion designers were well known. While her husband forged a distinctive social welfare program and identified himself with minorities and the poor, she validated the ethic of individual consumption that had gained new strength in post–World War II affluence. She was, according to one analyst, a "super consumer."[25]

Based on her mystique and that of the fashion designers and other celebrities, a new kind of celebrity reporting appeared. Columnist Eugenia Sheppard first employed it in her gossip column in the *New York Herald Tribune,* and it was perfected by the staff of *Women's Wear Daily.* This reportage involved the same kind of breezy and titillating style that Walter Winchell and others had earlier employed, but it added an even greater insouciance and willingness to shock. In addition, fashion now emerged as a significant variable in celebrity reporting. Not only were the personal doings of designers deemed newsworthy, but a designer attribution was also given to dresses worn to parties and other social events. The attribution functioned as a validation for women's taste, but it also served as an advertisement for the importance of consumerism in their lives.

In the 1960s the American public seemed fascinated by its celebrities, ever willing to buy the publications that chronicled their exploits and promoted their vogue. With the demise of many metropolitan newspapers and the disappearance of their gossip columns, scandal sheets like the *National Enquirer* and the *Star* appeared, which combined features of the old movie fan magazines with coverage of celebrities from a variety of fields and which corresponded to the diffusion in the sorts of popular heroes American culture was producing. These publications paved the way for the appearance in the 1970s of *People* and *Us,* magazines that catered to the American fascination with the private lives of the wealthy and famous.

Yet despite these modes of consumerism and self-absorption, the very real impact of 1960s rebelliousness must not be forgotten. Youths who in the 1950s had played football, cruised in cars, and worried about going steady now as eagerly seemed to take up uninhibited sex, drugs, mystical religions, natural foods, and a critical attitude toward the culture they had unthinkingly supported in the 1950s. Young women gave up wearing makeup and grew their hair long and straight. Because of their continued buying power, the commercial beauty culture was forced to incorporate their version of naturalness into its prevailing styles. The major hairdressers of the decade—Vidal Sassoon, Kenneth—developed new methods of cutting and styling hair, but their basic designs were geometric and straight.

For the first time in American history, non-European models of beauty were not only extolled by writers on beauty, but were actually presented as models for cultural emulation. Donyale Luna was the first black model to be featured in ads in general circulation fashion magazines like *Vogue.* "Black is Beautiful," the slogan of the black rebellion, penetrated white consciousness. Decrying the traditional vogue of hair straightening among blacks and identifying with their homeland, many blacks proudly wore their hair naturally and called it an Afro cut. By the end of the decade, the look became fashionable for white women who, when they did not wear their hair straight, had it frizzed into an approximation of the black style.

But arguing that even the commercial beauty culture presented blacks as beautiful does not mean that the popularity of traditional sorts of looks went out of style. Voluptuous blondes and elegant brunettes were still greatly admired. What is important about the 1960s is that the rigid standardization of physical appearance was broken to such an extent that, more than ever before, a variety of racial and ethnic looks could be seen as attractive. By the 1970s blacks and orientals (although in small numbers) even advanced to the finals of the Miss America pageant, while the Miss Universe contest presented as beautiful a worldwide selection of disparate faces and bodies. In this same period Barbra Streisand refused to reduce the size of her nose and still advanced to stardom. And where Fanny Brice, the 1920s comedienne she most resembled, was never considered as anything more than a comic, Streisand was presented as beautiful. In 1974 in the movie *The Way We Were,* she was even paired romantically with Robert Redford, a reigning matinée idol with classic looks.

This shattering of traditional styles of beauty continues. Its extension is based partly on the commercial realization that ethnic cultures with substantial buying power exist. But the increasing sophistication of businessmen and advertisers in targeting specific consumer populations alone cannot explain the continuing democratization of beauty. Young men and women of the 1960s may have cast off their rebelliousness in the process of maturation, but the memory of the freedom of styles in dress and appearance in that decade is not easily forgotten. Here, too, a paradoxical element enters. The very self-absorption of the last two decades itself may underlie the continuing democratization of beauty standards by implicitly validating each individual's claim to beauty.

In all these matters, we must not forget the continuing influence of feminism. Of all the radicalisms of the 1960s, feminism has continued to be one of diversity, naturalness, and pride in female identity. Feminist activism has re-emerged in recent years, and the movement of women into the work force, their advance in the professions, and the emergence of women's caucuses and organizations in a variety of disciplines and enterprises attest to the continuing strength of the movement. Because of this power, feminist ideals about naturalness in physical appearance and of beauty standards that take into account a variety of looks and are based on sound medical judgments about healthy bodies remain strong.

What about the future? We seem today to have entered a conservative, business-oriented era, reflected in longer hemlines, more mature-looking styles in dress, and recent vogues in very high-heeled shoes. Makeup seems slowly to be making a comeback. Heavy eye makeup has been in style for some years, and bright red lipstick may yet become universal. Yet comfortable clothing for home, sports, leisure, and work has not lost its popularity, and working women continue to wear a "uniform" reminiscent of the shirtwaist of the 1890s or the dress of the 1920s. In the 1960s it was the pants suit; more recently it has been blazers, skirts, and shirts.

Nancy Reagan, the current president's wife, like her predecessor Jacqueline Kennedy has become renowned for her expensive taste in clothing and home decoration. She seems to be setting expensive buying standards that the wealthy, enriched by her husband's economic policies, hurry to follow. On the other hand, as a model of beauty she may be an important indicator of a coming trend. As the age bulge in the population moves toward middle age and later years, we may see an end to the obsessive identification of beauty with youth that has long characterized this nation's standards of physical appearance for women.

It is possible that if the resurgent conservatism of the 1980s succeeds in its goal of re-creating domesticity as the dominant ideal for women, the empty-headed child-woman of the 1950s may re-emerge. Or the voluptuous woman may again triumph. Like many potential beauty models she can still be found—for example, in burlesque houses and pornographic pictures. A new technology may launch us into the fanciful costumes that science fiction writers have long fantasized. Yet it is difficult to imagine that the current emphasis on healthy bodies will decline, based as it is on solid medical knowledge, or that women in the work force, given current rates of inflation, will either retreat to the home or allow themselves to be doubly exploited by pretending that domesticity is their primary role. As it always has, feminism continues to play a major role in the determination of fashion.

Yet we continue to be "fashionables." In 1856 Emmeline Stuart-Wortley noted that all the women in New York City were wearing white shawls that made them look either like ghosts or Africans in burnooses. In the summer of 1981 the streets of New York were crowded with street vendors selling cheaper versions of the gold handbags, belts, and shoes featured in all the stores. What the gold signifies is open to a variety of interpretations: it may be either an extension of the gold chains fashionable for some years or a parody of them; it may be symbolic of the concern about economic conditions that has led many individuals recently to invest in gold; it may be a designer's tribute to the new conservative, Reaganite wealth and an acknowledgment that Americans now believe it is acceptable to display their wealth without concern for others. Whatever the gold fashion means, it is certain that, within a year or two or three, it will no longer sweep all before it. Once again, alterations in fashions will take place. But change will take place in a changed world and, therefore, will hold meaning that it did not have in the past.

Notes
Selected Bibliography
Index

Notes

INTRODUCTION

1. Roger Thompson, *Women in Stuart England and America: A Comparative Study* (London: Routledge & Kegan Paul, 1976), pp. 66–67; Jane Addams, *Twenty Years at Hull House* (New York: Macmillan, 1910), p. 192; Isadora Duncan, *My Life* (New York: Liveright, 1927), p. 237.

2. In "Fashion: From Class Differentiation to Collective Selection," *Sociological Quarterly* 10 (Spring 1969): 275–91, Herbert Blumer makes a similar point. "In women's dress, fashion is responsive to its own trends, to developments in fabrics and ornamentation, to developments in the fine arts, to exciting events that catch public attention, such as the discovery of the tomb of Tutankhamen, to political happenings, and to major social shifts such as the emancipation of women or the rise of the cult of youth." In other words, the analysis of fashion requires detailed historical understanding.

3. In their excellent introduction to the study of fashion in dress, Mary Ellen Roach and Kathleen Musa (*New Perspectives on the History of Western Dress* [New York: Nutri-Guides, 1980]) note Veblen's continued domination, apparent in major works like Quentin Bell, *On Human Finery,* 2d ed. (New York: Schocken, 1976).

4. The problem of recent versus contemporary interpretation is apparent in the writings of fashion analysts who adopt a Freudian model. The appealing argument that the widespread tightlacing of corsets was indicative of sadomasochism or sexual fetishism, for example, cannot really be proved. Contemporary American feminists had a simpler explanation: most women knew that tightlacing was unhealthy, but deceived themselves into believing that they were not lacing themselves tightly when, in fact, they were. The practice simply was fashionable: it made them feel modern, up-to-date, even rebellious. See Helene E. Roberts, "Submission, Masochism, and Narcissism: Three Aspects of Women's Role as Reflected in Dress," *Signs: Journal of Women in Culture and Society* 3 (Spring 1977): 7–29; and David Kunzle, *Fashion and Fetishism: A Social History of the Corset, Tight-lacing and Other Forms of Body Sculpture in the West* (Totowa, N.J.: Rowman & Littlefield, 1982).

5. Mrs. A. H. Emms, *How She Became Beautiful* (Albany: Brandow, 1890), p. 61; *The Ladies Companion, or Sketches of Life, Manners, and Morals of the Present Day, Edited by a Lady* (Philadelphia: n.p., 1854), pp. 37–38; James Bryce, *The American Commonwealth* (New York: Macmillan, 1893), p. 807; Frank Rossiter, *Charles Ives and His America*

(New York: Knopf, 1975), p. 27; Anna A. Rogers, *Why American Marriages Fail* (Boston: Houghton Mifflin, 1909).

6. Alan Dale, "Why Women Are Greater Actors Than Men," *Cosmopolitan* 41 (May 1906): 518; Elizabeth Linn Linton, *Modern Women and What Is Said of Them* (New York: Redfield, 1868), pp. 272–73.

7. Helen Gilbert Ecob, *The Well-Dressed Woman* (New York: Fowler and Wells, 1892), p. 299; *Decorum, A Practical Treatise on Etiquette and Dress of the Best American Society* (New York: Union, 1880), p. 178; Daniel Garrison Brinton and George Henry Napheys, *Personal Beauty* (Springfield, Mass.: W. J. Holland, 1870), p. 310; *Godey's Lady's Book* 46 (July 1852): 105. In addition, see almost any nineteenth-century beauty manual or advice book to women.

8. Herbert Dieckman, "Beauty," in Philip P. Wiener, ed., *Dictionary of the History of Ideas: Studies of Selected Pivotal Ideas,* 4 vols. (New York: Charles Scribner's Sons, 1973), 1:195; Susan Moller Okin, *Women in Western Political Thought* (Princeton, N.J.: Princeton Univ., 1979), pp. 17–20; Jefferson Butler Fletcher, *The Religion of Beauty in Woman and Other Essays on Platonic Love in Poetry and Society* (New York: Macmillan, 1911).

9. Una Stannard, "The Mask of Beauty," in Vivian Gornick and Barbara K. Moran, eds., *Women in Sexist Society: Studies in Power and Powerlessness* (New York: Basic, 1971), p. 121. Cf. Helene E. Roberts, "Marriage, Redundancy, or Sin: The Painter's View of Women in the First Twenty-five Years of Victoria's Reign," in Martha Vicinus, ed., *Suffer and Be Still: Women in the Victorian Age* (Bloomington, Ind.: Indiana Univ., 1972), p. 45; William Hogarth, *The Analysis of Beauty, Written With a View of Fixing the Fluctuating Ideas of Taste* (London: J. Reeves, 1753).

10. Edmund Burke, *Philosophical Inquiry Into the Origin of Our Ideas of the Sublime and Beautiful,* in *The Works of Edmund Burke, With a Memoir,* 3 vols. (New York: George Dearborn, 1836), 1:74–78; Oscar Moss, "Women's Dress," in *Modern Hygeian,* pamphlet, 1890, Schlesinger Library, Radcliffe College, p. 201; Ralph Waldo Emerson, "Beauty," in *The Complete Writings of Ralph Waldo Emerson* (New York: William Wise, 1929), p. 611.

11. On the derivation of the word "glamour," see *Oxford English Dictionary,* 12 vols. (Oxford: Oxford Univ., 1933), 4, 198. On Shaftesbury, see Dieckman, "Beauty," p. 205.

12. John Ruskin, *Sesame and Lilies* (Boston: Dana, Estes, n.d.), pp. 98–99; Frances Russell, "Lines of Beauty," in "Symposium on Women's Dress," *Arena* 6 (Sept. 1892): 499–507.

13. See Mario Praz, *The Romantic Agony* (New York: Milford, 1933); Martha Kingsbury, "The Femme Fatale and Her Sisters," in Linda Nochlin and Thomas Hess, eds., *Woman as Sex Object: Studies in Erotic Art, 1730–1970* (New York: Newsweek, 1972), pp. 182–205.

14. John Wesley Hanson, Jr., *Etiquette of Today* (Chicago: Robert G. Law, 1896), p. 3; *Denver Post,* Feb. 4, 1900; *Chicago Tribune,* Feb. 24, 1901.

15. The attempt to explore women's "separate culture" has recently been of interest to historians of women. See Carroll Smith-Rosenberg, "The Female World of Love and Ritual: Relations Between Women in Nineteenth-Century America," *Signs: Journal of Women in Culture and Society* 1 (Autumn 1975): 1–25. Space and time limitations have prevented me from investigating the important subject of racial and ethnic variations of beauty, which could easily absorb the pages of a lengthy monograph. My research indicates, however, that class rather than ethnicity was the key factor in the determination of beauty standards.

16. In his interesting attempt to define "Victorian" culture in the United States, Daniel Walker Howe has neglected its sexual aspects, which is a central concern of my work. "American Victorianism as a Culture," *American Quarterly* 27 (Dec. 1975): 507–32.

CHAPTER I

1. Marian Gouverneur, *As I Remember: Recollections of American Society During the Nineteenth Century* (New York: D. Appleton, 1911), p. 98. Throughout this book, I have followed the practice of calling women by the names they commonly used, even when this involved calling them by their husbands' names.

2. Linda K. Kerber, "Daughters of Columbia: Educating Women for the Republic, 1787–1805," in Stanley Elkins and Eric McKitrick, eds., *The Hofstadter Aegis: A Memorial* (New York: Knopf, 1974), p. 38; Anne Hollingsworth Wharton, *Social Life in the Early Republic* (Philadelphia: Lippincott, 1902), pp. 225–27; Tyrone Power, *Impressions of America, During the Years 1833, 1834, and 1835,* 2 vols. (Philadelphia: Carey, Lea, and Blanchard, 1836), 1:148; Elizabeth Duane Gillespie, *Book of Remembrances* (Philadelphia: Lippincott, 1901), p. 72; Mary E. W. Sherwood, *An Epistle to Posterity: Being Rambling Recollections of Many Years of My Life* (New York: Harper & Bros., 1897), pp. 49–50, 58–59; Frances Wright, *Views of Society and Manners in America,* ed. Paul R. Baker (1818; Cambridge, Mass.: Harvard Univ., 1963), p. 24.

3. Maria McIntosh, *Woman in America: Her Work and Her Reward* (New York: D. Appleton, 1850), p. 59; John Robert Godley, *Letters from America* (London: J. Murray, 1844), p. 44; Charles Dickens, *American Notes* (1842; London: Oxford Univ., 1957), p. 81; Frances Kemble Butler, *Journal of a Residence in America* (Paris: A. and W. Galignani, 1835), pp. 56–57.

4. *Lily,* July 8, 1854; Francis Lieber, *The Stranger in America* (Philadelphia: Carey, Lea, and Blanchard, 1835), pp. 67–68; Michel Chevalier, *Society, Manners, and Politics in the United States,* ed. John William Ward (Garden City, N.Y.: Anchor, 1961), p. 119; Francis Pulsky and Theresa Pulsky, *White, Red, and Black: Sketches of American Society,* 3 vols. (New York: Redfield, 1853), 1:267; Anne Royall, *Sketches of History, Life, and Manners in the United States* (New Haven: Royall, 1826), pp. 30, 57, 72; Julie Roy Jeffrey, *Frontier Women: The Trans-Mississippi West, 1840–1880* (New York: Hill & Wang, 1979), pp. 38, 73, 86.

5. Mrs. Felton, *American Life: A Narrative of Two Years' City and Country Residence in the United States* (London: Simpkin, Marshall, 1842), p. 84; Caroline Howard Gilman, *Recollections of a New England Bride and of a Southern Matron* (New York: G. P. Putnam, 1852); *Rev. Dr. Judson's Letter, to the Female Members of Christian Churches, in the United States of America* (Providence: M. H. Brown, 1832).

6. Bertha Damon, *Grandma Called It Carnal* (New York: Simon & Schuster, 1938), p. 202; Robert Tomes, *The Bazar Book of Decorum* (New York: Harper & Bros., 1877), p. 164; Constance Cary Harrison, "The Woman of Fashion," *Munsey's Magazine* 17 (Aug. 1897): 700. See also Christopher Crowfield [Harriet Beecher Stowe], *The Chimney Corner* (Boston: Ticknor and Fields, 1868), p. 247; Eliza Leslie, *The Behaviour Book: A Manual for Ladies* (Philadelphia: Willis P. Hazard, 1854), p. 299; Mrs. A. J. Graves, *Women in America* (New York: Harper & Bros., 1853), p. 94.

7. Barbara Mayer Wertheimer, *We Were There: The Story of Working Women in America* (New York: Pantheon, 1977), p. 60; Benita Eisler, *The Lowell Offering* (Philadelphia:

Lippincott, 1977), p. 50; Domingo Sarmiento, *Travels in the United States in 1847,* ed. and trans. Michael Rockland (Princeton, N.J.: Princeton Univ., 1970), p. 246; Frederika Bremer, *The Homes of the New World,* trans. Mary Howill, 2 vols. (New York: Harper & Bros., 1853), 1:210; Chevalier, *Society,* p. 128; Lucy Larcom, *A New England Girlhood* (1889; Gloucester, Mass.: Peter Smith, 1973), p. 232.

8. Francis J. Grund, *Aristocracy in America,* 2 vols. (London: Richard Bentley, 1839), 1:20; Lady Emmeline Stuart-Wortley, *Travels in the United States in 1849 and 1850,* 3 vols. (New York: Harper & Bros., 1851), 1:147; Charles Astor Bristed, *The Upper Ten Thousand* (New York: Stringer and Townsend, 1852), pp. 239–40; Edward Abdy, *Residence and Tour in the United States in 1833–34* (London: n.p., 1835), pp. 74–75; Lieber, *Stranger in America,* pp. 65–66.

9. Grund, *Aristocracy in America,* 1:151; Thomas Woody, *A History of Women's Education in the United States,* 2 vols. (New York: Science, 1929), 2:102; Katharine Anthony, *Susan B. Anthony: Her Personal History and Her Era* (New York: Russell & Russell, 1954), p. 84; Graves, *Women in America,* p. 109; Royall, *Sketches,* p. 261; Virginia Penny, *The Employments of Women: A Cyclopaedia of Women's Work* (Boston: Walker, Wise, 1863), p. 362; Catharine M. Sedgwick, *Means and Ends* (New York: Harper & Bros., 1842), p. 175; Lieber, *Stranger in America,* pp. 65–68.

10. Wertheimer, *We Were There,* pp. 59–106; Penny, *Employments of Women,* p. 303.

11. Penny, *Employments of Women,* pp. 302, 310, 315, 317.

12. Abba Gould Woolson, *Woman in American Society* (Boston: Roberts Bros., 1873), pp. 104–105.

13. *Decorum, Practical Treatise,* p. 122; Florence Howe Hall, *Social Customs* (Boston: D. Estes, 1911), p. 305; Stuart-Wortley, *Travels,* 1:4–5.

14. Elizabeth Cady Stanton, *Eighty Years and More: Reminiscences, 1815–1897* (1898; New York: Schocken, 1971), p. 196.

15. Barbara Smith Bodichen, *An American Diary, 1857–1858* (London: Routledge & Kegan Paul, 1972), p. 87; Sarah Grimké, *Letters on the Equality of the Sexes and the Condition of Woman* (Boston: L. Knapp, 1838), p. 70; Woolson, *Woman in American Society,* pp. 104–105; Celia Burleigh, "The Relation of Woman to Her Dress," in *Papers and Letters Presented at the First Woman's Congress of the Association for the Advancement of Women* (New York: Mrs. Wm. Ballard, 1874), p. 115.

16. Helen Watterson Moody, "American Woman and Dress," *Ladies' Home Journal* 18 (June 1901): 15.

17. Grund, *Aristocracy in America,* 1:149. See also David W. Mitchell, *Ten Years in the United States* (London: Smith, Elder, 1862), pp. 164–94; Captain Frederick Marryat, *A Diary in America* (1838; New York: Knopf, 1962), pp. 42–43; Oscar Comettant, *Trois ans aux États-Unis* (Paris: Pagnerre, 1857), p. 77. On the question of women and modernization, my conclusions differ from those of Nancy L. Cott, *The Bonds of Womanhood: "Women's Sphere" in New England, 1780–1835* (New Haven: Yale Univ., 1977).

18. James Burn, *Three Years Among the Working Classes During the War* (London: Smith, Elder, 1865), p. 91; Grund, *Aristocracy in America,* 1:149; Harriet Beecher Stowe, *Pink and White Tyranny* (Boston: Roberts Bros., 1871), p. 8.

19. Graves, *Women in America,* p. 58; Artemus Bowers Muzzey, *The Young Maiden* (Boston: W. Crosby, 1840), p. 115; *Harper's Bazar* 1 (Oct. 17, 1868): 802.

20. Nancy M. W. Woodrow, "How Fashions Are Set," *Cosmopolitan* 33 (July 1902): 253–61; Ralph G. Martin, *Jennie: The Life of Lady Randolph Churchill: The Romantic Years, 1854–95* (New York: Signet, 1969), p. 52; Maria Cummins, *The Lamplighter* (London: Willoughby, n.d.), p. 348.

21. William Dean Howells, *Indian Summer* (New York: E. P. Dutton and Sons, 1951), p. 16; *Ladies' Home Journal* 10 (April 1894): 10.

22. Kate Douglas Wiggin, *My Garden of Memories* (Boston: Houghton Mifflin, 1923), p. 29.

23. Grund, *Aristocracy in America,* 1:149; [Ferdinand Longchamps], *Asmodeus in New York* (New York: Longchamps, 1868), p. 289; Maria Theresa Longworth, *Teresina in America,* 2 vols. (London: Richard Bentley and Son, 1875), 2:270; Robert Ernst, *Immigrant Life in New York City, 1825–1863* (New York: Columbia, 1949), p. 67. My conclusions differ from those of Herbert G. Gutman, "Work, Culture, and Society in Industrializing America, 1815–1919," in his *Work, Culture, and Society in Industrializing America* (New York: Vintage, 1977), pp. 3–78, and of Carol Groneman, "Working Class Immigrant Women in Mid-Nineteenth Century New York: The Irish Woman's Experience," *Journal of Urban History* 4 (May 1978): 255–73. Both authors stress traditional values in the lives of the working class, although Gutman mentions the existence of a group which "shed these older ways to conform to new imperatives" (p. 15).

24. Burn, *Three Years,* p. 82; Mary Sargeant Gove Nichols, *Mary Lyndon* (New York: Stringer and Townsend, 1855), pp. 59, 306; Caroline Healy Dall, *The College, the Market, and the Court* (Boston: Lea and Shepard, 1867), pp. 13–14.

25. On colonial dress see Peter Copeland, *Working Dress in Colonial and Revolutionary America* (Westport, Conn.: Greenwood, 1977).

26. Elizabeth Linn Linton, *The Girl of the Period and Other Social Essays,* 2 vols. (London: Richard Bentley and Son, 1883), 1:67.

27. Damon, *Grandma Called It Carnal,* p. 115.

CHAPTER 2

1. Susan C. Dunning Power, *The Ugly-Girl Papers, or, Hints for the Toilet* (New York: Harper & Bros., 1875), pp. 86–87.

2. By the early nineteenth century, milliners often sold dry goods in addition to making hats and designing dresses and thus differed from the contemporary trend toward specialization in merchandising. In this, they provided an example for A. T. Stewart and other creators of department stores.

3. Francis Lieber, *The Stranger in America* (Philadelphia: Carey, Lea, and Blanchard, 1835), pp. 102–103; Thomas Hamilton, *Men and Manners in America* (Edinburgh: W. Blackwood, 1833), 1:33; Nathaniel Parker Willis, *Life Here and There: or Sketches of Society and Adventures* (Detroit: Kerr, 1853), p. 120.

4. *The Book of Beauty, Vigor, and Elegance* (New York: Hurst, 1874), p. 57; W. R. Andrews, *The American Code of Manners* (New York: W. R. Andrews, 1880), p. 234; Isabella Bird, *The Englishwoman in America* (1856; Madison: Univ. of Wisconsin, 1966), p. 361; Marion Pullan, *Beadle's Guide to Dress-Making and Millinery* (New York: Beadle, 1860).

5. A. Thomason [Andrew Bell], *Men and Things in America* (London: William Smith, 1838), p. 40; Andrews, *American Code of Manners,* p. 234; James D. McCabe, Jr., *Lights and Shadows of New York Life, or Sights and Sensations of the Great City* (Philadelphia: National, 1872), p. 169; Ishbel Ross, *Crusades and Crinolines: The Life and Times of Ellen Curtis Demorest and William Jennings Demorest* (New York: Harper & Row,

1963), pp. 20–23; Sarah Josepha Hale, *Manners: Or, Happy Homes and Good Society* (1868; New York: Arno, 1972), p. 237; Tyrone Power, *Impressions of America, During the Years 1833, 1834, and 1835,* 2 vols. (Philadelphia: Carey, Lea and Blanchard), 2:225; Olive Logan, *They Met By Chance: A Society Novel* (New York: Adams, Victor, 1873), pp. 200–201.

6. Anna Cora Mowatt, *Fashion: or Life in New York* (New York: Samuel French, 1849); Ann Ellis, *The Life of an Ordinary Woman* (Boston: Houghton Mifflin, 1929), pp. 90–91.

7. *Revolution* 7 (May 11, 1871).

8. Marie Louise Hankins, *Women of New York* (New York: M. L. Hankins, 1861), p. 34; Misses Mendell and Hosmer, *Notes of Travel and Life* (New York: Mendell and Hosmer, 1854), p. 282; *Home Journal,* May 13, 1854; Jean Philippe Worth, *Century of Fashion* (Boston: Little, Brown, 1928), p. 12; George Ellington, *The Women of New York* (New York: New York Book, 1869), p. 393; Mary Elizabeth Massey, *Bonnet Brigades: American Women and the Civil War* (New York: Knopf, 1966), pp. 250–51; *The Ladies' Hand-Book of Millinery and Dress-making* (New York: Redfield, 1843); Noel Gerson, *Queen of the Plaza: A Biography of Adah Isaacs Menken* (New York: Funk & Wagnalls, 1964), p. 126.

9. Oscar Comettant, *Trois ans aux États-Unis* (Paris: Pagnerre, 1857), p. 77. On tailoring and ready-to-wear, see Jesse Eliphalet Pope, *The Clothing Industry in New York* (Columbia, Mo.: Univ. of Missouri, 1905).

10. Pope, *Clothing Industry,* p. 17.

11. On Stewart's and the early history of the department store, I have used Harry E. Ressequie, "A. T. Stewart's Marble Palace: Department Store," *New-York Historical Society Quarterly* 48 (1964): 131–62; Lloyd Wendt and Herman Kogan, *Give the Lady What She Wants!* (Chicago: Rand McNally, 1952); John William Ferry, *A History of the Department Store* (New York: Macmillan, 1960); Robert Henrickson, *The Grand Emporiums: The Illustrated History of America's Great Department Stores* (New York: Stein & Day, 1979); and Gunther Barth, *City People: The Rise of Modern City Culture in Nineteenth-Century America* (New York: Oxford Univ., 1980), pp. 110–47.

12. Natalie Dana, *Young in New York: A Memoir of a Victorian Girlhood* (Garden City, N.Y.: Doubleday, 1963), p. 93. Ferry, *History of the Department Store,* p. 46; William Burns, *Life in New York, In Doors and Out of Doors* (New York: Bunce and Brother, 1851); Mary J. Windle, *Life in Washington, and Life Here and There* (Philadelphia: Lippincott, 1859), p. 243.

13. Ann S. Stephens, *The Reigning Belle* (Philadelphia: T. B. Peterson and Bros., 1872), p. 25.

14. Lady Emmeline Stuart-Wortley, *Travels, in the United States in 1849 and 1850,* 3 vols. (New York: Harper & Bros., 1851) 1:281.

15. Dana, *Young in New York,* p. 93.

16. Richard C. Wade, *The Urban Frontier: The Rise of Western Cities, 1790–1830* (Cambridge, Mass.: Harvard Univ., 1959), p. 315; J. Bennett Nolan, *Play at Reading Town: The Diversions of Our Ancestors* (Reading, Pa.: Feroe Press, 1935), plate 15.

17. Ressequie, "A. T. Stewart's Marble Palace," p. 156.

18. On Macy's, see Rowland M. Hower, *History of Macy's of New York: Chapters in the Evolution of a Department Store* (Cambridge, Mass.: Harvard Univ., 1943); on Genin, see Francis Pulsky and Theresa Pulsky, *White, Red, and Black: Sketches of American Society,* 3 vols. (New York: Redfield, 1853), 2:238; Hazel Hunton, *Pantaloons and Petticoats: The Diary of a Young American* (New York: Field, 1950), p. 107; Lillian

Foster, *Way-Side Glimpses, North and South* (New York: Rudd & Carleton, 1860), pp. 208-209.

19. Robert Seager II, *And Tyler, Too: A Biography of John and Julia Gardiner Tyler* (New York: McGraw-Hill, 1963), p. 35.

20. National Hairdressers and Cosmetologists Association, *NHCA's Gilded Years* (n.p.: Western, 1971), p. 5; McCabe, *Lights and Shadows,* p. 573. For a discussion of status anxieties in a similar profession, see Lois W. Banner, "Why Women Have Not Been Great Chefs," *South Atlantic Quarterly* 62 (Spring 1973): 198-212.

21. Power, *Ugly-Girl Papers,* p. 258; Gilbert Vail, *A History of Cosmetics in America* (New York: Toilet Goods, 1947), pp. 90-91. Cf. *Godey's Lady's Book* 39 (March 1849): 216.

22. Virginia Penny, *The Employments of Women: A Cyclopaedia of Women's Work* (Boston: Walker, Wise, 1863), p. 279; Julia Ward Howe, *Reminiscences, 1819-1899* (Boston: Houghton Mifflin, 1900), pp. 64-66; George William Curtis, *The Potiphar Papers* (New York: Harper & Bros., 1856), p. 32.

23. *New York World,* April 14, 1901; Hiram Fuller, *Belle Brittain on Tour, at Newport, and Here and There* (New York: Derby & Jackson, 1858), p. 279; Agnes Pryor, *Reminiscences of Peace and War* (New York: Macmillan, 1905), pp. 49-50.

24. Penny, *Employments of Women,* p. 279; *Godey's Lady's Book* 47 (Nov. 1853): 441. Throughout the early nineteenth century the word "saloon" was used to designate a large room with an elegant purpose. According to the *Oxford English Dictionary,* 12 vols. (Oxford: Oxford Univ., 1933), 9:57, in the 1870s the word was appropriated to designate a drinking bar, and "salon" was substituted for the former usage. My research indicates that "saloon" was first appropriated in the 1850s by entertainment entrepreneurs seeking respectability when they opened "concert saloons," which were a cross between music halls and drinking establishments.

25. Eliza Leslie, *The Behaviour Book: A Manual for Ladies* (Philadelphia: Willis P. Hazard, 1854), p. 299; Matthew Hale Smith, *Sunshine and Shadow in New York* (Hartford: J. B. Burr, 1868), pp. 352-53.

26. *Godey's Lady's Book* 47 (Nov. 1853): 441; Smith, *Sunshine and Shadow,* pp. 352-53.

27. Cf. Charles Haswell, *Reminiscences of New York by an Octogenarian* (New York: Harper & Bros., 1896), p. 96.

28. For the history of hairdressing and cosmetics I have used with profit the advertising flyers and other materials in the Bella C. Landauer Collection of Business and Advertising Art in the New-York Historical Society. The Fouladous card is the earliest hairdressing advertisement in the collection. On James of Seneca Falls, see Elizabeth Cady Stanton to Mary Gove Nichols, Aug. 31, 1852, Stanton Papers, Library of Congress.

29. *Revolution* 1 (Jan. 15, 1868): 25; John M. Lafoy, *The Complete Coiffeur* (New York: n.p., 1817), p. 29. See also Eliza Potter, *A Hairdresser's Experience in High Life* (Cincinnati: the Author, 1859).

30. On the history of cosmetics, I have used Maggie Angeloglou, *A History of Make-up* (New York: Macmillan, 1970); Richard Corson, *Fashions in Make-Up: From Ancient to Modern Times* (New York: Universe, 1972); and Fenja Gunn, *The Artificial Face: A History of Cosmetics* (London: Newton Abbot, 1973).

31. Anne Hollingsworth Wharton, *Social Life in the Early Republic* (Philadelphia: J. B. Lippincott, 1902), p. 158; "Wanted—Healthy Wife," *Harper's New Monthly Magazine* 13 (June 1856): 79.

32. On Blumenbach, see Fred W. Voget, *A History of Ethnology* (New York: Holt, Rinehart and Winston, 1975), pp. 105, 125. On the Circassian women, see N. M. Panzer,

The Harem (London: Spring, 1965), pp. 20–21, 122. Edmund Spencer, *Travels in Circassia in 1836,* 2 vols. (London: Henry Colburn, 1837), 1:243–44, noted that the Circassian women seemed of Greek type, with small aquiline noses, and that they used heavy cosmetics. "The American Face," *Harper's Bazar* 1 (Dec. 7, 1867): 82, pointed to the connection between the Circassian beauty and arsenic eating. E. S. Hallock, "The American Circus," *Century Magazine* 70 (Aug. 1905): 568–85, noted the connection between Blumenbach's discoveries and the Circassian women. The Circassian beauty became a feature of later dime museums. She was usually extremely fair-skinned, almost albino in complexion.

33. Robert Tomes, "Women's Beauty: How to Get and Keep It," *Harper's New Monthly Magazine* 37 (June 1868): 119. *Harper's Bazar* 1 (Dec. 7, 1867): 82, noted use of Fowler's solution, as do John S. Haller, Jr., and Robin M. Haller, *The Physician and Sexuality in Victorian America* (Urbana, Ill.: Univ. of Illinois, 1974), p. 144. On the American diet see Richard O. Cummings, *The American and His Food* (1941; New York: Arno, 1970).

34. Frances Trollope, *Domestic Manners of the Americans* (New York: Knopf, 1949), p. 300; Jane Aster, ed., *Ladies' and Gentlemen's Etiquette of the Best Society* (New York: G. W. Carleton, 1879), pp. 132–35; James Fenimore Cooper, *Notions of the Americans,* 2 vols. (1863; New York: Frederick Ungar, 1963), 1:195; Leslie, *Behaviour Book,* p. 99.

35. On cosmetics in the United States, see Vail, *History of Cosmetics.*

36. Chauncey Depew, *One Hundred Years of American Commerce, 1795–1895,* 2 vols. (New York: D. O. Haynes, 1895), 2:427; Eugene Rimmel, *The Book of Perfumes* (London: Chapman and Hall, 1868), passim; Penny, *Employments of Women,* pp. 395–96.

37. Lydia Maria Child, *Letters from New York* (New York: C. S. Francis, 1845), pp. 248–49. The 1868 Gouraud advertisement is in the Landauer Collection, New-York Historical Society.

38. George Ellington, *Women of New York,* p. 45, describes the Turkish baths.

39. The A. Simonson catalogue is in the Landauer Collection. For the derivation of fashion words, I have used the *Oxford English Dictionary,* 2:335; 3:81.

CHAPTER 3

1. Caroline Moseley, "Nineteenth-Century Parlor Songs" (lecture presented at the annual meeting of the American Studies Association, Minneapolis, Minnesota, September 1979).

   My use of the term "steel-engraving lady" is derived from Caroline Ticknor, "The New Woman and the Steel-Engraving Lady," *Atlantic Monthly* 88 (July 1901): 105–10.

2. Charles Astor Bristed, *The Upper Ten Thousand* (New York: Stringer and Townsend, 1852), p. 44; Ella Adelia Fletcher, *The Woman Beautiful* (New York: Brentano's, 1901), p. 26; George Makepeace Towle, *American Society,* 2 vols. (London: Chapman and Hall, 1870), 1:294; George Combe, *Notes on the United States of North America, During a Phrenological Visit in 1838-39-40,* 3 vols. (Edinburgh: MacLachlan, Steward, 1841), 2:124; A. Thomason [Andrew Bell], *Men and Things in America* (London: William Smith, 1838), p. 39; James Stuart, *Three Years in North America* (New York: J. & J. Harper, 1833), p. 30; William Hancock, *An Emigrant's Five Years in the Free States of America* (London: T. Cantley Newby, 1860); Frances Kemble Butler, *Journal of a Residence in America* (Paris: A. and W. Galignani, 1835), p. 155; James Fenimore

Cooper, *Notions of the Americans,* 2 vols. (1863; New York: Frederick Ungar, 1963), 1:187–93.

3. Fenja Gunn, *The Artificial Face: A History of Cosmetics* (London: Newton Abbot, 1973), pp. 6off; Geoffrey Squire, *Dress, Art, Society* (London: Studio Vista, 1974), pp. 72–80.

4. Samuel Richardson, *Pamela* (New York: Dutton, 1928), pp. 378, 391; Mary Wollstonecraft, *A Vindication of the Rights of Woman* (New York: W. W. Norton, 1967), pp. 53, 62, 68; Robert Palfrey Utter and Gwendolyn Needham, *Pamela's Daughters* (New York: Russell & Russell, 1936); Marlene Legates, "The Cult of True Womanhood in Eighteenth-Century Thought," *Eighteenth-Century Studies* 10 (Fall 1976): 21–39.

5. On Mademoiselle George and the Napoleonic ideal of beauty, see Edith Saunders, *Napoleon and Mademoiselle George* (New York: E. P. Dutton, 1959); George Crabb, *English Synonyms* (New York: J. & J. Harper, 1836), p. 118.

6. Christopher Crowfield [Harriet Beecher Stowe], *The Chimney Corner* (Boston: Ticknor and Fields, 1868), p. 131.

7. Robert Tomes, *The Bazar Book of Decorum* (New York: Harper & Bros., 1877), p. 191; *Harper's Bazar* 1 (Dec. 21, 1867): 114; Frederick Law Olmsted, *A Journey in the Seaboard Slave States* (New York: Mason Bros., 1856), p. 449; Abba Gould Woolson, *Woman in American Society* (Boston: Roberts Bros., 1873), p. 193.

8. *Revolution* 2 (Nov. 4, 1869): 292.

9. Marion Harland [Mary Virginia Terhune], *Eve's Daughters* (New York: Anderson & Allen, 1882), pp. 350–51.

10. Mary Livermore, "Health and Woman's Dress," in *Modern Hygeian* (pamphlet, Schlesinger Library, Radcliffe College), p. 6; Ethel Gale, *Hints on Dress* (New York: G. P. Putnam's Sons, 1872); *Godey's Lady's Book* 65 (Aug. 1887): 86.

11. *Harper's Bazar* 32 (Feb. 24, 1900): 176.

12. Marie Montaigne, *How to Be Beautiful* (New York: Harper & Bros., 1913); Theodore Stanton and Harriot Stanton Blatch, eds., *Elizabeth Cady Stanton as Revealed in Her Letters, Diary and Reminiscences,* 2 vols. (New York: Harper & Bros., 1922), 1:249; Suzanne Hilton, *The Way It Was—1876* (Philadelphia: Westminster, 1975), p. 52. See also Beatrice Fairfax [Marie Manning], *Ladies Now and Then* (New York: Dutton, 1944), p. 38; Mary E. W. Sherwood, *Manners and Social Usage* (New York: Harper & Bros., 1884), p. 214; Louisa May Alcott, *Little Women* (New York: Macmillan, 1962), p. 282.

13. Erving Goffman, *Gender Advertisements* (Cambridge, Mass.: Harvard Univ., 1979).

14. Mrs. A. Walker, *Female Beauty* (New York: Scofield and Voorhees, 1840); *Demorest's Monthly,* Jan. 1882, p. 224; *Ladies' Home Journal* 31 (Aug. 1914): 7. On medical attitudes toward women, see John S. Haller, Jr., and Robin M. Haller, *The Physician and Sexuality in Victorian America* (Urbana, Ill.: Univ. of Illinois, 1974); Ann Douglas, " 'The Fashionable Diseases': Women's Complaints and Their Treatment in Nineteenth-Century America," in Mary S. Hartman and Lois W. Banner, eds., *Clio's Consciousness Raised: New Perspectives on the History of Women* (New York: Harper & Row, 1974), pp. 1–22; and Carroll Smith-Rosenberg, "Puberty to Menopause: The Cycle of Femininity in Nineteenth-Century America," in Hartman and Banner, pp. 23–37.

15. Elizabeth Cady Stanton, "On the Social, Educational, Religious, and Political Position of Women in America. Delivered at Prince's Hall, 25 June 1833" (mss. speech, Stanton Papers, Library of Congress). See also Kemble Butler, *Journal,* p. 57; Francis J. Grund, *Aristocracy in America,* 2 vols. (London: Richard Bentley, 1839), 1:73; Thomason [Bell], *Men and Things,* p. 39; Misses Mendell and Hosmer, *Notes of Travel*

and Life (New York: Mendell and Hosmer, 1835), p. 172; James Reed Chadwick, "Health of American Women," *North American Review* 135 (Dec. 1882): 521.

16. Ruth Miller Elson, *Guardians of Tradition: American Schoolbooks of the Nineteenth Century* (Lincoln, Nebr.: Univ. of Nebraska, 1964), p. 66. On phrenology, see John D. Davies, *Phrenology, Fad and Science: A Nineteenth-Century American Crusade* (New Haven: Yale Univ., 1955). There is no study of the physiognomists, to whose theories my sources consistently refer. See Bristed, *Upper Ten Thousand*, p. 139; Kemble Butler, *Journal*, p. 5; *Pocket Lavater* (Hartford, Conn.: Andrus and Judd, 1836); Wilson Flagg, *Analysis of Female Beauty* (Boston: March, Caper, and Lyon, 1834), pp. v–vi; *Personal Beauty* (New York: Hurst, 1875), p. 13; A. Cazenave, *Beauty* (Cincinnati: Chase and Hall, 1877).

17. Woolson, *Woman in American Society*, p. 135; Amy Louise Reed, "Female Delicacy in the Sixties," *Century Magazine* 90 (Oct. 1915): 861–62.

18. Lucy Larcom, *A New England Girlhood* (1889; Gloucester, Mass.: Peter Smith, 1973), p. 106; Joseph Satterwaite, "The Tremulous Formula," *American Quarterly* 7 (Summer 1956): 99–113; *Revolution* 2 (Sept. 9, 1869): 155.

19. "The Weaker Sex," *Harper's Bazar* 1 (Oct. 10, 1868): 186; Woolson, *Woman in American Society*, p. 192; Nathaniel Hawthorne, *The Blithedale Romance* in *The Complete Novels and Selected Tales of Nathaniel Hawthorne*, ed. Norman Holmes Pearson (New York: Modern Library, 1937), p. 499; Catharine E. Beecher, *Letters to the People on Health and Happiness* (New York: Harper & Bros., 1855), pp. 124–29.

20. On tuberculosis, see Barbara Ehrenreich and Deirdre English, *Complaints and Disorders: The Sexual Politics of Illness* (Old Westbury, N.Y.: Feminist Press, 1973); René Dubos, *The White Plague: Tuberculosis, Man, and Society* (Boston: Little, Brown, 1952); Susan Sontag, *Illness as Metaphor* (New York: Farrar, Straus & Giroux, 1977). Ehrenreich and English, p. 19, cite 1865 tuberculosis mortality rates for women by age 20 as twice the mortality rates for men.

21. *Revolution* 2 (Sept. 9, 1869): 155.

22. See Barbara Welter, "The Cult of True Womanhood, 1800–1860," in Welter, *Dimity Convictions: The American Woman in the Nineteenth Century* (Athens, Ohio: Ohio Univ., 1976), pp. 21–41.

23. Caroline Howard Gilman, *Recollections of a New England Bride and of a Southern Matron* (New York: G. P. Putnam, 1852), p. 327. See also "An Uncommon Beauty," *Harper's Bazar* 10 (May 26, 1877): 322; Harriet Hubbard Ayer, *Harriet Hubbard Ayer's Book: A Complete and Authentic Treatise on the Laws of Health and Beauty* (New York: Home, 1899), pp. 289–99; *Scrap-book for "Homely Women" Only* (Boston: Brown, Sherbrook, 1884), p. 68; Garry Gaines, *The American Girl of the Period: Her Ways and Views* (Philadelphia: Lippincott, 1878), p. 61.

24. Artemus Bowers Muzzey, *The Young Maiden* (Boston: W. Crosby, 1840), pp. 111–12; Lydia Maria Child, *Letters from New York* (New York: C. S. Francis, 1845), pp. 279–80; W. E. Baxter, *America and the Americans* (London: George Routledge, 1855), pp. 96–98; Towle, *American Society*, 2:83.

25. *Ladies' Guide to Perfect Gentility*, p. 17; Crowfield [Stowe], *Chimney Corner*, pp. 248–49; *Godey's Lady's Book* 43 (June 1850): 370.

26. *Oxford English Dictionary*, 12 vols. (Oxford: Oxford Univ., 1933), 4:114–15; Mrs. Basil Hall, *The Aristocratic Journey (1827–1828)*, ed. Una Pope Hennessy (New York: G. P. Putnam's Sons, 1931), p. 89.

27. Frances Trollope, *Domestic Manners of the Americans* (New York: Knopf, 1949), p. 136; Thomas Colley Grattan, *Civilized America*, 2 vols. (London: Bradbury and Evans,

1859), 2:54; Combe, *Notes,* 2:155; "Our Prudes," *Harper's Bazar* 10 (April 7, 1877): 210; Maria Theresa Longworth, *Teresina in America,* 2 vols. (London: Richard Bentley and Son, 1875), 1:313: "They are particular even to straitlacedness in what they say, but not often what they do."

28. Maria Susan Cummins, *Haunted Hearts* (Boston: Tilton, 1864), p. 95; Elson, *Guardians of Tradition,* p. 305.

29. Woolson, *Woman in American Society,* pp. 192–93; "Symposium on Woman's Dress," *Arena* 6 (Sept.–Oct. 1892): 488–507, 621–34.

30. Josephine DeMott Robinson, *Circus Lady* (New York: Thomas Y. Crowell, 1926), p. 176.

31. Walter Hamilton, *The Aesthetic Movement in England* (London: Reeves and Turner, 1882), p. 76; *Revolution* 3 (Oct. 20, 1870): 248; Francis Lieber, *The Stranger in America* (Philadelphia: Carey, Lea, and Blanchard, 1835), p. 81; Towle, *Society in America,* 1:294.

32. James Silk Buckingham, *America, Historical, Statistic and Descriptive,* 3 vols. (London: Fisher and Son, 1884), 1:55–57; Isabella Bird, *The Englishwoman in America* (1856; Madison: Univ. of Wisconsin, 1966), p. 362; Marianne Finch, *An Englishwoman's Experience in America* (London: R. Bentley, 1853), p. 21; *Una,* Dec. 1853, p. 182.

33. Joseph Hatton, *Today in America: Studies for the Old World and the New,* 2 vols. (London: Chapman and Hall, 1881), 1:29–30. In *Our Old Home: A Series of English Sketches,* 2 vols. (London: Smith, Elder, 1863), 2:280–81, Hawthorne admitted that after some years in England, he no longer found American women so beautiful. Yet he "still resolved to uphold these fair creatures as angels, because I was sometimes driven to a half-acknowledgement that the English ladies, looked at from a lower point of view, were perhaps a little finer animals than they. The advantages of the latter . . . were all comprised in a few additional lumps of clay on their shoulders and other parts of their figures. It would be a pitiful bargain to give up the ethereal charm of American beauty for half a hundred-weight of clay."

34. On the Germans, I have used in particular Robert Ernst, *Immigrant Life in New York City 1825–1863* (New York: Columbia Univ., 1949); Albert Bernhardt Faust, *The German Element in the United States* (Boston: Houghton Mifflin, 1909); and "Germany in New York," *Atlantic Monthly* 19 (Jan.–June 1867): 555–64.

35. William Howitt, *The Rural and Domestic Life of Germany* (London: Longman, Brown, Green, and Longmans, 1842), pp. 51–52.

36. George Beard, *American Nervousness: Its Causes and Consequences* (New York: G. P. Putnam's Sons, 1881), p. 339; David Macrae, *Americans at Home: Pen-and-Ink Sketches of American Men, Manners, and Institutions* (New York: E. P. Dutton, 1875), p. 76; Israel Joseph Benjamin, *Three Years in America* (1862; New York: Arno, 1975), p. 192; Hutchins Hapgood, *Types from City Streets* (New York: Funk & Wagnalls, 1910), p. 117.

37. Lola Montez, "Beautiful Women," in Charles Chauncey Burr, ed., *The Lectures of Lola Montez* (Philadelphia: T. B. Peterson, 1858), pp. 86–123. "The Bosom," wrote Montez elsewhere, "is the 'greatest claim of a lovely woman' " (*The Arts of Beauty: or, Secrets of a Lady's Toilet* [New York: Dick & Fitzgerald, 1858], p. 50).

38. *Oxford English Dictionary,* 12:306.

39. Hans Jurgen Hansen, ed., *Late Nineteenth-Century Art* (New York: McGraw-Hill, 1972), p. 123; William Gerdts, *The Great American Nude: A History in Art* (New York: Praeger, 1974), passim; Charles Haswell, *Reminiscences of New York by an Octogenarian* (New York: Harper & Bros., 1896), p. 270, remembered that the exhibition of

the canvases was greatly criticized because of the nude figures, but that "as a result it was largely attended." Edward Strahan [Earl Shinn], *Art Treasures of America*, 3 vols. (Philadelphia: George Barrie, 1879), 1:53.

40. Ned Buntline [Edward Judson], *G'Hals of New York* (New York: DeWitt and Davenport, 1850), p. 55; George Ellington, *The Women of New York* (New York: New York Book, 1869), pp. 45–46. Gerdts, *Great American Nude*, pp. 91–93, notes the long nose of the Greek slave and her thick waist, coupled, however, with small breasts.

41. Members of the New York Press, *Night Side of New York* (New York: J. C. Haney, 1866), p. 11; Buntline, *G'Hals of New York*, pp. 82–83; Mark Gabor, *The Pin-Up: A Modest History* (New York: Universe, 1972), p. 36. For prostitutes on the frontier, see Julie Roy Jeffrey, *Frontier Women: The Trans-Mississippi West, 1840–1880* (New York: Hill & Wang, 1979), p. 109: "Hangtown gals are plump and rosy."

42. Hiram Fuller, *Belle Brittain on Tour, at Newport, and Here and There* (New York: Derby & Jackson, 1858), p. 278; Ellington, *Women of New York*, pp. 517–18.

43. Lieber, *Stranger in America*, p. 80; Henry Cooke, "Notes of a Loiterer in New York," *Bentley's Miscellany* 16 (1844): 599. *Demorest's Monthly*, Aug. 1870; Grattan, *Civilized America*, 2:56; Henry Collins Brown, *Brownstone Fronts and Saratoga Trunks* (New York: Dutton, 1935), p. 144.

44. Elizabeth Cady Stanton to [?], 1856, Stanton Papers, Library of Congress; Burleigh, "Relation of Woman to Dress," p. 119.

45. "A Fashion in Hands," *Harper's Bazar* 17 (June 21, 1884): 386; *Ladies' Guide to Perfect Gentility*, p. 36. Studies of Byron's impact in America include "Byronism," *Galaxy* 7 (June 1868): 777–81; Samuel C. Chew, "Byron in America," *American Mercury* 1 (March 1925): 335–44; William Ellery Leonard, *Byron and Byronism in America* (New York: Columbia, 1907).

46. *Revolution* 2 (Sept. 9, 1869): 155; Fletcher, *Woman Beautiful*, p. 26; Tomes, *Bazar Book*, p. 191; Fuller, *Belle Brittain*, p. 116; "Childe Harold's Pilgrimage," in *Works of Byron*, ed. Ernest Hartley Coleridge, 6 vols. (London: John Murray, 1899), 2:59; George Brandes, *Main Currents in Nineteenth Century Literature* (New York: Boni and Liveright, 1923), p. 330; Peter Quennell, *Byron: The Years of Fame* (New York: Viking, 1935), p. 73. Like many fashion historians, Michael Batterbery and Ariane Batterbery, *Mirror, Mirror: A Social History of Fashion* (New York: Holt, Rinehart and Winston, 1977), p. 220, repeat the Byron story without attribution. In his definitive biography of Byron, Leslie Marchand cites a variation of the remark in a letter Byron wrote about an Italian opera singer. See Marchand, *Byron: A Biography*, 3 vols. (New York: Knopf, 1957), 1,366: "A woman should never be seen eating or drinking, unless it be lobster salad and champagne, the only truly feminine and becoming viands." Interesting in Byron's work in this regard is the extent to which sumptuous feasts are a prelude to love-making. See, in particular, *Don Juan*.

47. "The Fair One with the Golden Locks," *Harper's Bazar* 11 (Sept. 21, 1878): 602.

48. Ivor Guest, *The Romantic Ballet in Paris* (Middletown, Conn.: Wesleyan Univ., 1966), p. 144. See also Guest, *Romantic Ballet in England* (London: Phoenix, 1954); *Fanny Elssler* (London: Black, 1970); Louis Maigron, *Le Romantisme et la Mode* (Paris: Champion, 1911), p. 14.

49. Ellington, *Women of New York*, pp. 517–18; Fuller, *Belle Brittain*, p. 222.

50. Guest, *Romantic Ballet in Paris*, p. 104. In person, Fanny Elssler was actually tall and slim.

51. Harnett Kane, *Queen New Orleans* (New York: Morrow, 1949), pp. 175–76; Maude Howe Elliott, *Uncle Sam Ward and His Circle* (New York: Macmillan, 1938), p. 269.

52. Alexander Walker, *The Ladies' Guide to Perfect Beauty* (New York: Derby & Jackson, 1861), p. 15.
53. Havelock Ellis, *Studies in the Psychology of Sex,* 2 vols. (1910; Philadelphia: F. A. Davis, 1924), 2:42. On men's fascination for small waists, cf. Maude Howe Elliott, *This Was My Newport* (Cambridge, Mass.: Harvard Univ., 1944), p. 133; Woolson, *Woman in American Society,* p. 135.

CHAPTER 4

1. Clara Morris, *Sensible Etiquette of the Best Society* (Philadelphia: Porter and Coates, 1878), p. 251.
2. Caroline Howard Gilman, *The Poetry of Travelling in the United States* (New York: S. Colman, 1848), pp. 84–85; Virginia Clay-Clopton, *A Belle of the Fifties* (New York: Doubleday-Page, 1904), p. 90.
3. David Grimsted, *Melodrama Unveiled: American Theater and Culture, 1800–1850* (Chicago: Univ. of Chicago, 1978), p. 58; Ben Graf Hennecke, "The Playgoer in America, 1752–1792" (Ph.D. diss., Univ. of Illinois, 1956); Frederika Bremer, *The Homes of the New World,* trans. Mary Howill, 2 vols. (New York: Harper & Bros., 1853), 2:102; Major H. Byng Hall, "New York As It Is," *St. James's Magazine* 8 (Aug.–Nov. 1853): 62–68. Claudia Johnson, "That Guilty Third Tier: Prostitution in Nineteenth-Century American Theaters," *American Quarterly* 27 (Dec. 1975): 575–84, overemphasizes the longevity of the third tier.
4. Lillian Foster, *Way-Side Glimpses North and South* (New York: Rudd & Carleton, 1860), pp. 154–55; Oscar Comettant, *Trois ans aux Étas-Unis* (Paris: Pagnerre, 1857), p. 7.
5. E. Berry Wall, *Neither Pest Nor Puritan* (New York: Dial, 1940), p. 73.
6. Foster, *Way-Side Glimpses,* p. 42; Charles Astor Bristed, *The Upper Ten Thousand* (New York: Stringer and Townsend, 1852), p. 146; Comettant, *Trois ans,* p. 253; Edward S. Sears, *Foxon's Illustrated Handbook of Summer Travel* (Boston: Foxon, 1875), p. 117; Harriet Martineau, *Society in America,* 2 vols. (New York: Saunders and Otley, 1837), 2:216.
7. Lloyd Morris, *Curtain Time: The Story of the American Theater* (New York: Random House, 1953), p. 138; Francis Courtney Wemyss, *Twenty-Six Years of the Life of an Actor and Manager,* 2 vols. (New York: Burgess, Stringer, 1847), 2:102; Comettant, *Trois ans,* p. 37.
8. Catharine Beecher, *Treatise on Domestic Economy* (New York: Harper, 1849), p. 27; A. Thomason [Andrew Bell], *Men and Things in America* (London: William Smith, 1838), p. 212.
9. Edward Pessen, *Jacksonian America: Society, Personality, and Politics* (New York: Dorsey, 1978), most strongly argues against social mobility. Too, Douglas T. Miller, *Jacksonian Aristocracy: Class and Democracy in New York City, 1830–60* (New York: Oxford Univ., 1967), stresses a widening class gulf. On the other hand, Frederick Jaher, "Nineteenth-Century Elites in Boston and New York," *Journal of Social History* 2 (Fall 1972): 32–77, stresses the decline of traditional elites during the 1830s and the rise of a nouveau riche class by the 1840s.
10. Francis J. Grund, *Aristocracy in America,* 2 vols. (London: Richard Bentley, 1839), 1:139–40; James D. McCabe, Jr., *Lights and Shadows of New York Life, or Sights and*

Sensations of the Great City (Philadelphia: National, 1872), pp. 135–41; George Foster, *New York Naked* (New York: Robert DeWitt, 185[?]), p. 53; Grund, *Aristocracy in America,* 1:100; Eliza Ware Farrar, *The Young Lady's Friend* (New York: Samuel and William Wood, 1857), p. 319.

11. See Anna Cora Mowatt, *Fashion: or Life in New York* (New York: Samuel French, 1849), passim.

12. George Combe, *Notes on the United States of North America, During a Phrenological Visit in 1838-39-40,* 3 vols. (Edinburgh: MacLachlan, Steward, 1841), 2:52–53; Grund, *Aristocracy in America,* 1:269; Thomas Colley Grattan, *Civilized America,* 2 vols. (London: Bradbury and Evans, 1859), 1:118; [Ferdinand Longchamps], *Asmodeus in New York* (New York: Longchamps, 1868), p. 40; "Ideas of Respectability," *Harper's Bazar* 1 (Aug. 22, 1868): 674; Thomason [Bell], *Men and Things,* p. 210; Dixon Wecter, *The Saga of American Society: A Record of Social Aspirations, 1607-1937* (New York: Charles Scribner's Sons, 1937), p. 101; Nathaniel Parker Willis, "Lecture on Fashion" in *The Complete Works* (New York: J. J. Redfield, 1846), p. 807.

13. Grattan, *Civilized America,* 1:109; Charles Dickens, *American Notes (*1842; London: Oxford Univ., 1957), p. 246; David W. Mitchell, *Ten Years in the United States* (London: Smith, Elder, 1862), p. 196; Thomas Butler Gunn, *Physiology of New York Boarding Houses* (New York: Mason Bros., 1857), passim; Comettant, *Trois ans,* pp. 4–7; William Hancock, *An Emigrant's Five Years in the Free States of America* (London: T. Cantley Newby, 1860), p. 80; George Ellington, *The Women of New York* (New York: New York Book, 1869), p. 568; Joseph S. Rubin and Charles Brown, *Walt Whitman of the Aurora* (State College, Pa.: Bald Eagle Press, 1950), pp. 22–23.

14. Josiah Gilbert Holland, *Every-Day Topics* (New York: Charles Scribner's Sons, 1876), p. 250; Mary Cable, *American Manners and Morals* (New York: American Heritage, 1969), p. 108.

15. Abram C. Dayton, *Last Days of Knickerbocker Life* (New York: George W. Harlan, 1882), pp. 96–97; George Foster, *New York in Slices: By an Experienced Carver* (New York: W. F. Burgess, 1848), pp. 65–66.

16. Gunn, *Physiology,* p. 68; Joel H. Ross, *What I Saw in New York* (New York: Auburn, Derby, and Miller, 1851), p. 148; Grattan, *Civilized America,* 1:102; Frances Kemble Butler, *Journal of a Residence in America* (Paris: A. and W. Galignani, 1835), p. 32; Anthony Trollope, *North America* (1865; New York: Knopf, 1941), p. 29.

17. Anna Cora Mowatt Ritchie, *Autobiography of an Actress: Or Eight Years on the Stage* (Boston: Ticknor, Reed, and Fields, 1854), p. 284; Artemus Bowers Muzzey, *The Young Maiden* (Boston: W. Crosby, 1840), p. 96; George Foster, *New York by Gaslight: With Here and There a Streak of Sunshine* (New York: DeWitt and Davenport, 1850), p. 68. Women wore dark dresses for nineteenth-century photographs partly because light colors reflected light and did not photograph well. See T. S. Arthur, "The Daguerreotypist," *Godey's Lady's Book* 39 (May 1849): 355.

18. Charles Haswell, *Reminiscences of New York by an Octogenarian* (New York: Harper & Bros., 1896), p. 355; Richard M. Dorson, "Mose the Far-Famed and World Renowned," *American Literature* 15 (Nov. 1943): 288–300.

19. Foster, *New York in Slices,* p. 120; Foster, *New York by Gaslight,* p. 107; McCabe, *Lights and Shadows,* p. 188; Alvin F. Harlow, *Old Bowery Days* (New York: D. Appleton, 1931), pp. 194–214.

20. Foster, *New York in Slices,* p. 113.

21. Ibid., p. 9; William Sanger, *The History of Prostitution* (New York: Harper & Bros., 1859), pp. 549–50; Larry Howard Whiteaker, "Moral Reform and Prostitution in

New York City, 1830–60" (Ph.D. diss., Princeton Univ., 1977), p. 60; Willis, *Rag-Bag*, in *Complete Works*, p. 583; Smith, *Sunshine and Shadow*, p. 427.

22. *Chambers' Miscellany of Useful and Entertaining Knowledge*, quoted by Cable, *American Manners and Morals*, pp. 106–107; W. G. Rogers and Mildred Weston, *Carnival Cross-roads: The Story of Times Square* (Garden City, N.Y.: Doubleday, 1960), p. 123; Foster, *New York by Gaslight*, p. 6.

23. Willis, *Rag-Bag*, in *Complete Works*, p. 685.

24. James Burn, *Three Years Among the Working Classes During the War* (London: Smith, Elder, 1865), p. 85; Anne Royall, *Sketches of History, Life, and Manners in the United States* (New Haven: Royall, 1826), p. 260.

25. Mary Elizabeth Wilson Sherwood, *A Transplanted Rose: A Story of New York Society* (New York: Harper & Bros., 1862), pp. 3–10.

26. Hiram Fuller, *Belle Brittain on Tour, at Newport, and Here and There* (New York: Derby & Jackson, 1858), p. 294; Foster, *New York by Gaslight*, p. 108.

27. Ellington, *Women of New York*, p. 346.

28. Octave Uzanne, *Fashions in Paris, 1797–1897* (London: Wm. Heinemann, 1928), p. 103. Max von Boehn, *Modes and Manners of the Nineteenth Century*, trans. M. Edwardes, 3 vols. (New York: E. P. Dutton, 1909), 3:90, traced the loudness of dress and manner in the 1840s to the grisette, the lower-class companion of the Parisian bohemian.

29. George Makepeace Towle, *American Society*, 2 vols. (London: Chapman and Hall, 1870), 1:303–305; David Macrae, *Americans at Home: Pen-and-Ink Sketches of American Men, Manners, and Institutions* (New York: E. P. Dutton, 1875), p. 511; "Are We a Polite People?" *Harper's New Monthly Magazine* 15 (Sept. 1857): 527; Nathaniel Parker Willis, *The Rag-Bag: A Collection of Ephemera* (New York: Charles Scribner's Sons, 1885), p. 167.

30. "Are We a Polite People?," p. 527; Kemble Butler, *Journal*, p. 141; Comettant, *Trois ans*, p. 282.

31. Julia Newberry, *Diary* (1870; New York: W. W. Norton, 1933), p. 147; Kemble Butler, *Journal*, p. 141. *Cosmopolitan* 42 (Nov. 1906): 42, dated the introduction of chaperonage to the 1880s. *Harper's Bazar* 34 (July 9, 1881): 434, found it "strange" that Americans were so slow to introduce chaperonage. See also Arthur Meier Schlesinger, *Learning How to Behave: A Historical Study of American Etiquette Books* (New York: Macmillan, 1946), pp. 44–46.

32. Willis, *Rag-Bag*, p. 263; "Are We a Polite People?," p. 527; Abba Gould Woolson, *Woman in American Society* (Boston: Roberts Bros., 1873), p. 118; Maria Theresa Longworth, *Teresina in America*, 2 vols. (London: Richard Bentley and Son, 1875), 1:387. Joseph Kett, *Rites of Passage: Adolescence in America, 1790 to the Present* (New York: Basic, 1977), p. 56: "In colleges, unchaperoned dating was the norm."

33. Grund, *Aristocracy in America*, 1:20; Albert Rhodes, "Shall the American Girl Be Chaperoned?," *Galaxy* 22 (Oct. 1877): 485; Camille Ferri-Pisani, *Prince Napoleon in America, 1861: Letters from His Aide-de-Camp*, trans. George J. Joyavy (Bloomington, Ind.: Indiana Univ., 1959), pp. 148–49.

34. Fuller, *Belle Brittain*, p. 313; Sigmund Diamond, ed. and trans., *A Casual View of America: The Home Letters of Salomon de Rothschild, 1859–1861* (Stanford, Calif.: Stanford Univ., 1961), p. 68.

35. Grattan, *Civilized America*, 1:61; Domingo Sarmiento, *Travels in the United States in 1847*, ed. and trans. Michael Rockland (Princeton, N.J.: Princeton Univ., 1970), p. 161; *Revolution* 7 (April 6, 1871); Comettant, *Trois ans*, p. 75; Longworth, *Teresina in America*, p. 313.

36. Marion Harland [Mary Virginia Terhune], *Marion Harland's Autobiography: The Story of a Long Life* (New York: Harper & Bros., 1910), p. 220; *Godey's Lady's Book* 81 (Nov. 1870): 428–29; Caresse Crosby, *The Passionate Years* (New York: Dial, 1953), pp. 47–48.

37. Grattan, *Civilized America,* 2:58–61; Henryk Sienkiewicz, *Portrait of America: Letters of Henryk Sienkiewicz,* ed. and trans. Charles Morley (New York: Columbia Univ., 1959), p. 26.

38. Newberry, *Diary,* pp. 52, 93; "Dancing," *Harper's Bazar* 1 (Feb. 29, 1868): 274; Henry James, *Daisy Miller* (New York: Harper & Bros., 1879), pp. 100–101.

39. *Ladies' Home Journal* 24 (Aug. 1907): 9; and (Oct. 1907): 12.

40. Towle, *American Society,* 2:139. On kissing games see Harland, *Autobiography,* p. 220; Bertha Damon, *Grandma Called It Carnal* (New York: Simon & Schuster, 1938), p. 255; Charles T. Harris, *Memories of Manhattan in the 60s and 70s* (New York: Derrydale, 1928), p. 119; Robert U. Johnson, *Remembered Yesterdays* (Boston: Little, Brown, 1923), p. 46; Mabel Osgood Wright, *My New York* (New York: Macmillan, 1926), pp. 133–34; Ledyard Sargent, ed., *Dudley Allen Sargent: An Autobiography* (Philadelphia: Lea and Febiger, 1927), p. 36; Walt MacDougall, *This Is the Life* (New York: Knopf, 1926), p. 27; and especially Esther Alice Peck, *A Conservative Generation's Amusements: A Phase of Connecticut's Social History* (Bangor, Me.: Jordan-Frost, 1938), pp. 85, 100.

41. Farrar, *Young Lady's Friend,* p. 331; Eliza Leslie, *The Behaviour Book: A Manual for Ladies* (Philadelphia: Willis P. Hazard, 1854), p. 263.

42. Grund, *Aristocracy in America,* 1:41; Marianne Finch, *An Englishwoman's Experiences in America* (London: R. Bentley, 1853), p. 19; Maria Daly, *Diary of a Union Lady,* ed. Harold Earl Hammond (New York: Funk & Wagnalls, 1962), p. 95; Baxter, *America and the Americans,* p. 95.

43. James, *Daisy Miller,* p. 83; Alexis de Tocqueville, *Democracy in America,* 2 vols. (London: Longmans, Green, 1889), 2:181.

44. Frederick Marryat, *A Diary in America* (1838; New York: Knopf, 1962), p. 411; Farrar, *Young Lady's Friend,* pp. 185–86; John Leng, *America in 1876* (Dundee: Dundee Advertiser, 1877), p. 254; Tocqueville, *Democracy in America,* 2:181.

45. Captain J. W. Oldmixon, *Transatlantic Wanderings: Or, a Last Look at the United States* (London: George Routledge, 1855), pp. 173, 182.

46. *Revolution* 7 (May 25, 1871).

CHAPTER 5

1. Amelia Bloomer, *Life and Writings,* ed. Dexter Bloomer (Boston: Arena, 1895), p. 65.

2. See Lois W. Banner, *Elizabeth Cady Stanton: A Radical for Woman's Rights* (Boston: Little, Brown, 1980), pp. 35, 55–57; Theodore Stanton and Harriot Stanton Blatch, eds., *Elizabeth Cady Stanton as Revealed in Her Letters, Diary and Reminiscences,* 2 vols. (New York: Harper & Bros., 1922), 2:257.

3. Stanton and Blatch, eds., *Elizabeth Cady Stanton,* 2:50.

4. Ibid., 2:171; *History of Woman Suffrage,* ed. Elizabeth Cady Stanton, Susan B. Anthony, and Matilda Jocelyn Gage, 6 vols. (New York: Fowler and Wells, 1881), 1:470.

5. Elizabeth Smith Miller, in "Symposium on Women's Dress," *Arena* 6 (Sept. 1892): 493–94; Stanton and Blatch, *Elizabeth Cady Stanton,* 2:171; Tyrone Power, *Impressions of America, During the Years 1833, 1834, and 1835* (Philadelphia: Carey, Lea and Blanchard, 1836), 1:155.

6. Mary J. Safford Blake essay in Abba Gould Woolson, *Dress Reform* (Boston: Roberts Bros., 1874), p. 31; Katharine Anthony, *Susan B. Anthony: Her Personal History and Her Era* (New York: Russell & Russell, 1954), p. 106.

7. Mary Sargeant Gove Nichols, *Mary Lyndon* (New York: Stringer and Townsend, 1855), p. 339; *Revolution* 1 (Jan. 29, 1868): 49–50. On Brook Farm, see Katherine Burton, *Paradise Planters: The Story of Brook Farm* (London: Longmans, Green, 1939), p. 81. On Oneida and New Harmony, see Mary E. Tillotson, *Progress versus Fashion: An Essay on the Sanitary and Social Influences of Women's Dress* (Vineland, N.J.: n.p., 1873), pp. 23, 89.

8. Richard H. Shryock, "Sylvester Graham and the Popular Health Movement, 1830–70," *Mississippi Valley Historical Review* 18 (Sept. 1931): 172–83; Stanton and Blatch, *Elizabeth Cady Stanton,* 2:171; *Godey's Lady's Book* 105 (Aug. 1887); Harry B. Weiss and Howard Kemble, *The Great American Water Cure Craze* (Trenton, N.J.: Past Times Press, 1967).

9. Harriot Hunt to Elizabeth Cady Stanton, Stanton Papers, Library of Congress.

10. Banner, *Stanton,* pp. 13–14, 28; George Combe, *Notes on the United States of North America, During a Phrenological Visit in 1838-39-40,* 3 vols. (Edinburgh: MacLachian, Steward, 1841), 2:125–27.

11. John R. Betts, "Mind and Body in Early American Thought," *Journal of American History* 54 (March 1968): 787–805; Thomas Woody, *A History of Women's Education,* 2 vols. (New York: Science, 1929), 2:98–133; Almira Phelps, *The Female Student; or Lectures to Young Ladies* (New York: Leavitt, Lord, 1836), p. 68. On the difference between calisthenics and gymnastics, see Lydia Maria Child, *Girls' Own Book* (New York: Clark, Austin, 1833), p. 110.

12. On Lewis, see Mary F. Eastman, *The Biography of Dio Lewis* (New York: Fowler and Wells, 1891); Dio Lewis, in "Health of American Women," *North American Review* 135 (Dec. 1882); Fred Leonard, *A Guide to the History of Physical Education* (Philadelphia: Lea and Febiger, 1923); Anne O'Hagan, "The Athletic Girl," *Munsey's Magazine* 25 (Aug. 1901): 729; Fred Leonard, *Pioneers of Modern Physical Training* (New York: Association Press, 1919), p. 83.

13. *Godey's Lady's Book* 46 (July 1852): 64–65; and 39 (Feb. 1849): 145.

14. Josephine Robinson, *Circus Lady* (New York: Thomas Y. Crowell, 1926), p. 208; Eastman, *Lewis,* p. 72; Thomas Low Nichols, *Forty Years of American Life, 1821–1861* (1864; New York: Stackpole Sons, 1937), p. 188; Harriet Martineau, *Society in America,* 2 vols. (New York: Saunders and Otley, 1837), 2:261; Misses Mendell and Hosmer, *Notes of Travel and Life* (New York: Mendell and Hosmer, 1835) p. 55, remarked that seeing the circus had inspired them to undertake an exercise regimen.

15. Frederick Rudolph, *The American College and University* (New York: Knopf, 1972), pp. 151–52; Robert Barney, "German Turners in America: Their Role in Nineteenth Century Exercise Expression and Physical Education Legislation," in Earle F. Ziegler, ed., *A History of Physical Education and Sport in the United States and Canada* (Champagne, Ill.: Stipes, 1975), pp. 111–12. On gymnasiums in San Francisco beer halls, see Joseph Benjamin, *Three Years in America* (1862; New York: Arno, 1975), p. 192.

16. Larry Howard Whiteaker, "Moral Reform and Prostitution in New York City, 1830–60" (Ph.D. diss., Princeton Univ., 1977), p. 28; Hazel Hunton, *Pantaloons and Petticoats: The Diary of a Young American* (New York: Field, 1950); John S. Haller,

Jr., and Robin M. Haller, *The Physician and Sexuality in Victorian America* (Urbana, Ill.: Univ. of Illinois, 1974), argue that many regular doctors opposed tightlacing. Like Dio Lewis, Sarah Hale came to believe in the efficacy of exercise when her mother recovered from a supposedly incurable illness through exercise. Mary L. Booth had a woman's rights background: she served as secretary of the woman's rights conventions at Saratoga in 1855 and New York City in 1860. Jane Cunningham Croly, who wrote under the pseudonym Jennie June, was a dress reformer and a leader of the women's club movement. On Hale, see Ruth E. Finley, *The Lady of Godey's* (Philadelphia: Lippincott, 1931). On Croly, see Elizabeth Bancroft Schlesinger, "The Nineteenth-Century Woman's Dilemma and Jennie June," *New York History* 42 (Oct. 1961): 365–79. On Booth, see the article by Madeleine B. Stern in Edward T. James et al., eds., *Notable American Women,* 2 vols. (Cambridge: Harvard Univ., 1971), 1:207–208.

17. Cf. Eliza Ware Farrar, *Young Lady's Friend* (New York: Samuel and William Hood, 1857), pp. 124–36; Rufus Wilmot Griswold, *The Republican Court: or American Society in the Days of Washington* (New York: D. Appleton, 1854), pp. 160–61, on Martha Washington. On Queen Victoria, see James T. Parton, "Queen Victoria," in James T. Parton et al., *Eminent Women of the Age* (Hartford: n.p., 1868), 405–38. Washington's mother, also named Mary, was another popular model of domestic virtue. Cf. Mrs. A. J. Graves, *Women in America* (New York: Harper & Bros., 1853), p. 206.

18. My analysis of women novelists differs from Ann Douglas's, *The Feminization of American Culture* (New York: Knopf, 1978). I have rather relied on Nina Baym, *Woman's Fiction: A Guide to Novels By and About Women in America, 1820–1870* (Ithaca: Cornell Univ., 1978). Baym makes clear that the old designations of this school as "domestic" or "sentimental moralistic" are inaccurate, although she has not coined a new and needed designation. See also Helen Waite Papashvilly, *All the Happy Endings* (New York: Harper & Bros., 1956).

19. Mary Jane Holmes, *Meadowbrook* (New York: C. M. Saxton, Barker, 1860), p. 22; Stowe, *Pink and White Tyranny,* p. 49.

20. Catharine M. Sedgwick, *Clarence* (New York: George P. Putnam, 1849), pp. 178, 205, 218, 254, 513.

21. Ibid., p. 444.

22. Russell, "Brief Survey of the Dress Reform Movement," *Arena* 6 (Sept. 1892): 325.

23. Bloomer, *Life and Writings,* p. 68; J. W. Oldmixon, *Transatlantic Wanderings: Or, a Last Look at the United States* (London: George Routledge, 1855), p. 48; Virginia Clay-Clopton, *Belle of the 50's* (New York: Doubleday-Page, 1904), p. 98; Nichols, *Forty Years,* p. 44; Mary E. Tillotson, *History of the Science Costume Movement in the U.S.A.* (Vineland, N.J.: Weekly-Independent Book and Job Office, 1885), pp. 5–15.

24. "Dress Reform," *The New Encyclopedia of Social Reform,* ed. William Dwight Porter Bliss (New York: Funk, 1908), p. 517; Mrs. Merrifield, *Female Costume: Dress as a Fine Art* (London: Arthur Hall, 1854), p. 79; Tillotson, *Progress versus Fashion,* p. 11.

25. Mrs. L. Abell, *Woman in Her Various Relations; Containing Practical Advice for American Females* (New York: W. Holdredge, 1851), pp. 305–11; Catharine E. Beecher, *Letters to the People on Health and Happiness* (New York: Harper & Bros., 1855), pp. 176–82.

26. "A Bloomer Among Us," *Godey's Lady's Book* 48 (May 1854): 396–402.

27. Oscar Comettant, *Trois ans aux États-Unis* (Paris: Pagnerre, 1857), pp. 202–203. On the connection between free love and feminism, see Banner, *Stanton,* pp. 112ff. On bloomers in brothels, see *New York Herald,* June 11, 1851, quoted in Paul Fatout, "Amelia Bloomer and Bloomerism," *New-York Historical Society Quarterly* 36 (Oct.

1952): 367; and William Sanger, *The History of Prostitution* (New York: Harper & Bros., 1859), p. 563.

28. "Our Daughters," *Harper's New Monthly Magazine* 16 (Dec. 1857): 77.

29. Lato, *So-Called Skirts, or Why Girls Should Not Wear 'Rationals'* (London: Simpkin, Marshall, Hamilton, Kent, 1906), p. 6; Tillotson, ' *Progress versus Fashion*, p. 20; Bloomer, *Life and Writings*, p. 260; Stanton and Blatch, *Elizabeth Cady Stanton*, 2:257; *New York Herald*, May 21, 1851, quoted by Fatout, "Amelia Bloomer," p. 367. In *Lily*, Sept. 1851, Amelia Bloomer asserted that many people seemed to think that wearing trousers would actually change a woman's personality.

30. Tillotson, *Progress versus Fashion*, p. 20; Beecher, *Letters to the People*, p. 113; Merrifield, *Female Costume*, p. 83. For general information, see Cecil Saint-Laurent, *A History of Ladies' Underwear* (London: Michael Joseph, 1968), and Elizabeth Ewing, *Fashions in Underwear* (London: B. T. Botsford, 1971).

31. Sarah M. Grimké to [Elizabeth Cady Stanton], March 30, 1854, Stanton Papers, Library of Congress; Elizabeth Smith Miller in *Arena*, "Symposium on Women's Dress," p. 494; Bloomer, *Life and Writings*, p. 72; Stanton and Blatch, *Elizabeth Cady Stanton*, 2:173.

32. Cady Stanton later confessed that she had always thought that the tights and tunic actress Ellen Tree wore in *Ion* would have been better looking and more comfortable than the bloomer costume. But this design would have been even more unacceptable to the public. See Elizabeth Cady Stanton to Elizabeth Smith Miller, Stanton Papers, Library of Congress; *Revolution* 3 (July 22, 1869): 41; S. Oakes Smith to M. G. Nichols, 1854, Stanton Papers, Library of Congress.

33. Ida Husted Harper, *The Life of Susan B. Anthony*, 3 vols. (Indianapolis: Hollenbeck, 1908), 2:117; "American Women and English Women," *Galaxy* 9 (July 1870): 29. Dee Brown, *The Year of the Century: 1876* (New York: Charles Scribner's Sons, 1966), p. 144, noted that feminist leaders generally wore dark dresses.

34. Russell, "Brief Survey of the Dress Reform Movement," p. 331; *Demorest's Monthly*, June 1868: "For thick walking boots we are indebted to Queen Victoria"; Marion Harland [Mary Virginia Terhune], *Marion Harland's Autobiography: The Story of a Long Life* (New York: Harper & Bros., 1910), p. 258.

35. A pelisse was a full-length coat or cloak; a redingote (adapted from the male English riding coat) was a three-quarter-length or full-length coat-dress worn over a skirt. See Stella Blum, *Victorian Fashions and Costumes from Harper's Bazar, 1867–1898* (New York: Dover, 1974), p. 294; Worth, *Age of Worth*, pp. 81–82.

36. Mary Elizabeth Massey, *Bonnet Brigades: American Women and the Civil War* (New York: Knopf, 1966), p. 47; Ishbel Ross, *Crusades and Crinolines: The Life and Times of Ellen Curtis Demorest and William Jennings Demorest* (New York: Harper & Row, 1963), p. 34; Woolson, *Dress Reform*, p. 163; *Godey's Lady's Book* 105 (Aug. 1887).

37. *Revolution* 2 (Nov. 18, 1869): 316; 7 (March 16, 1871); 7 (June 22, 1871).

38. *Revolution* 3 (Sept. 2, 1869): 129.

39. *Revolution* 1 (Jan. 22, 1868): 37; and 7 (May 25, 1871).

40. *Revolution* 7 (May 25, 1871).

41. Elisabeth Finley Thomas, *Ladies, Lovers, and Other People* (New York: Longmans, Green, 1935), pp. 7–13.

42. Ella Adelia Fletcher, *The Woman Beautiful* (New York: Brentano's, 1901), p. 10.

43. Farrar, *Young Lady's Friend*, p. 109; Graves, *Women in America*, p. 107; *Una*, April 1854; "How to Keep Well," *Harper's New Monthly Magazine* 14 (Dec. 1856): 57; Abell, *Woman*, pp. 310–11.

44. William A. Alcott, *The Young Woman's Guide* (New York: Clark, Austin, and Smith, 1852); Lydia Sigourney, *Letters to Mothers* (Hartford: Hudson and Skinner, 1838), p. 73; *Lily,* July 1851, pp. 49–51.

45. Susan C. Dunning Power, *The Ugly-Girl Papers, or, Hints for the Toilet* (New York: Harper & Bros., 1875), p. 227; Lydia Maria Child, *Mother's Book* (Boston: Carter and Hendee, 1832), p. 130; Christopher Crowfield [Harriet Beecher Stowe], *The Chimney Corner* (Boston: Ticknor and Fields, 1868), p. 238; *Demorest's Monthly,* June 1868, p. 209; Catharine M. Sedgwick, *Means and Ends* (New York: Harper & Bros., 1842), p. 170.

46. Graves, *Women in America,* p. 124; Ethel Gale, *Hints on Dress* (New York: G. P. Putnam and Sons, 1872), p. 24; Power, *Ugly-Girl Papers,* p. 21.

47. "Why We Get Sick," *Harper's New Monthly Magazine* 13 (Oct. 1856): 646; Caroline Howard Gilman, *Recollections of a New England Bride and of a Southern Matron* (New York: G. P. Putnam, 1852), p. 133.

48. *Revolution* 1 (Jan. 29, 1868): 4; Graves, *Women in America,* p. 52; Ernest Duvergier de Hauranne, *Huit mois en Amérique: Lettres et notes de voyage, 1864–65,* trans. and ed. Ralph A. Bowen (Chicago: Donnelley and Sons, 1975), p. 256.

   Recent demographers argue that there was no particular decline in the incidence of marriage or rise in the age of first marriage between the eighteenth and nineteenth centuries. Cf. Robert V. Wells, "Women's Lives Transformed: Demographic and Family Patterns in America, 1600–1970," in Carol Berkin and Mary Beth Norton, eds., *Women of America: A History* (Boston: Houghton Mifflin, 1979), pp. 20–21. Based on this evidence, one must conclude that the contemporary perception that marriage was decreasing in incidence was inaccurate and that it may have been related to changing courtship patterns and the end to arranged marriages—a phenomenon which placed more pressure on women to find husbands. On the other hand, Thomas P. Monahan, *The Pattern of Age at Marriage in the United States* (Philadelphia: Stephenson Bros., 1951), the standard monograph on which Wells and others depend, is ambiguous on the issue of a stable age of first marriage during these two periods. In fact, there may have been a rise in the age of first marriage, particularly in cities.

49. Caroline Lee Hentz, *Courtship and Marriage: or the Joys and Sorrows of American Life* (Philadelphia: T. B. Peterson, 1870), p. 277; Elizabeth Stuart Phelps, *What to Wear* (Boston: James R. Osgood, 1873), p. 74.

50. Olive Logan, *Before the Footlights and Behind the Scenes* (Philadelphia: Parmelee, 1870), pp. 24–25; Allison Delarue, *The Chevalier Henry Wikoff, Impresario, 1840* (Princeton, N.J.: Princeton Univ., 1968), p. 516; Rebecca Harding Davis, *Bits of Gossip* (Boston: Houghton Mifflin, 1904), pp. 224–25. According to *Harper's Bazar* 87 (Jan. 1903): 5, Sallie Ward had been famed in every state south of the Mason-Dixon Line. "In Kentucky to this day if a man has a perfect thing from a horse to a business proposition, he will say, 'I've got a regular Sallie Ward.' "

51. Challenged for her use of the word "queen" to refer to women in republican America, Elizabeth Ellet contended that the word was commonly used in ordinary conversation to refer to beautiful women. Ellet, *The Queens of American Society* (Philadelphia: Porter and Coates, 1873), p. 1.

   Anne Hollingsworth Wharton, *Social Life in the Early Republic* (Philadephia: J. B. Lippincott, 1902), p. 31; Elizabeth Ellet, *The Court Circles of the Republic, or the Beauties and Celebrities of the Nation* (Hartford: Hartford Publishing, 1869), pp. 36, 16; Hiram Fuller, *Belle Brittain on Tour, at Newport, and Here and There* (New York: Derby & Jackson, 1858), p. 191.

52. Power, *Ugly-Girl Papers,* p. 10.

53. Fuller, *Belle Brittain,* p. 319; Meade Minnegerode, *The Fabulous Forties: 1840–1850* (New York: G. P. Putnam's Sons, 1924), p. 292.

CHAPTER 6

1. Marion Harland [Mary Virginia Terhune], *Eve's Daughters* (New York: Anderson & Allen, 1882), p. 349; Margaret Hubbard Ayer and Isabella Taves, *The Three Lives of Harriet Hubbard Ayer* (Philadelphia: Lippincott, 1957), p. 236; Harold Brydges [James Harvard Bridge], *Uncle Sam at Home* (New York: Henry Holt, 1888), p. 46; David Macrae, *Americans at Home: Pen-and-Ink Sketches of American Men, Manners, and Institutions* (New York: E. P. Dutton, 1875), p. 40.

2. Francis M. Smith, *Health and Beauty* (New York: A. L. Burt, 1889), p. 20; George Beard, *American Nervousness: Its Causes and Consequences* (New York: G. P. Putnam's Sons, 1881), p. 338; Beard, "Physical Future of the American People," *Atlantic Monthly* 43 (June 1879): 726.

3. *History of Woman Suffrage,* ed. Elizabeth Cady Stanton, Susan B. Anthony, and Matilda Jocelyn Gage, 6 vols. (New York: Fowler and Wells, 1881), 2:190: Elizabeth Cady Stanton speech before Equal Rights Association, 1867.

4. Thomas Colley Grattan, *Civilized America* (London: Bradbury and Evans, 1859), 2:56. In 1858 Hiram Fuller noted New York City galleries of Düsseldorf, English, and French art and showings for charity of millionaires' collections of French and German paintings. Fuller, *Belle Brittain on Tour, at Newport, and Here and There* (New York: Derby & Jackson, 1858), p. 233.

5. Cf. Lillian B. Miller, *Patrons and Patriotism: The Encouragement of the Fine Arts in the United States, 1790–1860* (Chicago: Univ. of Chicago, 1966); and Neil Harris, *The Artist in American Society: The Formative Years, 1790–1860* (New York: Braziller, 1966).

6. David Howard Dickason, *The Daring Young Men: The Story of the American Pre-Raphaelites* (New York: Benjamin Blom, 1953), discusses pre-Raphaelite influence on American art but does not address the issue of physical appearance. Contemporary art critic Edward Strahan contended that before 1876 English paintings were rarely seen in the United States. Strahan [Shinn], *Fine Art of the International Exhibition* (Philadelphia: Gebbie & Barie [1877?]), p. 26.

7. Carl Bode, *The Anatomy of American Popular Culture* (Berkeley and Los Angeles: Univ. of California, 1959), pp. 60–61; *Appleton's Journal* 7 (Dec. 14, 1872): 674; Strahan [Shinn], *Fine Art of the International Exhibition;* Lillian B. Miller, "Engines, Marbles, and Canvases: The Centennial Exposition of 1876," in *Indiana Historical Society Lectures, 1972–3* (Indianapolis, Ind.: Indiana Historical Society, 1973), pp. 3–29; William George Constable, *Art Collecting in the United States of America* (London: Thomas Nelson, 1964).

8. Albert Boime, *The Academy and French Painting in the Nineteenth Century* (London: Phaidon, 1971).

9. On Bouguereau, see Robert Isaacson, *William-Adolphe Bouguereau* (London: Humphries, London, and Bradford, 1975), a catalogue of a collection at the New York Cultural Center in association with Fairleigh Dickinson; "Idealization and the Nude," *Art Pompier: Anti-Impressionism, Nineteenth-Century Salon Painting* (Long Is-

land: Emily Lowe Gallery, n. p., 1974) (catalogue of show); Louis Sonolet, "Bouguereau," in *Masters in Art: French School* (Boston: Bates and Guild, 1906), pp. 389–419; Frank Fowler, "The Lesson of Bouguereau," *Scribner's Magazine* 38 (Dec. 1905): 765–68; and Carroll Beckwith, "Bouguereau," *Cosmopolitan* 8 (Jan. 1890): 259–64. On Mrs. Astor's ballroom, see Elizabeth Drexel Lehr, *"King Lehr" and the Gilded Age* (Philadelphia: Lippincott, 1935), p. 88.

10. Justin McCarthy, "The Pre-Raphaelites in England," *Galaxy* 21 (June 1876): 727. Henry James, "Du Maurier and London Society," in J. B. and J. L. Gilder, *Trilbyana* (New York: [?], 1895), newspaper clipping, noticed the "Botticellian" women on London streets and the lack of them in the United States.

11. Ronald Persall, *The Worm in the Bud: The World of Victorian Sexuality* (New York: Macmillan, 1959), pp. 102–10; Richard Jenkyns, *The Victorians and Ancient Greece* (Cambridge, Mass.: Harvard, 1980).

12. See Margaret Bieber, *The Sculpture of the Hellenistic Age* (New York: Columbia, 1955).

13. Calvin Tompkins, *Merchants and Masterpieces: The Story of the Metropolitan Museum of Art* (New York: Dutton, 1970), p. 17; Michael Batterbery and Ariane Batterbery, *On the Town in New York: From 1776 to the Present* (New York: Charles Scribner's Sons, 1973), p. 144; William Gerdts, *The Great American Nude: A History in Art* (New York: Praeger, 1974), p. 103; Richmond Brooks Barnett, *Good Old Summer Days: Newport, Narragansett Pier, Saratoga, Long Branch, Bar Harbor* (Boston: Houghton Mifflin, 1952), p. 32.

14. Richard Ettinghausen, *Jean-Léon Gérôme* (Dayton, Ohio: Dayton Art Institute, 1972); David Sonstroem, *Rossetti and the Fair Lady* (Middletown, Conn.: Wesleyan Univ., 1970), pp. 63–66; Johanna Richardson, "Winterhalter: Portrait of an Artist," *History Today* 23 (May 1973): 331–35.

15. Gerdts, *Great American Nude,* pp. 27–91. For the argument regarding motherhood, see Mary P. Ryan, *Womanhood in America: From Colonial Times to the Present* (New York: Franklin Watts, 1975), p. 158. On epic statuary and the Statue of Liberty, see Marvin Trachtenberg, *The Statue of Liberty* (New York: Viking, 1976), p. 104.

16. S. Weir Mitchell, *Fat and Blood* (Philadelphia: J. B. Lippincott, 1887), pp. 9–16; Mitchell, *Wear and Tear, Or Hints for the Overworked* (Philadelphia: Lippincott, 1871), pp. 29–41; Natalie Dana, *Young in New York: A Memoir of a Victorian Girlhood* (Garden City, N.Y.: Doubleday, 1963), p. 53.

17. *New York Clipper,* Sept. 17, 1881; Ayer and Taves, *Three Lives,* p. 236; Tomes, "Woman's Form," *Harper's New Monthly Magazine* 38 (July 1868): 202.

18. *Current Literature* 34 (April 1903): 489; Henry Collins Brown, *Brownstone Fronts and Saratoga Trunks* (New York: Dutton, 1935), p. 144; Helen MacKnight Doyle, *A Child Went Forth: The Autobiography of Helen MacKnight Doyle* (New York: Gotham House, 1934), p. 63: Harriet Hubbard Ayer, *Harriet Hubbard Ayer's Book* (1899; New York: Arno, 1974), p. 252; Phillip Kaplan, "America Pin-Ups, 1870–1900," in *Saturday Book,* vol. 31, ed. John Hatfield (London: Hutchinson, 1931), pp. 218–19; Annie Wolfe, *The Truth About Beauty* (New York: Lovell, Coryell, 1892), pp. 62–63.

19. Edith Saunders, *The Age of Worth: Couturier to the Empress Eugénie* (London: Longmans, Green, 1954), p. 28; Henry W. Knepler, *The Gilded Stage: The Lives and Careers of Four Great Actresses* (London: Constable, 1968), p. 72; Lucy H. Hooper, "Fig Leaves and French Dresses," *Galaxy* 18 (Oct. 1874): 505; Justin McCarthy, "Eugénie, Empress of the French," *Galaxy* 9 (April 1870): 513.

20. Johanna Richardson, *The Courtesans: The Demi-Monde in Nineteenth-Century France* (London: Weidenfeld and Nicholson, 1967), pp. 9, 20, quoting Jacques Mardoche and Pierre Desgenais, *Les Parisiennes.*

21. Émile Zola, *Nana* (1879; New York: Modern Library, 1927), pp. 17, 27, 34.

22. I have been influenced in this argument by Eric Trudgill, *Madonnas and Magdalens* (New York: Holmes & Meier, 1976) and by Morse Peckham, "Victorian Counterculture," *Victorian Studies* 18 (March 1975): 257–76, who argue that Victorian repression in England had only limited success in mastering the dominant permissiveness.

23. George Ellington, *The Women of New York* (New York: New York Book, 1869), pp. 317–25; Mary Henderson, *The City and the Theatre: New York Playhouses from Bowling Green to Times Square* (Clifton, N.J.: James T. White, 1973), pp. 103–108.

24. Garff B. Wilson, *A History of American Acting* (Bloomington, Ind.: Indiana Univ., 1966), pp. 110–39; Lucy H. Hooper, "How Dumas Wrote Camille," *Ladies' Home Journal* 10 (Jan. 1893): 5; Amelia Ransome Neville, *The Fantastic City: Memoirs of the Social and Romantic Life of San Francisco* (1932; New York: Arno, 1975), p. 227; Clayton Hamilton, *Seen on the Stage* (New York: Henry Holt, 1920), p. 73: "The role of Camille became for actresses the same kind of acting challenge that Hamlet has always posed for actors."

25. "*The Black Crook,*" newspaper clipping, no attribution, *Black Crook* File, Harvard Theatre Collection; Fuller, *Belle Brittain,* p. 290; Lloyd R. Morris, *Incredible New York: High Life and Low Life of the Last Hundred Years* (New York: Random House, 1951), p. 30.

26. Cf. Noel Gerson, *Queen of the Plaza: A Biography of Adah Isaacs Menken* (New York: Funk & Wagnalls, 1964), passim.

27. Michael B. Leavitt, *Fifty Years in Theatrical Management, 1859–1909* (New York: Broadway, 1912), p. 63.

28. Ibid., pp. 79, 183; Henderson, *City and the Theatre,* p. 108; George William Curtis, "Editor's Easy Chair," *Harper's New Monthly Magazine* 24 (Feb. 1862): 409; Edward Crapsey, *Nether Side of New York: or, The Vice, Crime, and Poverty of the Great Metropolis* (New York: Sheldon, 1872), p. 162. Ellington, *Women of New York,* pp. 187, 348.
    The impact of the Civil War on general social behavior has never been studied. Some information is contained in Bell Irwin Wiley, *The Life of Billy Yank: The Common Life of the Soldier* (Indianapolis: Bobbs-Merrill, 1951), pp. 257–62; Mary Elizabeth Massey, *Bonnet Brigades: American Women and the Civil War* (New York: Knopf, 1966), pp. 242–65; William Leach, *True Love and Perfect Union: The Feminist Reform of Sex and Society* (New York: Basic, 1980), pp. 5–15; Herbert Asbury, *The Gangs of New York* (Garden City, N.Y.: Doubleday, 1927), p. 174; Emerson David Fite, *Social and Industrial Conditions in the North During the Civil War* (New York: Frederick Ungar, 1963), pp. 260–71; Milton Rugoff, *Prudery and Passion: Sexuality in Victorian America* (New York: G. P. Putnam's Sons, 1971), p. 124.

29. Charles Gallaudet Trumbull, *Anthony Comstock, Fighter* (New York: Fleming H. Revell, 1913), p. 39; John William De Forest, *A Volunteer's Adventures: A Union Captain's Record* (New Haven: Yale Univ., 1946), pp. 41, 80. Wiley, *Life of Billy Yank,* p. 340, discusses the grouping of northern soldiers around their mess units.

30. William Howard Russell, *My Diary North and South* (New York: Harper & Bros., 1954), p. 13; Maria Daly, *Diary of a Union Lady,* ed. Harold Earl Hammond (New York: Funk & Wagnalls, 1962), p. 280.

31. Elizabeth Ellet, *The Queens of American Society* (Philadelphia: Porter and Coates, 1873), pp. 456–57; *Harper's Bazar* 1 (Sept. 12, 1868): 722.

32. John H. Warren, Jr., *My Thirty Years' Battle with Crime* (Poughkeepsie, N.Y.: A. J. White, 1874), p. 37; Don Seitz, *The Dreadful Decade: Detailing Some Phases in the History of the United States from Reconstruction to Resumption, 1869–1879* (Indianapolis: Bobbs-Merrill, 1926); Walt Whitman, *Democratic Vistas, and Other Papers* (New York: Walter Scott, 1888), p. 12.

33. Herbert Asbury, *All Around the Town* (New York: Knopf, 1934), p. 77.

34. Ibid., pp. 23, 68–74; *New York World,* Dec. 18, 1870. See also [Ferdinand Long-champs], *Asmodeus in New York* (New York: Longchamps, 1868), p. 18; *Harper's Bazar* 1 (Oct. 10, 1868); Ellington, *Women of New York,* p. 47; Olive Logan, *The Mimic World, and Public Exhibitions: Their History, Their Morals, and Effects* (Philadelphia: New-World, 1871), p. 79.

35. Rheta Childe Dorr, *Susan B. Anthony: The Woman Who Changed the Mind of a Nation* (New York: A.M.S. Press, 1970), p. 245; Charles Dickens, *Barnaby Rudge* (1841; New York: E. P. Dutton, 1972), p. 304.

36. For some information on theatrical censorship in the United States, see Abe Laufe, *The Wicked Stage: A History of Theater Censorship and Harassment in the United States* (New York: Frederick Ungar, 1978). For censorship in England, see Richard Find-later, *Banned! A Review of Theatrical Censorship in Britain* (London: MacGibbon & Kee, 1967). Logan, *Mimic World,* p. 364, contended that the puritanical element in the United States did not control the theater as it did in England. Frederick Van Wyck, *Recollections of an Old New Yorker* (New York: Liveright, 1932), p. 183.

37. Historians of the theater are beginning to have misapprehensions about earlier stud-ies of their subject. For example, as Julian Mates points out in *"The Black Crook* Myth," *Theatre Survey* 7 (May 1966): 31–43, *The Black Crook* was neither the first spectacle in the United States nor the first production to feature chorus girls in tights. Similarly, I have discovered that vaudeville managers of the 1870s were responsible for the myth that all variety theaters that preceded them had been salacious and that respectable patrons stayed away. The concert saloon expansion after the Civil War tainted the reputation of all variety theaters. See Noah M. Ludlow, *Dramatic Life as I Found It* (1880; New York: Benjamin Blom, 1966), pp. 703–74; John L. Jennings, *Theatrical and Circus Life* (St. Louis: M. S. Barnett, 1882), pp. 389–91; Robert Grau, *Forty Years Observation of Music and the Drama* (New York: Broadway, 1909), p. 9; Leavitt, *Fifty Years,* p. 184.

38. H. E. Cooper, "Pink Tights and British Blondes," *Dance Magazine,* Oct. 1926, p. 62.

39. The blonde hair may have developed from the use of blonde women as angels in the "transformation" scenes that climaxed traditional British Christmas shows and be-came standard in later spectacles. J. Mortimer Crandall contended that Englishmen had long liked big blonde chorus girls, while those on the French stage were smaller and darker ("The American Chorus Girl," *Metropolitan Magazine* 4 [April 1895]: 173–75).

40. Samuel L. Clemens, *Mark Twain's Travels with Mr. Brown,* ed. Franklin Walter and G. Ezra Dane (New York: Knopf, 1940), pp. 84–87; William Dean Howells, "The New Taste in Theatricals," *Atlantic Monthly* 23 (May 1869): 635–44; Howells, "Some Lessons from the School of Morals," *Suburban Sketches* (Boston: Houghton Mifflin, 1888), pp. 220–39; Olive Logan, *Apropos of Women and Theatres* (New York: G. W. Carleton, 1869), pp. 128–30; Richard Grant White, "The Age of Burlesque," *Galaxy* 8 (Aug. 1869): 262. See also Marilyn A. Moses, "Lydia Thompson and the British Blondes in the United States" (Unpub. diss., Univ. of Oregon, 1978).

41. Howells, "New Taste in Theatricals," pp. 640–41; "Interview with Lydia Thompson," *New York Sunday Herald,* May 26, 1901, British Blondes File, Harvard Theatre Collection; White, "Age of Burlesque," p. 260.

42. White, "Age of Burlesque," p. 260; Howells, "Some Lessons," p. 238; *Spirit of the Times,* Oct. 3, 1868, p. 29; "Interview with Thompson," *New York Sunday Herald.*

43. See "Niblo's Garden: *The Black Crook,*" newspaper clipping, no citation, *Black Crook* File, Harvard Theatre Collection; David John Russell, "The Genesis of the Variety Theatre: *Black Crook* Comes to St. Louis," *Missouri Historical Review,* no citation, clipping, *Black Crook* File, New York Public Library Theatre Collection, noted that women of all social classes in St. Louis came to the production; Dana, *Young in New York,* p. 123, recorded that women veiled their faces, but George Templeton Strong, *Diary of George Templeton Strong: Post-War Years, 1865–75,* ed. Allan Nevins and Milton Halsey Thomas (New York: Macmillan, 1952), p. 164, noted without comment that his wife went to see *The Black Crook* with some friends. Several sources remarked on the press agentry of Commodore Tooker: Grau, *Forty Years Observation,* p. 128. William A. Brady, *Showman* (New York: E. P. Dutton, 1937), p. 131, contended that Tooker planted the moral attacks on *The Black Crook* as a way of stimulating attendance. Mabel Osgood Wright, *My New York* (New York: Macmillan, 1926), pp. 124–31.

44. Olive Logan. *Before the Footlights and Behind the Scenes* (Philadelphia: Parmelee, 1870), pp. 535, 585; White, "Age of Burlesque," pp. 257, 261.

45. White, "Age of Burlesque," pp. 258, 261; Brown, *Brownstone Fronts,* p. 278; *Spirit of the Times,* May 15, 1875, quoting Cincinnati newspaper clipping, Eliza Weathersby File, New York Public Library Theatre Collection.

46. Howells, "New Taste in Theatricals," pp. 639–40.

47. Moses, "Lydia Thompson and the British Blondes," notes the origin of the name. Markham's remark is contained in an interview in the *New York World,* Jan. 20, 1805. See also "The Fair One with Golden Locks," *Harper's Bazar* 12 (Sept. 21, 1878): 602.

48. Sol Bloom, *The Autobiography of Sol Bloom* (New York: G. P. Putnam's Sons, 1948), pp. 41–43; *Spirit of the Times,* Oct. 3, 1868, p. 112.

49. Howells, "Some Lessons," pp. 239–40.

50. Logan, *Apropos of Women and Theatres,* p. 133. It is perhaps not accidental that the success of the British Blondes' engagement came at a time of sizable feminist activity in New York City. In 1868 Sorosis, the nation's first women's club, was founded; a woman's building to house feminist activities opened; and Cady Stanton and Anthony founded the *Revolution* and agitated the Hester Vaughan infanticide case. The indirect influence of feminist activity on women's general behavior is hard to chart, and Anthony and Cady Stanton themselves were critical of the British Blondes' performances as prurient. Nonetheless, the "woman question" was very much in the air in 1868, and the British Blondes offered an interesting role model for women.

51. William Davidge, *Footlight Flashes* (New York: American News, 1866), p. 171, drew a distinction between the soubrette and the singing chambermaid to differentiate the latter's musical ability. Elaine Sylvia Small Klein ("The Development of the Leading Feminine Character in Selected Librettos of American Musicals from 1900 to 1960" [Ph.D. diss., Columbia Univ., 1962], p. xii) argued that the soubrette was an active, clever young woman who had to work. Frederick Nicolls, "The Tendencies of Recent Fiction," *Arena* 32 (July 1904): 10–18, noted the popularity of the soubrette in late nineteenth-century fiction. John Hollingshead, *Gaiety Chronicles* (Westminster, Eng.: Constable, 1898), p. 200, traced the origin of the soubrette to William Congreve's *Love for Life.*

52. The first soubrette star on the American stage was Clara Fisher in the 1830s. She was short, her body "just reaching, but not exceeding, a delicate plumpness" (H. P. Phelps, *Players of a Century: A Record of the Albany Stage* [New York: Werner, 1890], p. 114). On Crabtree, see Constance Rourke, *Troupers of the Gold Coast: or the Rise of Lotta Crabtree* (New York: Harcourt, Brace, 1928).

53. *Police Gazette,* Jan. 21, 1885.

54. Anna Cora Mowatt, *Mimic World: Or Before and After the Curtain* (Boston: Ticknor and Fields, 1856), p. 57; Dora Ranous, *Diary of a Daly Débutante* (New York: Duffield, 1910).

55. White, "Age of Burlesque," p. 262. George Augusta Sala, *America Revisited* (London: Vizetelly, 1882), p. 53, underlined the continuing mythology of post–Civil War variety actresses: "When a businessman comes to financial grief in New York and is accused by his creditors of having lived extravagantly, it is generally urged against him that he lived in 'a brownstone house with a marble façade, kept fast trotting horses, and gave champagne suppers to the "blonde belles of *The Black Crook* burlesque." ' "

CHAPTER 7

1. Robert Grau, *Forty Years Observation of Music and the Drama* (New York: Broadway, 1909), pp. 166–68. In 1874 police officer John Warren contended that concert saloon waitresses were being chosen for their "amplitude of proportions," that they were "huge-limbed and squabbly": John H. Warren, Jr., *My Thirty Years' Battle with Crime* (Poughkeepsie, N.Y.: A. J. White, 1874), p. 117.

2. Natalie Dana, *Young in New York: A Memoir of a Victorian Girlhood* (Garden City, N.Y.: Doubleday, 1963), p. 53; Lucy Duff-Gordon, *Discretions and Indiscretions* (New York: Frederick A. Stokes, 1932), p. 78; Tomes, "Woman's Form," *Harper's New Monthly Magazine* 38 (July 1868): 202; *Phrenological Journal of Science and Health,* Sept. 1895, clipping, Elizabeth Cady Stanton Papers, Library of Congress; Alan Dale [Alfred Cohen], *Familiar Chats with Queens of the Stage* (New York: G. W. Dillingham, 1890), p. 87.

3. Cf. William Banting, *Letter on Corpulence Addressed to the Public* (San Francisco: A. Roman, 1865). On the development of scientific knowledge of nutrition, see Richard O. Cummings, *The American and His Food* (1941; New York: Arno, 1970).

4. Cf. Dale [Cohen], *Familiar Chats,* p. 87; *Spirit of the Times,* Feb. 15, 1868; Francis W. Crowninshield, *Manners for the Metropolis: An Entrance Key to the Fantastic Life of the 400* (New York: D. Appleton, 1909), pp. 29–30; *Oxford English Dictionary,* 1:659.

5. Richmond Brooks Barnett, *Good Old Summer Days: Newport, Narragansett Pier, Saratoga, Long Branch, Bar Harbor* (Boston: Houghton Mifflin, 1952), p. 108.

6. Calvin Tompkins, *Merchants and Masterpieces: The Story of the Metropolitan Museum of Art* (New York: E. P. Dutton, 1970), p. 43; Dana, *Young in New York,* p. 53; Fairfax Downey, *Portrait of an Era as Drawn by C. D. Gibson* (New York: Charles Scribner's Sons, 1936), p. 226. In his study of Newport, Richard O'Connor contended that the Newport elites followed the Lillian Russell look and that they began to diet only after the Florodora girls became the rage in 1900—in this case "society aping the stage" (*The Golden Summers: An Antic History of Newport* [New York: G. P. Putnam's Sons, 1974], p. 187).

7. Edward Strahan [Earl Shinn], *Art Treasures of America*, 3 vols. (Philadelphia: George Barrie, 1879), 1:120. On Sargent, see Charles Merrill Mount, *John Singer Sargent: A Biography* (New York: W. W. Norton, 1955).

8. Sol Smith, *Theatrical Management in the South and West* (New York: Harper & Bros., 1868), pp. 237-38; Michael B. Leavitt, *Fifty Years in Theatrical Management, 1859-1909* (New York: Broadway, 1912), p. 308; Olive Logan, *The Mimic World, and Public Expectations: Their History, Their Morals and Effects* (Philadelphia: New-World, 1871), p. 565. See also John L. Jennings, *Theatrical and Circus Life* (St. Louis: M. S. Barnett, 1882), p. 236; Laurence Hutton, *Curiosities of the American Stage* (New York: Harper & Bros., 1891), p. 182; Joseph Hatton, *Today in America: Studies for the Old World and the New*, 2 vols. (London: Chapman and Hall, 1881), 1:17.

9. Grau, *Forty Years Observation*, pp. 9, 51.

10. Arthur Train, *Puritan's Progress* (New York: Charles Scribner's Sons, 1931), pp. 283, 293; J. W. C., "Social New York," from *Macmillan's Magazine*, quoted in *Eclectic Magazine* 16 (1872): 205.

   On the social purity movement see David Pivar, *Purity Crusade: Sexual Morality and Social Control* (Westport, Conn.: Greenwood, 1973). On Anthony Comstock, see Heywood Broun and Margaret Leech, *Anthony Comstock: Roundsman of the Lord* (New York: Albert and Charles Boni, 1927). On divorce, see Nelson Manfred Blake, *The Road to Reno* (New York: Macmillan, 1962). On abortion, see James Mohr, *Abortion in America: The Origins and Evolution of National Policy, 1800-1900* (New York: Oxford Univ., 1978).

11. See Lucy Kavalier, *The Astors* (New York: Dodd, Mead, 1966).

12. Arthur Meier Schlesinger, *Learning How to Behave: A Historical Study of American Etiquette Books* (New York: Macmillan, 1946), p. 35.

13. Dana, *Young in New York*, p. 90; Julia Newberry, *Diary* (1870; New York: W. W. Norton, 1933), p. 147; May King Van Rensselaer, *The Social Ladder* (New York: Henry Holt, 1924), p. 45; Clarence Day, *Life with Father* (New York: Knopf, 1935), p. 5.

14. Malcolm Cowley, *After the Genteel Tradition* (New York: Norton, 1937), p. 10; William Dean Howells, *Indian Summer* (New York: Dutton, 1951), p. 15.

15. Arthur Pember, *The Mysteries and Miseries of the Great Metropolis* (New York: D. Appleton, 1874). On the later period, cf. Miriam Young, *Mother Wore Tights* (New York: McGraw-Hill, 1944), p. 575; Billie Burke (with Cameron Shipp), *With a Feather on My Nose* (New York: Appleton-Century-Crofts, 1949), pp. 80-81; Beatrice Fairfax [Marie Manning], *Ladies Now and Then* (New York: E. P. Dutton, 1944), p. 95.

16. Logan, *Mimic World*, p. 575; James L. Ford, "New York of the Seventies," *Scribner's Magazine* 63 (June 1923): 742-48; Rudolph Aaronson, *Theatrical and Musical Memoirs* (New York: McBride, Nast, 1913), p. 27.

17. Otis Skinner, *Footlights and Spotlights: Recollections of My Life on the Stage* (Indianapolis: Bobbs-Merrill, 1923), p. 87. Leander Richardson, "Beauty as an Element in Stage Success," *Metropolitan Magazine* 7 (July 1898), contended that newspapermen derided the Kiralfy choruses as looking as though they had been recruited from "the Old Ladies' Home." W. A. Darlington, *The World of Gilbert and Sullivan* (New York: Crowell, 1950), p. 9.

18. Emily Soldene, *My Theatrical and Musical Recollections* (London: Gilbert and Rivington, 1897), p. 159; Lloyd Morris, *Curtain Time: The Story of the American Theater* (New York: Random House, 1953), p. 218.

19. Marie Dressler, *My Own Story, as Told to Mildred Harrington* (Boston: Little, Brown, 1935), p. 86.

My analysis of Lillian Russell is based on Parker Morrell, *Lillian Russell: The Era of Plush* (New York: Random House, 1940); John Burke, *Duet in Diamonds: The Flamboyant Saga of Lillian Russell and Diamond Jim Brady in America's Gilded Age* (New York: G. P. Putnam's Sons, 1972); Lillian Russell, "Lillian Russell's Reminiscences," *Cosmopolitan* 72 (Feb., March, April 1922); and especially the clipping files at the Harvard and New York Public Library Theatre Collections.

20. Lewis C. Strang, *Prima Donnas and Soubrettes of Light Opera and Musical Comedy in America* (Boston: L. C. Page, 1900), p. 30; Morrell, *Russell*, p. 300; *San Francisco Examiner*, Sept. 1, 1912.

21. Clarence Day, "Appearing with Lillian Russell," *Saturday Evening Post* 208 (Oct. 26, 1935): 90; Fairfax [Manning], *Ladies*, p. 27; *New York World*, Feb. 14, 1902, clipping, Lillian Russell File, Harvard Theatre Collection; Edna Ferber, *A Peculiar Treasure* (1938; Garden City, N.Y.: Doubleday, 1960), p. 12.

22. Albert Stevens Crockett, *Peacocks on Parade* (New York: Sears, 1931), p. 159; *Dramatic Mirror*, Feb. 28, 1891, p. 7.

23. Remarks about the American Beauty rose abound in the day's literature. Cf. Very Rev. S. Reynolds Hole, *A Little Tour in America* (1895; Freeport, N.Y.: Books for Libraries Press, 1971), pp. 100–101.

24. On the esthetic painters, see William Gaunt, *The Aesthetic Adventure* (London: Jonathan Cape, 1945); On Lillie Langtry, see Noel G. Gerson, *Lillie Langtry* (London: Robert Hale, 1971); Pierre Sichel, *The Jersey Lily: The Story of the Fabulous Mrs. Langtry* (Englewood Cliffs, N.J.: Prentice-Hall, 1958), and "English Beauties," *Harper's Bazar* 13 (April 3, 1880): 215.

25. Gerson, *Langtry*, p. 101.

26. Emily Faithfull, *Three Visits to America* (Edinburgh: David Douglas, 1884), pp. 338–39; *Police Gazette*, Dec. 23, 1882.

27. Amy Leslie, *Some Players: Personal Sketches* (New York: Duffield, 1906), p. 401; Henry Lepel Griffin, *The Great Republic* (New York: Scribner and Welford, 1884), pp. 53–56; *Spirit of the Times*, Nov. 15, 1882, clipping, Lillie Langtry File, New York Public Library Theatre Collection; Duff-Gordon, *Discretions and Indiscretions*, p. 26.

28. "Beauty in Art and Nature," in *The Woman's Atheneum* (New York: Woman's Atheneum, 1912), p. 182; clipping [1901?], Lillie Langtry File, New York Public Library Theatre Collection. *Music and Drama*, Nov. 11, 1882, complained about her large hands and feet (clipping, Langtry File, New York Public Library Theatre Collection).

29. Robert Tomes, *The Bazar Book of Decorum* (New York: Harper & Bros., 1877), p. 36; Edna Woolman Chase and Ilka Chase, *Always in Vogue* (Garden City, N.Y.: Doubleday, 1954), p. 29.

30. George Odell, *Annals of the New York Stage*, 15 vols. (New York: Columbia Univ., 1927–49), 12:3; *Music and Drama*, Nov. 18, 1882, clipping, Langtry File, New York Public Library Theatre Collection.

31. William G. Anderson, *Light Gymnastics* (New York: Effingham, Maynard, 1889), p. 3.

32. John Habberton, "Open Air Recreation for Women," *Outing* 7 (Nov. 1885): 161.

33. *Union Standard*, Jan. 2, 1890.

34. Henry T. Finck, *Romantic Love and Personal Beauty* (New York: Macmillan, 1887), p. 404; Carol Wald, *Myth America: Picturing Women, 1865–1945* (New York: Pantheon, 1975), p. 56; Harriet Hubbard Ayer, *Harriet Hubbard Ayer's Book: A Complete and Authentic Treatise on the Laws of Health and Beauty* (New York: Home, 1899), p. 244.

35. Julia B. Foraker, *I Would Live It Again: Memories of a Vivid Life* (New York: Harper & Bros., 1932), p. 185. On Delsarte, see "Delsarte," *Atlantic Monthly* 55 (May 1871): 614–20; M. V. O'Shea, "Physical Training in the Public Schools," *Atlantic Monthly* 85 (Feb. 1895): 246–54; *New York Daily Tribune,* May 13, 1900.

36. Anne O'Hagan, "Athletic Girl," *Munsey's Magazine* 25 (Aug. 1901): 731.

37. Ellen W. Gerber et al., *American Women in Sport* (Reading, Mass.: Addison-Wesley, 1974), p. 4; Suzanne Hilton, *The Way It Was—1876* (Philadelphia: Westminster, 1975), p. 104; Edith Wharton, *A Backward Glance* (New York: D. Appleton-Century, 1934), p. 46; "The Athletic Age," *Godey's Lady's Book* 104 (Aug. 1889): 204.

38. Sophia Foster Richardson, "Tendencies in Athletics for Women in Colleges and Universities," *Popular Science Monthly* 50 (Feb. 1897): 517–26.

39. Van Rensselaer, *Social Ladder,* p. 223; Frederick Townsend Martin, *Passing of the Idle Rich* (1911; New York: Arno, 1975), pp. 230–31.

40. Foster Rhea Dulles, *A History of Recreation: America Learns to Play* (New York: Appleton-Century-Crofts, 1965), p. 193; Adelaide Louise Sampson, "Women's Gymnasiums in New York," *Metropolitan Magazine* 3 (Jan. 1896): 33.

41. Lila Rose McCabe, *The American Girl at College* (New York: Dodd, Mead, 1893), p. 16; Richardson, "Tendencies in Athletics"; O'Hagan, "Athletic Girl."

42. David F. Burg, *Chicago's White City of 1893* (Lexington, Ky.: Univ. of Kentucky, 1976), p. 193; Mary Taylor Bissell, "Athletics for City Girls," *Popular Science Monthly* 46 (Dec. 1894): 145–55; Dudley Sargent, "The Physical Development of Women," *Scribner's Magazine* 5 (Feb. 1889): 181.

43. Margaret Bisland, "Bowling for Women," *Outing* 16 (April 1890): 16; Sargent, "Physical Development," p. 181.

44. Sampson, "Women's Gymnasiums in New York," p. 33. See also Robert Dunn, "The Country Club: A National Expression: Where Woman Is Really Free," *Outing* 30 (Nov. 1905): 160–73.

45. Teresa Dean, *How to Be Beautiful* (Chicago: T. Howard, 1889), p. 42; Henry Collins Brown, *In the Golden Nineties* (New York: Valentine's, 1928), pp. 48, 53.

46. Charles E. Clay, "Fair Riders on Modern Wheels," *Outing* 18 (Jan. 1891): 305–307; Mary Roberts Rinehart, *My Story* (New York: Farrar & Rinehart, 1931), p. 34.

47. *Vogue* 5 (March 5, 1895): 167. As early as 1886 the *Police Gazette* used the term "daisy" to refer to an independent woman. See *Police Gazette,* June 26, 1886.

48. Cf. James Fullerton Muirhead, *The Land of Contrasts: A Briton's View of His American Kin* (London: John Land, 1898), p. 127.

49. *Vogue* 4 (Nov. 2, 1894): 274; Elizabeth Drexel Lehr, *"King Lehr" and the Gilded Age* (Philadelphia: J. B. Lippincott, 1935), p. 139.

50. *Vogue* 3 (Jan. 7, 1893): 49; *New York World,* Jan. 18, 1895.

51. *Harper's Bazar* 8 (June 12, 1875): 379; *Harper's Weekly,* Jan. 28, 1893.

52. *Godey's Lady's Book* 105 (Nov. 1884): 518. Marion Harland noted the similarity between the spencer and the shirtwaist. See Marion Harland [Mary Virginia Terhune], *Marion Harland's Autobiography: The Story of a Long Life* (New York: Harper & Bros., 1910), p. 258.

53. Alexandra Gripenberg, *A Half Year in the United States,* ed. and trans. Ernest J. Moyne (Newark: Univ. of Delaware, 1954), p. 204; Elizabeth Stuart Phelps, "Décolletée in Modern Life," *Forum* 9 (Aug. 1890): 674–75.

54. Henry Collins Brown, *Brownstone Fronts and Saratoga Trunks* (New York: Dutton, 1935), p. 150; Brown, *In the Golden Nineties,* p. 23; *Woman's Journal* 27 (Oct. 3, 1896): 313. Margaret Hubbard Ayer and Isabella Taves, *The Three Lives of Harriet Hubbard*

Ayer (Philadelphia: Lippincott, 1957), pp. 256–57; David L. Cohn, *The Good Old Days: A History of American Morals and Manners as Seen Through the Sears, Roebuck Catalogs, 1905 to the Present* (New York: Simon & Schuster, 1940), p. 294.

55. Nora Waugh, *Corsets and Crinolines* (London: Batsford, 1954), pp. 79–85.

56. Natalie Dana, *Young in New York: A Memoir of a Victorian Girlhood* (Garden City, N.Y.: Doubleday, 1963), pp. 89, 95; *New York World,* May 19, 1901.

57. *Harper's Bazar* 26 (April 1, 1893); *Vogue* 11 (June 20, 1901).

58. Katharine Anthony, *Feminism in Germany and Scandinavia* (New York: Henry Holt, 1915), pp. 55–56; "Fashion as a Dress Reformer," *Independent* 76 (Oct. 23, 1913): 151.

59. Dana, *Young in New York,* p. 118; Ferber, *Peculiar Treasure,* pp. 111–12; Margaret Sanger, *Margaret Sanger: An Autobiography* (1938; New York: Dover, 1971), p. 37.

60. *Metropolitan Magazine* 1 (April 1895): 152.

61. Malcolm Tenny, "Living Pictures and the Nude in Art," *Metropolitan Magazine* 1 (March 1895): 76.

62. Clippings, Frankie Bailey File, New York Public Library Theatre Collection; Crockett, *Peacocks on Parade,* p. 159.

63. David Graham Phillips, *Susan Lenox: Her Fall and Rise,* 2 vols. (New York: D. Appleton, 1917), 1:18, 222–23.

64. Young, *Mother Wore Tights,* p. 131.

CHAPTER 8

1. Cf. Robert Howard Russell, "How Charles Dana Gibson Started," *Ladies' Home Journal* 19 (Oct. 1902): 7; *Charles Dana Gibson: A Study of the Man and Some Recent Examples of His Best Work* (New York: P. F. Collier and Son, 1905). For Gibson's work, I have used in particular the large collection in the Library of Congress.

2. Mark Sullivan, *Our Times: The Turn of Century, America Finding Itself,* 6 vols. (New York: Charles Scribner's Sons, 1926), 2:194.

3. Cf. Morton Keller, *The Art and Politics of Thomas Nast* (New York: Oxford, 1968), passim.

4. John Mitchell, "Contemporary American Caricature," *Scribner's Magazine* 6 (Dec. 1889): 728–45.

5. Ibid., 740; Constance C. Harrison, *The Well-Bred Girl in Society* (New York: George W. Harlan, 1882), p. 116. See also F. Weitenkampf, *American Graphic Art* (New York: Henry Holt, 1912); and William Murrell, *A History of American Graphic Humor, 1865–1938* (New York: Macmillan, 1938).

6. Fairfax Downey, *Portrait of an Era as Drawn by C. D. Gibson* (New York: Charles Scribner's Sons, 1936), pp. 101–102.

7. Norman Rockwell, as told to Thomas Rockwell, *My Adventures as an Illustrator* (Garden City, N.Y.: Doubleday, 1960), p. 69; Susan E. Meyer, *America's Great Illustrators* (New York: Harry N. Abrams, 1978), p. 225.

8. Charlotte Perkins Gilman, *Women and Economics,* ed. Carl N. Degler (1898; New York: Harper & Row, 1966), p. 148.

9. Downey, *Portrait of an Era,* p. 265; Caresse Crosby, *The Passionate Years* (New York: Dial, 1953), p. 31.

10. *San Francisco Examiner,* April 13, 1912; *New York Herald,* April 14, 1907; Richard Harding Davis, "The Origin of a Type of the American Girl," *Quarterly Illustrator,* Jan.–March 1895, pp. 3–8; Helena Rubinstein, *My Life for Beauty* (London: The Bodley Head, 1964), p. 56.

11. Cora Potter, *Beauty and Health: The Secrets of Beauty and Mysteries of Health* (New York: Paul Elder, 1908), pp. 242–43; Belle Livingstone, *Belle Out of Order* (New York: Henry Holt, 1959), pp. 42–43; Winfield Scott Moody, "Daisy Miller and the Gibson Girl," *Ladies' Home Journal* 21 (Sept. 1904): 17; *New York Herald,* June 5, 1905; *New York World,* Nov. 1, 1903. Modern-day analysts of the Gibson girl continue the controversy over her meaning. James R. McGovern, "The American Woman's Pre–World War I Freedom in Manners and Morals," *Journal of American History* 40 (Sept. 1968): 315–33, sees her as a conservative image. Martha Kingsbury, "The Femme Fatale and Her Sisters," in Linda Nochlin and Thomas Hess, eds., *Woman as Sex Object: Studies in Erotic Art, 1730–1970* (New York: Newsweek, 1972), pp. 182–205, stresses the eroticism in her thrown-back head and lowered eyes drawn, Kingsbury argues, from the femme-fatale configuration of late nineteenth-century art.

12. *Denver Post,* Jan. 20, 1907; Robert Grant, "Charles D. Gibson: The Man and His Art," *Collier's,* Jan. 3, 1901; *New York World,* Nov. 8, 1903.

13. Russell, "How Gibson Started," p. 7; J. M. Bulloch, "Charles Dana Gibson," *Studio* 8 (June 8, 1896): 75–81; Spencer Coon, "Gibson's American Girl," *Metropolitan Magazine* 4 (Dec. 1896).

14. Grant, "Gibson," passim.

15. *New York World,* Dec. 9, 1900.

16. Josephine Gibson Knowlton, *Longfield: The House on the Neck* (Providence: Oxford Press, 1956), p. 311.

17. Knowlton, *Longfield,* p. 320. On Du Maurier, see Leonée Ormond, *George Du Maurier* (London: Routledge & Kegan Paul, 1969). Robert H. Sherard, "The Author of Trilby: An Autobiographical Interview with Mr. George Du Maurier," *McClure's Magazine* 4 (April 1895): 391–400, in *Trilbyana,* Regarding the Venus de Milo bust in his study, Du Maurier said, "There is my great inspiration."

18. Constance Cary Harrison, *Recollections Grave and Gay* (New York: C. Scribner's Sons, 1911), p. 355.

19. Weitenkampf, *American Graphic Art,* p. 234. Journalist Beatrice Fairfax thought that Gibson had been a force for reform. Fairfax [Marie Manning], *Ladies Now and Then* (New York: E. P. Dutton, 1944), pp. 147–48: "Goodness knows where all [the extravagance] might have ended if C. D. Gibson had not come along and begun to impale 'society' on the point of his clever pencil."

20. Michael Astor, *Tribal Feeling* (London: John Murray, 1963), p. 26; Henry Collins Brown, *In the Golden Nineties* (New York: Valentine's, 1928), p. 185.

21. Charles Wilbur de Lyon Nichols, *The Ultra-Fashionable Peerage of America* (1904; New York: Arno, 1975), p. 27.

22. Brown, *In the Golden Nineties,* p. 69; Charles Belmont Davis, "Mr. Charles Dana Gibson and his Art," *Critic* 34 (Jan. 1899): 50; Peter Casill, *New York Memories of Yesteryear: Life and Times at the Turn of the Century, 1890–1910* (New York: Exposition, 1964), p. 15. One analyst of Gibson's vogue thought that his decision to focus on the elites grew out of a calculating business sense ("Charles Dana Gibson, Illustrator," *Brush and Pen* 7 [Feb. 1901]: 282–84).

23. H. I. Brock, "From the Cotillion to the Supper Dance," *New York Times Magazine,* May 6, 1934, p. 12. Both Joseph Pulitzer and the editor of the *Denver Post* contended

that the massive circulations of their newspapers rested on their appeal to women (Emily Faithfull, *Three Visits to America* [Edinburgh: David Douglas, 1884], pp. 344–45; *Denver Post,* Oct. 8, 1906).

24. Paul Bourget, *Outre-Mer: Impressions of America* (New York: Charles Scribner's Sons, 1895), p. 86; Harrison, *Well-Bred Girl,* p. 3.

25. Eleanor Robson Belmont, *The Fabric of Memory* (New York: Farrar, Straus, and Cudahy, 1957), p. 61; *Denver Post,* Oct. 9, 1904.

26. Consuelo Vanderbilt Balsan, *The Glitter and the Gold* (New York: Harper & Bros., 1952); Michael Strange, *Who Tells Me True* (New York: Charles Scribner's Sons, 1940), p. 26.

27. *Vogue* 5 (Nov. 2, 1895): 274.

28. Woody Gelman, ed., *The Best of Charles Dana Gibson* ([?]: Bounty Books, [?]), p. ix.

29. "Charles Dana Gibson," obituary, *New York Times,* Dec. 24, 1944; Ann Uhry Abrams, "Frozen Goddess: The Image of Woman in Turn-of-Century American Art," in Mary Kelley, ed., *Woman's Being, Woman's Place: Female Identity and Vocation in American History* (Boston: G. K. Hall, 1979), pp. 93–96.

30. *New York Herald,* Oct. 26, 1902; *New York World,* Jan. 5, 1913.

31. See William Wasserstrom, *Heiress of All the Ages: Sex and Sentiment in the Genteel Tradition* (Minneapolis: Univ. of Minnesota, 1959); and Paul John Eakin, *The New England Girl: Cultural Ideals in Hawthorne, Stowe, Howells, and James* (Athens, Ga.: Univ. of Georgia, 1976).

32. Oscar Comettant, *Trois ans aux États-Unis* (Paris: Pagnerre, 1857), p. 70; Josephine DeMott Robinson, *Circus Lady* (New York: Thomas Y. Crowell, 1926), pp. 120–21; Captain Frederick Marryat, *A Diary in America* (1838; New York: Knopf, 1962), pp. 148–49; Fred Stone, *Rolling Stone* (New York: McGraw Hill, 1945), p. 64.

33. *Vogue* 15 (Aug. 15, 1905): iii; Edward Strahan [Earl Shinn], *Fine Art of the International Exhibition* (Philadelphia: Gebbie & Barie [1877?]), pp. 38, 79; John G. Cawalti, "America on Display: The World's Fairs of 1876, 1893, 1933," in Frederic Cople Jaher, ed., *The Age of Industrialism in America* (New York: Free Press, 1968), p. 340: "To our eyes, those statues look rather like monumental versions of the Gibson Girl...."

34. Agatha Young, *Women and the Crisis* (New York: McDowell, Obolensky, 1959), p. 95; E. McClung Fleming, "The American Image as Indian Princess, 1765–1783," *Winterthur Portfolio* 2 (1965): 65–81, and "From Indian Princess to Greek Goddess: The American Image, 1783–1815," Ibid. 3 (1966): 37–66.

35. Sir Alfred Maurice Low, *America at Home* (London: George Newnes, 1908), p. 70; Alexander Black, *Miss America: Pen and Camera Sketches of the American Girl* (New York: Charles Scribner's Sons, 1898), p. 50.

36. Cf. Charles Victor de Varigny, *Women of the United States,* trans. Arabella Ward (New York: Dodd, Mead, 1895), p. 84; Henry Lepel Griffin, *The Great Republic* (New York: Scribner and Welford, 1884), pp. 68–69; Catherine Bates, *A Year in the Great Republic,* 2 vols. (London: World and Downey, 1887), 1:53; John Walter Cross, *Impressions of Dante and of the New World* (Edinburgh: William Blackwood, 1893), pp. 273, 279; Marion Harland [Mary Virginia Terhune], *Eve's Daughters* (New York: Anderson & Allen, 1882), p. 125; Émile Félix Deschamps, *Les Femmes d'Oncle Sam* (Paris: J. Maisonneuve et Fils, 1913). *Police Gazette,* Nov. 22, 1884, noted the popularity of the Wild West stage heroine, of lowly origin, always with red hair and the ability to sing and dance because her knowledge of the world came from the concert saloon.

37. Moody, "Daisy Miller," p. 17.

38. See Larzer Ziff, *The American 1890s: Life and Times of a Lost Generation* (New York: Viking, 1966).

39. Francis Hyde Bangs, *John Kendrick Bangs: Humorist of the Nineties* (New York: Knopf, 1941), p. 151; Amelia Ransome Neville, *The Fantastic City* (1932; New York: Arno, 1975), p. 254; George Du Maurier, *Trilby* (New York: Harper & Bros., 1894), p. 18; *Denver Post*, Oct. 9, 1904.

40. Du Maurier, *Trilby*, p. 16. My analysis of the Progressive novelists is based on my own reading; on Beatrice Kevitt Hofstadter and Richard Hofstadter, "Winston Churchill: A Study in the Popular Novel," *American Quarterly* 2 (Spring 1950): 229–39; and especially on Karen Anderson, "The Progressives as Unquestioning Conservatives: The Muckraking Novelists" (Senior thesis, Princeton Univ., 1978).

41. Richard Harding Davis, *Soldiers of Fortune* (New York: Charles Scribner's Sons, 1916), pp. 21, 167.

42. Ibid., pp. 149, 151.

43. Ibid., p. 329.

44. Gilman, *Women and Economics*, p. 148.

CHAPTER 9

1. *New York World,* Jan. 5, 1913. On Lobster Palace Society and the dance craze, see Lewis Erenberg, *Stepping Out: New York Nightlife and the Transformation of American Culture, 1890–1930* (Westport, Conn.: Greenwood, 1981).

2. David Graham Phillips, *The Price She Paid* (New York: D. Appleton, 1912), pp. 323–26; Richard Harding Davis, "Her First Appearance," in *Van Bibber and Others* (New York: Charles Scribner's Sons, 1916).

3. Ben L. Bassham, *The Theatrical Photographs of Napoleon Sarony* (Kent, Ohio: Kent State Univ., 1978); Ralph Stein, *The Pin-Up: From 1852 to Now* (Secaucus, N.J.: Chartwell, 1974); Henry Collins Brown, *New York in the Elegant Eighties* (New York: Valentine's, 1927), p. 176; Josiah Leeds, "The Relation of the Press and the Stage to Purity," in Aaron Macy Powell, ed., *The National Purity Congress* (New York: American Purity Alliance, 1896), p. 326.

4. See Alan Dale [Alfred Cohen], *Familiar Chats with Queens of the Stage* (New York: G. W. Dillingham, 1890), pp. 371–72.

5. Lloyd Morris, *Incredible New York: High Life and Low Life of the Last Hundred Years* (New York: Random House, 1951), p. 181; Mary Henderson, *The City and the Theatre: New York Playhouses from Bowling Green to Times Square* (Clifton, N.J.: James T. White, 1973), pp. 105–108.

6. Dale [Cohen], *Familiar Chats,* p. 39; Mary Elizabeth Coolidge, *Why Women Are So* (1912; New York: Arno, 1972), p. 128.

7. Sarah Bernhardt, "Comparative Impressions of America," *Appleton's Booklover's Magazine,* June 1906, clipping, Sarah Bernhardt File, Harvard Theatre Collection; Jacques Offenbach, *America and the Americans* (London: William Reeves, 1876), p. 78.

8. *Revolution* 3 (Feb. 11, 1869): 85; *Munsey's Magazine* 17 (Oct. 1896): 34; Henry Collins Brown, *Brownstone Fronts and Saratoga Trunks* (New York: E. P. Dutton, 1935), p. 283; Sarah Truax, *A Woman of Parts: Memories of a Life on Stage* (New York: Longmans, Green, 1949), p. 99; Frances Shaw, "The Matinée Girl," *Metropolitan Magazine* 9 (June 1900): 616–21.

9. Albert Rhodes, "Shall the American Girl Be Chaperoned?" *Galaxy* 24 (Oct. 1877): 456; William A. Brady, *Showman* (New York: E. P. Dutton, 1937), p. 130; Franklin Fyles, "The Theatre and Its People," *Ladies' Home Journal* 16 (Oct. 1899): 18.

10. Paul Bourget, *Outre-Mer: Impressions of America* (New York: Charles Scribner's Sons, 1895), p. 61; Beatrice Fairfax [Marie Manning], *Ladies Now and Then* (New York: E. P. Dutton, 1944), p. 141.

11. *Cincinnati Evening Star,* 1887, newspaper clipping, Eliza Weathersby File, New York Public Library Theatre Collection; Elsie Janis, *So Far, So Good! An Autobiography* (New York: Dutton, 1932), p. 91; Billie Burke (with Cameron Shipp), *With a Feather on My Nose* (New York: Appleton-Century-Crofts, 1949), p. 104.

12. *Denver Post,* Sept. 21, 1902. Information on chorus girls is contained in Derek Parker and Julia Parker, *The Natural History of the Chorus Girl* (London: David and Charles, 1975); Elizabeth Kendall, *Where She Danced* (New York: Knopf, 1980); Olive Logan, *Apropos of Women and Theatres* (New York: Carleton, 1869); George Ellington, *The Women of New York* (New York: New York Book, 1869); Cecil Smith, *Musical Comedy in America* (New York: Theater Arts Books, 1950); John L. Jennings, *Theatrical and Circus Life* (St Louis: M. S. Barnett, 1882); Olive Logan, *The Mimic World, and Public Exhibitions: Their History, Their Morals, and Effects* (Philadelphia: New-World, 1871).

   On hostility to ballet girls, see Clara Morris, *Stage Confidences: Talks About Players and Play Acting* (Boston: Lathrop, 1902), p. 13. On the decline in popularity of ballet girls, cf. Leander Richardson, "Beauty as an Element in Stage Success," *Metropolitan Magazine* 7 (July 1898): 103.

   On women in musical productions, see John Hollingshead, *My Lifetime* (London: S. Low, Marston, 1805); Felix Isman, *Weber and Fields: Their Tribulations, Triumphs, and Their Associates* (New York: Boni and Liveright, 1924); George Jean Nathan, *The Theatre, the Drama, the Girls* (New York: Knopf, 1921); Nathan, *The Popular Theatre* (New York: Knopf, 1918); Nathan, *The World in Falseface* (New York: Knopf, 1923). Henry Collins Brown, *New York in the Elegant Eighties* (New York: Valentine's, 1925), p. 268: "The Casino Girl was equivalent to the Follies Girl." Hedda Hopper, *From Under My Hat* (Garden City, N.Y.: Doubleday, 1952), p. 50: "The Weber and Fields chorus girls were as famous as the Florodora sextette or the Ziegfeld Girls." Nathan, *Theatre, Drama, Girls,* p. 303, contended that Lederer was primarily responsible for the chorus girl vogue, particularly by planting stories about their supposed glamorous lives.

13. Nellie Revell, *Right Off the Chest* (New York: George H. Doran, 1923), p. 254; George L. Wilson, "Green Room Glimpses," *Metropolitan Magazine* 1 (May 1895): 284–85.

14. Clipping, Apr. 26, 1905, *New York Herald Tribune,* Aug. 23, 1936, *Florodora* File, Harvard Theatre Collection; Nathan, *Theatre, Drama, Girls,* pp. 327–28; Allen Churchill, *The Great White Way* (New York: Dalton, 1962), p. 309.

15. Churchill, *Great White Way,* pp. 8–9.

16. Clipping, Lillie Langtry File, New York Public Library Theatre Collection; clipping, Dec. 18, 1901, Lillian Russell File, Harvard Theatre Collection.

17. Cf. Ray McCardell, *The Show Girl and Her Friends* (New York: Street and Street, 1904); Belle Livingstone, *Belle of Bohemia: The Memoirs of Belle Livingstone* (New York: Barse [n.d.]).

18. "What It Means to be a Chorus Girl," *Ladies' Home Journal* 27 (March 1910): 16, 58; Campbell Cusard, "Behind the Scenes with the Real Chorus Girls," *Broadway Maga-*

zine 13 (Dec. 1904): 32; *New York World,* Dec. 18, 1904; Theodore Dreiser, *Sister Carrie,* ed. Donald Pizer (New York: Norton, 1970), p. 276.

19. *Ladies' Home Journal* 27 (March 1910): 16, 58.

20. *Denver Post,* Sept. 21, 1902; J. Mortimer Crandall, "The American Chorus Girl," *Metropolitan Magazine* 1 (April 1895): 173–80.

21. John Higham, "The Reinterpretation of American Culture in the 1890s," in John Weiss, ed., *The Origins of Modern Consciousness* (Detroit: Wayne State Univ., 1965), pp. 25–48. See also F. Mooney Hughson, "Songs, Singers, and Society, 1890–1945," *American Quarterly* 6 (Fall 1954): 221–32.

22. Jefferson DeAngelis, *A Vagabond Trouper* (New York: Harcourt, Brace, 1931), p. 290. On the Nethersole case, see also Abe Laufe, *The Wicked Stage: A History of Theater Censorship and Harassment in the United States* (New York: Frederick Ungar, 1978). On Little Egypt, cf. Edo McCullough, *World's Fair Midways* (1966; New York: Arno, 1976); Bernard Sobel, "The Historic Hootchy-Kootchy," *Dance Magazine* 20 (Oct. 1946): 13–15.

23. "The Licentious Drama," *Metropolitan Magazine* 11 (June 1901): 649; *Denver Post,* Feb. 4, 1900.

24. *Police Gazette,* Oct. 24, 1885; Bettina Knapp and Myra Chipman, *That Was Yvette: The Biography of the Great Diseuse* (New York: Holt, Rinehart and Winston, 1964), p. 164.

25. On Ziegfeld and Held, see Charles Higham, *Ziegfeld* (Chicago: Henry Regnery, 1972); Anna Held, *Mémoires: Une Étoile française au ciel de l'Amérique* (Brussels: George Houyoux, 1955); and the Anna Held clipping files at the Harvard and New York Public Library Theatre Collections.

26. *New York World,* May 1897, clipping, Anna Held File, Harvard Theatre Collection.

27. Dorothy Russell, "My Mother, Lillian Russell," *Liberty Magazine* 6 (Nov. 2, 1929): 55; *Vogue* 8 (Oct. 1, 1896): 218.

28. Albert F. MacClean, Jr., "Eva Tanguay," *Notable American Women,* ed. Edward T. James et al., 3 vols. (Cambridge, Mass.: Harvard, 1971), 3:425–27.

29. Katherine Graves Busbey, *Home Life in America* (New York: Macmillan, 1910), pp. 118–19; Mary Gay Humphreys, "Women Bachelors in New York," *Scribner's Magazine* 10 (August 1896): 633. On the conservatism of middle-class women of this period, see Peter Gabriel Filene, *Him/Her/Self: Sex Roles in Modern America* (New York: Harcourt Brace Jovanovich, 1974), pp. 35–68.

30. Lydia Commander, *The American Idea* (New York: A. S. Barnes, 1907), p. 135.

31. Robert Wiebe, *The Search for Order, 1877–1920* (New York: Hill & Wang, 1967); Lewis Corey, "Problems of the Peace: The Middle Class," *Antioch Review* 5 (Spring 1945): 68–87.

32. C. Wright Mills, *White Collar: The American Middle Classes* (New York: Oxford Univ., 1951), p. 64. Cf. Albert F. MacClean, Jr., *American Vaudeville as Ritual* (Lexington, Ky.: Univ. of Kentucky, 1965); Charles E. Funnell, *By the Beautiful Sea: The Rise and High Times of That Great Resort, Atlantic City* (New York: Knopf, 1975); Elaine Tyler May, *Great Expectations: Marriage and Divorce in Post-Victorian America* (Chicago: Univ. of Chicago, 1980).

33. Louise Collier Willcox, "Wives as Companions," *Harper's Bazar* 44 (Aug. 1910): 499; Anna A. Rogers, *Why American Marriages Fail, and Other Papers* (Boston: Houghton Mifflin, 1909), pp. 174–75; Theodore Stanton and Harriot Stanton Blatch, eds., *Elizabeth Cady Stanton as Revealed in Her Letters, Diary and Reminiscences* (New York: Harper & Bros., 1922), 2:350; MacClean, *American Vaudeville,* p. 41.

34. Richard Harding Davis, "Miss Delamarr's Understudy," in *The Exiles and Other Stories* (New York: Charles Scribner's Sons, 1916), p. 228; Constance Cary Harrison, *Good Americans* (New York: Century, 1898), p. 23.

35. Cf. Albert Payson Terhune, *To the Best of My Memory* (New York: Harper & Bros., 1930), p. 122; Edna Woolman Chase and Ilka Chase, *Always in Vogue* (Garden City, N.Y.: Doubleday, 1954), p. 28; Madame Theresa Blanc, *The Condition of Woman in the United States,* trans. Abby Langdon Alger (1895; Freeport, N.Y.: Books for Libraries, 1972), p. 266; Winifred Sothern, "The Truth About the Bachelor Girl," *Munsey's Magazine* 25 (May 1901): 282.

36. Terhune, *To the Best of My Memory*, p. 123.

37. Cornelius Vanderbilt, *Queen of the Gilded Age: The Fabulous Story of Grace Wilson Vanderbilt* (New York: McGraw-Hill, 1956), pp. 149–50; Elizabeth Drexel Lehr, *"King Lehr" and the Gilded Age* (Philadelphia: Lippincott, 1935), p. 121.

38. Vanderbilt, *Queen,* pp. 149–50; Lehr, *"King Lehr,"* p. 121; Helen Worden, *Society Circus: From Ring to Ring, with a Large Cast* (New York: Covici, Friede, 1936), p. 180.

39. *Vogue* 11 (June 20, 1901).

40. Richmond Brooks Barnett, *Good Old Summer Days: Newport, Narragansett Pier, Saratoga, Long Branch, Bar Harbor* (Boston: Houghton Mifflin, 1952), p. 119; Elinor Glyn, *Romantic Adventure: Being the Autobiography of Elinor Glyn* (New York: E. P. Dutton, 1937), p. 136; Peter Casill, *New York Memories of Yesteryear: Life and Times at the Turn of the Century, 1890–1910* (New York: Exposition, 1964), p. 209.

41. Ralph Pulitzer, *New York Society on Parade* (New York: Harper & Bros., 1910), p. 180.

42. Edith Wharton, *The Custom of the Country* (New York: Charles Scribner's Sons, 1913), p. 72.

43. Cf. "The Vulgarization of Salome," *Current Literature* 45 (Oct. 1908): 437–40; Elsie de Wolfe, *After All* (New York: Harper & Bros., 1935), p. 132; Julia Hoyt, "The Modern Generation," *Liberty* 1 (Aug. 16, 1924): 5–6.

44. Margaret Mead, *Blackberry Winter: My Earlier Years* (New York: Morrow, 1972), p. 28; Dorothy Richardson, *The Long Day: The Story of a Working Girl as Told by Herself* (New York: Century, 1905).

45. Jane Addams, *The Spirit of Youth and the City Streets* (New York: Macmillan, 1910), pp. 6–7.

46. *Ladies' Home Journal* 24 (June 1907): 5; Terhune, *To the Best of My Memory*, p. 129; Addams, *Spirit of Youth,* p. 88.

47. Gary Kyriazi, *The Great Amusement Parks: A Pictorial History* (Secaucus, N.J.: Citadel, 1976), p. 13; Abram Dayton, *Last Years of Knickerbocker Life* (New York: George W. Harlan, 1882), pp. 171–74.

48. George Ellington, *Women of New York* (New York: New York Books, 1869), pp. 319–27; James D. McCabe, Jr., *Lights and Shadows of New York Life, or Sights and Sensations of the Great City* (Philadelphia: National, 1872), pp. 597–604.

49. Lillian W. Betts, *The Leaven in a Great City* (New York: Dodd, Mead, 1903), p. 142; Rollin Lynde Hartt, "The Amusement Park," *Atlantic Monthly* 99 (June 1907): 668. See also Kathy Piess, "Dance Madness: New York City Dance Halls and Working Class Sexuality, 1900–1920" (paper, Berkshire Conference on Women's History, June 1981).

50. Cleveland Amory, *Who Killed Society?* (New York: Harper & Bros., 1940), p. 541; *New York World,* Feb. 8, 1914; *San Francisco Examiner,* Jan. 17, 1897; *Chicago Tribune,* Feb. 24, 1901; *San Francisco Examiner,* March 21, 1897. *San Francisco Examiner,* March

24, 1912: "The 'bunny-hug' was danced ten years ago in San Francisco by the lower classes."

51. *Ladies' Home Journal* 17 (Sept. 1899); Robert A. Woods and Albert J. Kennedy, *Young Working Girls: A Summary of Evidence from Two Thousand Social Workers* (Boston: Houghton Mifflin, 1913), p. 105; Betts, *Leaven in a Great City*, p. 251; Mary Kingsbury Simkhovitch, *The City Worker's World in America* (New York: Macmillan, 1917), p. 130.

52. Belle Lindner Israels, "The Way of the Girl," *Survey* 22 (July 3, 1919): 486–97.

53. Rollin Lynde Hartt, *People at Play* (Boston: Houghton Mifflin, 1909), pp. 200, 207.

54. Richardson, *Long Day*, p. 95; Jane Addams, *Twenty Years at Hull House* (New York: Macmillan, 1910), p. 192.

55. Hutchins Hapgood, *Types from City Streets* (New York: Funk & Wagnalls, 1910), p. 129; Hartt, *People at Play*, pp. 214–15; Israels, "Way of the Girl," p. 486; Helen Woodward, *Through Many Windows* (New York: Harper & Bros., 1932), p. 148.

56. Hapgood, *Types*, p. 129; Richardson, *Long Day*, passim.

57. Massachusetts Commission for the Investigation of the White Slave Traffic, *Report of the Commission for the Investigation of the White Slave Traffic, so-called* (Boston: Wright & Parton, 1914), p. 43; Peggy Killam, "Vice in Baltimore: An Investigation of the Maryland Vice Commission Report," Senior Honors Paper, University of Maryland, Baltimore County, 1981; Bernard Sobel, *Broadway Heartbeat: Memoirs of a Press Agent* (New York: Hermitage House, 1953), p. 19; Henry Seidel Canby, *The Age of Confidence: Life in the Nineties* (New York: Farrar & Rinehart, 1934), p. 162; James Montgomery Flagg, *Roses and Buckshots* (New York: G. P. Putnam's Sons, 1946), p. 49. Mark Thomas Connelly, *The Response to Prostitution in the Progressive Era* (Chapel Hill, N.C.: Univ. of North Carolina, 1980), argues that early twentieth-century antiprostitution campaigns were as much a response to the heightened sexuality of that era as to commercial prostitution.

58. Clara Laughlin, *The Work-a-Day Girl, A Study of Some Present-Day Conditions* (New York: Fleming H. Revell, 1913), p. 143; Addams, *Twenty Years*, p. 433.

59. Alice Duer Miller, "The New Dances and the Younger Generation," *Harper's Bazar* 46 (May 1912): 225.

CHAPTER 10

1. The cosmetic advertisements and wrappers in the Warshaw Collection of Business Americana, Smithsonian Institution, regularly include a statement that the product does not contain poisonous ingredients.

2. *Denver Post*, Sept. 3, 1899; *San Francisco Examiner*, Nov. 23, 1899.

3. *Denver Post*, Oct. 26, 1902; *Vogue* 22 (Nov. 15, 1912): 19; The Family Doctor, "Fashions in Hygiene," in *Woman: A Collection of 156 Articles . . . Taken from the Chautauquan, Between 1892 and 1906* (Cleveland: [?], 1919), p. 592; *Denver Post*, Jan. 24, 1904; *New York World*, Sept. 19, 1909.

4. *San Francisco Examiner*, Sept. 11, 1898; *Denver Post*, May 1, 1904.

5. Sara Schmucker, "If You Want Beauty, Think Beauty," *Woman Beautiful* 4 (Jan. 1910): 39; Lillian Russell, "Beauty as a Factor in Success on the Stage," *Woman Beautiful* 4 (April 1910): 39; *Pittsburgh Gazette Times*, Jan. 27, 1907, clipping, Lillie Langtry File, New York Public Library Theatre Collection.

6. Grace Peckham Murray, *The Fountain of Youth: or Personal Appearance and Personal Hygiene* (New York: Frederick A. Stokes, 1904), p. 9.
7. Henry Finck, *Romantic Love and Personal Beauty* (New York: Macmillan, 1887).
8. Alexander Black, "A Modern Standard of Feminine Beauty," *Monthly Illustrator* 4 (April 1895): 22–23; Annie Jenness Miller, "Dress Improvement," in *Congress of Women,* ed. Mary Kavanaugh Eagle (Philadelphia: International, 1895), p. 696.
9. Luke North, *Nature's Secret of Beauty* (San Diego: Brushwood, 1904), p. 3.
10. Gertrude Lynch, "Racial and Ideal Types of Beauty," *Cosmopolitan* 38 (Dec. 1904): 233; Howard Chandler Christy, *The American Girl, as Seen and Portrayed by Howard Chandler Christy* (New York: Moffat, Yard, 1906), pp. 11–13.
11. See *Woman's Journal,* 1870–1914.
12. Margaret Hubbard Ayer and Isabella Taves, *The Three Lives of Harriet Hubbard Ayer* (Philadelphia: Lippincott, 1957), p. 255; Annette Kellermann, *Physical Beauty: How to Keep It* (New York: George H. Doran, 1918), pp. 15–16, 22.
13. Julia B. Foraker, *I Would Live It Again: Memories of a Vivid Life* (New York: Harper & Bros., 1932), p. 61.
14. Henry Collins Brown, *Brownstone Fronts and Saratoga Trunks* (New York: E. P. Dutton, 1935), p. 154; David L. Cohn, *The Good Old Days: A History of American Morals and Manners as Seen Through the Sears, Roebuck Catalogs, 1905 to the Present* (New York: Simon & Schuster, 1940), p. 319.
15. Cf. Wendy Cooper, *Hair: Sex, Society, Symbolism* (London: Alders, 1971).
16. Bertha Damon, *Grandma Called It Carnal* (New York: Simon & Schuster, 1938), p. 187.
17. "The Clothes Mania," *Atlantic Monthly* 23 (May 1869): 540.
18. The references to business advertising in this chapter, unless otherwise cited, come from circulars and cards in the Bella Landauer Collection of Business and Advertising Art, New-York Historical Society.
19. Brown, *Brownstone Fronts,* pp. 154–55.
20. *McCall's Magazine,* April 1976, p. 24: reproduction of 1878 article. The 1886 New York City business directory (the first directory to list "ladies' hairdressers" as a separate category) lists 61 such specialists, in comparison with 1,176 barbers and male hairdressers. By 1892 the figures had risen to 139 and 1,792, respectively. See *Wilson's Business Directory of New York City* (New York: Trow City Directory, 1886); *The Trow Business Directory of New York City* (New York: Trow Directory, Printing, and Bookbindery, 1892).
21. Harriet Hubbard Ayer, *Harriet Hubbard Ayer's Book: A Complete and Authentic Treatise on the Laws of Health and Beauty* (New York: Home, 1899), p. 283.
22. Virginia Penny, *The Employments of Women: A Cyclopaedia of Women's Work* (Boston: Walker, Wise, 1863), p. 412; Rachel Rhona, *Boudoir Companion or Guide to Beauty* (Chicago: Poole Bros., 1889); Mary Moss, "Machine-Made Human Beings," *Atlantic Monthly* 94 (Aug. 1904): 267–68; Emily Faithfull, *Three Visits to America* (Edinburgh: David Douglas, 1884), p. 304.
23. William Woodbury, *Beauty Culture* (New York: Dillingham, 1910), p. 21.
24. Cf. Lois W. Banner, "Harriet Hubbard Ayer," in Lina Mainiero, ed., *Guide to American Women Writers* (New York: Frederick Ungar, 1979).
25. Cf. Dora M. Morrell, "Helps to Beauty," in *Woman: A Collection; Ladies' Home Journal* 25 (Jan. 1908): 17–18; 27 (Sept. 1910); and 29 (Nov. 1912); "The Transformation of a Face," *Metropolitan Magazine* (Oct. 1895), advertising supplement.
26. *Woman Beautiful* 3 (March 1910): 33.

27. *Woman Beautiful* 1 (Sept. 1908): 58.

28. *Harper's Bazar* 26 (April 8, 1893): 274.

29. Anne O'Hagan, "The Quest for Beauty," *Munsey's Magazine* 29 (June 1903): 409; Anne Hard, "The Beauty Business," *American Magazine* 69 (Nov. 1919): 79, 84.

30. *Woman Beautiful* 2 (Feb. 1908): 33; and 1 (Jan. 1908): 7; Woodbury, *Beauty Culture,* p. 13.

31. *Woman Beautiful* 3 (Nov. 1908): 46; Helen Bullitt Lawrey, "Black Magic of Beauty Parlors," *New York Times,* Sept. 18, 1921, p. 8.

32. Neville Williams, *Powder and Paint: A History of the English Woman's Toilet: Elizabeth I–Elizabeth II* (London: Longmans, Green, 1957), p. 119; Cohn, *Good Old Days,* p. 226; Frank W. Crowninshield, *Manners for the Metropolis: An Entrance Key to the Fantastic Life of the 400* (New York: D. Appleton, 1909), p. 37.

33. Elizabeth Reid, "What the American Woman Pays for Cosmetics," *Woman Beautiful* 4 (Nov. 1910): 29.

34. *New York World,* Sept. 11, 1910; Lillian Wald, *The House on Henry Street* (New York: Henry Holt, 1915), p. 192.

35. Helena Rubinstein, *My Life for Beauty* (London: Bodley, Head, 1964), pp. 58–59.

36. *Woman Beautiful* 3 (Aug. 1908): 23, and (Dec. 1908): 45.

37. David Graham Phillips, *The Price She Paid* (New York: D. Appleton, 1912), p. 229.

38. Knight Dunlap, *Personal Beauty and Racial Betterment* (St. Louis: C. V. Mosby, 1920), p. 39; Mme. Lina Cavalieri, *My Secrets of Beauty* (New York: Circulation Syndicate, 1914), p. 45; *New York World,* Sept. 8, 1918.

39. Elinor Glyn, *Romantic Adventure: Being the Autobiography of Elinor Glyn* (New York: E. P. Dutton, 1937), p. 151.

40. On old age, I have depended on David Hackett Fisher, *Growing Old in America* (New York: Oxford Univ., 1977), and W. Andrew Achenbaum, *Old Age in the New Land: The American Experience Since 1790* (Baltimore: Johns Hopkins, 1978). My interpretation, however, differs from both, since neither has considered women as a variable.

41. *Home Journal,* Apr. 1, 1854; see also Lois W. Banner, "Religion and Reform in the Early Republic: The Role of Youth," *American Quarterly* 23 (Dec. 1971): 677–95.

42. "The Passing of the Old Lady," *Atlantic Monthly* 99 (June 1907): 874; *Vogue* 4 (Dec. 20, 1894): 414.

43. Jane Addams, "Need a Woman Over Fifty Feel Old?," *Ladies' Home Journal* 31 (Oct. 1914): 7; *Vogue* 5 (March 7, 1895): 146.

44. Caroline Kirkland, "Growing Old Gracefully," *Home Journal,* May 17, 1851.

45. Robert Tomes, *The Bazar Book of Decorum* (New York: Harper & Bros., 1877), p. 33; "The Growing Youthfulness of Age," *Harper's Bazar* 18 (Jan. 3, 1885); *Vogue* 41 (Jan. 1, 1913).

46. Margaret Fuller, *Woman in the Nineteenth Century* (1845; New York: W. W. Norton, 1971), p. 99.

47. John William De Forest, *Miss Ravenel's Conversion from Secession to Loyalty,* ed. Gordon S. Haight (New York: Rinehart, 1955), p. 17; Lois W. Banner, *Elizabeth Cady Stanton: A Radical for Woman's Rights* (Boston: Little, Brown, 1980), pp. 123–24.

48. Anne H. Wharton, "The Prolongation of Youthfulness in Modern Women," in *Woman: A Collection;* Mrs. Wilson Woodrow, "The Woman of Fifty," *Cosmopolitan* 23 (March 1903): 505–12.

49. *Revolution* 3 (Sept. 29, 1870): 196; Grace M. Johnson, "The New Old Maid," *Woman Beautiful* 2 (May 1909): 68.

50. Banner, *Elizabeth Cady Stanton,* p. 110.

51. *Denver Post,* Oct. 5, 1902; *Current Literature* 34 (April 1903): 489.
52. Cf. *New York Herald Tribune,* March 23, 1902.
53. *Harper's Bazar* 25 (June 11, 1892).

CHAPTER 11

1. Horace Bushnell, *Woman Suffrage: The Reform Against Nature* (New York: Charles Scribner, 1869), p. 51; *San Francisco Examiner,* March 3, 1895; Henry T. Finck, "The Influence of Beauty on Love," *Cosmopolitan* 30 (April 30, 1901): 598.
2. For prints of the delicate man, see Harry T. Peters, *Currier and Ives: Printmakers to the American People* (Garden City, N.Y.: Doubleday, Doran, 1929–31), passim; *Harper's Weekly,* Jan. 28, 1860; James Burn, *Three Years Among the Working Classes During the War* (London: Smith, Elder, 1865), p. 3; Oliver Wendell Holmes, "The Autocrat of the Breakfast Table," *Atlantic Monthly* 1 (May 1858): 881. See also Frederika Bremer, *Homes of the New World,* trans. Mary Howill, 2 vols. (New York: Harper & Bros., 1853), 1:64; A. Thomason [Andrew Bell], *Men and Things in America* (London: William Smith, 1838), p. 39; James Stuart, *Three Years in North America* (New York: J. & J. Harper, 1833), p. 30.
3. *Harper's Weekly,* Jan. 28, 1860; Charles Dickens, *American Notes* (1842; London: Oxford Univ., 1957), p. 249; Nathaniel Parker Willis, *Rag-Bag: A Collection of Ephemera* (New York: Charles Scribner, 1855), p. 22.
4. Francis J. Grund, *Aristocracy in America,* 2 vols. (London: Richard Bentley, 1839), 1:98; William Burns, *Life in New York: In Doors and Out of Doors* (New York: Bunce & Brothers, 1851); Willis, *Rag-Bag,* p. 22. According to Virginia Penny, women liked both the "effeminacy" of dry goods salesmen and their knowledge of the latest fashion gossip. See Penny, *Think and Act: A Series of Articles Pertaining to Men and Women, Work and Wages* (Philadelphia: Claxton, Remsen, & Haffelfinger, 1869), p. 228.
5. George Augusta Sala, *America Revisited* (London: Vizatelly, 1882), p. 65.
6. Dickens, *American Notes,* p. 81; Henry Lunettes [Margaret Conkling], *The American Gentlemen's Guide to Politeness and Fashion* (New York: Derby & Jackson, 1857), p. 27.
7. Sala, *America Revisited,* p. 65.
8. David Macrae, *Americans at Home: Pen-and-Ink Sketches of American Men, Manners and Institutions* (New York: E. P. Dutton, 1875), pp. 33–34; Two Englishmen [Rivington and Harris], *Reminiscences of America in 1869* (London: Sampson, Low, Son, and Marston, 1870), p. 53.
9. Macrae, *Americans at Home,* pp. 400–402; Walt McDougall, *This Is the Life* (New York: Knopf, 1926), p. 39: Every parlor contained a spittoon, often made of "alabaster, near-Jade, and gem-studded gold-plate." Charles Berry, *The Other Side: How It Struck Us* (New York: E. P. Dutton, 1880), pp. 15–16: "I often think the American chews quid in bed."
10. Charles Haswell, *Reminiscences of New York by an Octogenarian* (New York: Harper & Bros., 1896), p. 88.
11. Cf. John William Ward, *Andrew Jackson: Symbol for an Age* (New York: Oxford Univ., 1955); on "man-milliner," see Lois W. Banner, *Elizabeth Cady Stanton: A Radical for Woman's Rights* (Boston: Little, Brown, 1980), p. 43.

12. Frances Hodge, *Yankee Theatre: The Image of America on Stage, 1825–50* (Austin, Tex.: Univ. of Texas, 1964); Thomas Colley Grattan, *Civilized America* (London: Bradbury and Evans, 1859), p. 82; Francis Pulsky and Theresa Pulsky, *White, Red, and Black: Sketches of American Society,* 3 vols. (New York: Redfield, 1853), 2:141; *Home Journal,* May 13, 1854; Richard M. Dorson, *America in Legend: Folklore from the Colonial Period to the Present* (New York: Pantheon, 1973), pp. 108–21. For a positive appraisal of the Yankee, see Bremer, *Homes of the New World,* 1:188.

13. Willis, *Rag-Bag,* p. 26; Lady Emmeline Stuart-Wortley, *Travels in the United States in 1849 and 1850,* 3 vols. (New York: Harper & Bros., 1851), 1:54–55.

14. John R. Betts, *America's Sporting Heritage, 1850–1950* (Reading, Mass.: Addison-Wesley, 1974), p. 39; Sigmund Diamond, ed. and trans., *A Casual View of America: The Home Letters of Salomon de Rothschild, 1859–1861* (Palo Alto, Calif.: Stanford Univ., 1961), p. 38. See also Foster Rhea Dulles, *A History of Recreation: America Learns to Play* (New York: Appleton-Century-Crofts, 1965), and Leo Stein's collection of articles in *The Sporting Set* (New York: Arno, 1975).

15. "The Clothes Mania," *Alantic Monthly* 23 (May 1869): 533.

16. George Beard, "Physical Future of the American People," *Atlantic Monthly* 43 (June 1879): 725; Dexter William Fellows and Andrew A. Freeman, *This Way to the Big Show: The Life of Dexter Fellows* (New York: Viking, 1936), p. 93; Donald Barr Chidsey, *John the Great* (Garden City, N.Y.: Doubleday, Doran, 1942), p. 147.

17. Oscar Comettant, *Trois ans aux États-Unis* (Paris: Pagnerre, 1857), p. 3; Camille Ferri-Pisani, *Prince Napoleon in America, 1861: Letters from His Aide-de-Camp,* trans. George J. Joyavy (Bloomington, Ind.: Indiana Univ., 1959), p. 60; Grattan, *Civilized America,* pp. 318–19; Henryk Sienkiewicz, *Portrait of America: Letters of Henryk Sienkiewicz,* ed. and trans. Charles Morley (New York: Columbia Univ., 1959), p. 119.

18. Mrs. Felton, *American Life: A Narrative of Two Years' City and Country Residence in the United States* (London: Simpkin, Marshall, 1842), p. 74; Edwin T. Freedley, *Philadelphia and Its Manufacturers* (Philadelphia: Edward Young, 1859), pp. 220–24; "Clothes Mania," p. 546.

19. Charles Day, *Hints on Etiquette* (New York: A. V. Blake, 1843), p. 68; Harriet Martineau, *Society in America,* 2 vols. (New York: Saunders and Otley, 1837), 1:254; Sala, *America Revisited,* p. 66.

20. Christopher Crowfield [Harriet Beecher Stowe], *House and Home Papers* (Boston: Ticknor and Fields, 1865), p. 174; Max Von Boehn, *Modes and Manners of the Nineteenth Century,* trans. M. Edwards, 3 vols. (New York: E. P. Dutton, 1909), 3:128; Haswell, *Reminiscences,* p. 75.

21. "Men's Clothes," *Nation,* Jan. 26, 1882, p. 79.

22. Margaret Hubbard Ayer, *The Three Lives of Harriet Hubbard Ayer* (Philadelphia: Lippincott, 1957), pp. 26–27.

23. "The Clothes Mania," passim.

24. On facial hair and the presidents, see John Durant and Alice Durant, *Pictorial History of American Presidents* (South Brunswick, N.J.: A. S. Barnes, 1955). For some information on the history of beards, see Reginald Reynolds, *Beards: An Omnium Gatherum* (London: George Allen & Unwin, 1950).

25. *Home Journal,* Nov. 15, 1851; Virginia Clay-Clopton, *A Belle of the Fifties* (New York: Doubleday-Page, 1904), p. 98; Mabel Osgood Wright, *My New York* (New York: Macmillan, 1926), p. 122.

26. Richard J. Walsh, *The Making of Buffalo Bill: A Study in Heroics* (Indianapolis: Bobbs-Merrill, 1928), p. 137.

27. Ellen Moers, *The Dandy: Brummel to Beerbohn* (London: Secker and Warburg, 1960), pp. 12–13.
28. Asa Green, *A Glance at New York,* in Warren S. Tryon, *My Native Land: Life in America* (Chicago: Univ. of Chicago, 1971), pp. 94–95.
29. *Harper's New Monthly Magazine* 23 (Oct. 1890): 718.
30. Charles Astor Bristed, *The Upper Ten Thousand* (New York: Stringer and Townsend, 1852), pp. 134–35, 248; George William Curtis, *The Potiphar Papers* (New York: Harper & Bros., 1856), p. 94; Everetta Van Vorst, "Story of New York's Social Life," *Ladies' Home Journal* 16 (Feb. 1899): 4; John H. Warren, Jr., *My Thirty Years' Battle with Crime* (Poughkeepsie, N.Y.: A. J. White, 1874), p. 93.
31. Louisa May Alcott, *Little Women* (New York: Macmillan, 1962), pp. 268–69, 450; Sala, *America Revisited,* p. 66.
32. Ned Buntline [Edward Z. Judson], *Mysteries and Miseries of New York* (New York: Berford, 1848), p. 57.
33. Edgar Fawcett, *Social Silhouettes: Being the Impressions of Mr. Mark Manhattan* (Boston: Ticknor, 1885), p. 161. Fawcett noted that the word "dude" was of recent use in the East, but William Cody, "Buffalo Bill," used it in the West as early as 1872 (*Making of Buffalo Bill,* pp. 173–74).
34. John L Jennings, *Theatrical and Circus Life* (St. Louis: M. S. Barnett, 1882), pp. 48, 243–94; James Laver, *Taste and Fashion: From the French Revolution to Today* (London: G. G. Harrap, 1937), p. 45; E. Berry Wall, *Neither Pest Nor Puritan* (New York: Dial, 1940), p. 64. The influence of the subculture of sensuality on elite men can also be seen in the fact that the tuxedo, adopted as standard elite male evening attire in the 1890s and named after the exclusive Tuxedo Park community where it presumably originated, actually first was worn in the dance halls of the lower East Side (Herbert Asbury, *All Around the Town* [New York: Knopf, 1934], p. 261).
35. Jennings, *Theatrical and Circus Life,* p. 55; Dreiser, *Sister Carrie,* p. 3.
36. Lewis Feuer, *The Conflict of Generations: The Character and Significance of Student Movements* (New York: Basic Books, 1969).
37. George Parsons Lathrop, *Newport* (New York: Charles Scribner's Sons, 1884), p. 164; Henry Collins Brown, *New York in the Elegant Eighties* (New York: Valentine's, 1925), p. 135.
38. Chidsey, *John the Great,* p. 281. In 1877 the *Galaxy* noted that ten years previously cigarette smoking had been rare, but that it had since become popular, that stores in the cities vied with each other in selling leading brands, and that 30 percent of the smoking tobacco consumed in the United States was in the form of cigarettes (*Galaxy* 23 [April 1877]: 470).
39. Constance Cary Harrison, *The Circle of a Century* (New York: Century, 1899), p. 159.
40. Brown, *New York in the Elegant Eighties,* p. 269.
41. My analysis of the turn-of-the-century college is based especially on Frederick Rudolph, *The American College and University* (New York: Knopf, 1972); Clayton Sedgwick Cooper, "The American Undergraduate," *Century* (Jan. 1912), in James C. Stone and Donald P. DeNevi, *Portraits of the American University* (San Francisco: Jossey-Bass, 1971); George E. Peterson, *The New England College in the Age of the University* (Amherst, Mass.: Amherst College, 1964); Henry Seidel Canby, *Alma Mater: The Gothic Age of the American College* (New York: Farrar & Rinehart, 1936).
42. Canby, *Alma Mater,* p. xii.
43. Ibid., pp. 31, 52; Russell, "Reminiscences," p. 68; Aleck Quest, "The Fast Set at Harvard University" (1888), in Stein, ed., *The Leisure Class,* pp. 546–49.

44. Rudolph Aaronson, *Theatrical and Musical Memories* (New York: McBride, Nast, 1913), p. 207.

45. Elizabeth Cady Stanton, handwritten ms. of Speech Before the Young Men's Suffrage Association in Plympton Hall, 1870. Stanton Mss., Library of Congress.

46. C. Wright Mills, *White Collar: The American Middle Classes* (New York: Oxford Univ., 1951), p. 64; Albert J. Beveridge, *The Young Man and the World* (New York: D. Appleton, 1905), pp. 26, 28, 50. Stephan Thernstrom, *The Other Bostonians: Poverty and Progress in the American Metropolis, 1880–1970* (Cambridge, Mass.: Harvard Univ., 1973), pp. 35, 76, finds that rural migrants to the city constituted a major proportion of white-collar workers and that there was a 20 percent movement from blue-collar to white-collar work. Jürgen Kocka, *White Collar Workers in America: A Social-Political History in International Perspective,* trans. Maura Kealey (London: Saye, 1980), reaches similar conclusions.

47. Augustus Thomas, *The Print of My Remembrance* (New York: Charles Scribner's Sons, 1922), p. 261; Francis Hyde Bangs, *John Kendrick Bangs: Humorist of the Nineties* (New York: Knopf, 1941), p. 69; Arthur Howell, "A New York Childhood: Cigarette Pictures," *New Yorker* 5 (May 1929): 25; Margaret T. Chanler, *Roman Spring: Memoirs* (Boston: Little, Brown, 1934), pp. 238–40.

48. Cf. Allen Churchill, *Park Row* (New York: Rinehart, 1958).

49. Gerald Langford, *The Richard Harding Davis Years: A Biography of a Mother and Son* (New York: Holt, Rinehart & Winston, 1961), p. 10.

50. James D. Hart, *The Popular Book: A History of America's Literary Taste* (New York: Oxford Univ., 1950), p. 156; Paul Bourget, *Outre-Mer: Impressions of America* (New York: Charles Scribner, 1895), p. 135.

51. Malcolm Bingay, *Of Me I Sing* (Indianapolis: Bobbs-Merrill, 1949), p. 88; Hutchins Hapgood, *Types from City Streets* (New York: Funk & Wagnalls, 1910), pp. 74, 95.

52. Cf. Langford, *Richard Harding Davis Years;* Scott Compton Osborn, "Richard Harding Davis: The Development of a Journalist" (Ph.D. diss., Univ. of Kentucky, 1953); Charles Dana Gibson, "The First Glimpse of Davis," *Scribner's Magazine* 60 (July 1916): 90.

53. Lionel Barrymore, *We Barrymores* (New York: Appleton-Century-Crofts, 1951), p. 77.

54. See John G. Cawelti, *The Six-Gun Mystique* (Bowling Green, Ohio: Bowling Green Univ., 1971).

CHAPTER 12

1. On the Miss America contest, see Frank Defore, *There She Is: The Life and Times of Miss America* (New York: Viking, 1971); Charles E. Funnell, *By the Beautiful Sea: The Rise and High Times of That Great Resort, Atlantic City* (New York: Knopf, 1975); William McMahon, *So Young . . . So Gay* (Atlantic City: Atlantic City Press, 1970); and especially contemporary issues of the *New York Times, New York World, Atlantic City Daily Press,* and *Atlantic City Evening Union.*

2. *Vogue* 13 (Sept. 8, 1898): 160. On the observance of May Day in England, see Horatio Smith, *Festivals, Games, and Amusements* (London: Colburn and Bentley, 1831). On May Day and Catholicism, see Marina Warner, *Alone of All Her Sex: The Myth and Cult of the Virgin Mary* (New York: Knopf, 1976), pp. 281–82.

3. Scattered examples of beauty competitions can be found during the colonial era. Thus the events celebrating St. Andrews's Day (Nov. 30), in Hanover County, Virginia, in 1737, included a beauty competition among "Country Maids" for the entertainment of "Ladies and Gentlemen" (*Virginia Gazette* [1737], in *Virginia Historical Register* 6 [1853]: 99–101). I am grateful to Douglass Greenberg for sharing this information with me.

4. Lydia Maria Child, *Girl's Own Book* (New York: Clark, Austin, 1833), p. 25; Jessie Benton Frémont, *Souvenirs of My Time* (Boston: D. Lathrop, 1887), pp. 12–13; Carolina Lee Hentz, *Eoline, or Magnolia Vale* (Philadelphia: T. B. Peterson and Bros., 1852), pp. 76–77; Mary Caroline Crawford, *The College Girl of America* (Boston: L. C. Page, 1905). Frederika Bremer, *The Homes of the New World,* trans. Mary Howill, 2 vols. (New York: Harper & Bros., 1853), 2:572, noted the absence of festivals in the United States, but also observed a "new" movement to hold floral fêtes in May and June. Carl Wittke, *Refugees of Revolution: The German Forty-eighters in America* (Philadelphia: Univ. of Pennsylvania, 1952), pp. 284–87, traced this new movement to the Germans. For photographs of May Day queens, see Robert Taft, *Photography and the American Scene: A Social History, 1839–1889* (New York: Macmillan, 1942), p. 331; *Scribner's Magazine* 21 (May 1897); *Harper's Weekly,* May 18, 1901, p. 505.

5. On the tributes to Washington, see Rufus Wilmot Griswold, *The Republican Court; or American Society in the Days of Washington* (New York: D. Appleton, 1854), p. 129; on those to Lafayette, see Jane Bacon McIntire, *Lafayette: The Guest of the Nation* (Newton, Mass.: Simone, 1967); Edgar Ewing Brandon, *Lafayette: Guest of the Nation,* 2 vols. (Oxford, Ohio: Oxford Historical Society, 1954); and Virginia Tatnall Peacock, *Famous American Belles of the Nineteenth Century* (Philadelphia: Lippincott, 1901), p. 195. On the continuing fame of the "Lafayette Girls," see Marian Gouverneur, *As I Remember: Recollections of American Society During the Nineteenth Century* (New York: D. Appleton, 1911), p. 238. A similar tribute was held in New Orleans to honor Andrew Jackson after the 1815 Battle of New Orleans. See John William Ward, *Andrew Jackson: Symbol for an Age* (New York: Oxford Univ., 1955), p. 101.

6. Anne Hollingsworth Wharton, *Social Life in the Early Republic* (Philadelphia: Lippincott, 1902), p. 313; Clara Fisher Maeder, *Autobiography of Clara Fisher Maeder,* ed. Douglass Taylor (1807; New York: Burt Franklin, 1957), p. 23.

On the southern tournament, see Rollin G. Osterweis, *Romanticism and Nationalism in the Old South* (New Haven: Yale Univ., 1949) and especially Esther J. Crooks and Ruth W. Crooks, *The Ring Tournament in the United States* (Richmond, Va.: Garrett and Massie, 1936). On the United States and the Eglinton tournament, see George Combe, *Notes on the United States of North America, During a Phrenological Visit in 1838–39–40,* 3 vols. (Edinburgh: Maclachlan, Steward, 1841), 3:103; and Ian Anstruther, *The Knight and the Umbrella: An Account of the Eglinton Tournament, 1839* (London: Geoffrey Bles, 1963).

7. Cf. Ellis Paxton Oberholtzer, *Philadelphia: A History of the City and Its People,* 4 vols. (Philadelphia: S. J. Clarke, 1912), 1:274–76; Allen Lesser, *Enchanting Rebel: The Secret of Adah Isaacs Menken* (Philadelphia: Jewish Book Club, 1947), p. 76; *Harper's Weekly* 9 (Oct. 7, 1865): 636–37.

8. Some information on American festivals can be found in Robert Eugene Meyer, *Festivals: U.S.A. and Canada* (New York: Washburne, 1970), and in Jack B. Ludwig, *The Great American Spectaculars* (Garden City, N.Y.: Doubleday, 1976). Reports on the festivals can be found in contemporary newspapers. Cf. *San Francisco Examiner,* March 15, 1896; May 1, 1896; June 7, 1896. For the Pasadena Rose Parade, I have used the programs and mimeographed background material graciously provided me by the

official Tournament of Roses Committee. For the Portland Rose Festival I have used material from the clipping file on the event at the Portland Historical Society.

9. See *Denver Post,* Sept. 3, 1899, and Sept. 17, 1899, on the Festival of Mountain and Plain. For the Ak-Sar-Ben Festival and the Veiled Prophet's Ball, see Cleveland Amory, *Who Killed Society?* (New York: Harper & Bros., 1940), pp. 227–28. On the St. Paul Winter Carnival and the St. Petersburg Festival of States, I have used programs and other mimeographed materials graciously sent me by the official committees of these events.

10. Information on the Mardi Gras is derived from Robert Tallant, *Mardi Gras* (Garden City, N.Y.: Doubleday, 1948), and *The Romantic New Orleanians* (New York: E. P. Dutton, 1950).

11. Michel Chevalier, *Society, Manners, and Politics in the United States,* ed. John William Ward (Garden City, N.Y.: Anchor, 1961), pp. 305–308.

12. Ibid.

13. *San Francisco Examiner,* April 22, 1900.

14. On Barnum, see M. R. Werner, *Barnum* (New York: Harcourt, Brace, 1923); Irving Wallace, *The Fabulous Showman: The Life and Times of P. T. Barnum* (New York: Knopf, 1959); Neil Harris, *Humbug: The Art of P. T. Barnum* (Boston: Little, Brown, 1973); and the seven editions of Barnum's autobiography published between 1855 and 1891. I have used the 1871 edition in particular, which Werner recommends: Phineas T. Barnum, *Struggles and Triumphs: or Forty Years' Recollections* (New York: American News, 1871). In none of these editions does Barnum discuss his beauty contest.

   On Franconi's Hippodrome, see Arthur Hornblow, *A History of the Theatre in America,* 2 vols. (Philadelphia: Lippincott, 1919), 2:171.

15. Throughout the nineteenth and early twentieth centuries, baby competitions were as popular as beauty contests. In 1854 a national baby show was held in Springfield, Ohio, with 120 babies in competition (*Lily,* Nov. 1854). An extensive description of such a contest is contained in Alfred Pairpont, *Uncle Sam and His Country: Or, Sketches of America, in 1854-55-56* (London: n.p., 1857), pp. 41–43. The most famous baby contest was held in Asbury Park, New Jersey, beginning in 1891 and remaining popular into the 1920s. Beginning in 1900, an adult queen and court were also elected. See, e.g., *New York Herald Tribune,* Sept. 2, 1906; *New York World,* Aug. 30, 1922. Barnum, *Struggles and Triumphs,* p. 372; Thomas Low Nichols, *Forty Years of American Life, 1821-61* (1864; New York: Stackpole Sons, 1937), p. 473; Wayne Caldwell Neely, *The Agricultural Fair* (New York: Columbia Univ., 1935), pp. 193–94.

16. Oscar Comettant, *Trois ans aux États-Unis* (Paris: Pagnerre, 1857), pp. 32–33.

17. The quotations from *Humphrey's Journal* are contained in Richard Rudisell, *The Influence of the Daguerreotype on American Society* (Albuquerque: Univ. of New Mexico, 1971), pp. 156–57. They are duplicated in "Barnum's Gallery of American Beauty," circular, Chicago Historical Society. See also George O'Dell, *Annals of the New York Stage,* 15 vols. (New York: Columbia Univ., 1927–49), 6:398. It is probable that the photographs were destroyed in a fire that destroyed the museum in the 1860s.

18. John L. Jennings, *Theatrical and Circus Life* (St. Louis: M. S. Barnett, 1882), p. 515. As with his 1854 beauty contest, Barnum made no mention of his abortive 1889 beauty contest in his memoirs.

19. *World's Fair Bulletin: Published in the Interest of the Louisiana Purchase Exposition* 3 (Feb. 1902): 20–29, courtesy of Missouri Historical Society; *Denver Post,* May 8, 1904, and Dec. 8, 1906; *San Francisco Examiner,* Sept. 10, 1905; Jan. 28, 1906; and Sept. 1, 1912; *St. Louis Post-Dispatch,* 1906. On competitions for models of sculpture, cf. *San*

Francisco Examiner, Sept. 27, 1896, on Montana's silver statue of justice for the Chicago World's Fair. *New York World,* Dec. 2, 1900, and *Denver Post,* Dec. 9, 1900, on the emblem for the 1901 Buffalo Pan-American Exposition. *San Francisco Examiner,* March 2, 1902, on the "Ideal Girl" of Colorado to adorn the dome of the new state capitol.

20. Cf. *Denver Post,* Sept. 18, 1904; *New York World,* March 10, 1905. James Huneker, "Is There an American Type of Feminine Beauty?," *Everybody's* 17 (Aug. 1907): 238–47, reprints photographs of many winners. See also Imogene Graham, "The Real Della Carson," *Woman Beautiful* 1 (Sept. 1908): 63.

21. *Ladies' Home Journal* 24 (March 1907): 5 and 28 (March 1911): 3.

22. On the circus and the dime museum, which has yet to find its historian, see Felix Isman, *Weber and Fields: Their Tribulations, Triumphs, and Their Associates* (New York: Boni and Liveright, 1924), pp. 25–27; E. S. Hallock, "The American Circus," *Century Magazine* 70 (Aug. 1905): 568–85; Fred Allen, *Much Ado About Me* (Boston: Little, Brown, 1956), pp. 81–83; Clarence Day, *Life with Father* (New York: Knopf, 1935), p. 163; and especially George Middleton, *Circus Memories: As Told to and Written by his Wife* (Los Angeles: George Rice, 1913).

23. Alexander Woollcott, *Shouts and Murmurs* (New York: Century, 1922), p. 215; Middleton, *Circus Memories.*

24. *Police Gazette,* Dec. 2, 1882; and Dec. 30, 1882; *Spirit of the Times,* Nov. 15, 1882, clipping, Lillie Langtry File, New York Public Library Theatre Collection.

25. On the carnival, see Joe McKennon's anecdotal but useful *Pictorial History of the American Carnival,* vol. 1 (Sarasota, Fla.: Carnival Publishers, 1971).

26. David F. Burg, *Chicago's White City of 1893* (Lexington, Ky.: Univ. of Kentucky, 1976), p. 218; S. C. de Soissons, *A Parisian in America* (Boston: Estes and Lauriat, 1896), pp. 138–39.

27. Norman Shavin, "The Great Cotton Exposition of 1895," *Atlanta* 5 (Oct. 1965): 32–37; Elmer Vance Clarkson, "Atlanta's Beauty Show," *Metropolitan Magazine* 2 (Dec. 1895): 390–94.

28. McKennon, *Carnival,* p. 51. The Elks' employment of carnivals may have stemmed from their origin as a fraternity of actors and writers. The name "Elks" came from an elk's head in Barnum's museum. Charles W. Ferguson, *Fifty Million Brothers: A Panorama of American Lodges and Clubs* (New York: Farrar & Rinehart, 1937), p. 281.

29. *New York World,* Nov. 22, 1903; Heywood Broun and Margaret Leech, *Anthony Comstock: Roundsman of the Lord* (New York: Albert and Charles Boni, 1927), pp. 236–37; Henry Collins Brown, *New York in the Elegant Eighties* (New York: Valentine's, 1925); *New York American,* April 23, 1904, quoted by Mark Sullivan, *Our Times: The Turn of Century, America Finding Itself,* 6 vols. (New York: Charles Scribner's Sons, 1926), 2:67–68.

30. George Ellington, *The Women of New York* (New York: New York Book, 1869), pp. 519–21; George Holme, "Artists' Models," *Munsey's Magazine* 10 (Feb. 1894): 527–31.

31. Thomas Beer, *Mauve Decade: American Life at the End of the Nineteenth Century* (New York: Knopf, 1926), p. 36. *New York World,* Sept. 10, 1910; *New York Herald,* March 18, 1906.

32. John Brisbane Walker, "Beauty in Advertising Illustrations," *Cosmopolitan* 33 (Sept. 1902): 491–500; *San Francisco Examiner,* Feb. 1, 1903. My information on perfume cards in the latter part of the century is derived from the Warshaw Collection of Business Americana, Museum of American History, Smithsonian Institution.

33. Lucy Duff-Gordon, *Discretions and Indiscretions* (New York: Frederick A. Stokes, 1932), p. 135; *Outlook* 105 (Nov. 22, 1913): 673–74.

34. *New York Herald,* Feb. 11, 1906, and Feb. 25, 1906; Elisabeth Finley Thomas, *Ladies, Lovers and Other People* (New York: Longmans, Green, 1935), pp. 152–53.

35. John Robert Powers, *The Powers Girls* (New York: E. P. Dutton, 1941), pp. 11–23.

36. See Lois W. Banner, "Clara Bow," in Barbara Sicherman and Carol Hurd Green, *Notable American Women: The Modern Period* (Cambridge, Mass.: Harvard Univ., 1980), pp. 95–97.

37. Jacque Mercer, *How to Win a Beauty Contest* (Phoenix, Ariz.: Curran, 1960).

38. *New York Times,* September 11, 1920; *Atlantic City Daily Press,* September 7, 1921. On the floral parades at resorts, see Marian Lawrence Peabody, *To Be Young Was Very Heaven* (Boston: Houghton Mifflin, 1967), p. 25; George Waller, *Saratoga: Saga of an Impious Era* (Englewood Cliffs, N.J.: Prentice-Hall, 1966), p. 185. On the Rehoboth Beach contest, see Defore, *There She Is.* On the Coney Island festival, cf. *New York World,* Sept. 10, 1910, and Sept. 12, 1922.

39. *Demorest's Monthly,* June 1867, p. 185.

40. Katherine Graves Busby, *Home Life in America* (New York: Macmillan, 1910), pp. 78–79; Cohn, *Good Old Days,* pp. 394–95.

41. On Sennett, see Mack Sennett (as told to Cameron Shipp), *King of Comedy* (Garden City, N.Y.: Doubleday, 1954); DeWitt Bodeen, "All the Sad Young Bathing Beauties," *Films in Review* 19 (Autumn 1974): 33–35; Robert Giroux, "Mack Sennett," *Films in Review* 19 (Dec. 1968): 593–612, and 20 (Jan. 1969): 1–28; Kalton C. Lahue and Terry Brewer, *Kops and Custards: The Legend of Keystone Films* (Norman, Okla.: Univ. of Oklahoma, 1968); *Photoplay,* May 1915; Adela Rogers St. John, "Goodbye, Bathing Girl," *Photoplay,* Sept. 1921.

42. On Kellermann, see the clipping file in the New York Public Library Theatre Collection. Robert Grau, *Forty Years Observation of Music and the Drama* (New York: Broadway, 1909), p. 40, observed that he had never seen anything like the "extraordinary sensationalism" of Kellermann's publicity, masterminded by her press agent-manager-husband James Sullivan. Contra Sennett, Kellermann contended that she was the originator of the "bathing beauty." The story of her arrest is told by Duncan Crow, *Edwardian Woman* (London: Allen and Unwin, 1971), pp. 118–19.

43. *Atlantic City Daily Press,* Sept. 9, 1922; "The Vulgarest Thing in America," *Outlook* 138 (Sept. 1924): 45; *New York Times,* Sept. 8, 1921.

44. *New York Times,* Sept. 8, 1921.

45. *Atlantic City Daily Press,* Sept. 11, 1922. On the judging, see Norman Rockwell's amusing account of the controversies in *My Adventures as an Illustrator,* as told to Thomas Rockwell (Garden City, N.Y.: Doubleday, 1960).

46. Defore, *There She Is,* pp. 83–88.

CHAPTER 13

1. Helen Landreth, "The Beautiful and the Bobbed," *Collier's* 76 (Dec. 26, 1925): 11; Jeanette Eaton, "The Cosmetic Urge," *Harper's,* 162 (Feb. 1931): 323–30; Paul W. White, "Our Booming Beauty Business," *Outlook* 154 (Jan. 22, 1930): 133–35; Morris Fishbein, "Cult of Beauty," *American Mercury* 7 (Feb. 1926): 161–68; Ida Con-

nolly, *Beauty Operator on Broadway* (Fresno: Academy Library Guild, 1954), passim.

2. In the 1880s Bible salesman David H. McConnell found that his customers were more interested in the free perfume samples he provided with his Bibles than in the Scriptures, so he abandoned piety for profits, beginning the practice of selling cosmetic products by salespeople door to door. Margaret Allen, *Selling Dreams* (New York: Simon & Schuster, 1981), pp. 43, 45-55; Norman Sklarewitz, "This Business of Beauty," *Coronet* 39 (Feb. 1956): 149-52. On Tussy, DuBarry, and Tangee, see *Vogue* 99 (Jan. 1942): 17; *Vogue*, 109 (Jan. 1947): 36.

3. Andrew Tobias, *Fire and Ice: The Story of Charles Revson* (New York: William Morrow, 1976), pp. 47-115, 120; "It's the Ad That Sells Cosmetics," *Business Week,* Dec. 3, 1952, p. 63.

4. Shirley Polykoff, *Does She or Doesn't She? And How She Did It* (Garden City, N.Y.: Doubleday, 1975); Vance Packard, *The Hidden Persuaders* (New York: David McKay, 1957), p. 85.

5. Kathrin Perutz, *Beyond the Looking Glass: America's Beauty Culture* (New York: William Morrow, 1970), p. 22.

6. Allen, *Selling Dreams,* p. 251; Walter Goodman, "The Lipstick War: All's Fair," *Nation* 182 (Jan. 21, 1956): 47-49.

7. Nora Scott Kinzer, *Put Down and Ripped Off: The American Woman and the Beauty Culture* (New York: Crowell, 1977), p. 83.

8. T. Swann Harding, "The Revised Food and Drugs Bill—What It Means to You," *Scientific American* 150 (Feb. 1934): 150; Allen, *Selling Dreams,* p. 193.

9. *Vogue* 47 (June 1916): 80, 61; and 53 (Jan. 15, 1922): 58; Woods Hutchinson, "Health and Sports Suits," *Saturday Evening Post* 198 (Aug. 1, 1925): 20-21, 37; Rose Feld, "Yes, My Darling Daughter," *Collier's* 79 (June 25, 1927): 11, 40; Ethel G. Hoyle, "Dressing the Outdoor Woman," *Outing* 47 (Feb. 1922): 79. On sports clothes and the development of the American ready-to-wear industry, I have used Margaret C. Christman and Claudia B. Kidwell, *Suiting Up: The Democratization of Clothing in America* (Washington, D.C.: Smithsonian Institution, 1974); Jessica Daves, *Ready-Made Miracle: The American Story of Fashion for the Millions* (New York: G. P. Putnam's Sons, 1967); Paul Nystrom, *Economics of Fashion* (New York: Ronald Press, 1928); Virginia Pope, "The Development of American Creativity in Fashion," in Jeanette A. Jarnow and Beatrice Judelle, eds., *Inside the Fashion Business* (New York: John Wiley and Sons, 1965), pp. 70-71.

10. See Edmonde Charles-Roux, *Chanel: Her Life, Her World, and the Woman Behind the Legend She Created,* trans. Nancy Amphoux (New York: Knopf, 1975).

11. John R. Betts, *America's Sporting Heritage, 1850-1950* (Reading, Mass.: Addison-Wesley, 1974), pp. 250-87; Stephanie L. Twin, ed., *Out of the Bleachers: Writings on Women and Sport* (Old Westbury, N.Y.: Feminist Press, 1979); Paul Gallico, *Farewell to Sport* (New York: Knopf, 1938), pp. 40-46; Sonja Henie, *Wings on My Feet* (New York: Prentice-Hall, 1940).

12. Gallico, *Farewell to Sport,* p. 250; John R. Tunis, "Women and the Sport Business," *Harper's Magazine* 159 (July 1929): 211-21; Elizabeth Halsey, "The New Sportswoman," *Hygeia,* Sept. 5, 1927, p. 444.

13. Leo Rosten, *Hollywood: The Movie Colony: The Moviemakers* (New York: Harcourt, Brace, 1941), passim; Frederick Lewis, "Fashion's Sun Rises in the West," *Liberty* 13 (Nov. 2, 1940): 54-55; Eleanor Kinsella McDonnell, "Fashion and the Hollywood Handicap," *Saturday Evening Post* 207 (May 18, 1935): 27.

14. Frederick Lewis Allen, *Since Yesterday* (New York: Harper & Bros., 1940), pp.

147–50; Daves, *Ready-Made Miracle,* pp. 147–49; Betty Thomley Stuart, "In Short," *Collier's* 26 (Feb. 24, 1934): 20.

15. Lois W. Banner, "Clara Bow," in Barbara Sicherman and Carol Hurd Green, eds., *Notable American Women: The Modern Period* (Cambridge, Mass.: Harvard Univ., 1980), pp. 95–97; Marjorie Rosen, *Popcorn Venus: Women, Movies & the American Dream* (New York: Coward, McCann & Geoghegan, 1973), p. 86. On women in the movies, I have also used Andrew Bergman, *We're in the Money: Depression America and Its Films* (New York: Harper & Row, 1971); Molly Haskell, *From Reverence to Rape: The Treatment of Women in the Movies* (New York: Holt, Rinehart & Winston, 1973); Lary May, *Screening Out the Past: The Birth of Mass Culture and the Motion Picture Industry* (New York: Oxford Univ., 1980); Mary P. Ryan, "The Projection of a New Womanhood: The Movie Moderns in the 1920s," in Jean E. Friedman and William G. Shade, eds., *Our American Sisters: Women in American Life and Thought,* 2d ed. (Boston: Allyn and Bacon, 1976), pp. 366–84; June Sochen, "Mildred Pierce and Women in Film," *American Quarterly* 30 (Spring 1978): 3–20.

    On the 1920s youth culture, see Paula Fass, *The Damned and the Beautiful: American Youth in the 1920s* (New York: Oxford Univ., 1977); and Kenneth A. Yellis, "Prosperity's Child: Some Thoughts on the Flapper," *American Quarterly* 12 (Spring 1969): 44–64. On women in general in the twentieth century, see Lois W. Banner, *Women in Modern America: A Brief History* (New York: Harcourt Brace Jovanovich, 1974); and William H. Chafe, *The American Woman: Her Changing Social, Economic, and Political Roles, 1930–1970* (New York: Oxford Univ., 1972).

16. Joan Crawford, *Portrait of Joan* (Garden City, N.Y.: Doubleday, 1962), p. 118; Lawrence J. Quirk, *The Films of Joan Crawford* (New York: Citadel, 1968), p. 16; Bob Thomas, *Joan Crawford: A Biography* (New York: Simon & Schuster, 1978), p. 83.

17. Elsa Schiaparelli, *Shocking Life* (New York: E. P. Dutton, 1954), p. 76; Irene Sharaff, *Broadway and Hollywood: Costumes Designed by Irene Sharaff* (New York: Van Nostrand Reinhold, 1976), p. 59.

18. Rosen, *Popcorn Venus,* p. 108, presents the argument for oppression.

19. Helen Merrell Lynd and Robert S. Lynd, *Middletown in Transition: A Study in Cultural Conflicts* (New York: Harcourt Brace, 1937), p. 262.

20. On the 1950s I have used Douglas T. Miller and Marion Nowak, *The Fifties: The Way We Really Were* (Garden City, N.Y.: Doubleday, 1977).

21. Sharaff, *Broadway and Hollywood,* p. 59.

22. Twin, *Out of the Bleachers,* passim.

23. On the 1960s fashion industry and high society, see Marylin Bender, *The Beautiful People* (New York: Coward-McCann, 1967). On "mod" culture and the general history of the 1960s, see William L. O'Neill, *Coming Apart: An Informal History of America in the 1960s* (New York: Quadrangle, 1971).

24. Bender, *Beautiful People,* p. 46.

25. Ibid., 76–77.

Selected Bibliography

In formulating the structure and contents of this book, my debts to the work of fellow colleagues in the field of women's history are many. Of special value have been Gerda Lerner, "Placing Women in History: A 1974 Perspective," in Berenice Carroll, ed., *Liberating Women's History: Theoretical and Critical Essays* (Urbana, Ill.: Univ. of Illinois, 1976); Carroll Smith-Rosenberg, "The Female World of Love and Ritual: Relations Between Women in Nineteenth-Century America," *Signs: Journal of Women in Culture and Society* 1 (Autumn 1975): 1–29; William H. Chafe, *Women and Equality: Changing Patterns in American Culture* (New York: Oxford Univ., 1977); Robert V. Wells, "Women's Lives Transformed: Demographic and Family Patterns in America, 1600–1970," in Carol Ruth Berkin and Mary Beth Norton, *Women of America: A History* (Boston: Houghton Mifflin, 1979); and all of the contributors to Mary S. Hartman and Lois W. Banner, eds., *Clio's Consciousness Raised: New Perspectives on the History of Women* (New York: Harper & Row, 1974).

Writings on the history and sociology of fashion, central to any study of physical appearance, are numerous, but many suffer from being either overly popular or overly theoretical, with insufficient grounding in factual data. Among the most insightful are Michael Batterbery and Ariane Batterbery, *Mirror, Mirror: A Social History of Fashion* (New York: Holt, Rinehart and Winston, 1977); François Boucher, *A History of Costume in the West* (London: Thames and Hudson, 1967); Margaret Braun-Ronsdorf, *Mirror of Fashion: A History of European Costume, 1789–1929* (New York: McGraw-Hill, 1964); Anne Buck, *Dress in Eighteenth-Century England* (New York: Holmes & Meier, 1979); Cecil Willett Cunnington, *English Women's Clothing in the Nineteenth Century* (London: Faber and Faber, 1937); Alison Gernsheim, *Fashion and Reality, 1840–1914* (London: Faber and Faber, 1963); James Laver, *Taste and Fashion: From the French Revolution to Today* (London: G. G. Harrap, 1937); Diana de Marly, *The History of Haute Couture, 1850–1950* (New York: Holmes & Meier, 1980); Blanche Payne, *History of Costume from the Ancient Egyptians to the Twentieth Century* (New York: Harper & Row, 1965); Geoffrey Squire, *Dress, Art, Society* (London: Studio Vista, 1974); Octave Uzanne, *Fashions in Paris, 1797–1897* (London: Heinemann, 1928); Max Von Boehn, *Modes and Manners of the Nineteenth Century*, trans. M. Edwardes, 3 vols. (New York: E. P. Dutton, 1909); and Nora Waugh, *Corsets and Crinolines* (London: Botsford, 1954). On fashions in dress in the United States, the major study, Elizabeth McClellan, *Historic Dress in America, 1607–1870,* 2 vols. (Philadelphia: G. W. Jacobs, 1904), is out-of-date.

On the sociology of fashion, I have found most useful Bernard Barber and Lyle S. Lobel, "Fashions in Women's Clothes and the American Social System," *Social Forces* 31 (Dec. 1952): 124–31; Quentin Bell, *On Human Finery,* 2d ed. (New York: Schocken, 1976); Herbert Blumer, "Fashion: From Class Differentiation to Collective Selection," *Sociological Quarterly* 10 (Spring 1969): 275–91; René König, *A la Mode: On the Social Psychology of Fashion,* trans. F. Bradley (New York: Seabury, 1973); and Georg Simmel, "Fashion," *American Journal of Sociology* 62 (1957): 541–58 (reprint of 1904 publication). Thorstein Veblen, whose work still dominates the field, is crucial. See Veblen, *The Theory of the Leisure Class* (New York: Macmillan, 1899). Mary Ellen Roach and Kathleen Musa, *New Perspectives on the History of Western Dress* (New York: NutriGuides, 1980), provides an excellent introduction to the subject, as does Alison Lurie, *The Language of Clothes* (New York: Random House, 1981), although her theoretical component is more obscuring than enlightening. Kenneth Clark, *Feminine Beauty* (New York: Rizzoli, 1980), is idiosyncratic and disappointing. For fashions in dress in recent years, Kennedy Fraser, *The Fashionable Mind: Reflections on Fashion, 1970–1981* (New York: Knopf, 1981), is indispensable.

Writings on nineteenth-century Victorianism, particularly those dealing with England, have informed my discussion of sexual and social modes. Of special benefit have been Morse Peckham, "Victorian Counterculture," *Victorian Studies* 18 (March 1975): 257–76; Ronald Persall, *The Worm in the Bud: The World of Victorian Sexuality* (New York: Macmillan, 1959); and Eric Trudgill, *Madonnas and Magdalens* (New York: Holmes & Meier, 1976). To understand general cultural trends in Europe and on the Continent, I have used Alice Chandler, *A Dream of Order: The Medieval Ideal in Nineteenth-Century English Literature* (Lincoln, Neb.: Univ. of Nebraska, 1970); C. Willet Cunnington, *Feminine Attitudes in the Nineteenth Century* (London: Heinemann, 1935); Mark Girouard, *The Return to Camelot: Chivalry and the English Gentleman* (New Haven: Yale Univ., 1981); Siegfried Kracauer, *Orpheus in Paris: Offenbach and the Paris of His Time,* trans. Gwenda David and Eric Mosbacher (New York: Knopf, 1938); Louis Maigret, *Le Romantisme et les moeurs* (Paris: Libraire Ancienne, 1910); Morse Peckham, ed., *Romanticism: The Culture of the Nineteenth Century* (New York: Braziller, 1965); Johanna Richardson, *The Courtesans: The Demi-Monde in Nineteenth-Century France* (London: Weidenfeld and Nicholson, 1967); Edith Saunders, *The Age of Worth: Couturier to the Empress Eugénie* (London: Longmans, 1954); and Robert Palfrey Utter and Gwendolyn Needham, *Pamela's Daughters* (New York: Russell & Russell, 1936).

On women and Romanticism the available literature is slim. I have used in particular George Boas, *Romanticism in America* (Baltimore: Johns Hopkins, 1940); Irene Taylor and Genia Luria, "Gender and Genre: Women in British Romantic Literature," in Marlene Springer, ed., *What Manner of Women: Essays on English and American Life and Literature* (New York: New York Univ., 1977); Mario Praz, *The Romantic Agony* (New York: Milford, 1933); and Edward Peter Michael Strickland, "Metamorphoses of the Muse: A Study of Women as Symbol of the Romantic Imagination" (Ph.D. diss., York Univ., 1976).

With the exception of heterosexual sexuality, the area of American Victorian social mores remains largely unstudied. On the issue of sexuality, one should consult John S. Haller, Jr., and Robin M. Haller, *The Physician and Sexuality in Victorian America* (Urbana, Ill.: Univ. of Illinois, 1974), and Carl N. Degler, *At Odds: Women and the Family in America from the Revolution to the Present* (New York: Oxford Univ., 1980), for a sensible discussion of the controversy over the issue. For some insight into modes and manners, the best works are Mary Cable, *American Manners and Morals* (New York: American Heritage, 1969); Sidney Ditzion, *Marriage, Morals, and Sex in America: A History of Ideas* (New York: Octagon, 1969); Milton Rugoff, *Prudery and Passion: Sexuality in Victorian America* (New York: G. P. Putnam's Sons, 1971); and Arthur Meier Schlesinger, *Learning How to Behave: A Historical Study of American Etiquette Books* (New York: Macmillan, 1946).

The history of popular culture, long scorned by historians, is now beginning to receive attention in works notable for imagination and scholarly precision, and these writings have been crucial in enabling me to understand the forces that shaped women's self-perception. One might mention Carl Bode, *The Anatomy of American Popular Culture* (Berkeley and Los Angeles: Univ. of California, 1959); Lewis Erenberg, *Stepping Out: New York Nightlife and the Transformation of American Culture, 1890–1930* (Westport, Conn.: Greenwood, 1981); Charles E. Funnell, *By the Beautiful Sea: The Rise and High Times of That Great Resort, Atlantic City* (New York: Knopf, 1975); David Grimsted, *Melodrama Unveiled: American Theater and Culture, 1800–1850* (Chicago: Univ. of Chicago, 1968); John F. Kasson, *Amusing the Millions: Coney Island at the Turn of the Century* (New York: Hill & Wang, 1978); Albert F. MacClean, Jr., *American Vaudeville as Ritual* (Lexington, Ky.: Univ. of Kentucky, 1965); Lary May, *Screening Out the Past: The Birth of Mass Culture and the Motion Picture Industry* (New York: Oxford Univ., 1980); and William Wasserstrom, *Heiress of all the Ages: Sex and Sentiment in the Genteel Tradition* (Minneapolis: Univ. of Minnesota, 1959). John Higham, "The Reorientation of American Culture in the 1890s," in John Weiss, ed., *The Origins of Modern Consciousness* (Detroit: Wayne State Univ., 1965), offers major insights into the 1890s. Marjorie Rosen, *Popcorn Venus: Women, Movies & the American Dream* (New York: Coward, McCann & Geoghegan, 1973), is crucial to understanding models of physical appearance in the twentieth century.

The history of the theater proved to be a major area of my research, and I hope that I have contributed to understanding the centrality of this overlooked institution in shaping American mores. Unfortunately, histories of the theater suffer from scholarly imprecision and lack of imagination, and for this reason the subject has failed to have much impact on general historical writing. Exceptions to this prevailing weakness include Grimsted and MacClean, cited above; Lloyd R. Morris, *Curtain Time: The Story of the American Theater* (New York: Random House, 1953); Cecil Smith, *Musical Comedy in America* (New York: Theatre Arts, 1950); Robert Toll, *Blacking Up: The Minstrel Show in Nineteenth-Century America* (New York: Oxford Univ., 1969); and Toll's *On With the Show!: The First Century of Show Business in America* (New York: Oxford Univ., 1976).

A number of perceptive contemporary analyses and autobiographies of theater people exist. Outstanding among these are the works of Olive Logan, including *Apropos of Women and Theatres* (New York: Carleton, 1869); *Before the Footlights and Behind the Scenes* (Philadelphia: Parmelee, 1870); and *The Mimic World, and Public Exhibitions: Their History, Their Morals, and Effects* (Philadelphia: New-World, 1871). Also useful are Rudolph Aaronson, *Theatrical and Musical Memories* (New York: McBride, Nast, 1913); William A. Brady, *Showman* (New York: E. P. Dutton, 1937); Robert Grau, *Forty Years Observation of Music and the Drama* (New York: Broadway, 1909); John L. Jennings, *Theatrical and Circus Life* (St. Louis: M. S. Barnett, 1882); Michael B. Leavitt, *Fifty Years in Theatrical Management, 1859–1909* (New York: Broadway, 1912); George Jean Nathan, *The Theatre, the Drama, the Girls* (New York: Knopf, 1921), *The Popular Theatre* (New York: Knopf, 1918), and *The World in Falseface* (New York: Knopf, 1923); George Odell, *Annals of the New York Stage*, 15 vols. (New York: Columbia Univ., 1927–49); Otis Skinner, *Footlights and Spotlights: Recollections of My Life on the Stage* (Indianapolis: Bobbs-Merrill, 1923); and Emily Soldene, *My Theatrical and Musical Recollections* (London: Gilbert and Rivington, 1897). Finally, on the history of the theater, I have used the exceptional collections of clippings at the Harvard Theatre Collection and the New York Public Library Theatre Collection, located at the Lincoln Center for the Performing Arts.

One of the most difficult research problems I encountered concerned the image of women in nineteenth-century art, partly because so little work exists on the French salon painters, the most popular artists in post–Civil War America, and partly because few art historians have addressed themselves to the subject of the image of women in art. The most helpful works are Albert Boime, *The Academy and French Painting in the Nineteenth Century* (London: Phaidon, 1971); William Brown et al., *American Art* (New York: Harry Abrams, 1979); William George Constable, *Art Collecting in the United States of America* (London: Thomas Nelson, 1964); William Gaunt, *The Aesthetic Adventure* (London: Jonathan Cape, 1945); William Gerdts, *The Great American Nude: A History in Art* (New York: Praeger, 1974); James Harding, *Artistes Pompiers: French Academic Art in the Nineteenth Century* (New York: Rizzoli, 1979); Linda Hyman, "The Greek Slave by Hiram Powers: High Art as Popular Culture," *Art Journal* 35 (Spring 1976); Samuel Isham, *The History of American Painting* (New York: Macmillan, 1927). Oliver Larkin, *Art and Life in America* (New York: Rinehart, 1957); Leonée Ormond, *George Du Maurier* (London: Routledge & Kegan Paul, 1969); Johanna Richardson, "Winterhalter: Portrait of an Artist," *History Today* 23 (May 1973): 331–35; Edward Strahan [Earl Shinn], *Art Treasures of America,* 3 vols. (Philadelphia: George Barrie, 1879); and F. Weitenkampf, *American Graphic Art* (New York: Henry Holt, 1912). Aside from the still valuable Fairfax Downey, *Portrait of an Era as Drawn by C. D. Gibson* (New York: Charles Scribner's Sons, 1936), there is no up-to-date study of the Gibson girl or of Charles Dana Gibson. My analysis is based substantially on the writings of contemporaries, which are scattered throughout the popular literature of the period.

Dress and exercise reform, plus the growing importance of sports for women, were major influences in the genesis of the natural woman as a model of beauty for women. On dress reform, see Robert Riegel, "Women's Clothes and Women's Rights," *American Quarterly* 15 (Fall 1963): 390–401, and Paul Fatout, "Amelia Bloomer and Bloomerism," *New-York Historical Society Quarterly* 36 (Oct. 1952): 361–75. The best contemporary analysis is contained in National Council of Women of the United States, "Symposium on Women's Dress," *Arena* 6 (Aug., Sept., Oct., 1892): 325–39, 488–507, 621–34. Stella Mary Newton, *Health, Art, and Reason: Dress Reformers in the Nineteenth Century* (London: John Murray, 1974), covers the English movement.

On exercise and health reform, see Dorothy Ainsworth, *The History of Physical Education in Colleges for Women* (New York: A. S. Barnes, 1930); John R. Betts, "Mind and Body in Early American Thought," *Journal of American History* 54 (March 1968): 787–805; Fred Leonard, *A Guide to the History of Physical Education* (Philadelphia: Lea and Febiger, 1923); Sheila M. Rothman, *Woman's Proper Place: A History of Changing Ideals and Practices, 1870 to the Present* (New York: Basic, 1978); Richard H. Shryock, "Sylvester Graham and the Popular Health Movement, 1830–70," *Mississippi Valley Historical Review* 18 (March 1968): 172–83; and Earle F. Ziegler, ed., *A History of Physical Education and Sport in the United States and Canada* (Champagne, Ill.: Stipes, 1975).

The literature on the history of sports is rapidly expanding, although there is yet no detailed study of women's participation. See John R. Betts, *America's Sporting Heritage, 1850–1950* (Reading, Mass.: Addison-Wesley, 1974); Foster Rhea Dulles, *A History of Recreation: America Learns to Play* (New York: Appleton-Century-Crofts, 1965); Leo Stein, ed., *The Sporting Set* (New York: Arno, 1975); and Stephanie L. Twin, ed., *Out of the Bleachers: Writings on Women and Sport* (Old Westbury, N.Y.: Feminist Press, 1979).

On the bicycle, important in women's acceptance of sports, see Robert A. Smith, *A Social History of the Bicycle: Its Early Life and Times in America* (New York: American Heritage, 1972); and Richard Harmond, "Progress and Flight: An Interpretation of the American Cycle Craze of the 1890s," *Journal of Social History* 2 (Winter 1971–72): 235–57. Central to an understanding of American sports are the articles in *Outing* magazine, the journal of the burgeoning sports movement.

Like actresses, New York society women were an important source of beauty models in the late nineteenth and early twentieth centuries. There is yet no satisfactory study of this group of women. Some information is contained in popular studies like Allen Churchill, *The Splendor Seekers* (New York: Grosset & Dunlap, 1974); Virginia Cowles, *The Astors* (New York: Knopf, 1979); Ralph Pulitzer, *New York Society on Parade* (New York: Harper & Bros., 1910); Cornelius Vanderbilt, *Queen of the Gilded Age: The Fabulous Story of Grace Wilson Vanderbilt* (New York: McGraw-Hill, 1956); and Helen Worden, *Society Circus: From Ring to Ring, with a Large Cast* (New York: Covici, Friede, 1936). A more scholarly analysis is presented by Frederick Cople Jaher, "Nineteenth-century Elites in Boston and New York," *Journal of Social History* 2 (Fall 1972): 66–77. Contemporary analyses and autobiographies provide valuable information. These include Consuelo Vanderbilt Balsan, *The Glitter and the Gold* (New York: Harper & Bros., 1952); H. I. Brock, "From the Cotillion to the Supper Dance," *New York Times Magazine,* May 6, 1934, p. 12; Margaret T. Chanler, *Roman Spring: Memoirs* (Boston: Little, Brown, 1934); Juliana Cutting, "From Cotillion to Jazz," *Saturday Evening Post* 205 (April 1, May 6, June 24, 1933); Elizabeth Drexel Lehr, *"King Lehr" and the Gilded Age* (Philadelphia: J. B. Lippincott, 1935); Michael Strange, *Who Tells Me True* (New York: Charles Scribner's Sons, 1940); Charles Wilbur de Lyon Nichols, *The Ultra-Fashionable Peerage of America* (1904; New York: Arno, 1975); and the pages of *Vogue* magazine, especially during the 1890s. Perhaps the most insightful analysis of the New York elite is contained in Richmond Brooks Barnett, *Good Old Summer Days: Newport, Narragansett Pier, Saratoga, Long Branch, Bar Harbor* (Boston: Houghton Mifflin, 1952).

In order to understand the culture of middle-class women in the late nineteenth and early twentieth centuries, I have relied in particular on Katherine Graves Busby, *Home Life in America* (New York: Macmillan, 1910); Lydia Commander, *The American Idea* (New York: A. S. Barnes, 1907); Peter Gabriel Filene, *Him/Her/Self: Sex Roles in Modern America* (New York: Harcourt Brace Jovanovich, 1974); C. Wright Mills, *White Collar: The American Middle Classes* (New York: Oxford Univ., 1951).

For working-class women I have used Jane Addams, *Twenty Years at Hull House* (New York: Macmillan, 1910), and *The Spirit of Youth and City Streets* (New York: Macmillan, 1910); Michael Davis, *Exploitation of Pleasure: A Study of Commercial Recreations in New York City* (New York: Russell Sage, 1917); Grace H. Dodd, *Thoughts of Busy Girls* (New York: Cassell, 1892); Richard Henry Edwards, *Popular Amusements* (New York: Association, 1915); Emma Goldman, "The Traffic in Women," in *Anarchism and Other Essays* (New York: Dover, 1969); Hutchins Hapgood, *Types from City Streets* (New York: Funk & Wagnalls, 1910); Belle Lindner Israels, "The Way of the Girl," *Survey* 22 (July 3, 1909): 486–97; Clara Laughlin, *The Work-A-Day Girl: A Study of Some Present-Day Conditions* (New York: Fleming H. Revell, 1913); Frank Hatch Streightoff, *The Standard of Living Among the Industrial People of America* (Boston: Houghton Mifflin, 1911); Leslie Woodcock Tentler, *Wage-Earning Women: Industrial Work and Family Life in the United States, 1900–1930* (New York: Oxford Univ., 1979); Robert A. Woods, ed., *The City Wilderness: A Settlement Study* (Boston: Houghton Mifflin, 1898); and Robert A. Woods and Albert J. Kennedy, *Young Working Girls: A Summary of Evidence from Two Thousand Social Workers* (Boston: Houghton Mifflin, 1913).

The subject of male roles is beginning to interest historians. For preliminary analyses, see Joe L. Dubbert, *A Man's Place: Masculinity in Transition* (Englewood Cliffs, N.J.: Prentice-Hall, 1979); Filene, *Him/Her/Self;* and James McGovern, "David Graham Phillips and the Virility Impulse of the Progressives," *New England Quarterly* 29 (Sept. 1966): 334–55. My own thinking has been influenced by Henry Seidel Canby, *Alma Mater: The Gothic Age of the American College* (New York: Farrar & Rinehart, 1936); R. Gordon Kelley, *Mother Was a Lady: Self and Society in Selected American Children's Periodicals, 1865–1890* (Westport, Conn.: Greenwood, 1974); James McLachlan, *American Boarding Schools: A Historical Study* (New York: Charles Scribner's Sons, 1970); and Stow Persons, *The Decline of American Gentility* (New York: Columbia Univ., 1973).

Primary source materials on all the above issues are scattered throughout contemporary biographies, autobiographies, foreign travellers' accounts, etiquette and beauty manuals, novels, journals, and newspapers. On the social history of New York City, I have used in particular Peter Cassill, *New York Memories of Yesteryear: Life and Times at the Turn of the Century, 1890–1910* (New York: Exposition, 1964); Albert Stevens Crockett, *Peacocks on Parade* (New York: Sears, 1931); Abram Dayton, *Last Days of Knickerbocker Life* (New York: George W. Harlan, 1882); George Ellington, *Women of New York* (New York: New York Books, 1869); George Foster, *New York in Slices: By an Experienced Carver* (New York: W. F. Burgess, 1848); George Foster, *New York Naked* (New York: DeWitt, 185[?]); Thomas Butler Gunn, *Physiology of New York Boarding Houses* (New York: Mason Bros., 1857); Charles Haswell, *Reminiscences of New York by an Octogenarian* (New York: Harper & Bros., 1896); James D. McCabe, Jr., *Lights and Shadows of New York Life, or Sights and Sensations of the Great City* (Philadelphia: National, 1872); Members of the New York Press, *Night Side of New York* (New York: J. C. Haney, 1866); Matthew Hale Smith, *Sunshine and Shadow in New York* (Hartford: J. B. Burr, 1868); John H. Warren, Jr., *My Thirty Years' Battle with Crime* (Poughkeepsie, N.Y.: A. J. White, 1874); and Mabel Osgood Wright, *My New York* (New York: Macmillan, 1926).

The following secondary works on New York City have also been helpful: Grace Mayer, *Once Upon a City: New York from 1890–1910* (New York: Macmillan, 1956); and especially the works of Herbert Asbury, *The Gangs of New York* (Garden City, N.Y.: Doubleday, 1927), and *All Around the Town* (New York: Knopf, 1934).

Among the most valuable contemporary analyses of general manners and mores are Charles Astor Bristed, *The Upper Ten Thousand* (New York: Stringer and Townsend, 1852); James Fenimore Cooper, *Notions of the Americans,* 2 vols. (1863; New York: Frederick Ungar, 1963); Bertha Damon, *Grandma Called It Carnal* (New York: Simon & Schuster, 1938); Hiram Fuller, *Belle Brittain on Tour, at Newport, and Here and There* (New York: Derby & Jackson, 1858); Dio Lewis, *Our Girls* (New York: Harper & Bros., 1891); Virginia Penny, *The Employments of Women: A Cyclopaedia of Women's Work* (Boston: Walker, Wise, 1863); William Sanger, *The History of Prostitution* (New York: Harper & Bros., 1859); Catharine M. Sedgwick, *Means and Ends* (New York: Harper & Bros., 1842); Christopher Crowfield [Harriet Beecher Stowe], *The Chimney Corner* (Boston: Ticknor and Fields, 1868); Arthur Train, *Puritan's Progress* (New York: Charles Scribner's Sons, 1931); and the incomparable works of Henry Collins Brown, *Brownstone Fronts and Saratoga Trunks* (New York: E. P. Dutton, 1935), *In the Golden Nineties* (New York: Valentine's, 1928), and *New York in the Elegant Eighties* (New York: Valentine's, 1927).

In addition, one can with profit consult George Beard, *American Nervousness: Its Causes and Consequences* (New York: G. P. Putnam's Sons, 1881); Catharine E. Beecher, *Letters to the People on Health and Happiness* (New York: Harper & Bros., 1855); Mrs. A. J. Graves, *Women in America* (New York: Harper & Bros., 1847); Elizabeth Linn Linton, *The Girl of the Period and Other Social Essays,* 2 vols. (London: Richard Bentley and Son, 1883); Misses Mendell and Hosmer, *Notes of Travel and Life* (New York: Mendell and Hosmer, 1854); and Mary J. Windle, *Life in Washington, and Life Here and There* (Philadelphia: J. B. Lippincott, 1859). Furthermore, on the early nineteenth century and on male attitudes, I have found the writings of Nathaniel Parker Willis, especially his *Home Journal* and his *Rag-Bag: A Collection of Ephemera* (New York: Charles Scribner's, 1855), to be especially interesting.

Among the many biographies and autobiographies I have consulted, the following are the most rewarding: Margaret Hubbard Ayer and Isabella Taves, *The Three Lives of Harriet Hubbard Ayer* (Philadelphia: J. B. Lippincott, 1957); Sol Bloom, *The Autobiography of Sol Bloom* (New York: G. P. Putnam's Sons, 1948); Billie Burke (with Cameron Shipp), *With a Feather on My Nose* (New York: Appleton-Century-Crofts, 1949); Edna Woolman Chase and Ilka Chase, *Always in Vogue* (Garden City, N.Y.: Doubleday, 1954); Virginia Clay-Clopton, *A Belle of the 50's* (New York: Doubleday-Page, 1904); Josephine DeMott Robinson, *Circus Lady* (New York: Thomas Y. Crowell, 1926); Lucy Duff-Gordon, *Discretions and Indiscretions* (New York: Frederick A. Stokes, 1932); Beatrice Fairfax [Marie Manning], *Ladies Now and Then* (New York: E. P. Dutton, 1944); Edna Ferber, *A Peculiar Treasure* (1938; Garden City, N.Y.: Doubleday, 1954); and Julia B. Foraker, *I Would Live It Again: Memories of a Vivid Life* (New York: Harper & Bros., 1932).

Additional insightful autobiographies and biographies include Marian Gouverneur, *As I Remember: Recollections of American Society During the Nineteenth Century* (New York: D. Appleton, 1911); Elinor Glyn, *Romantic Adventure: Being the Autobiography of Elinor Glyn* (New York: E. P. Dutton, 1937); Marion Harland [Mary Virginia Terhune], *Marion Harland's Autobiography: The Story of a Long Life* (New York: Harper & Bros., 1910); Hazel Hunton, *Pantaloons and Petticoats: The Diary of a Young American* (New York: Field, 1950) [a fictionalized account]; Gerald Langford, *The Richard Harding Davis Years: A Biography of a Mother and Son* (New York: Holt, Rinehart and Winston, 1961); Mary Roberts Rinehart, *My Story* (New York: Farrar & Rinehart, 1931); Ishbel Ross, *Crusades and Crinolines: The Life and Times of Ellen Curtis Demorest and William Jennings Demorest* (New York: Harper & Row, 1963); Mary E. W. Sherwood, *An Epistle to Posterity: Being Rambling Recollections of Many Years of My Life* (New York: Harper & Bros., 1897); and Edith Wharton, *A Backward Glance* (New York: D. Appleton-Century, 1934).

Foreign travellers' accounts of American manners and mores form a particularly valuable source. Surprisingly, historians have only occasionally utilized them for this subject. The most insightful include Paul Bourget, *Outre-Mer: Impressions of America* (New York: Charles Scribner's Sons, 1895); Charles Dickens, *American Notes* (1842; London: Oxford Univ., 1957); Emily Faithfull, *Three Visits to America* (Edinburgh: David Douglas, 1884); Thomas Colley Grattan, *Civilized America,* 2 vols. (London: Bradbury and Evans, 1859); Francis J. Grund, *Aristocracy in America,* 2 vols. (London: Richard Bentley, 1839); Maria Theresa Longworth, *Teresina in America,* 2 vols. (London: Richard Bentley and Son, 1875); Donald Macrae, *Americans at Home: Pen-and-Ink Sketches of American Men, Manners, and Institutions* (Glasgow: J. S. Marr & Sons, 1875); Captain J. W. Oldmixon, *Transatlantic Wanderings: Or, a Last Look at the United States* (London: George Routledge, 1855); Francis Pulsky and Theresa Pulsky, *White, Red, and Black: Sketches of Society* (New York: Redfield, 1853); George Augustus Sala, *America Revisited* (London: Vizetelly, 1882); and Frances Trollope, *Domestic Manners of the Americans* (New York: Knopf, 1949). Alexis de Tocqueville, *Democracy in America,* 2 vols. (London: Longmans, Green, 1889), is characteristically insightful on these matters, as is the overlooked Oscar Comettant, *Trois ans aux États-Unis* (Paris: Pagnerre, 1857).

Etiquette books and beauty manuals were a major source for this work, and in their pursuit I used the libraries of Harvard and Princeton, the Boston Public Library, the New York Public Library, and the Library of Congress, the last of which contains an especially large collection of beauty manuals. Many of both kinds of advice books are repetitive and uninformative; those I found most informative are cited in the footnotes. In reconstructing the history of beauty parlors and nineteenth-century commercial advertising more generally, the Bella C. Landauer Collection of Business and Advertising Art at the New-York Historical Society was of inestimable value. I also benefited from the Warshaw Collection of Business Americana at the Smithsonian Institution.

Analyses of physical appearance and related social mores are scattered throughout the day's periodical literature. I have used with profit articles in the following magazines: *American Magazine; Atlantic Monthly; Cosmopolitan; Current Literature; Everybody's; Forum; Harper's Monthly Magazine; North American Review;* and *Scribner's Magazine.* The *Galaxy,* which lasted between 1868 and 1874, proved very valuable, as did the *Police Gazette* and the *Metropolitan Magazine,* which lasted through the decade of the 1890s.

Magazines directed toward women were also crucial to the investigation of physical appearance. They included *Godey's Lady's Book; Demorest's Monthly; Harper's Bazar; Woman Beautiful; Vogue,* and *Ladies' Home Journal.* Women's reform journals were also helpful, including the *Lily;* the *Woman's Journal;* and Elizabeth Cady Stanton's *Revolution,* a major source of nineteenth-century social commentary. Finally, I utilized Sunday supplements in major metropolitan newspapers from 1890 to World War I, including the *New York World,* the *Chicago Tribune,* the *San Francisco Examiner,* the *Denver Post,* and the *St. Louis Post-Dispatch.* Constituting a major source for the social history of these years, these newspaper journals have rarely been examined by historians.

When used in connection with other sources, novels provide key insights into social history. The works of popular women novelists in the early nineteenth century constitute a significant vehicle of reform views, while their late-century descendants in the Progressive school used similar themes in a more sophisticated manner. On the early-century novelists, the best analysis is Nina Baym, *Women's Fiction: A Guide to Novels By and About Women in America, 1820–1870* (Ithaca, N.Y.: Cornell Univ., 1978). There is no published analysis of the novelists on whom I have focused for the late nineteenth century, although I have found of benefit Richard Hofstadter and Beatrice Kevitt Hofstadter, "Winston Churchill: A Study in the Popular Novel," *American Quarterly* 2 (Spring 1950): 229–39, and especially Karen Anderson, "The Progressives as Unquestioning Conservatives: The Muckraking Novelists" (senior thesis, Princeton Univ., 1978).

Finally, I must once again acknowledge my debt to the legacy of Elizabeth Cady Stanton, whose works aided me immeasurably in understanding the dynamics of feminism and fashion in the nineteenth century. Her most trenchant comments are contained in the *Revolution* and in her speeches, some of which have been published in the massive *History of Woman Suffrage* and in Ellen Dubois, ed., *Elizabeth Cady Stanton–Susan B. Anthony: Correspondence, Writings, Speeches* (New York: Schocken, 1981).

Index

PHOTO CREDITS

[1-7] Division of Costume, The National Museum of American History, Harry T. Peters Collection, Smithsonian Institution, Washington, D.C.; [8] Seneca Falls Historical Society; [9] The New-York Historical Society; [10] Division of Costume, The National Museum of American History, Harry T. Peters Collection, Smithsonian Institution, Washington, D.C.; [11] Library of Congress; [12] Sterling and Francine Clark Art Institute; [13] Lauros-Giraudon; [14] Library of Congress; [15] Library of Congress; [16] Metropolitan Museum of Art, Gift of an Association of Gentlemen, 1873; [17] Metropolitan Museum of Art, Bequest of Catharine Lorillard Wolfe, 1887; [18-21] Library of Congress; [23] Theater Collection, New York Public Library; [25-26] Library of Congress; [27] Harvard Theater Collection; [29] Butterick Archives; [30-34] Library of Congress; [35] Courtesy of Butterick Patterns; [36] Revlon; [37-39] Kobal Collection.

A NOTE ABOUT THE AUTHOR

Lois Banner was born in Los Angeles, California, in 1939. She received
her B.A. from the University of California at Los Angeles and her M.A.
and Ph.D. from Columbia University. She has taught at Rutgers University, Princeton University, the University of Scranton, the University
of Maryland, and George Washington University, and she has been a
fellow of both the Bunting Institute of Radcliffe College and the
Rockefeller Foundation. She is the co-editor with Mary S. Hartman of
Clio's Consciousness Raised: New Perspectives on the History of Women (1974)
and the author of *Women in Modern America: A Brief History* (1974)
and *Elizabeth Cady Stanton: A Radical for Woman's Rights* (1979).

A NOTE ON THE TYPE

The text of this book was set in a computer version of Garamond, a
modern rendering of the type first cut in the sixteenth century by
Claude Garamond (1510–1561). Garamond was a pupil of Geoffrey
Troy and is believed to have based his letters on the Venetian models,
although he introduced a number of important differences. It is to him
we owe the letter which we know as old style. He gave to his letters a
certain elegance and a feeling of movement which won for himself an
immediate reputation and the patronage of King Francis I of France.

Composed by American–Stratford Graphic Services, Inc.,
Brattleboro, Vermont
Printed and bound by The Murray Printing Company,
Westford, Massachusetts

Designed by Judith Henry